BLOOD TIES

BLOOD TIES

Religion, Violence, and the Politics of Nationhood in Ottoman Macedonia, 1878–1908

İPEK YOSMAOĞLU

CORNELL UNIVERSITY PRESS
Ithaca & London

Copyright © 2014 by Cornell University

All rights reserved. Except for brief quotations in a review, this book, or parts thereof, must not be reproduced in any form without permission in writing from the publisher. For information, address Cornell University Press, Sage House, 512 East State Street, Ithaca, New York 14850.

First published 2014 by Cornell University Press
First printing, Cornell Paperbacks, 2014

Library of Congress Cataloging-in-Publication Data
Yosmaoğlu, İpek, author.
  Blood ties : religion, violence, and the politics of nationhood in Ottoman Macedonia, 1878–1908 / İpek K. Yosmaoğlu.
      pages cm
  Includes bibliographical references and index.
  ISBN 978-0-8014-5226-0 (cloth : alk. paper)
  ISBN 978-0-8014-7924-3 (pbk. : alk. paper)
  1. Macedonia—History—1878–1912. 2. Nationalism—Macedonia—History. 3. Macedonian question. 4. Macedonia—Ethnic relations. 5. Ethnic conflict—Macedonia—History. 6. Political violence—Macedonia—History. I. Title.
  DR2215.Y67 2013
  949.76'01—dc23   2013021661

Cornell University Press strives to use environmentally responsible suppliers and materials to the fullest extent possible in the publishing of its books. Such materials include vegetable-based, low-VOC inks and acid-free papers that are recycled, totally chlorine-free, or partly composed of nonwood fibers. For further information, visit our website at www.cornellpress.cornell.edu.

Cloth printing   10 9 8 7 6 5 4 3 2 1
Paperback printing   10 9 8 7 6 5 4 3 2 1

To Josh

Contents

Acknowledgments	ix
Note on Transliteration	xiii
Introduction	1
1. The Ottoman Empire, the Balkans, and the Great Powers on the Road to Mürzsteg	19
2. Education and the Creation of National Space	48
3. Territoriality and Its Discontents	79
4. Fear of Small Margins	131
5. A Leap of Faith: Disputes over Sacred Space	169
6. Logic and Legitimacy in Violence	209
Conclusion	289
Bibliography	295
Index	311

Acknowledgments

During the writing of this book I have accrued a large debt of gratitude to colleagues, mentors, friends, family members, and various institutions that generously funded my project. I apologize in advance for any omissions I may commit in acknowledging them here.

First, I thank the many scholars whose previous work on Macedonia made mine possible, and apologize to those whom I was not able to cite directly in this book. I regret that Keith Brown's excellent work on the Macedonian revolutionaries, *Loyal unto Death* (Indiana, 2013) came to my attention after this book was already in production, which prevented me from directly engaging with it here. I thank him for sharing his work with me before publication.

I wish to acknowledge the American Research Institute in Turkey and the National Endowment for the Humanities for the postdoctoral fellowship that allowed me to start the research project that resulted in this book; the Institute for Advanced Study in Princeton and the Andrew W. Mellon Foundation for the year of leave during which I completed the writing process; and the Graduate School at University of Wisconsin–Madison for the summer research grants they provided. At Northwestern University I acknowledge the Buffett Center for International Studies for the funds they provided for research in Turkey; the Alice Kaplan Institute for the Humanities for funding a quarter of leave for manuscript revision; the Dean's Office for their assistance with the production of this book; and the History Department for their ongoing support.

I thank the staff of the Başbakanlık Archives in Istanbul, Turkey; the Archives du Ministère des Affaires Étrangères in Nantes, France; the Bibliothèque Nationale de France in Paris, France; the Gennadius Library of the American School of Classical Studies at Athens, Greece, especially Robert Bridges and Charis Kalliga; Despina Syrri, Basil Gounaris, Iakovos Michailidis and Vlasis Vlasidis at the Museum of the Macedonian Struggle in Thessaloniki, Greece; AnnaLee Pauls at the Manuscript and Rare Books collection of Firestone Library, Princeton; and Patricia Crone, Avishai Margalit, Julia Bernheim, Maria Mercedes Tuya, and Marian Zelazny at the Institute for Advanced Study, School of Historical Studies. Many thanks also go to Edhem Eldem, who shared images from his own collection, and to the staff at the Thessaloniki Museum of Photography, who reproduced images from the Leonidas Papazoglou collection. I am grateful to Christos Golobias for granting me permission to use these striking images in the book.

I was fortunate to pursue and complete my graduate studies at Princeton University's Department of Near Eastern Studies, which provided me not only with generous financial support but allowed me to become part of an exceptional scholarly community. I learned about the late Ottoman Empire from the very best: Şükrü Hanioğlu, who patiently guided me through my continuously morphing dissertation project, and continued to mentor me as I was trying to establish my early academic career. I cannot say enough thanks to Peter Brown for taking the time to get involved in my project and encouraging me to find my own voice. During the year he was at Princeton, Rifa'at Abou-El-Haj singlehandedly challenged and changed the way a generation of students thinks about Ottoman history—and I was lucky enough to be one of them. Thanks to Norman Itzkowitz and Heath W. Lowry, I can pretend to know a few things about the Ottomans before the nineteenth century. The semester I spent with my peers in a seminar room with Hanioğlu, Abou-El-Haj, Itzkowitz, and Lowry is an indelible memory, and also the reason I ended up as a historian rather than reverting to my earlier career plan of economics—not a good decision perhaps, for pecuniary considerations, but one that I have yet to regret. The Program in Hellenic Studies at Princeton was an immense intellectual and social resource, all thanks to its director, Dimitri Gondicas. I am grateful to him above all for asking me the question "Have you considered Greek?" and following up on it.

Heartfelt thanks go to my circle of friends (and family) at Princeton for the exceptional conviviality and the intellectual enrichment they provided: to Şuhnaz Yılmaz, Baki Tezcan, Janet Klein, Mustafa Aksakal, Christine Philliou, Milen Petrov, Jocelyn Sharlet, Jessica Tiregol, Michael Reynolds, Orit Bashkin, Berrak Burçak, Rebecca Graves, Ahmet Bayazıtoğlu, Adam Becker, Arang Keshavarzian, Peter Turner, Leyla Aker, George Gavrilis, Hongyung Anna Suh, Arindam Dutta, Marton Dornbach, and the late Sakura Handa. I am forever indebted to Cole Crittenden for supporting me through every tough spot I encountered with good humor, and to Leo Coleman for helping me survive various moves across the country, and for the stimulating conversations, some of which found their way into this book.

I thank Nur Bilge Criss for tirelessly being my mentor, role model, virtual mother, critic, and friend for most of my grown-up life; Kerem Öktem for years of intellectual engagement and unwavering friendship; Dimitris Antoniou for his ideas and the *parea*; Margarita Poutouridou for her *Pontic* spirit of solidarity; Nikolas Lakiotakis and René Poutou for making research in France something to look forward to; Sibel Zandi Sayek and Ali Yaycıoğlu for the exquisite camaraderie and intellectual stimulation that started at Cambridge, and has kept up since; and Jessica Winegar and Hamdi Attia for making Evanston feel like home. Special thanks to Rita Koryan and Kaya

Şahin for sharing the most stressful and joyful moments of my life in the past few years.

I would like to acknowledge the support of my colleagues and mentors at the University of Wisconsin–Madison, especially David McDonald, Francine Hirsch, Robert Kaiser, Michael Chamberlain, and David Morgan, who read and commented on earlier versions of the manuscript, and also made Madison a most welcoming place.

I have presented sections of the book at various workshops and seminars and benefited from the insights of the commentators, especially those of Peter Holquist, Ryan Gingeras, and Dimitar Bechev. I am indebted to Fatma Müge Göçek and Ronald Grigor Suny for taking the time to participate in a manuscript workshop at Northwestern and giving me invaluable feedback and advice. John Bushnell has read more versions of this book than anyone else and provided extensive comments each time, for which I am truly grateful.

Parts of chapters 3 and 4 have been published earlier and are published here with permission from the University of Georgia Press and Cambridge University Press: "Constructing National Identity in Ottoman Macedonia," in *Understanding Life in the Borderlands,* edited by William Zartman (Athens: University of Georgia Press, 2010), 160–88; and "Counting Bodies, Shaping Souls: The "1903 Census" and National Identity in Ottoman Macedonia," *International Journal of Middle East Studies* 38 (2006), 55–77.

I appreciate the collegial environment Northwestern University's History Department has provided since my arrival here in 2010. I would like to acknowledge the support and friendship I have received from my colleagues, especially Ben Frommer, Peter Carroll, Carl Petry, Amy Stanley, Scott Sowerby, and Regina Grafe. I am grateful to Peter Hayes for going beyond the call of duty in finding extra resources toward the completion of this project.

I am indebted to John Ackerman and the editorial staff at Cornell University Press who produced this book. Their integrity and professionalism have made what could have been a stressful process run as smoothly and pleasantly as possible.

Writing this book has been a long journey that started when I came to the United States for my graduate work. My only regret is the long distance this has put between my family and me. I am grateful to them—Muammer and Mehper Zeynep Yosmaoğlu, Reyyan, Hakan, and Nazlı Hacievliyagil, and Cahit Kocaömer—for their understanding, unconditional support, and love. Finally, I would like to thank my husband, Joshua L. Cox. I could not have seen through this project without his patient support and love. This book is dedicated to him.

Note on Transliteration

Selânik/Thessaloniki/Solun/Salonika/Salonica/Saloniki. These are just a few versions of the name of the largest city in Ottoman Macedonia, and it was hard to choose one that would be used consistently throughout the book (I opted for Salonika in the end). I hope the reader will understand the "hybrid" method I have used for place names based on this example. For large cities such as Salonika and Monastir I have used the version most common in contemporary English transliteration. For smaller towns I have tried to use the Ottoman version, transliterated in modern Turkish, followed by the contemporary name in parentheses the first time it is mentioned (e.g., Demirhisar (Sidirokastro)). Given the subject matter of the book, a large number of small villages are mentioned, especially in the last three chapters, and these were the most challenging: again, I tried to provide the Ottoman Turkish version (which could vary depending on transliteration) followed by alternative spellings and the current name of the locale in parenthesis (e.g., Graçen/Gratsiani (Agiohori)). I hope this will make it easier to identify the exact locations of these villages. I have used modern Turkish spelling for Ottoman Turkish transliteration, and the Library of Congress style for Greek. For the sake of convenience, all dates have been converted into the Gregorian calendar.

BLOOD TIES

Introduction

> Macedonia is the most frightful mix of races ever imagined. Turks, Albanians, Greeks and Bulgarians live there side by side without mingling—and have lived so since the days of St. Paul.
> —John Reed, *The War in Eastern Europe*, 1916

From the Congress of Berlin to the outbreak of the Balkan Wars, a potent combination of zero-sum imperialism, irredentist nationalism, and modernizing states transformed southeast Europe into a violent conflict zone. As empires collapsed and the boundaries of nation-states were drawn, first on paper and then through the land, a long period of suffering started for the people inhabiting an area stretching from Eastern Europe though the Black Sea littoral and Asia Minor into the Fertile Crescent; they were caught in the riptide of geopolitics, and worse was yet to come. The demarcation lines drawn on paper cut through not only topographical markers but also ordinary people's lives, which no longer were that ordinary. Communal solidarities broke down, time and space were rationalized, the fluidity of vernaculars was replaced by the rigid rules of literary languages, and the immutable form of the nation and the boundaries of the nation-state replaced the polyglot associations and ways of life that had formerly characterized people's connections with those beyond their immediate kin or community.

The residents of the Ottoman Balkans, including Macedonia, were not entirely unfamiliar with coercive violence, lawlessness, and depredations. All were occasionally visited on them by a variety of bandits and state agents—who sometimes were one and the same. The violence that sprang up in the nineteenth century and escalated to the point of all-out war at the turn of the twentieth century, however, was qualitatively different: it was systemic, was pervasive, and pitted one community against another, whether the members of those communities desired to be active participants in this struggle or not. Back then it was called a "war of races." Today it is called "ethnic conflict." The principal question I raise in this book is how a region inhabited by a population that had not experienced any sustained, systemic, or high level of intercommunity violence until the turn of the twentieth century turned into one synonymous with ethnic conflict.

The association of the name *Macedonia* with ethnic conflict has a long history. Writing during World War I, John Reed described it as "the most frightening mix of races ever imagined,"[1] and he was not the first to have said so. In 1925, A. Pallis called the situation "chronic racial warfare" caused by "the inextricable mixture of Greeks, Bulgars, Turks, and others."[2] It is true that Macedonia was home to an unusual diversity of "races," even by the standards of the notoriously mixed Ottoman Empire, and it is also true that it was a frightening place by the time of Reed's visit; it was definitely a zone of violence. Reed and Pallis, like many at the time and since, assumed wrongly that the "fear" was an outcome of this presumably anomalous "mixture of races." The violence that accompanied the unmixing of the same people should have taught them otherwise. The "racial" violence in Macedonia was not the natural outcome of (presumably) mutually hostile groups of people living in close proximity to one another; it was, instead, the combined result of three factors: adoption by the elites of the neighboring Balkan states of an exclusionary nation-state model as the only path to modernization and prosperity; the determined refusal of Ottoman statesmen to accept any political reorganization, such as autonomy, that might result in their loss of these territories; and the reckless pursuit by the Great Powers of a policy that would preserve the European balance of power until, obviously, they could not. The bizarre mingling of several languages, dialects, religions, and sects in an area roughly the size of Maryland was secondary to this tension and became a pretext for violence only after the scramble for territory had already started.

Macedonia was hardly unique in its ethnic, linguistic, and religious makeup; heterogeneity was the rule, not the exception, in imperial territories ruled by the Habsburg or the Romanov dynasties such as Transylvania, Moravia, Bohemia, Galicia, and the Caucuses. Although the path to national consolidation differed in each of these territories, the goals were the same and in each case involved violent social upheavals and transformative population movements. The transition from empire to nation-state created citizens out of subjects even as it transformed some populations into minorities in their former homelands, who were then forced to leave in campaigns of deportation and emigration, cynically called repatriation.

In the words of Ernest Gellner, nationalism is "the general imposition of a high culture on society, where previously low cultures had taken up the lives of the majority, and in some cases of the totality, of the population."[3] Although his theory has helped to shape the debate about nations and nationalism for the last four decades, it has also been subjected to a good

---

1. John Reed, *The War in Eastern Europe*, 1916.
2. A. Pallis, "Racial Migrations in the Balkans during the years 1912–1924," *Geographical Journal* 66, no. 4 (1925), 316.
3. Ernest Gellner, *Nations and Nationalism* (Ithaca, 1983), 57.

deal of criticism.[4] Like all such theoretical approaches to nationalism, Gellner's presents a universal framework to explain an ideology that has adapted and replicated itself in different guises with the resilience of tuberculosis bacteria.[5] The success of nationalism in contexts where the connection between elites and agro-literate masses was tenuous at best and nonexistent at worst is particularly difficult to explain. To speak of imposition from above is to suggest strict limits on the agency of the very masses whose collaboration was necessary for the completion of the elites' nationalist agendas. Yet it is hard to deny the universal role played by the elites and the high culture they represented—even as they embraced a romantic notion of the *volk* as the essence of the nation—in initiating the process that culminated in the foundation of nation-states. The nationalist movements in the Ottoman Empire were no exception to this pattern.

But how did the masses connect with the elites if they did not already share similar values and aspirations? To answer this question, I explain in this book the transition to nationhood not through a textual analysis of the record left behind by national visionaries but through the experience of the common folk. I trace the paths to nationhood "in terms of the assumptions, hopes, needs, longings and interests of ordinary people, which are not necessarily national and still less nationalist," as Eric Hobsbawm urges.[6] This is not to deny the importance of works that have analyzed the course of nationalism in the Balkans based on the written work, activities, and testimony of national leaders, intellectuals, and elites.[7] Rather, I build here on that framework to understand the dynamics of nation-making that depended on the diffusion among the peasant masses of what was essentially an elite ideology.

This book therefore has two axes: one follows the agendas and actions of state and nonstate political actors with competing visions for the region, and the other traces the experiences of the people who continued to make a living in the territory staked out between these competitors. At the center of my argument are the ways in which difference—religious, sectarian,

---

4. For a comprehensive evaluation and critique of Gellner's theory of nationalism, see the collection of essays in John Hall, ed., *The State of the Nation: Ernest Gellner and the Theory of Nationalism* (Cambridge, 1998). For an emphatic defense, see David McCrone, *The Sociology of Nationalism* (New York, 1998), 64–84.

5. The exceptional adaptability of nationalism can be explained more easily if it is treated "as if it belonged with 'kinship' and 'religion,'" as Benedict Anderson suggests, rather than as ideology. *Imagined Communities* (London, 1991), 5.

6. Eric J. Hobsbawm, *Nations and Nationalism since 1780: Programme, Myth, Reality* (Cambridge, 1990), 10.

7. Historiography is particularly rich in this regard for the Greek case; see, among many others, Paschalis Kitromilides, *The Enlightenment as Social Criticism: Iosipos Moisiodax and Greek Culture in the Eighteenth Century* (Princeton, 1992); Stathis Gourgouris, *Dream Nation* (Stanford, 1996); Peter Mackridge, *Language and National Identity in Greece, 1766–1976* (Oxford, 2009).

4 → Introduction

linguistic—was constructed and compounded.[8] While acknowledging the roles played by literary elites and competing educational establishments, I do not consider these the factors that dismantled the "complex structure of local groups" (pace Gellner). In Ottoman Macedonia, elites and the peasants were brought together through the reappropriation of existing markers of collectivity, such as religion, and through the politicization of those reworked differences through violence.

Nationhood, Nationalism and Eastern Backwardness

As the Cold War came to an end and communism seemed to collapse like a house of cards, nationalism experienced a resurgence that proved how powerful it still was. It became "the hegemonic discourse of sovereignty and the unavoidable language of those who want to play the game of statehood."[9] Decades later, the nation-state, far from withering after an interlude of vitality, has proved extremely well suited to the globalizing world capitalist system, which presumably thrives on transnationalism rather than nationalism. Because the nation-state retains its robust presence, it is all the more difficult to avoid a teleological bias when analyzing the emergence of nationhood, regardless of the context and period. Therefore, it is important, first, to separate nationalism from nationhood: the former is a basis of political legitimacy, whereas the latter is a basis for collective identity. We might assume that nationalism follows naturally from nations, collectivities mobilized for attaining the ultimate goal of nationalism, namely statehood, or, as Gellner put it, "the congruence of the boundaries of state with those of the nation."[10] The case studies detailed in this book demonstrate a different trajectory, however, outlining the historical process by which the category "nation" came to complete the ideology of nationalism.[11] I consider the category "nation" primarily as an interest group and nationalism as a mobilizing ideology that creates nations where they did not exist before.[12] I engage with the micro rather

---

8. See Fredrik Barth, ed., *Ethnic Groups and Boundaries: The Social Organization of Cultural Difference* (London, 1969). Barth's amended model resonates better with studies on ethnicity outside the field of anthropology; see Fredrik Barth, "Enduring and Emerging Issues in the Analysis of Ethnicity," in *The Anthropology of Ethnicity: Beyond Ethnic Groups and Boundaries*, edited by Hans Vermeulen and Cora Govers (Amsterdam, 1994), 11–32.

9. Ronald Grigor Suny, *The Revenge of the Past: Nationalism, Revolution, and the Collapse of the Soviet Union* (Stanford, 1993) 14.

10. Gellner, *Nations and Nationalism*, 1.

11. Some have even argued in favor of entirely doing away with "nation" as an analytical category; see Valery A. Tishkov, "Forget the 'Nation': Post-Nationalist Understanding of Nationalism," *Ethnic and Racial Studies* 23 (2000), 625.

12. The Gellnerian tone of this statement is obvious; however, by locating the roots of nationhood in the process of mobilization, I veer from a strictly Gellnerian framework. In fact, the definitions here owe much to Barry Barnes's theory of interest groups, which posits that an

than the macro level of the transition to nationness and, therefore, focus more on the *process* of nationalist mobilization than on its putative inspiration.

To speak about the emergence of nationhood as a process is to place oneself firmly within the modernist camp of the scholarship on nationalism.[13] I do not, however, subscribe to a strictly modernist reading of nationhood, not least because the usual trappings of modernity did not reach the majority of the people whose lives were nevertheless being claimed by fighters for the national cause. I do acknowledge the roots of nationalist mobilization in earlier markers of belonging, especially in religious belonging. After all, even Gellner followed his famous declaration that "nationalism is not the awakening of nations to self consciousness" with the acknowledgment that it "does need some pre-existing differentiating marks to work on, even if ... these are purely negative."[14] I frame the central question about the emergence of nationhood in the following manner: How does a transition to nationhood occur in the absence of the commonly accepted prerequisites for that process such as public education, universal conscription, industrialization, and the spread of print culture? The answer developed in this book is that the early subscribers of nationalism in Ottoman Macedonia — including members of the nascent bourgeoisies, state elites, the men and women of letters, and young political activists — understood well the need to recast it in a new and overtly religious language. Nationalism and mass political participation went hand in hand to redefine the basis of political legitimacy in the nineteenth century. If the same trend were to have any shot at prevailing in the Ottoman Balkans, it was exigent to make it accessible to the only demographic contingent that had the potential to carry it to the mainstream — the peasantry. The operative realm of religion was the most effective medium through which the gospel of nationalism could be preached to a skeptical audience, and the ultimate catalyst in the process that would render free-floating allegiances hard and fixed was political violence. In other words, violence was not a by-product of but a real force in the genesis of nation-ness.

Having spelled out violence and religion as the two major factors in the popularization of nationhood in Ottoman Macedonia, I find it necessary to briefly address the possibility that the arguments of this book will be associated with two of the famous canards attributed to Balkan history and historiography. The first of these is the notion, peddled especially by western media outlets during the breakup of Yugoslavia, that nationalism in the Balkans

---

interest group is constituted by the very process of its mobilization; Barry Barnes, *The Elements of Social Theory* (Princeton, 1995).

13. Theories on the origins of nationhood are aplenty, and they do not fall into neat clusters. However, it is fair to say that the most visible demarcation line is between modernists and primordialists. Elie Kedouri's *Nationalism* (London, 1960) was a milestone in the establishment of what later would be called the *modernist paradigm* or, alternatively, *modernist orthodoxy* by its critics.

14. Ernest Gellner, *Thought and Change* (London, 1964), 168.

is, and has always been, atavistic and innately violent. The second is the primordialist conception of religion as the vault where nations preserved their core values through centuries of subordination under the Ottomans.

This book directly challenges these two stereotypes, which have long burdened the study of the Balkans. Fortunately it does not stand alone; since 1993, when Michael Ignatieff associated the term *ethnic hatred* with former Yugoslavia and Robert Kaplan introduced "ghosts" that apparently haunted the same country, scholarship on the Balkans has come a long way toward shedding the weight of such ahistorical notions as "national awakenings" and "ancient hatreds."[15] The Ottoman period has become better integrated into historiography in the Balkans as professional historians have distanced themselves from the official establishment narratives of national history and revisionism has become more common.[16] Unfortunately, the attraction of facile classifications and Manichean divisions block the effect of scholarly writings that might trickle their way into works of general readership. At the same time, despite modest gains, the resistance of education ministries in the Balkans to revisions in history textbooks means that students are indoctrinated in the same narratives of national liberation and are conditioned to think of history as National History.[17] Rogers Brubaker calls primordialism a "long-dead horse that writers on ethnicity and nationalism continue to flog."[18] In the realm of banal nationalism, however, the horse seems to be in rude health and still kicking.[19]

Historiographically, this book is part of a growing literature that seeks to normalize Ottoman and southeast European history. It shows that the transition to nationhood as experienced in Ottoman Macedonia was not an aberration to the purportedly serene progress of civic values enjoyed elsewhere. It contends that ethnic nationalism, commonly used to refer to Balkan nationalist movements, including those that precipitated the fall of the Ottoman Empire, is an analytically redundant categorization because violence, symbolic or physical, is the midwife of nation-ness, even in its

---

15. Michael Ignatieff, *Blood and Belonging* (New York, 1993); Robert D. Kaplan: *Balkan Ghosts: A Journey through History* (New York, 1993). For a corrective, see Mark Mazower, *The Balkans: A Short History* (New York, 2002).

16. Yet the gains have so far been modest and uneven across countries in southeast Europe; for a review, see Ulf Brunnbauer, ed., *(Re)Writing History: Historiography in Southeast Europe after Socialism* (Münster, 2004).

17. For an evaluation of the records of the individual Balkan countries on this issue, see Christina Koulouri, ed., *Clio in the Balkans: The Politics of History Education* (Thessaloniki, 2002).

18. Rogers Brubaker, *Nationalism Reframed: Nationhood and the National Question in the New Europe* (Cambridge, 1996), 15.

19. Michael Billig, *Banal Nationalism* (London, 1995). As Ronald G. Suny argues, "there is a selective affinity between nation, essentialism, and primordialism." "Constructing Primordialism: Old Histories for New Nations," *Journal of Modern History* 73, no. 4 (2001), 892. Despite what historians and theoreticians of nationalism have been writing for decades, primordialism, it seems, is here to stay.

"civic" version.[20] The ethnic versus civic distinction, originally developed by Hans Kohn and further elaborated by John Plamenatz, has served primarily as a typology that distinguishes nationalism in its "eastern" versus "western" versions.[21] Political scientists and historians alike have widely adopted this categorization, primarily to explain the volatility of late-comer (read: eastern) nationalisms as opposed to the stability enjoyed through the "daily plebiscite" of earlier nations.[22] More recently, the civic versus ethnic division was implicit in the liberal defense of nationalism because it allowed the easy attribution of the destructive, oppressive manifestations of bigotry and xenophobia around the globe to the "dark gods" of nationalism and the prosperity of western democracies, presumably, to its better angels.[23] Nationalism, according to this scheme, is a benign, even progressive ideology and the best foundation we have for political modernization and social equality; yet it can go haywire in certain "cultural" contexts. Notable exceptions notwithstanding, scholars usually see the Balkans as exhibiting this cultural proclivity to ethnic violence.[24]

There are quite a few problems with this approach. To begin with, considering the semantic proximity of and the highly elastic conceptual distinctions theorists have drawn between the categories "ethnie" and "nation," pitting the term *ethnic* against *civic* to qualify different forms of nationalism serves only to bolster the assumption that ethnic nationalism is deviant from the norm, unique to cultures that have been late in making the leap from ethnie to nation.[25] The categories "ethnie" and "nation" are different

---

20. On the analytical shortcomings of the civic versus ethnic nationalism distinction, see Brubaker, "The Manichean Myth: Rethinking the Distinction between 'Civic' and 'Ethnic' Nationalism," in *Nation and National Identity: The European Experience in Perspective*, edited by Hanspeter Kriesi, Klaus Armingeon, and Hannes Siegrist (Zürich, 1999), 55–71. Brubaker proposes that a "less ambiguous" distinction would be between "state-framed" and "counter-state" understandings of nationalism. The term *civic nationalism* has also been critiqued as a by-product of the necessary lore-making by the nation-state to obfuscate the origins of its historical evolution. For a discussion, see Bernard Yack, "The Myth of the Civic Nation," *Critical Review* 10, no. 2 (1996): 193–211; Nicholas Xenos, "Civic Nationalism: An Oxymoron?" *Critical Review* 10, no. 2 (1996): 213–31.

21. Hans Kohn, *A History of Nationalism in the East* (New York, 1929); Hans Kohn, *The Idea of Nationalism: A Study in Its Origins and Background* (New York, 1944); John Plamenatz, "Two Types of Nationalism," in *Nationalism: The Nature and Evolution of an Idea*, edited by Eugene Kamenka (London, 1976), 23–36.

22. See, for instance, Aviel Roshwald, *Ethnic Nationalism and the Fall of Empires: Central Europe, Russia & the Middle East, 1914–1923* (London, 2001). Gellner also subscribes to this distinction, which he finds consistent with his time zones model of nationalism in Europe; *Nations and Nationalism*, 97–101.

23. For a sophisticated defense of liberal nationalism, see Craig Calhoun, *Nations Matter: Culture, History, and the Cosmopolitan Dream* (New York, 2007).

24. Roshwald, *Ethnic Nationalism*, 6. Valère P. Gagnon takes exception to Balkan exceptionalism and the presumed link between ethnic difference and violence in *The Myth of Ethnic War: Serbia and Croatia in the 1990s* (Ithaca, 2004).

25. The state, or state-seeking, occupies a great place in discussions concerning the differences between an ethnie and a nation. According to Craig Calhoun, for instance, "a crucial difference between ethnicities and nations is that the latter are envisioned as intrinsically

yet cognate concepts, and they are similarly contingent and process-dependent. In the late nineteenth and early twentieth centuries, ethnographers described them as objectively distinct entities along an evolutionary or ideological spectrum. The designation *ethnic nationalism,* in seeking an analytical distinction between these two categories, duplicates the same assumptions that nineteenth- and early-twentieth-century ethnographers made (if with the best of intentions) while categorizing social groups.

Second, the *civic* designation is imprecise at best and cynical at worst, considering that it refers to nationalisms that motivated colonialist ventures, drew impenetrable boundaries between citizens and imperial subjects, and sustained slavery. The legacy of civic nationalism cannot be separated from the qualities of its flip side—state consolidation, religious purges, colonialism, and racism—which ultimately made possible the homogeneity that the nation-state required.[26] Or, as John Hall puts it, "liberal tolerance is easy once there is actually little to tolerate."[27]

Finally, even after admitting that nationhood imbues people with a sense of solidarity and coherence, laying the ideal social foundation for a smoothly functioning and egalitarian political system, we cannot overlook the historical connection between mass political participation and the move toward national homogenization—through violence when necessary. This is why Michael Mann has aptly called ethnic cleansing the "dark side of democracy."[28]

By questioning the civic versus ethnic categorization, I do *not* argue that nationalism is inherently and necessarily violent. We need to recognize, however, that changing the basis of sovereignty and establishing a nation-state, which is the ultimate goal of nationalism, requires certain social and political processes that cannot easily be separated from violence.[29] Even Craig Calhoun, who has written most empathically of nations as the ideal basis of democratic polities concedes the "the founding of a new nation has never

---

political communities, as sources of sovereignty, while this is not central to the definition of ethnicities." "Nationalism and Ethnicity," *Annual Review of Sociology* 19 (1993), 229.

26. For the exclusionary and violent backgrounds to European civic nations, see Anthony Marx, *Faith in Nation: Exclusionary Origins of Nationalism* (Oxford, 2003). See also Michael Mann, *The Dark Side of Democracy: Explaining Ethnic Cleansing* (Cambridge, 2005), 42–54.

27. John A. Hall, "Conditions for National Homogenizers," in *Nationalism and its Futures,* edited by Umut Özkırımlı (New York, 2003), 25. Hall uses the terms *ethnic nationalism* and *civic nationalism* but argues that "civic nationalism may be as resolutely homogenizing as is ethnic nationalism." John A. Hall, "Conditions for National Homogenizers," in *Nationalism and Its Futures,* edited by Umut Özkırımlı (New York, 2003), 28. Another theoretical possibility, according to him, is *civil nationalism,* but he adds that this is mostly a "prescriptive" suggestion and extremely hard to achieve in practice.

28. Mann, *Dark Side of Democracy.*

29. Note that state-seeking is not the exclusive goal of nationalist projects. As Rogers Brubaker argues, another type consists of "nationalisms that aim to nationalize an existing polity." *Nationalism Reframed,* 79. However, the nationalisms discussed in this book all belonged to the former category.

been simply the uncoerced and egalitarian project of all potential citizens."[30] Instituting the will of the nation as the source of political legitimacy requires social homogenization; it requires cultural, temporal, linguistic, and, in most cases, religious unity that can be attained only through violent means, physical or symbolic. Whether the resulting political formations legitimize this violence is another matter, but one that is immaterial as far as the relationship between nation-making and violence is concerned.

Names and Places

The territory that was once Ottoman Macedonia now lies within the borders of four nation-states: the eponymous Republic, which gained its independence relatively recently and just as soon found itself embroiled in a diplomatic fight with Greece over who had the historical copyright to the name *Macedonia;* Greece, the self-proclaimed descendant of Alexander the Great, which contains a region called Macedonia, otherwise known as Aegean Macedonia; Bulgaria, the principal claimant to the entire region at the turn of the twentieth century, which had to give up hope of recreating the borders of San Stefano Bulgaria but still includes Pirin Macedonia within its national borders; and finally, Albania, which currently holds a diminutive section of historical Macedonia in Mala Prespa and Golo Bardo, slivers of territory that flank the western shores of the Prespa and Ohrid lakes. Despite the wars, campaigns of ethnic cleansing, and assimilation, and use of demographic engineering tools such as population exchanges that have taken place since the turn of the twentieth century, Macedonia is still an ethnically diverse place, but that diversity pales compared to what it was a century ago. Given the ultimate historical triumph of the nation-state, it is difficult to envision a time when it was not the norm, but we still need to explain how exactly those nations were forged and, more important, how that process affected the lives of those who for the first time became acquainted with nationhood, whether they wanted to or not.

A few words are in order concerning the term *Ottoman Macedonia*, which, it could fairly be argued, is an oxymoron because the Ottomans themselves never had a province called Macedonia. The questions of what and who constitute Macedonia and the Macedonians has generated speculation since the early nineteenth century. "Macedonia is a field of illusions where nothing is entirely real," wrote Maurice Gandolphe, a journalist who toured the region

---

30. Calhoun, *Nations Matter,* 155. He adds, however, that even the "subjugation of large populations" that coincided with the creation of nations does not bring their legitimacy into question because "the new nations, especially where they embraced democracy, did create conditions for continued struggles for fuller citizenship" (155).

after the Ilinden Uprising in 1903.[31] Gandolphe's professionalism may be subject to debate in that he was rumored to have completed his inquiries in the pay of Sultan Abdülhamid II and the book relating his experiences was unusually favorable to the Ottoman government, but his words did capture the elusiveness of a definition for *Macedonia* quite well. "A field of illusions" was an apt metaphor for Macedonia, not because it was "false" in a positivist sense but because Macedonia was and is still a topos that evokes mutually exclusive realities for different groups of people. Its people, on the other hand, with what seemed like an unnerving mix of languages and religions even to the best-equipped ethnographer, defied the researcher's resolve to categorize them. It must have been this frustration that inspired one of them to declare, "Verily no country ever was in such need of a herald's office or of a lunatic asylum, as Macedonia. It may be described as a region peopled with new-born souls wandering in quest of a body, and losing themselves in the search."[32] As for the geographical boundaries of the region, there was never a consensus on where they started and where they ended, except in the descriptions of those who fought for an independent Macedonia: "the topographic features of Macedonia are quite irregular and rather mountainous; the geographic boundaries of the country are, for the most part, natural," one of them asserted.[33] Henry Roberts Wilkinson, who compared "natural frontiers" of Macedonia based on ethnographic maps of southeast Europe, none of which seemed to agree with another one, concluded that "of all attempts to define Macedonia, that which makes its appeal to physical geography is the least profitable, and also the easiest to refute."[34]

Nonetheless, I use the term *Ottoman Macedonia* in the title and throughout the present book without further befuddling qualifiers. The logic that justifies such a choice was inspired by the correspondence of the superintendent of Bulgaria, a high-level functionary of the Ottoman government. The superintendent was in trouble for having uttered the word *Macedonia* during an interview with a reporter from *Neue Freie Presse* in March 1903. During the time of Abdülhamid II, the Ottoman bureaucracy was not allowed to use the word *Macedonia* (along with many others considered harmful and seditious) in its official correspondence because the mere designation was considered a heinous concession to all the parties, especially the insurgents fighting in the region, that anticipated the Ottomans' imminent and complete departure from Europe. The superintendent defended his choice by indicating he had explained to the reporter that calling the

---

31. Maurice Gandolphe, *La Crise Macédonienne: Enquête dans les Vilayets Insurgés (Sept.–Dec. 1903)* (Paris, 1904), 1. Compare this with, for instance, Gaston Routier, *La Macédoine et les Puissances, l'Enquête du Petit-Parisien* (Paris, 1904).
32. George F. Abbott, *The Tale of a Tour in Macedonia* (London, 1903), 81.
33. Christ Anastasoff, *The Tragic Peninsula* (St. Louis, ca. 1934), 10.
34. Henry R. Wilkinson, *Maps and Politics: A Review of the Ethnographic Cartography of Macedonia* (Liverpool, 1951), 2.

"contagious imperial provinces [vilâyât-i mütelâhike-i Şâhâne]" with the "inappropriate name of Macedonia [tâbir-i nâsavabin]" was akin to calling contemporary France "Gaul," and he reaffirmed that he had used this term only in reference to the "malice committees [fesad komiteleri]."[35]

His apparent attachment to the sycophantic rules of the Hamidian bureaucracy and desire to save his skin notwithstanding, the superintendent made a good point: Macedonia was indeed the name of an ancient kingdom that occasionally graced historical atlases, but in reference to a region, not a political entity. On the other hand, it made no sense (although he did not push this point too strongly) to retort with a cumbersome alternative each time the issue was invoked because the presence of armed political committees that called themselves Macedonian made the term *Macedonia* as current as it could be. Likewise, it was somewhat pedantic to insist on the term *European Provinces of the Ottoman Empire* to avoid using the word *Macedonia*, not least because these provinces included areas that did not fall under even the most generous delimitations accorded to Macedonia, but also because the term had been firmly placed in international parlance by the 1900s. Even though *Rumeli,* the word the Ottomans used to describe the territories on the western side of the Bosphorus, remained in use and *Turkey in Europe* continued to be the international designation of choice, the insurgency completed the task that the European geographers had started a generation earlier. They shifted the meaning of *Macedonia* from an ancient and legendary kingdom to that of a territory with a particularly volatile mix of populations. In other words, my adoption of the term *Ottoman Macedonia* here is not meant to assign historical credence to the insurgents or the geographers over the Ottomans but, rather, a choice of convenience.

To continue the question of terminology, it is also necessary to explain the names I use throughout the book in reference to the main protagonists, namely the many "racial" groups of Macedonia. Finding names for the complex mass of humanity that made up the population of Macedonia is not an easy task; none of the ethnographers who undertook this endeavor seemed to get it right, at least according to their critiques, and one divided them up into no less than twenty-one distinct groups.[36] Using these names accurately is quite another matter; one, it must be admitted, that can never fully be accomplished. Static epithets such as Bulgarian or Greek certainly fall short of describing what essentially was a situation in flux.[37] On the

---

35. BOA, Y.PRK.MK, April 3, 1903.
36. Sax, Carl. "Ethnographische Karte der Europäischen Türkei und ihrer Dependenzen zu Aufang des Jahres," *Mittheilungen der Wiener Geographischen Gesellschaft,* Vol. 21 (Wien, 1878), plate III.
37. For more on the problem of terminology, see Anastasia Karakasidou, *Fields of Wheat, Hills of Blood: Passages into Nationhood in Greek Macedonia, 1870–1990* (Chicago, 1997), 21–24. How a person's nationality was to be determined became problematic, especially after the formation of nation-states that sought to homogenize their populations through

other hand, introducing additional terminology such as *proto-Greeks* or *ultra-Bulgarians,* following Jeremy King's use of "Ultra-Czech" and "Ultra-German" Bohemians,[38] would not only be cumbersome but would also imply that it is somehow possible to objectively distinguish the various stages in the transformation of Christian peasants into nationals. My solution, dictated by necessity, is to use terms such as "Greek," "Bulgarian," and "Vlach" in quotation marks and to convey the complexity of the situation by refraining from using ethnic epithets wherever possible. In direct quotations from Ottoman documents I use the term *Rum,* which the Greek Orthodox overwhelmingly used for self-reference, rather than Greek (Greeks from the Hellenic kingdom were called *Ellines*). For nationals of the Hellenic kingdom and the Bulgarian principality, the terms *Greek* and *Bulgarian,* respectively, are used without quotation marks.[39] Religious affiliation, also extremely fluid at the time, is treated in a similar manner, the terms *Greek Orthodox, Patriarchist,* and *Exarchist* refer to self-declared followers of the Patriarchate and the Exarchate.[40]

Equally (if not more) fraught is the choice of a designation for the Balkan Slavic dialects spoken by the residents of Macedonia at the time. There is a good argument to be made in favor of *Bulgarian* because this was the term of choice for most of the contemporaries, including the locals. Yet this is a highly problematic choice because the distinction between *Macedonian* and *Bulgarian* is a result of locally variant dialects and was certainly discernible in the nineteenth century, not least because Bulgarian had already been codified based on the dialect spoken in the northeastern parts of the country (especially that of Veliko Turnovo). It is important to understand that South Slavic dialects constitute a geographical continuum with zones of transition and that the differences between the modern standard versions of these languages rely heavily on the dialect that was chosen to be the basis of the national language during the period of standardization, this choice itself being constitutive of the national identities it presumably reflected.[41]

---

demographic and social engineering tools such as "population exchanges." See, for instance, Theodora Dragostinova, *Between Two Motherlands: Nationality and Emigration among the Greeks of Bulgaria, 1900–1949* (Ithaca, 2011).

38. Jeremy King, *Budweisers into Czechs and Germans: A Local History of Bohemian Politics* (Princeton, 2002).

39. Greek or Bulgarian citizenship, of course, was not necessarily isomorphic with Greco/Bulgarophony. For more on this issue, see Victor Friedman, "Macedonian Language and Nationalism during the Nineteenth and Early Twentieth Centuries," *Balkanistica* 2 (1975): 83–98. Many thanks to Dimitar Bechev for pointing out that for the Slavs, "risjanin" (Christian) or "Bugar" were commonly used in self-reference.

40. The Ecumenical Patriarchate of Constantinople did not recognize the Exarchate as a legitimate Orthodox church after the Schism of 1872.

41. Victor Friedman, "Language in Macedonia as an Identity Construction Site," in *When Languages Collide: Perspectives on Language Conflict, Language Competition, and Language Coexistence,* edited by Brian D. Joseph, Johanna Destefano, Niel G. Jacobs, and

Where does this leave us, then, with regard to naming the Slavic dialects spoken across Macedonia at the turn of the twentieth century? What difference does it make as far as daily patterns of speech are concerned that there certainly existed—at least among the intellectuals—a consciousness about geographical variance in Slavic dialects and that some argued in favor of a split between Macedonian and Bulgarian? It means that someone from Plovdiv would not be speaking the same dialect as a resident of Ohrid circa 1900. This does not, however, change the fact that both would likely have called the language they spoke Bulgarian and found common ground between them to communicate with few, if any, difficulties, especially if the Ohrid resident had been through formal schooling. In other words, although we need to acknowledge this variance, we should not ascribe a national meaning or national preference to the terms people used for the language they spoke. This is not only because nationality and language were not isomorphic in this context but also because neither had yet acquired the exclusive meanings that the nation-state assigned them. Moreover, we should not assume that language built insurmountable barriers between communities. Interactions in the marketplace were common enough between speakers of Greek (or Rumca or Romaika, as the locals would have called it) and Slavic—not to mention all the other languages used by the residents of Macedonia.[42] More strikingly, intermarriages were also common enough among Greek and Slavic speakers.[43] In most of these cases, the marriage served as an agent of Hellenization—which underscores the point that the struggle of Bulgarian and Macedonian intellectuals against the hegemony of Greek over the Slavic speakers of Macedonia was more vital than their own differences as to which dialect should serve as the basis of a standardized language.[44]

Almost all the case studies discussed in this book, especially in the last three chapters, come from communities in the district of Serres and neighboring

---

Ilse Eliste (Columbus, 2003), 257–98. It has been argued that the Central Macedonian dialect was chosen to form the basis of standard literary Macedonian because it also happened to be the dialect "most unlike Serbian and Bulgarian." Stephen E. Palmer Jr. and Robert R. King, *Yugoslav Communism and the Macedonian Question* (Hamden, 1971), 155.

42. Anastasia Karakasidou showcases the role of the marketplace, which she calls a "forum of cross-boundary transaction" in creating communities that overcame linguistic barriers. *Fields of Wheat, Hills of Blood*, p. 75; for more on the marketplace, or the *aghora*, see esp. 54–76.

43. Karakasidou notes that after the Balkan wars Slavic-speaking women from other villages around Guvezna, a Greek-speaking village, who had married Guvezna men were "actively forbidden by their husbands to speak Slavic at home or to teach it to their children." Ibid., 125. Mixed marriages also occurred among Greeks and Bulgarians in Bulgaria, some families following the Greek custom of the husband living with the family of the wife; Dragostinova, *Between Two Motherlands*, 182–83.

44. In the nineteenth century, marrying into a Hellenizing family indicated upward social mobility; Galia Valtchinova, "Nationalism at Symbolic Work: Social Disintegration and the National Turn in Melnik and Stanimaka," in *Conflicting Loyalties in the Balkans: The Great Powers, the Ottoman Empire and Nation-Building*, edited by Hannes Grandits, Nathalie Clayer and Robert Pichler (London, 2011), 231.

areas in the province of Salonika, roughly corresponding to the southern Struma Valley. This region is currently divided between Bulgaria and Greece, in Pirin and Aegean Macedonia, respectively. Starting with the Balkan Wars, successive waves of emigration, deportation, ethnic cleansing, and assimilation sorted its population in nation-states aspiring for homogeneity. At the turn of the twentieth century, the outlook was strikingly different: these communities were suspended in the quickly narrowing space between empire and nation. Not only were people's self-ascriptions of identity labile and fluid, but so too was the content of the languages that facilitated daily interaction. Therefore, the term *Bulgarian* as it is used in this book should be understood to refer to the territorial dialects of Macedonia (which are quite different than standard Macedonian) as well as standard Bulgarian.

I must add that by making this distinction I am not taking a position on the question of Macedonian ethnogenesis. This book is a plea to understand the dynamics behind the makings of nationhood—but a genealogy of the Macedonian nation it is not. All nation-making efforts involve projecting the putative nation into antiquity, as if it were a stable entity with a shelf life of millennia, and the Macedonian case is no exception to this practice. The issue here is not to test the validity of modern Macedonian nationalists' claims against the claims of competing national agendas.[45] As long as there are thousands of people who call themselves Macedonians, as distinct from Greeks or Bulgarian Macedonians, the insistence that they are confusing a communist supra-identity with genuine nationhood—however we define it—is intellectual thuggery. Their sense of belonging to a particular nation is no less valid than that of any other national group, and their national identity is no less authentic than others. On the other hand, this does not mean that we should read the events that took place in Macedonia at the turn of the twentieth century in a manner consistent with the official historiography of the Republic of Macedonia, which maintains that the revolutionary movement against Ottoman rule in Macedonia was a liberation struggle of the Macedonian nation, or espouse the Skopje-based notion that all Slavs who inhabit geographic Macedonia are the co-nationals of modern Macedonians.[46]

---

45. For a discussion of the contested meanings of *Macedonian* see Jane K. Cowan and Keith Brown, "Introduction: Macedonian Inflections," in *Macedonia: The Politics of Identity and Difference*, edited by Jane K. Cowan (London, 2000), 1–28. Hugh Poulton's *Who Are the Macedonians?* (Bloomington, 2000) focuses on the citizens of the contemporary Republic. Even though it focuses on the conflict between Greece and the Republic of Macedonia over ownership of the term *Macedonian,* Loring Danforth's anthropological study, which is based on ethnographic research done in Melbourne, Australia, remains a reference on the topic of modern Macedonian nationhood; Loring M. Danforth, *The Macedonian Conflict: Ethnic Nationalism in a Transnational World* (Princeton, 1995).

46. Ulf Brunnbauer notes that, although the "first generation of Macedonian historians traced the emergence of the Macedonian nation back to the beginning of the nineteenth century," an important break occurred after the Stalin-Tito split (Ulf Brunnbauer, "Historiography,

It is not, to be sure, only Macedonian nationalist historians who saw the first indications of a Macedonian national identity in the Internal Macedonian Revolutionary Organization (IMRO; Internal Organization)[47] agenda and conflict with the Exarchate.[48] There was, in fact, an undeniable attachment to the ideas of autonomy for Macedonia and action independent of Bulgaria in the program and manifestos of IMRO from its inception, which can reasonably be considered as indication of a separate Macedonian identity. Whether that attachment should be viewed exclusively as one borne out of nationalism is, however, a different matter. The modern Macedonian historiographic equation of demands for autonomy with a separate and distinct national identity does not necessarily jibe with the historical record. A rather obvious problem is the very title of the organization, which included the word *Thrace* in addition to *Macedonia*—Thrace was a region, as Tchavdar Marinov points out, "whose population was never claimed by modern Macedonian nationalism."[49] As for the tension between the Exarchate and the Internal Organization, that has been read as symptomatic of IMRO uneasiness with Bulgarian influence; we should not lose sight of the facts that promoting membership in the Exarchate was the principal means of IMRO propaganda and mobilization, and that the schoolteachers who doubled as IMRO recruiters were appointed to their posts by the Exarchate.

There is, moreover, the not less complicated issue of what *autonomy* meant to the people who espoused it in their writings. According to Hristo Tatarchev, one of the leaders of IMRO, their demand for autonomy was motivated not by an attachment to Macedonian national identity but out of concern that an explicit agenda of unification with Bulgaria would provoke

---

Myths and the Nation in the Republic of Macedonia," in Brunnbauer, *(Re)Writing History*, 178.) Now, the origins were traced further back in time, to the medieval empire of Tsar Samuil, who was appropriated as Macedonian rather than Bulgarian. In the 1990s, when Greece started a campaign to deny the use of the name *Macedonia* to the newly independent Republic, Macedonian historiography carried the origins back even earlier, to antiquity. For more on the myths of origin of the Macedonian nation, see Brunnbauer, "Historiography, Myths and the Nation in the Republic of Macedonia," 176–86.

47. I use the common acronym IMRO for this organization throughout the book, even though it is not strictly accurate; this acronym dates from 1918. Over the years, the organization acquired many different names that can be Latinized in various forms, and it originally included *Adrianople* in its title, so VMRO, IMARO, VMORO, and TMARO are alternative acronyms. For the various titles and short biographies of the leaders of IMRO see Dimitar Bechev, *The Historical Dictionary of the Republic of Macedonia* (Plymouth and Maryland, 2009).

48. See, for instance, Fikret Adanır, *Die Makedonische Frage: Ihre Entstehung und Entwicklung bis 1908* (Wiesbaden, 1979).

49. Bulgarian and Macedonian nationalists have different reasons for disputing the various names of the organization. Marinov notes that, even though to date no record has been found to verify the claim, Bulgarian historians assume that the original name was Bulgarian Macedonian-Adrianopolitan Revolutionary Committees; Tchavdar Marinov, "We, the Macedonians," in *We, the People: Politics of National Peculiarity in Southeastern Europe*, edited by Diana Mishkova (Budapest, 2009), 114–15.

other small Balkan nations and the Great Powers to action.[50] Macedonian autonomy, in other words, can be seen as a tactical diversion, or, as Marinov calls it, the "Plan B" of Bulgarian unification.[51] As problematic as it is to accept the plans for an autonomous entity modeled after Switzerland as the progenitor of the modern Macedonian nation-state, simply capitulating to Bulgarian nationalists' claims (i.e., that Macedonian Slavs were in fact Bulgarian) or to Greek nationalists' dismissal (i.e., that Macedonian Christians did not know what they were) does not do justice to the people who lost their lives as these competing national projects claimed their loyalty.[52] Here, it would behoove us to pause and consider whether by thinking of them as *either* this *or* that we place ourselves in an analytical straight jacket symptomatic of our own internalization of the notion that national consciousness is inherently exclusive and immutable.[53] It is instructive to note that Jane Sandansky, the fiercely independent leader of the IMRO left wing, had a slightly different justification for demanding autonomy, which involved keeping Macedonia within the Ottoman framework to maintain its territorial integrity. These plans did not necessarily include an ethnic purge as the basis of a nation-state. An important distinction that often gets lost in the tunnel vision of nation-states is that state-seeking is not necessarily indicative of nation-state-seeking, at least in the sense that we overwhelmingly understand the nation-state to be—ethnically homogenous and territorially stable. Despite the myths of national purity and continuity that came to dominate the official historiographies in the Balkans—as elsewhere—there is not much to be gained from a search for Macedonian national lineage as if it was already there to be discovered and tagged. The *politics* of modern Macedonian nationhood, on the other hand, is another matter altogether, the defining elements of which were shaped more in the decades following World War II than in the prelude to World War I.[54]

The struggle for Macedonia at the turn of the twentieth century is a difficult story to relate because it was not simply a war fought between states with conventional armies. It was not a purely diplomatic crisis either. It was a protracted conflict, finally a civil war, fought as an insurgency, where the

---

50. It is important to note that Tatarchev wrote this in 1928 in Bulgaria; Mehmet Hacısalihoğlu, *Jön Türkler ve Makedonya Sorunu* (Istanbul, 2008), 47.

51. Marinov, "We, the Macedonians," 119.

52. Dimo Hadzidimov was the chief architect of the federative Switzerland model; see Hacısalihoğlu, *Jön Türkler ve Makedonya Sorunu*, 122.

53. For comparison, see Marinov's discussion of the *Lozars*' (publishers of the literary magazine *Loza* [The Vine]) seemingly perplexing loyalty to both the Bulgarian and Macedonian causes, which, as he points out, was "hardly surprising." Marinov, "We, the Macedonians," 120–21.

54. The classic work on communism and the politics of Macedonian nationality in the English language is Palmer and King, *Yugoslav Communism and the Macedonian Question*. Marinov's recent work focuses more explicitly on the link between Yugoslav communism and the construction of Macedonian national consciousness and also covers the period after the disintegration of Yugoslavia; Tchavdar Marinov, *La Question Macédonienne de 1944 à Nos Jours: Communism et Nationalisme dans les Balkans* (Paris, 2010).

lines separating fighter from civilian, perpetrator from victim, traitor from hero, were not clearly drawn. When it comes to Macedonia, we should keep in mind that even the commemoration of national heroes is fraught well beyond the selective reading and polishing of history common to all nationalist hagiographies.[55]

Organization of the Book

In this book, I engage with historiography at three main levels: the construction of nationhood and nation-states, Ottoman imperial disintegration, and, finally and more specifically, the role of violence in these two processes. I contend that looking at violence as incidental to nation-making and imperial disintegration obscures the role that violence actually played as an independent variable in creating the differences and animosities that were purportedly its cause. In the first two chapters, I introduce the better-known historical actors of the Macedonian Question and summarize the events that constituted the larger background against which the remaining four chapters should be read. The first chapter provides the historical background to the crisis in Macedonia, starting with the integration of the Ottoman Empire into the Concert of Europe after the Crimean War, and its transformation into the *sick man of Europe,* and ending with the period of European-enforced reforms in Ottoman Macedonia and the Constitutional revolution in 1908 (otherwise known as the "Young Turk" revolution) in the Ottoman Empire, which, despite the initial euphoria it generated, precipitated a much worse conflict and hastened the end of Ottoman presence in Europe. The second chapter, "From Ecclesiastical to National Space," focuses on the religious and secular elites' (often divergent) agendas of national consolidation. I discuss the establishment of the Exarchate, one of the formative events in the struggle for Macedonia, as well as the rivalry between the Greek and Bulgarian camps to socialize the youth of Macedonia into a national mold through education.

In the third chapter, I trace the development of an interest in the cartography and the ethnography of the European provinces of the Ottoman Empire in the early nineteenth century. A series of geographical works and ethnographic maps demonstrates how the nation first was imagined as a blueprint on a map before its boundaries were drawn across the land and the people. In the fourth chapter, I take up the highly controversial and

---

55. For more on this issue, see James Frussetta, "Common Heroes, Divided Claims: IMRO between Macedonia and Bulgaria," in *Ideologies and National Identities: The Case of Twentieth-Century Southeastern Europe,* edited by John Lampe and Mark Mazower (Budapest, 2004), 110–30. The ambiguous place of Ilinden in Macedonian historiography is discussed in Keith Brown, "A Rising to Count On: Ilinden between Politics and History in Post-Yugoslav Macedonia," in *The Macedonian Question: Culture, Historiography, Politics,* edited by Victor Roudometof (Boulder: East European Monographs, 2000), 143–72.

politicized issue of population counts. The main focus of this chapter is the population count of 1905–1906, which recorded people's sectarian affiliations on their identity cards. The experience of those counted (the inhabitants of Macedonia) as well as the counters shows how this exercise of state power influenced people's self-perceptions of their ethnic and religious identities.

In the fifth chapter, I analyze the escalation of the sectarian tension within the Orthodox Church into a full-blown conflict and its absorption into the fight for territorial gain through struggles over sacred spaces, such as church buildings and parish schools. Here I contrast the visions of nationalist leaders and state actors with the reality of the peasants' worldview and expose how the actions of nationalist elites and guerrilla leaders politicized religion, making it a frame of reference for national belonging. The sixth and final chapter, is a taxonomy of physical violence and the conceptual culmination of the book as a whole. In this chapter, I substantiate the image of a world coming undone using archival evidence read against a framework informed by recent theoretical literature on political violence, most notably the work of Stathis Kalyvas. I analyze the process through which neighbors became enemies and people lost their trust in all the institutions they should have relied on for protection: the state, the military, the guerrillas, and the national elites—and even representatives of European Powers stationed in the region. The questions of indigenous violence and the motives and degree of involvement of civilians in acts of violence against members of rival groups take center state in this chapter, whereby a pattern and logic to the seemingly all-pervasive and indiscriminate violence emerge.

CHAPTER ONE

The Ottoman Empire, the Balkans, and the Great Powers on the Road to Mürzsteg

The primary and most essential factor in the problem [of the Near East] is then, the presence, embedded in the living flesh of Europe, of an alien substance. That substance is the Ottoman Turk.
—J. A. R. Marriott, 1917

The Crimean War marked the accession of the Ottoman Empire into the Concert of Europe, which, ironically, was also a confirmation of Ottoman dependency on external power to preserve its territorial integrity.[1] The positive publicity and sympathy the Crimean War generated in favor of the Ottomans faded as quickly as it appeared. No sooner had the ink on the Paris Treaty dried than the Ottomans found themselves back in the position they would occupy until the end of the empire: as an entity too big to be dismantled without major disruption to the European balance of power. Even though the Great Powers kept up the appearance of preserving Ottoman sovereignty on paper, this policy did not extend to cases where the Sublime Porte could be coerced into concessions that would not directly alter the status quo to the point of causing an open conflict among the Powers. Crises such as the uprising in Crete and the violent conflict in Mount Lebanon were resolved with the intervention of the Great Powers and resulted in special administrative status for the island and an internal constitution for Mount Lebanon. For this reason, understanding the shifting relations between the European Powers and their ambitions beyond southeastern Europe would become the cornerstone of

---

1. In the words of Ahmed Cevdet Pasha: "While Rumelia, the most precious of European lands was under Ottoman control, the Europeans refused to consider the Sublime State as European. After the Crimean War, the Sublime State was included in the European state system." Ahmed Cevdet Paşa, *Ma'ruzat* (Istanbul, 1980), 2, quoted in Selim Deringil, *The Well-Protected Domains: Ideology and the Legitimation of Power in the Ottoman Empire, 1876–1909* (London, 1999), 135-49. The wording of the treaty, while confirming the membership of the Ottoman Empire in the Concert of Europe, did not explicitly guarantee territorial integrity; Roderic Davison, "Ottoman Diplomacy and Its Legacy," in *The Imperial Legacy,* edited by L. Carl Brown (New York, 1996), 174–201. As later crises showed, this was an important omission, and the Ottomans sought a formal alliance with a European Power until the outbreak of World War I; Mustafa Aksakal, *The Ottoman Road to War in 1914: The Ottoman Empire and the First World War* (Cambridge, 2008).

Ottoman foreign policy, which, despite its obvious shortcomings, managed to preserve the standing of the empire as a member of the European Powers until the dawn of the twentieth century.

As the Ottomans responded to their growing loss of prestige among the European Powers with successive reform attempts, they met with obstacles from within and without that demonstrated the limited potential of these reforms for lasting change. Their diplomatic and military dependency was accompanied by growing indebtedness to European financial institutions, which eventually resulted in the Ottomans' loss of control over their public finances when they became unable to service their debt and had to declare bankruptcy in 1876.[2] The financial crisis was partially averted in late 1879 when the government reached an agreement with domestic creditors to forgo its "indirect revenues from stamp, spirits, and fishing taxes, the silk tithe, and salt and tobacco monopolies."[3] When the arrangement, overseen by the Ottoman Bank and other local creditors, turned out to be a success, it drew the ire of foreign debtors, who wanted a restructuring of the Ottoman foreign debt and lobbied their governments to force the Ottomans to the negotiation table. The result was the establishment of the Public Debt Administration in 1881, which essentially handed direct control over Ottoman public finances to debtor governments by forcing the Ottoman government to agree to relinquish a considerable part of its tax revenues for the payment of the foreign debt.[4]

As the financial crisis unfolded, a series of crises of another nature was brewing in the Balkans that would culminate in one of the worst disasters of the nineteenth century for the Ottomans. The first sign of trouble came from Hercegovina. Facing a financial crisis and dwindling tax revenues from Anatolia following the double calamities of draught and flood in the early 1870s, the government had put an undue tax burden on the peasants of Rumeli. In 1874, the peasants of Hercegovina rebelled, refusing to pay their taxes. Soon the rebellion had spread to Bosnia, and it seemed that Bulgaria and Serbia were getting ready to join in a general insurrection. Despite promises of reform by the Sublime Porte, the insurgents were not satisfied and pushed on against the Ottoman troops sent to quell the revolt. Coinciding with the first phase of the Ottoman government insolvency crisis, the situation was dire enough to warrant Great Power intervention, which came in the form of a note presented to the Sublime Porte in January 1876.[5]

---

2. For developments leading up to the financial crisis of 1875 and the subsequent establishment of the Public Debt Administration, see Edhem Eldem, "Ottoman Financial Integration with Europe: Foreign Loans, the Ottoman Bank and the Ottoman Public Debt," *European Review* 13, no. 3 (2005): 431–45.

3. Ibid., 441.

4. For the restructuring of Ottoman debt and the institutional composition of the Public Debt Administration, see Emine Kıray, *Osmanlı'da Ekonomik Yapı ve Dış Borçlar* (Istanbul, 1995).

5. F. A. K. Yasamee, *Ottoman Diplomacy: Abdülhamid II and the Great Powers* (Istanbul, 1996).

The Andrassy note, as it was called after Habsburg Foreign Minister Gyula Count Andrássy, who drafted it, required further reforms than those already promised by the Ottomans concerning local representative governance, tax reform, and religious liberty. The Sublime Porte accepted the note with the exception of the provision calling for direct local taxation in Bosnia Hercegovina; the insurgents, however, were not satisfied.[6]

In early May 1876, the Ottomans had to confront another diplomatic nightmare in Salonika when a Muslim mob, agitated by news that a Bulgarian girl who had come to town to convert to Islam had been seized by Christians and taken to the U.S. vice consul's residence, attacked and killed the French and German consuls who were trying to mediate the conflict.[7] It seemed that there was no end to troubles in spring 1876, and the worst was yet to come. In April, a group of Bulgarian revolutionaries gathered outside Panagiurishte to discuss the course of action for a rebellion soon to take place. One among their numbers was an informer, who went straight to the Ottoman authorities to report the plans, and the revolutionaries were ambushed. When they retaliated and were soon joined by groups elsewhere in the region, the April Uprising began.[8] The rebellion lasted about a fortnight and was brutally suppressed by the Ottomans with assistance from groups of *başıbozuks*, or irregulars, many of whom were apparently Circassian refugees from the Caucasus who had settled in the area after being driven out by the tsar's armies in the 1860s.[9] The worst of the atrocities occurred in Batak.[10] The final death toll was estimated to be 10,000–15,000. As the irregulars went on a murderous rampage, local Muslim peasants reportedly "gave shelter to the revolutionaries on occasion, refused payment, and did not inform the authorities."[11]

---

6. Ibid. See also John A. R. Marriott, *The Eastern Question: An Historical Study in European Diplomacy* (Oxford, 1947), 318–25.

7. Mark Mazower, *Salonika, City of Ghosts: Christians, Muslims and Jews, 1430–1950* (New York, 2004), 160–63.

8. The starting date was in April, according to the Julian calendar. Duncan Perry, *Stefan Stambolov and the Emergence of Modern Bulgaria, 1870–1895* (Durham, 1993), 29–30.

9. Marin V. Pundeff, "Bulgarian Nationalism," in *Nationalism in Eastern Europe*, edited by Peter F. Sugar and Ivo J. Lederer (Seattle, 1969), 118; Justin McCarthy, *Death and Exile: The Ethnic Cleansing of Ottoman Muslims, 1821–1912* (Princeton, 1996), 60. Large numbers of Circassians, escaping Russian armies, were settled in the Ottoman Empire starting in 1862. According to Kemal Karpat, these migrations "radically affected the social, ethnic, and religious composition of the Ottoman state." *Ottoman Population, 1830–1914* (Madison, 1985), 66.

10. The Batak massacre was the subject of a national controversy in Bulgaria in 2008, when Martina Baleva and Ulf Brunnbauer organized a conference with the main theme of the memory of the massacre in Bulgarian national consciousness. The conference did not take place because of protests, but the would-be presentations were published as Martina Baleva and Ulf Brunbauer, eds., *Batak: Das Bulgarischer Erinnerungsort* (Berlin, 2008). The protesters were not just a fringe group of extreme nationalists but also included, among others, members of the Bulgarian Academy of Sciences. For a critical evaluation of the Batak controversy, see Evelina Kelbechova, "The Short History of Bulgaria for Export," in *Religion, Ethnicity, and Contested Nationhood in the Former Ottoman Space*, edited by Jørgen Nielsen (Leiden, 2012), 223–48.

11. Perry, *Stefan Stambolov*, 31.

The massacres, or the "Bulgarian horrors," as the tragic event was named by William Gladstone's pamphlet, irrevocably destroyed what little remained of the positive publicity the Ottomans had briefly enjoyed at the time of the Crimean Wars. Gladstone, British member of Parliament and former premier, used the reports of unspeakable violence to rejuvenate his political career by attacking the conservative government, which, in his estimation, had stood by while innocent Christians were massacred. Gladstone also gave voice to what would remain the liberal European public opinion of Ottoman Turks, who were, in his memorable words, "upon the whole, from the black day when they first entered Europe, the one anti-human specimen of humanity."[12] The Ottomans certainly did not fail to deliver more material to confirm this opinion, as racist as it may have been, during the decades that followed. The notion that the "Turks" must be thrown out of Europe with their "bag and baggage" was only reinforced as news of further atrocities against Bulgarians, Armenians, and other Christian communities periodically circulated, followed by increasingly hollow-sounding promises of reparation, retribution, and reform.[13]

The month of May had one more crisis in store before it came to a close: a coup d'état in Istanbul deposed Sultan Abdülaziz and brought to the throne his nephew Murad V, who had a psychological breakdown only three months after his accession and was replaced by Abdülhamid II in August 1876. As the rebellion in Bosnia went on, Serbia and Montenegro declared war on the Ottoman Empire in July. Montenegrin forces were able to hold their own, but the ill-prepared Serbian army proved to be no match for the Ottoman forces. Worse, hopes of a general Balkan rebellion were dashed, and Russia was not initially forthcoming with military assistance. In October, after the Ottoman army started to advance into the Morava valley, Russia finally intervened and presented an ultimatum to the Sublime Porte.[14] In November an armistice was signed, but the Bosnian rebellion carried on. In December the Great Powers convened in Constantinople to discuss the terms of a new reform program that would be imposed on the Sublime Porte. Sultan Abdülhamid II took them by surprise by announcing that a parliamentary constitution had been proclaimed, making the reform proposals redundant. Count Pavel Ignatieff, the Russian representative, immediately withdrew from the conference, but the remaining diplomats formulated a revised set of demands and presented them to the Sublime Porte. The new terms included "concession of autonomy to Bosnia and Hercegovina and Bulgaria under an international commission."[15] The conference broke up after the sultan

---

12. William E. Gladstone, *The Bulgarian Horrors and the Question of the East* (London, 1876), 9.
13. Ibid., 31.
14. Charles Jelavich and Barbara Jelavich, *The Establishment of the Balkan National States, 1804–1920* (Seattle, 1986), 145.
15. Marriott, *Eastern Question*, 332–33.

categorically refused these terms. Russia had threatened war, and now it seemed inevitable.

The Russo-Ottoman war of 1877–1878, one of the pivotal events of European history, started on June 22, after the Russian army, already mobilized at the Romanian border, marched south across the Danube. The other theater of war was in the Caucasus, where the Russians advanced as far as Erzurum. On the Balkan front, they were met with unexpected resistance in Pleven, which the Ottoman troops held until December. The fall of Pleven changed the course of the war, galvanizing Serbia and Greece to commit to the action, albeit a little too late. By the time they mobilized, the Russians had signed an armistice with the Ottomans.[16] Adrianople fell on January 20, 1878, and the Russian army proceeded to Agia Stefanos, or San Stefano, a suburb of the imperial capital. The peace treaty of San Stefano, signed on March 3, 1878, came as a shock to Serbia, Romania, and Greece, as well as Austria-Hungary. Bulgaria was the indisputable winner: the borders of "Greater Bulgaria" drawn up by the San Stefano treaty could satisfy even the most ambitious Bulgarian nationalists' territorial aspirations. They were formed by the Danube in the north, the Rhodope Mountains in the south, the Black Sea coast in the east, and Vardar and Morava valleys in the west. The territories included most of Macedonia and even had an opening to the Aegean near Kavala and the Gulf of Orfano, although Salonika and Edirne, two other prizes the Bulgarians would have liked, were left out.[17] Montenegro, having nearly tripled its territory, was the other winner.

The treaty was in complete violation of the Reichstadt Convention of July 1876, an agreement between the Russian and Habsburg foreign ministers in which the two countries pledged to partition the Ottoman Balkans if the Balkan states won a victory against the Ottomans, "but with the provision that no great Balkan state should be established."[18] The British were not happy with its terms either, which, according to Lord Beaconsfield (Benjamin Disraeli), would "make the Black Sea as much a Russian Lake as the Caspian." A detachment of the British fleet, which was already at Besika Bay, was ready to sail into the Marmara Sea, ostensibly for "the protection of British subjects in Constantinople," but action was halted after the sultan, fearing a Russian reaction, pleaded with the British to remain where they were.[19] Pressure to revise the terms of the treaty was mounting from another side—the Austrians, mobilized in the Carpathians, and the Emperor Francis

---

16. Jelavich and Jelavich, *Establishment of the Balkan National States*, 153.
17. The Russian ambassador, Count Ignatieff, who had played an active role in the establishment of the Bulgarian Exarchate was also the "chief architect" of the St. Stefano treaty Bulgaria and, apparently, at one point had considered including Salonika within its borders because it was "the birthplace of Cyril and Methodius." Pundeff, "Bulgarian Nationalism," 120.
18. Jelavich and Jelavich, *Establishment of the Balkan National States*, 147.
19. Marriott, *Eastern Question*, 339.

Joseph demanded that a congress be held in Vienna. As Şükrü Hanioğlu puts it: "Russian territorial gains at the expense of the Ottomans were one thing; the wholesale transformation of the Balkans into a Slavic federation under Russian hegemony was another matter altogether."[20] Finally, the Russians agreed to a revision, but the congress would be held in Berlin, not Vienna, under Otto von Bismarck's "honest brokerage."[21]

The status of the Ottoman Empire as a secondary power at the congress could not have been made clearer than in the words of the host, Chancellor Bismarck, apparently fortified with "full tumblers of port": "If you think the Congress has met for Turkey," he told Karatheodoris Pasha, a Phanariot diplomat and the head of the Ottoman delegation, "disabuse yourselves. San Stefano would have remained unaltered, if it had not touched certain European interests."[22] It certainly was altered: Bulgaria, which appeared as an immense satellite of Russia in the Balkans, was now partitioned in a way that did not threaten British and Austrian zones of influence. None of the Balkan states sat at the table during the congress. They were relegated to the kids' table, so to speak, having been allowed to send representatives to participate in a separate session that did not have any binding power over the outcome. In the end, Macedonia was restored to the Ottomans on the condition of their implementing reforms to improve the living conditions of its Christian inhabitants. Similar reforms were called for in the Six Provinces of Eastern Anatolia to protect the Armenian population from the exactions of Kurdish and Circassian marauders. What remained of Bulgaria was divided into two parts: the Principality in the north, between the Balkans and the Danube, and the province of Eastern Rumelia in the south. The latter would nominally remain under Ottoman sovereignty but retain autonomy under a Christian governor approved by the Great Powers. In sum, the Bulgaria that emerged out of the Congress of Berlin had only 37.5 percent of the territory accorded to the Bulgaria of the San Stefano treaty, which for Bulgarians remained "the real Bulgaria" so that "the new Bulgarian state was to enter into life with a ready-made programme for territorial expansion and a burning sense of the injustice meted out to it by the great powers."[23]

None of the Balkan states returned from Berlin with a territorial gain that satisfied its desires. Nor was the restoration of Ottoman sovereignty in Macedonia and Thrace a diplomatic victory for the Ottomans. On the contrary, it essentially marked the end of centuries of Ottoman presence in the Balkans. The Ottoman Turks, the "alien substance" in the "living flesh

---

20. Şükrü Hanioğlu, *A Brief History of the Late Ottoman Empire* (Princeton, 2008), 121.
21. Wilkinson, *Maps and Politics,* 67–68. Apparently Lord Beaconsfield (Benjamin Disraeli) dominated the congress with his personality, prompting the following remark from Bismarck: "Der alte Jude, das ist der Mann." Quoted in Marriott, *Eastern Question,* 341.
22. Quoted in Leften S. Stavrianos, *The Balkans since 1453* (New York, 2000), 410.
23. Richard J. Crampton, *A Concise History of Bulgaria* (Cambridge, 1997), 83–84.

of Europe" were on their way out of the continent for good.[24] The Ottoman Empire had lost "more than a third of its territory and much of its non-Muslim population."[25] It had to cede control of Bosnia Hercegovina to Austria. Russia retained Bessarabia as well as its acquisitions in the east: Batum, Kars, and Ardahan. Britain took control of Cyprus under a separate convention. Serbia, Montenegro, and Romania were recognized as independent states. Greece was not immediately accorded any territorial gains, but a conference held in Berlin two years later made a frontier settlement in its favor. As a result, the Hellenic Kingdom extended its borders to include Thessaly and Epirus in 1882. All these border changes were accompanied by voluntary and involuntary emigrations of large numbers of Muslims from former Ottoman territories into the receding empire.[26] The aim of the Congress of Berlin had been to prevent a total breakdown of the Concert of Europe; this it did, but only temporarily and at a high cost. Its higher aim, to settle the Eastern Question, was quite far from fulfilled. The political map of southeastern Europe that emerged as a result of the Congress of Berlin would precipitate decades of violent struggle for territory and set in motion events that ultimately resulted in the deaths, deportations, and ethnic cleansing of thousands of people. The epicenter of the first round of the struggle was Macedonia, a region that did not easily lend itself to partition along ethnic lines.

The Establishment of the Internal Macedonian Revolutionary Organization and the Supreme Committee

When the Bulgarian Principality united with Eastern Rumelia in 1885 as the result of a swift coup by revolutionaries on either side of the Balkans, and with the acquiescence of Alexander of Battenberg, the prince of Bulgaria, a diplomatic crisis ensued. The Russians withdrew their support of the Bulgarian military, which left Bulgaria unprepared against the Serbian aggression that followed the unification. The dream of a pan-Slavist federation under Russian tutelage had crumbled to pieces. Despite the lack of support from Russia, the Bulgarian army prevailed over the Serbian forces and was stopped from proceeding to Belgrade only by the intervention of Austria-Hungary.[27] The military victory did not bring much in terms of territorial gains, but the unification of Bulgaria was complete—although

---

24. Marriott, *Eastern Question*, 3.
25. Caroline Finkel, *Osman's Dream: The Story of the Ottoman Empire, 1300–1923* (New York, 2006), 486.
26. Alexandre Toumarkine, *Les Migrations des Populations Musulmanes Balkaniques en Anatolie* (Istanbul, 1995).
27. Crampton, *Concise History of Bulgaria*, 91.

Macedonia still remained an unfulfilled promise.[28] After the abdication of Prince Alexander in 1886, an interim regency consisting of the Prime Minister Petko Karavelov and Stefan Stambolov, the former revolutionary (later, speaker of the *sûbranie*), took charge until a suitable replacement for Alexander could be found. Prince Ferdinand of Saxe-Coburg-Gotha was instituted as the new regent of Bulgaria in 1887, without Great Power support or endorsement.[29] The person who really was in charge until 1894, however (and has given the period his name, *Stambolovshtina*), was Stefan Stambolov.

The Stambolov-Ferdinand team was not without its detractors, including those who were in favor of a more proactive policy in Macedonia. An important figure among them was Major Kosta Panitsa, who was of Macedonian origin and a close ally of the former prince. Panitsa was convinced that mending relations with Russia was the only option Bulgaria had for furthering its cause in Macedonia. To achieve this, he hatched a plan to assassinate Prince Ferdinand in February 1889, but when his valet spilled the beans about the planned coup, the assassination was aborted and Panitsa arrested and executed.[30] After the coup attempt, Stambolov resolved to use diplomacy to further Bulgarian interests in Macedonia; at this he proved to be quite successful. He had a long-term vision for the Bulgarianization of Macedonia through churches and schools rather than using weapons.[31] The good relations of the Stambolov regime with the Sublime Porte bore their first results in 1890 in the form of *berats* for new bishoprics in Uskub, Monastir, and Ohrid. The Exarchate was also allowed to publish a newspaper in Constantinople and establish direct relations with the Bulgarians in the Adrianople province.[32] Despite these accomplishments, his determined pursuit and suppression of Macedonian revolutionary activity made Stambolov many enemies within the Macedonian circles in Bulgaria.[33] In 1891, there was another assassination attempt, this time on Stambolov, which he survived.[34] He then tightened his grip on the pro-Macedonian circles even further. As Bulgaria moved further away from Russian influence (and favor) during the Stambolov regime, things could not have been

---

28. The treaty signed in Bucharest to end the conflict essentially preserved the status quo; Pundeff, "Bulgarian Nationalism," 126.

29. Duncan Perry, *The Politics of Terror: The Macedonian Liberation Movements, 1893–1903* (Durham, 1988), 32.

30. His sentence was carried out by a firing squad of fellow Macedonians; Crampton, *Concise History of Bulgaria*, 105–6.

31. Perry, *Politics of Terror*, 32–33.

32. These concessions also helped to mend the relations between the Stambolov government and the church in Bulgaria. In 1889, the Bulgarian government had suspended the payment of subsidies to the Exarchate because the clergy in Bulgaria refused to pray for Ferdinand, who was a Catholic; Crampton, *Concise History of Bulgaria*, 106–7.

33. Pundeff, "Bulgarian Nationalism," 129.

34. Duncan Perry and R. J. Crampton differ on the dates of the assassination attempt on the prince; Perry mentions that it was after the attempt on Stambolov in 1891, but according to Crampton the plan had been foiled a year earlier.

rosier with the Sublime Porte. Despite Russian attempts to disrupt the visit, Sultan Abdülhamid II hosted Stambolov and his wife with great pomp and circumstance in Istanbul in August 1892. During his visit, Stambolov also met with the Exarch and left the city having secured further privileges for the Bulgarian community from the Sublime Porte: the Exarch's seat would be moved to Pera, where all the embassies were located, and Bulgarian schools in Macedonia would be granted autonomy.[35]

Meanwhile, the experience of political autonomy and representative government in Bulgaria and the success of the Exarchate in expanding its base in Ottoman Macedonia gave the local dissidents hope, but many of them were convinced they could obtain their goals only through armed struggle. In the 1880s, a number of them had started to organize in small paramilitary bands, but these remained under the radar of Ottoman officials. A group of young men based around Salonika started the conspiracy that to organize these paramilitary groups into an army of insurgents fighting for Macedonian autonomy. They were Damian "Dame" Gruev, Georgi "Gotse" Delchev, Ivan Hadzi Nikolov, Andon Dimitrov, and Hristo Tatarchev. Gruev had been educated in Serbia and Bulgaria and had briefly been jailed in connection with the assassination attempt against Stambolov. Delchev was a cadet in the Bulgarian army, and Hadzi Nikolov was a schoolteacher. They were all natives of Macedonia who decided to go back there to start a revolutionary movement in 1891. Dimitrov was another teacher who happened to meet Gruev and Hadzi Nikolov in Salonika. Soon Tatarchev, a physician who had recently returned from Zurich and, incidentally, had been treating Gruev for eczema, joined them. The other two founding members, Petûr Poparsov and Hristo Batandzhiev were also schoolteachers. These men constituted the core group that formed the Internal Macedonian Revolutionary Organization (IMRO) in Salonika in 1893.

In Bulgaria, opposition against Stambolov was mounting with the connivance of Prince Ferdinand, whom Stambolov had single-handedly propped up during his early years as the unwanted Bavarian, mentored, and literally saved from death. Finally, Ferdinand and his supporters managed to force the prime minister–president's resignation in May 1894, although not without resorting to a number of vaudevillian tricks.[36] The former prime minister–president was brutally murdered on a Sofia street only fourteen months after his resignation.[37] After Stambolov's resignation, the tenor of the relations between the Sublime Porte and Bulgaria changed considerably.[38] The Armenian massacres in 1894 led to the commonly held opinion

---

35. Perry, *Stefan Stambolov*, 190–91.
36. Stambolov was accused, among other things, of having had an affair with a minister's wife; Crampton, *Concise History*, 110.
37. The assassins hacked him to pieces; Crampton, *Concise History*, 109. His funeral became another scene of scandal when his widow was insulted and the supporters of one of his rivals chanted as he was being laid to rest; Perry, *Stefan Stambolov*, 209–33.
38. Jelavich and Jelavich, *Establishment of the Balkan National States*, 168.

1. Dame Grueff with companions. Courtesy Princeton University Library.

2. Dame Grueff's detachment. Courtesy Princeton University Library.

3. Detachments in meeting. Courtesy Princeton University Library.

in Bulgaria that it was only a matter of time before the Ottoman Empire crumbled and a rapprochement with Russia brought benefits.[39] The new, pro-Russian regime quickly shelved Stambolov's policy toward the Sublime Porte, and the leaders looked favorably on plans to incite a rebellion in Macedonia that might invite European intervention.

In 1895, a second organization for Macedonian independence had been founded in Sofia, the Supreme Committee, or the Vŭrhovists (also known as the External Organization). The Supreme Committee attempted a rebellion the same year with the support of officials from the Bulgarian army, which would presumably have put pressure on the Sublime Porte to approve the Exarchate petition for new *berats* for more bishoprics.[40] But the revolt was a failure; the Ottoman army apparently expected it and responded swiftly, but, more important, the Supremists were not successful in convincing the local population to participate.[41] On the other hand, the revolt did serve as

---

39. The symbolic culmination of the rapprochement with Russia was the baptism of Prince Ferdinand's son as an Orthodox Christian with Tsar Nicholas II in attendance as the godfather; Crampton, *Concise History*, 110–11; Fikret Adanır, *Makedonya Sorunu*, translated by İhsan Catay (Istanbul, 1996), 112.
40. Adanır, *Makedonya Sorunu*, 124.
41. Boris Sarafov, a former officer in the Bulgarian army who eventually rose to leadership of the IMRO-Supremist merger, made his reputation during this revolt by managing (temporarily) to capture Menlik.

enough of a threat that Abdülhamid II approved a new reform program for Macedonia shortly afterward, which, alas, remained a dead letter.[42]

In the meantime, IMRO was occupied with setting up a secret network throughout the region, accumulating weapons and recruiting supporters to form village *chetas* (militias) which would later be mobilized for a general uprising. It had chapters that coincided with local administrative units such as the *kazas* and *sancaks,* and each *sancak* was assigned a *voyvoda* (leader). IMRO also acted like a shadow government within the Ottoman domains, dispensing "justice" and collecting "taxes" through the local chapters—not to mention its control over the means of coercion. The taxes were supposed to be voluntary contributions paid in liras and recorded in the currency unit of the organization to be paid back after independence, but more often than not they were exacted from the population at gunpoint.

The Ottoman authorities did not detect the existence of IMRO for years, thanks to its secretive methods of recruitment and organization and its ruthless punishment of any violation of its rules. It was only chance that gave it away in November 1897.[43] That month, a group had crossed the border from the Bulgarian principality into Uskub, to rob one of the local notables, which was the main method of fund-raising for the organization. After robbing and murdering a landowner, the band apparently took off with 800 liras.[44] The incident, which normally might have been considered a common act of brigandage revealed the existence of a wide-reaching organization when the authorities found caches of weapons and ammunitions in peasants' houses during the search for the "brigands." It was clear that the disturbances in the region could not be attributed solely to infiltrations from across the border and that there was a homegrown movement developing. The Exarchist population, now collectively branded as subversives, bore the brunt of the insurgents' activities and suffered at the hands of the Ottoman military and paramilitary forces. Following the searches, most schools in the region were closed after their teachers were arrested, and the Exarchate was dealt a major blow to the (relatively) favorable relations it had been enjoying with the Sublime Port.

Gotse Delchev and Gorce Petrov established an external branch of the IMRO in Sofia in 1896 to foster connections with the immigrants in the principality and the Supremists. Relations between the two organizations were not extremely harmonious in the beginning. Supremists insisted on having

---

42. Adanır, *Makedonya Sorunu,* 125.
43. Duncan Perry cites two prior incidents when IMRO mules were seized and arrested, and he argues that it is extremely unlikely that the Ottoman authorities were completely unaware of the existence of the organization until the Vinitza affair but that they probably considered it to be "inconsequential"; *Politics of Terror,* 61–78.
44. Christ Anastasoff, *Tragic Peninsula,* 48. Given that the going rate for 50 kilos of wheat was about 30 kuruş, 800 liras was a considerable sum.

Bulgarian army officers dominate their actions, whereas IMRO wanted to stay independent of government control. Delchev and Petrov envisioned a local grassroots revolt, whereas the Supremists favored tactics such as forming small militias and influencing public opinion through demonstrations and publications.[45] In 1899, IMRO and the Supremists temporarily merged under the leadership of Boris Sarafov.[46] The change in leadership was not sufficient for the two factions to work out their differences, however, and now they disagreed on the timing of the planned rebellion. The Supremists wanted to act faster because they were convinced that sufficient effort had been expanded for agitating the peasants and a widespread popular revolt was a utopian idea. The safest bet, according to the Supremists, was to start a rebellion with the help of the Bulgarian military and have the European Powers intervene on behalf of Macedonians.

The Internal Organization, on the other hand, considered that a rebellion was premature. Its members had been preparing by extending the *cheta* networks throughout the regions. These bands regularly carried out attacks against noncooperating Christians or Muslims as part of the IMRO agitation campaign, the purpose of which was to stigmatize the population. These operations required considerable financial outlay because they needed to maintain the *chetas* and provide them with weapons and ammunition. The "contributions" collected from peasants were not sufficient to support such an enterprise, even when supplemented with the spoils from robberies; this induced the IMRO leaders to turn to more inventive methods of raising cash, such as kidnappings. After a few amateurish and failed attempts, the guerrillas hit the jackpot when they seized Miss Ellen Stone, a U.S. missionary, and her companion Mrs. Tsilka, a Bulgarian Protestant, in Razlog in 1901.[47] As protracted negotiations went on for the delivery of the ransom, Stone and Tsilka, who was pregnant during the time of the kidnapping, were forced to hike into the mountains by Jane Sandansky's *cheta*. This was Sandansky's first (and arguably most) high-profile action, and his name would soon become known throughout the region. Stone and Tsilka were released, exhausted but unharmed, after spending six months with guerrillas, during which time the pregnant Tsilka gave birth to a girl and, it seems, Stone developed an early case of Stockholm syndrome.[48] The

---

45. Adanır, *Makedonya Sorunu*, 155–56.
46. Perry, *Politics of Terror*, 82.
47. The first three people kidnapped by IMRO, two Muslim landowners and a Greek moneylender, managed to flee and almost kill their kidnappers; Laura Beth Sherman, *Fires on the Mountain: The Macedonian Revolutionary Movement and the Kidnapping of Ellen Stone* (Boulder, 1980), 8. During the Stone kidnapping, the target had apparently been someone else, Dr. House, another missionary, who happened to change his itinerary, so Stone and her companion were taken instead; Anastasoff, *Tragic Peninsula*, 67.
48. The affair was especially sensational because Miss Ellen Stone was evidently the "first

amount that IMRO received was 14,500 liras, significantly discounted from the original demand of 25,000 but still sufficient to buy the rebels 5,000 rifles and 200,000 rounds of ammunition.[49] The kidnapping had the added bonus of generating considerable international publicity for the Macedonian independence movement.

Support for the Macedonian revolutionary organization from Bulgaria and Russia had considerably been toned down by 1902. The crisis in Crete, which had resulted in a war between the Ottoman Empire and Greece, had proved that the Ottomans were not yet ready to throw in the towel. Russia, meanwhile, was more interested in pursuing its goals in the Far East and preferred that the Macedonian issue lay dormant in the meantime. In early 1902, Bulgarian Minister President Stoyan Danev asked the Russians for financial help. He was told that such help would be provided only if Bulgaria agreed to curb the activity of the Macedonian revolutionaries.[50] Danev accepted the condition and started taking measures against the Macedonian activists, but these measures were in the main designed to convince the Sublime Porte and the Great Powers that the Bulgarian government was in control of the situation. In reality, the Supremists remained largely unchecked because a great part of the Bulgarian officer corps actively supported them.

The Supremists were actually preparing for another rebellion, which finally took place in September 1902, despite the IMRO opposition to it. The Gorna Dzhumaia, or Cuma-i Bâlâ (today Blagoevgrad), revolt, named after the district where it started, was another failure for the Supremists. Popular support was low, IMRO refrained from participating, and the disturbances did not spread over a large area. The Ottoman army suppressed the revolt by November. The purpose of the revolt was never entirely clear, but the most likely explanation, according to Duncan Perry, is that the Supremists were trying to take control and show the IMRO committees that "professional military leaders in Macedonia were much more effective than schoolteachers."[51] The reprisals were harsh, and the regrettably predictable script of burned villages, murdered noncombatants, and violated women was played out once again.[52] A large number of the inhabitants of the region

---

American to be kidnapped outside the continental United States." Stone was full of praise for her kidnappers and wrote articles in support of their cause upon her release. Sherman, *Fires on the Mountain*, 37. See also Teresa Carpenter, *The Miss Stone Affair: America's First Modern Hostage Crisis* (New York, 2003). Martin Wills, another victim kidnapped in summer 1905 was not as lucky; he had to escape on his own and, having lost an ear for the ransom note, his thoughts for his kidnappers were quite different than those of Miss Stone. Martin Wills, *A Captive of the Bulgarian Brigands, Englishman's Terrible Experiences in Macedonia* (London, 1906).

49. Anastasoff, *Tragic Peninsula*, 68.
50. Crampton, *Concise History of Bulgaria*, 127.
51. Perry, *Politics of Terror*, 117.
52. There are contradicting reports on exactly how many villages were burnt; Adanır puts the number at fifteen and Perry at twenty-eight; Adanır, *Makedonya Sorunu*, 163; Perry, *The Politics of Terror*, 117. No matter which is correct, the damage was significant.

fled to Bulgaria. Fikret Adanır notes that the Cuma uprising was significant in terms of signaling the growing control of the Supreme Committee; the Supremists now dominated the movement and they had demonstrated that Macedonia was a national issue for Bulgaria by engaging Bulgarian officers.[53] Moreover, the Macedonian question was now developing into an issue that the European Powers could not ignore for long.

After the Cuma uprising, Austria and Russia took the initiative for instituting reform in Macedonia. Agenor Maria Goluchowski, the Austro-Hungarian foreign minister, and Heinrich Freiherr von Calice, the Austro-Hungarian ambassador in Constantinople, along with their Russian counterparts, Vladimir Lamsdorff and I. A. Zinoviev, exercised great influence on the successive reform attempts.[54] Abdülhamid II was aware of the imminent imposition of radical reforms and preempted them by introducing his own program in December 1902.[55] The program was not directed only at the "Macedonian" *vilâyets* (provinces) of Monastir, Salonika and Kosovo; all provinces of the empire in Europe were made subject to the new measures, which added Yanya, İşkodra, and Edirne to the new administrative unit, called the Rumeli Umum Müfettişliği (General Inspectorate of Rumeli). Hüseyin Hilmi Pasha, a veteran of Ottoman administration who had held, among other posts, the governorship of Adana and Yemen, was appointed to head the inspectorate with the title Rumeli Vilâyetleri Müfettiş-i Umûmîsi (General Inspector of Rumeli Provinces).

The reform program pledged to ameliorate problems with public works and services, which would presumably improve the lot of the locals and mend their relations with the government. A new gendarmerie force would be recruited from among the Christian as well as the Muslim population. Criminal law was to be put under the jurisdiction of new local courts, and legal clerks would be appointed equally from Christian and Muslim communities. A school would be provided to any village with more than fifty households, and 5 percent of the provincial revenues would be allocated for public works.[56] Goluchowski and Lamsdorff did not find these measures satisfactory. Calice and Zinoviev, the Austrian and Russian ambassadors, drafted supplementary measures for the program to be presented to the other Great Powers. In addition to the original proposals of the Sublime Porte, the "Wiener Punktation" (as it was later named) called for the introduction of Christian fieldguards in Christian areas, the expansion of *valis'* (governors') authority, financial regulations that involved separate budgets for the three Macedonian provinces and supervision by the Ottoman Bank,

---

53. Adanır, *Makedonya Sorunu*, 164.
54. Steven Sowards, *Austria's Policy of Macedonian Reform* (Boulder, 1989), 17–23.
55. Abdülhamid II had commissioned a proposal for this purpose before the uprising, in July 1902; Adanır, *Makedonya Sorunu*, 166.
56. Ibid., 167; Sowards, *Austria's Policy of Macedonian Reform*, 23.

the protection of the population from Albanian excesses, amnesty for political prisoners, and a predetermined tenure for the general inspector.[57] These proposals were presented to the Ottoman government in February 1903 and were immediately accepted—but they remained a dead letter in terms of implementation.

The Ilinden Uprising

The consensus among the Great Powers was in favor of maintaining the status quo in Macedonia rather than supporting autonomy, but nothing short of independence would satisfy the leaders of the Macedonian movement, especially after the example of Crete, which had gained its autonomy despite the failure of Greece in the war with the Ottoman Empire in 1897. Danev, the Bulgarian minister president, was feverishly trying to control the Supremists, but his efforts, such as banning the organization and arresting some of its leaders in January 1903, only drew the ire of the Macedonian circles and nationalist Bulgarians. So, another minister president buckled under pressure from the pro-Macedonian camp and had to resign in April 1903. He was replaced by Racho Petrov, a general in the Bulgarian army.[58]

The Gemidzis, an anarchist fraction that had branched off from the Macedonian revolutionary movement based in Salonika, carried out a series of bombings in Salonika in April 1903.[59] The *Guadalquivir*, a French steamer in the harbor, was the faction's first target, followed a day later by a bomb planted on the railroad tracks at the main train station, which exploded when the train arriving from Istanbul rolled over it. An attack on the gas plant left the city in darkness the following day, preparing the stage for a more spectacular attack: the Ottoman Bank and the neighboring German bowling club blew up in flames as dynamite charges set in tunnels under the bank exploded. The German school also suffered a great deal of damage from the explosion. Attacks on a café, the post office, and the Russian consulate were next, and these were stopped only after a show of force by the squadrons of European Powers that were in the bay. These operations did not, however, publicize the Macedonian cause, as had been hoped, because these acts harmed mostly European interests and the reaction in Europe was far from favorable.[60] The attacks were followed by reprisals by the Ottoman

---

57. Adanır, *Makedonya Sorunu*, 170–71; Sowards, *Austria's Policy of Macedonian Reform*, 24–26.
58. Perry, *Politics of Terror*, 129.
59. Ibid., 100. For more on this group, see Giannis Megas, Oi *"Varkarides" tēs Thessalonikēs: ē Anarchikē Voulgarikē Omada kai oi Vomvistikes Energeies tou* (Athens, 1994).
60. The principal exception to the condemnation coming from the European press was Victor Bérard, a long-time supporter of the Macedonian revolutionaries. In an article published in *La Revue de Paris* on June 15, 1903, he made the following remarks about the activists:

army and irregulars in the countryside, and more IMRO operatives were arrested. The IMRO changed its course of action partly because of the negative reaction generated by the activities of this radical group. In May 1903, IMRO held a congress in Smilevo, in Monastir province and decided to prepare for a general uprising in the summer. Thanks to the combined efforts of Patriarchists and Ottoman officials organized by Germanos Karavangelis, the charismatic Metropolitan of Kastoria, to chase the *chetas* out of the region, IMRO suffered several blows to its operations during spring and summer 1903.[61] Despite these setbacks, the uprising broke out in Monastir province on August 2, the day of Saint Elijah, or Ilinden.

The insurgents first cut telegram lines and disabled the railroads to halt communications across the region. The greatest accomplishment of the rebels was the capture of Kruševo, where they proclaimed a short-lived republic after they set government buildings on fire and killed the officials.[62] After a few days, on the Feast of the Transfiguration, or Preobrazhenie, the rebellion spread to Adrianople province, where the rebels were briefly able to set up a government in Strandja. In principle, the uprising was meant to be an invitation to the entire population, without respect to language or religion, to rise up against tyranny, but in practice this proved to be an improbable ideal. In fact, in many places the insurgents did attack Patriarchists and Muslims despite prior orders to the contrary. Other acts such as singing Bulgarian marching songs and waving the Bulgarian flag undermined the committee claim that this was a general uprising and associated the insurgents—more or less accurately—with Bulgaria.[63]

By September, the Ottoman army had suppressed the rebellion and hundreds of villages were left devastated after the guerrillas pulled out and the soldiers and militias exacted the toll from the local population.[64] The Macedonians' plight did garner sympathy in Europe, and relief missions were organized and sent to the smoldering villages, but contrary to the expectations of the committee, the European Powers did not intervene on behalf of the Slav population, let alone demand autonomy for Macedonia.[65] The revolt

---

"Their crime is, perhaps, inexcusable, but their courage was without any doubt, of the most heroic!" Quoted in Michel Paillarès, *l'Imbroglio Macédonienne* (Paris, 1907), 13. (Michel Paillarès was rumored to be in the pay of the Greek government.)

61. Adanır, *Makedonya Sorunu*, 193–94.

62. On the Kruševo Republic and its place in Macedonian national memory, see Keith Brown, *The Past in Question: Modern Macedonia and the Uncertainties of Nation* (Princeton, 2003).

63. Ibid., 196–99.

64. According to Adanır, the auxiliary Albanian militias, not the regular infantry troops, were responsible for the atrocities following the uprising; *Makedonya Sorunu*, 203.

65. Ibid., 195–206. For the aftermath of the uprising, see Henry Brailsford, *Macedonia, Its Races and Their Future* (London, 1906), which provides a detailed, although pro-Bulgarian, account of the devastation in the countryside. For an evaluation of "humanitarian" motives of the European intervention in Macedonia, see Davide Rodogno, "The European Powers' Intervention in Macedonia, 1903–1908: An Instance of Humanitarian Intervention?" in

had come as a surprise and cast doubt on the effectiveness of the reform attempts. Nevertheless, again under Austrian and Russian leadership, the idea of reform within Ottoman sovereignty was accorded another chance. The Mürzsteg Reform Program, as it came to be known, was accepted by the Sublime Porte in November 1903.

Implementation of the Mürzsteg Reform Program

The Mürzsteg Program was not fundamentally different from the previous "Wiener Punktation," except for the provisions it introduced for implementation of the measures. The program was criticized for being merely a continuation of the agreement between Russia and Austria dating from 1897 to not disturb the status quo in Macedonia.[66] Whether the program was indeed prepared with such a cynical agenda would be hard to ascertain, but it is true that, having been formulated and implemented under the stewardship of Russia and Austria, it had a decidedly conservative tone. Under the program, Austria-Hungary and Russia would directly oversee its progress through the two special civil agents whom they appointed. Even though they carefully limited the interference of other European Powers in the design of the program, as a concession Austria-Hungary and Russia invited other signatories to the Berlin Treaty to participate in the discussions. The status of the civil agents became a continuous source of conflict between the Great Powers and the Sublime Porte. Proponents of more efficacious reforms considered the civil agents to be a half-hearted attempt by Austrian and Russian diplomats to give the illusion that they had some purchase on the actions of the Ottoman government, embodied by Inspector General Hüseyin Hilmi Pasha. They were "not representatives of European control," writes Draganoff, "but functionaries who are to be absolutely at his disposal and whose office is to lighten the responsibility in the eyes of Europe."[67] The Sublime Porte, on the other hand, viewed even this concession a potential breach of sovereignty and insisted that Hüseyin Hilmi Pasha's authority be paramount in the region and over the implementation process, and that the civil agents' role not exceed that of assistance.

Establishing stability and ensuring the security of the inhabitants were the two priorities of the program. Consequently, the reorganization of the gendarmerie, which the Great Powers considered to be the prerequisite for

---

Humanitarian Intervention: A History, edited by Brendan Simms and David J. B. Trim (Cambridge, 2011), 205-25.

66. Draganoff, *Macedonia and the Reforms* translated by Victor Bérard (London, 1908), 8.

67. Ibid., 61.

both goals, became the primary focus. The French consul in Salonika, Louis Steeg, had made a similar proposal a year earlier, emphasizing the important role that a reformed gendarmerie, "well paid, well selected and commanded by first-class officers," could play in preventing the activities of the revolutionary bands and the abuses of the "Turkish gendarmerie, who are recruited from a bad class, irregularly paid, and obliged to 'live on the inhabitants.'"[68] Steeg's proposal, which had not found an enthusiastic audience at the time he drafted it, now seemed to constitute the centerpiece of the reform program, and it indeed had potential to ease the tension in the region if implemented in good faith. There were, however, too many obstacles to this good faith effort. The reforms got off to a slow start due to the difficulty of accommodating varying desires of the Great Powers as well as the difficulty of persuading the Ottoman government to agree to the plan once it was drafted. Colonel Wladimir Giesl, the military attaché of Austria-Hungary in Istanbul, conceived the original plan, which proposed that a large force of foreign officers command the reformed gendarmerie.[69] The Austrians recommended that an Italian officer be in charge of the organization, which was accepted by all the Powers, and the Sublime Porte formally asked Italy to appoint one of its officers to the mission.[70] General Emilio Degiorgis was thus appointed to command the reformed gendarmerie.

The first disputes over the plan broke out over the proposed headgear for the officers.[71] Giesl had suggested that the uniform be identical to that of Ottoman soldiers, including the *fez*, which became an issue of discord, presumably because of ideological connotations. This issue was temporarily resolved with a compromise suggested by the Russians: instead of the quintessentially "Turkish" *fez*, the officers could don *kalpaks*, which were also used by the Ottoman army but did not have the same connotations. But the *kalpak* could also pose a small problem: "It appears," remarked General Degiorgis, "that in the regions where the foreign officers will be operating, the *kalpak* is the habitual headgear of the Bulgarians, and could expose the officers to danger."[72] The resourceful general added that they would "look for a different model of *kalpak* that did not resemble that of the Bulgarians," and the headgear issue was resolved.[73] Another bone of contention was the

---

68. Ibid., 54–55.
69. Sowards, *Austria's Policy of Macedonian Reform*, 35.
70. MAE, Turquie, vol. 415, Ministère des Affaires Étrangères, memo to embassies in London, Istanbul, St. Petersburg, Berlin, Vienna, and Rome, January 4, 1904; French Embassy in Rome to the Ministry, Rome, January 9, 1904. The French ambassador in Rome attributed the Italians' being overjoyed at having been accorded this mission to "national vanity" and downplayed the importance of the decision, which "had been known for a long time."
71. MAE, Constantinople Serie E 145, Verbal Proceedings of the Sessions on February 18–21, 1904.
72. MAE, Constantinople Serie E 145, Verbal Proceedings of the Session on February 20, 1904.
73. The headgear issue occupied more working hours than it should have, and the

issue of command; instead of forming mixed battalions from different countries, as has been originally envisioned, the final resolution favored the division of officers according to their countries with a specific zone accorded to each division. This was tantamount to creating spheres of influence, which, not surprisingly, generated another round of struggle among the European Powers.

The final plan demanded that the foreign officers be authorized to give direct orders to their Ottoman subordinates and to dismiss officers and soldiers whom they deemed unfit for their mission. The foreign officers would be appointed at one rank above the one they held in their country of origin and would be allotted generous salaries and benefits.[74] The total budget was estimated to be around a quarter of a million liras, which would be secured through the Ottoman Public Debt Administration.[75] The proposals were presented to the Sublime Porte on February 29, 1904, and promptly refused.

As the talks were going on, the uniform problem surfaced again; this time, the issue was not the headgear but the fabric, color, and style of the officers' garb.[76] The dispute was apparently settled by accepting the original proposal, which was a uniform similar to the one worn by the Ottoman officers with a *kalpak* as the headgear. A new draft proposal, which toned down the European demands from the Ottoman side concerning command, was formulated. Now the adjoint generals' orders would be transmitted through Ottoman officers, and the right to dismiss unfit soldiers was rephrased as the right to transfer them outside the Macedonian command. The total number of foreign officers was reduced to sixty.[77] The Italian *carabinieri* model would be adapted for a gendarmerie school to be established in Salonika to train the new recruits.[78] The final arrangement of zones was as following: in Kosovo, the district of Uskub was assigned to Austria-Hungary: in Monastir, the town of Monastir as well as Kastoria and Serfice were to be under Italian command; and the province of Salonika was to be divided among the Russians, British, and French, who took over the *sancaks* (subprovince) of

---

sultan's insistence on the *fez* made matters more complicated. When it was finally resolved, the Austrians, Russians, and French opted for the *kalpak*, whereas the Italian and English agreed to the *fez*; Colonel Léon Lamouche, *Quinze Ans d'Histoire Balkanique* (Paris, ca. 1928), 45.

74. MAE, Constantinople Serie E 145, Verbal Proceedings of the Session on February 20, 1904.

75. Lamouche, *Quinze Ans d'Histoire Balkanique*, 35–41.

76. General Degiorgis suggested a style reminiscent of the battle dress of the English army; meanwhile the French were getting impatient with what they called the general's "Italianismes"; MAE, Turquie, vol. 415, Verbal Proceedings, March–April 1904. Apparently the German government made the uniform controversy a point of dispute in St. Petersburg, and the German ambassador in Istanbul, talking to the French chargé d'affaires in Pera made a joke on the subject, which his French colleague found in bad taste, especially given that his country was not sending officers to the Macedonian gendarmerie; MAE, Turquie, vol. 415, Chargé d'affaires to Delcassé, Istanbul, April 15, 1904.

77. MAE, Turquie, vol. 415, Embassy to the Ministry, March 10, 1904.

78. Lamouche, *Quinze Ans d'Histoire Balkanique*, 49

Armed Activity and the Appearance of Greek and Serbian Bands

A short-lived détente between Bulgaria and the Ottoman Empire resulted in an agreement signed by the two countries in March 1904, according to which Bulgaria pledged to suppress Macedonian insurgent bands and the Ottoman Empire promised a general amnesty.[80] With the general amnesty, in April 1904 all political prisoners, including participants and organizers of the Ilinden Uprising, were set free, which created a temporary sense of joy among the population. Shortly afterward, the recently liberated rebels took up arms again and the Ottomans were back in pursuit.

In 1904, the first incursions of Greek bands or *andartes* into the region started. The activity was in retaliation for Bulgarian support of the *komitajis* that menaced the Patriarchist, especially the Slavic-speaking Patriarchist population, and to curb the growing Bulgarian influence in a region to which Greeks maintained they could lay at least as legitimate a claim. Similarly, Serbian bands started to organize in the northwest, in the areas of Kosovo that the Serbs considered to be part of "Old Serbia." Into this mix was added the Muslim and Albanian bands, the self-proclaimed protectors of the Muslim population, who menaced Christian villages in retaliation for attacks against Muslims.[81]

IMRO, after the Ilinden Uprising, was a "shadow of its former self," and the Supremists used this opportunity to take over the organization.[82] Fragmentation within the organization started shortly afterward, and two camps emerged, known as the right wing and the left wing. The right wing were the Supremists such as Ivan Garvanov and Boris Sarafov, who favored close relations with Bulgaria.[83] The left wing was dominated by the

---

79. Partition was a touchy subject given the different and contradicting interests of the Great Powers in the region. Austria-Hungary was not content with Italian control over Monastir but had to strike a compromise that allowed it control over Skopje, which was strategically more significant because of its proximity to Bosnia-Hercegovina; Routier, *Macédoine et les Puissances*, 19. Areas in the north where the Albanian population was the overwhelming majority were not included in the reform; Lamouche, *Quinze Ans d'Histoire Balkanique*, 44.

80. Adanır, *Makedonya Sorunu*, 231.

81. The Ottoman government vehemently denied the existence of these bands, but they were undeniably active by 1905; Şükrü Hanioğlu, *Preparation for a Revolution* (Oxford, 2001), 221. See also Nadine Lange-Akhund, *The Macedonian Question 1893–1908 from Western Sources* (Boulder, 1998), 199.

82. Perry, *Politics of Terror*, 141.

83. This was not a monolithic group either; Boris Sarafov espoused more radical and violent activities even when there was a tendency within the group, under the influence of

Serres-Strumnitza group and was under the leadership of Jane Sandansky, who supported autonomy for Macedonia. The Congress of the Revolutionary Organization at the Rila Monastery in October 1905 did not succeed in bringing together the opposing factions.[84] On the contrary, Sandansky was expelled from the group, and the Supremists decided to tone down armed activity and instead channel their energies toward "educating" the population.[85] The two groups staked out two separate zones of influence: the right wing dominated the Monastir and Uskub region, whereas the left wing was in charge of the south, the districts of Salonika, Serres, and Strumnitza, where its primary engagement was with the Greek bands.[86] The two camps convened separately for the next congress: the Supremists (rightists) in Sofia in January 1907 and the leftists in Doubnitza a month later. By this time, the rift within the organization was beyond repair. There were failed attempts on Sandansky's life by the Supremists. In retaliation, Sandansky's associates assassinated Boris Sarafov and Ivan Garvanov, after which point the separation of the two groups became irreconcilable.[87]

Meanwhile, there was a dramatic increase in Greek armed activity in Macedonia. It was no coincidence that this development occurred after the appointment of Lambros Koromilas as consul general of Greece in Salonika in May 1904.[88] Early signs of armed activity came from Kastoria, where Germanos Karavangelis, the district Metropolitan, attempted to organize a band and buy off IMRO members; however, this venture failed to transform into a tangible network.[89] Against the rise in the perceived threat to Greek interests, civil organizations and paramilitaries coordinated their efforts with that of the state in a common cause in Macedonia. The first forays into Ottoman territory were initiated by officers of the Greek army, such as the legendary Pavlos Melas, with the support of Cretan volunteers, who could travel into the region with ease because of their official status as Ottoman

---

moderates such as Damian Gruev, to renounce violence. Some sources indicate that he even considered a "central committee" separate from IMRO; Lange-Akhund, *Macedonian Question*, 206–7.

84. For more information on the contentious issues of the congress, see ibid., 231–38.
85. Hanioğlu, *Preparation for a Revolution*, 245.
86. Ibid.
87. Ibid.; Lange-Akhund, *Macedonian Question*, 263.
88. Koromilas served as consul until October 1907. His predecessor, Eugenios Eugeniadēs, had been appointed to the job at a critical time, after the Greek-Ottoman war of 1897, and had managed to maintain good relations with the Ottoman establishment despite the post-war bitterness and the ongoing crisis in Crete. He was one of the early architects of the Greek policy that favored collaboration with the Ottomans in Macedonia until the greater common enemy (i.e., the Bulgarians) could be eliminated. For a summary account of the two consuls' activities in Macedonia, see Vasileios Laoudras, *To Ellinikon Genikon Proxeneion Thessalonikēs* (Thessaloniki, 1961).
89. Douglas Dakin, *The Greek Struggle in Macedonia, 1897–1913* (Thessaloniki, 1966), 120–24; Adanır, *Makedonya Sorunu*, 191.

subjects.⁹⁰ At this stage, local Patriarchists did not have a significant presence in the armed activities. Consuls such as Lambros Koromilas in Salonika and Antonios Sachtouris in Serres assisted in supplying weapons, facilitated recruitment, and protected the interests of the Patriarchate through methods not always approved by the Patriarchate itself.⁹¹ Their task was facilitated by the indifference—and even active collaboration—of the Ottoman authorities, who saw the Greek bands as a welcome counterweight against the Bulgarian "bandits." The local Muslim population also actively collaborated with them, and apparently, "Greek committees that did not have Turkish members were rare."⁹²

Despite the reforms and the European presence in the area, security did not improve; in fact, it deteriorated between 1904 and 1908. With the exception of brief interruptions in armed activity, the monthly casualty records told a grim story. One estimate puts the number of people killed in Macedonia between 1903 and 1908 at 8,000; of these 3,500 were guerrillas and the rest civilians.⁹³

Problems with Financial Reform and the Customs Duty Increase

Financial difficulties beleaguered the gendarmerie reorganization from the start. The Ottomans had pledged to finance the new force, but the truth of the matter was that this new commitment imposed an enormous burden on a budget already bursting at the seams. This problem was the basis of the reluctance by the administration to accept more foreign "advisors," an issue brought up again by Austria-Hungary and Russia late in 1904. The treasury was in such a dreary situation that oftentimes Hüseyin Hilmi Pasha himself had to plead with the Allatini brothers, owners of the largest mill in the region, in Salonika, which supplied flour to Macedonian garrisons, to continue shipments despite payments being in arrears so that the soldiers would have bread to eat. On occasion, the government had to borrow money from the Salonika industrialists, including the Allatinis and the Kapanzades, so that it could pay soldiers, orphans, and widows. Or the government dipped

---

90. The young and dashing Pavlos Melas became the proto-martyr of the Greek cause in Macedonia when he was killed in a skirmish with Ottoman forces in Siatista on October 13, 1904. His death was considered a turning point that finally shook Athens to take action to protect Greek interests in Macedonia; Alexandros D. Zannas, *O Makedonikos Agōn (Anamnēseis)* (Thessaloniki, 1960), 19.

91. For a list of local participants from the Serres region, see Iakōvos D. Michaēlidēs and Kōnstantinos S. Papanikolaou, eds., *Aphaneis Gēgeneis Makedonomachoi (1903-1913)* (Thessaloniki, 2008), 138-60.

92. Letter from Dr. Nâzım to Bahaeddin Şakir, cited in Hanioğlu, *Preparation for a Revolution*, 222.

93. Sowards, *Austria's Policy of Macedonian Reform*, 76.

into the purses of the Anatolian provinces, which hardly had any extra funds to spare.[94]

Work toward a financial commission that would serve as an advisory body to solve the budgetary problems in Macedonia started shortly after the gendarmerie reforms in 1904. Calice and Zinoviev were the architects of the early proposals. Compared with later proposals, these were rather conservative schemes that essentially aimed to rectify the revenue base without creating any major upheaval of the existing framework. One of the major concerns at this stage was the payments to the civil personnel that were in arrears, which, the civil agents held, should take priority over payments to the military. After Hüseyin Hilmi Pasha warned that this kind of prioritization might cause a military revolt, another proposal that balanced the needs of the Ottoman administration with the demands of the European Powers was formulated. According to this plan, revenues from the Macedonian provinces would be allocated to cover both civil and military expenses, but the amount earmarked for military expenses would be capped at peacetime levels and the difference would be covered by an extraordinary fund supplied by the imperial center.[95] The Ottoman Bank was instituted as the treasurer for Macedonia.

In December 1904, Lord Landsowne (Henry Charles Keith Petty-Fitzmaurice) was not content with the work of Zinoviev and Calice, and was already sounding the alarm about a looming crisis because of financial difficulties. He proposed that an international commission be established to oversee the financial reforms.[96] In February 15, 1905, the Sublime Porte made a formal request to increase the rate of custom duties from 8 to 11 percent to defray the costs of the reforms. Austria-Hungary and Russia were in favor of accepting the increase provided that the Ottoman state met certain conditions regarding the administration of the extra revenue.[97] But the tariff increase would prove to be one of the most problematic issues in the execution of the Mürzsteg Program, as benign a proposal as it might seem. Even though all the Great Powers concurred on the need to raise additional resources to finance the rising expenditures, there was hardly any consensus on how to raise them. A tariff increase was a measure that directly interfered with British commercial interests in the Ottoman Empire.

---

94. I have documented these dealings between the Allatini brothers and Hüseyin Hilmi Paşa, and the extraordinary measures taken to procure bread for the troops in İpek K. Yosmaoğlu, "*Ekmek Parası:* The Allatini Brothers and the Ottoman Army in Macedonia at the Turn of the Twentieth Century," paper presented at the conference on Local and Imperial Histories: Approaches to Ottoman/Greek Civilization, Chios, Greece, September 2000. The correspondence between the Allatinis and other army contractors can be found in, BOA,TFR.I.SL 1/25, December 21, 1902; TFR.I.SL 8/782, April 7, 1903; TFR.I.ŞKT 9/185, April 27, 1903; TFR.I.SL 48/4724, July 25, 1904.
95. Sowards, *Austria's Policy of Macedonian Reform,* 51–52.
96. Draganoff, *Macedonia and the Reforms,* 63–64.
97. Dakin, *Greek Struggle in Macedonia,* 303.

The Anglo-Ottoman Convention of Baltalımanı in 1838 had abolished all internal customs in the Ottoman Empire, ensuring an open market for British goods. Since then, Britain had established a profitable market for its manufactured goods and dominated the foreign trade of the empire.[98] Despite the facts that the current tariff rates were among the lowest in Europe and that increasing that rate was the only unexplored source of revenue that could be diverted for the benefit of the reforms, Britain found this an undesirable measure and jealously protected its interests even though that meant jeopardizing the implementation of the reforms.

Another obstacle in the way of financial restructuring was the objections raised by the Sublime Porte against the proposed financial commission, which it considered to be a violation of its sovereignty. Between the Ottoman objections and the assorted attempts by the European Powers to assert their own concerns, the shape and function of the financial commission were revised six times from the beginning of 1905 until the year's end, with the proposals delivered to the Sublime Porte with a *note verbale* each time.[99] In November 1905, a seventh *note verbale* was presented, which included not only the new proposal concerning the financial commission but also a bundle that contained the renewal of the foreign officers' and the civil agents' contracts, and the reappointment of Hilmi Pasha. This seventh *note* was also rejected, precipitating a demonstration of gunboat diplomacy by the Great Powers. With the exception of Germany, all the Powers contributed to a fleet that appeared before the port of Mytilene in the northern Aegean on November 26, 1905.[100] After the demonstrators threatened to move to Lemnos, the Sublime Porte agreed to all the demands: the tenures of the inspector general, general of the gendarmerie, civil agents, and adjoints were extended for two more years, and the International Commission for Financial Control in Macedonia was officially recognized.[101]

The financial commission was not a body under the leadership of Austria-Hungary and Russia; all six Great Powers had an equal say in its functioning, which proved to be a recipe for delays and inefficiency and seriously hampered the progress of the proposals. With the Ottoman agreement to the financial commission, the issue of the tariff increase was revived. Drafting an agreement that satisfied all the Powers and the Sublime Porte at the same time took another year after the financial commission authorization, and then it took another six months for the increase to come into effect. The British aversion to the idea and mistrust of the management of the tariff revenue were largely responsible for the delay. Each time a *note verbale*

---

98. Reşat Kasaba, *Ottoman Empire and the World Economy, the Nineteenth Century* (Albany, 1988).
99. Sowards, *Austria's Policy of Macedonian Reform*, 55–59.
100. Draganoff, *Macedonia and the Reforms*, 65.
101. Sowards, *Austria's Policy of Macedonian Reform*, 63.

on the conditions for a tariff increase was presented to the Sublime Porte, Britain heaped another set of demands on the original text, seeking further concessions for its commercial associates, which confirmed the prevailing opinion that the British government was "acting in bad faith."[102] Finally, on July 12, 1907, the tariff increase was put into effect. Steven Sowards notes that "[w]hen the protocols [for the tariff increase] were signed in April, the Macedonian garrison had been paid just once in the preceding six months, the civil administration only twice."[103] Meanwhile, Britain had obtained every single concession it sought, including the regulation of porters in the Salonika harbor.

End of the Leadership a Deux, End of Reforms

Judicial reform had been included among the provisions of the Ottoman reform proposal of 1902, as well as in the Mürzsteg Program, but until 1907 not much attention had been paid to this part of the plan; in fact, there were very few complaints about judicial abuse in Macedonia.[104] In March 1907, a new set of measures were put into effect that called for an increase in the number of courts, better pay for the judiciary, curbs on corruption, semi-annual inspections, and assurance of judicial autonomy.[105] These measures were not found to be satisfactory by the European Concert, which meant that additional demands were made of the Sublime Porte and, consequently, another chapter of protracted struggle among the Powers and with the Ottoman government began. After long negotiations, two alternative plans were drafted in June 1907 by Zinoviev and Johann Markgraf von Pallavicini, the Russian and Austro-Hungarian ambassadors. The plans were essentially the same and called for the financial commission to be involved in the judiciary reform through its chancery and to appoint the judicial inspectors who would supervise the courts. The discord stemmed from Pallavicini's conviction that the Ottomans would not accept an arrangement in which they would not have some degree of control over the appointment of inspectors, whereas Zinoviev insisted on complete European control. The question of the degree of Ottoman control over the judiciary deepened the rifts among the Great Powers, and the final *note verbale* drafted in December 1907, which favored Zinoviev's position, was more the result of a begrudging compromise than a real consensus.

---

102. Ibid., 69.
103. Ibid., 72.
104. Dakin, *Greek Struggle in Macedonia*, 347. This may also be attributed to the local population's lack of trust in the Ottoman judicial system.
105. Ibid., 346.

As the year came to a close, the civil agents' and other reform personnel's mandates, which had been approved for another two years by the Sublime Port in November 1905, were again about to expire. The request for renewal of the mandate was presented along with the judiciary proposal in a *note verbale* to the Sublime Porte on December 15, 1907. The response received "said nothing of the extension and proposed that the foreign agents in Macedonia be taken into Ottoman service."[106] An identical *note* was sent a week later, but the Great Powers lacked the cohesion necessary to convince the Sublime Porte to accept the extension. Sir Edward Grey, the British foreign secretary, found the performance of the Ottoman administration since the reforms started to be far from satisfactory and was vocal about his disapproval of a plan that would continue to defer to Ottoman authorities. The leadership of the program, which had been assumed by the Austro-Hungarian and Russian alliance, was no longer in effect. It had already been eroded by the financial commission, which relied on all six powers equally, and further eroded by the resignation of important diplomats who had originally conceived of the plan. The Russian and Austro-Hungarian foreign ministers, Lamsdorff and Goluchowski, and Ambassador Calice had all left office in 1906.[107] The death knell for the alliance sounded when Austria-Hungary obtained the concession of the Uvać-Mitrovico railroad.[108]

Russia blamed the Dual Monarchy for engaging in secret dealings with the Ottoman Empire to obtain commercial concessions in return for favorable conditions in the reform proposals. Britain suspected that Germany was involved in the deal. Even though there is no evidence to suggest that this was the case, the railroad concession effectively ended the collaboration between the Dual Monarchy and Russia, which did not bode well for the future of Macedonian reforms.[109] It seemed that the leadership was gravitating toward Britain, and now that the former alliance was broken, a new alliance was being formed between Britain and Russia, making it more likely that subsequent European demands for reform from the Sublime Porte would be more extreme than ever. In fact, on March 3, 1908, Sir Edward Grey repeated his proposal in a formal *note* that the number of regular Ottoman troops in the region be reduced and that of the gendarmerie be augmented. In addition, the influence of the palace had to be reduced to a minimum if the reforms were to be effective, and this would be achieved only with a truly autonomous, European-appointed Turkish governor, answering only to the Powers.[110] Despite Austro-Hungarian commitment to the conservative reform scheme, Russia seemed

---

106. Hanioğlu, *Preparation for a Revolution*, 233.
107. Sowards, *Austria's Policy of Macedonian Reform*, 66–70.
108. Hanioğlu, *Preparation for a Revolution*, 234.
109. Hanioğlu, *Preparation for a Revolution*; Sowards, *Austria's Policy of Macedonian Reform*, 87.
110. Hanioğlu, *Preparation for a Revolution*, 235; Sowards, *Austria's Policy of Macedonian Reform*, 90–91.

to be willing to cooperate with Britain. To avert further British demands, on March 13, 1908, Sultan Abdülhamid II preemptively renewed the mandate of the civil agents and the program until July 1914.[111]

Despite the long diplomatic work hours devoted to it, the Mürzsteg Program had accomplished little in the way of ensuring the safety of the local population. To the contrary, it indirectly contributed to the increase in armed activity and violence. One of its major flaws was the provision that provincial administration be rearranged according to national principles, which the fighting camps understood as clear indication that the next stage of the reforms was autonomy and partition according to national boundaries. Another outcome of the reforms was the effect they had on the local Muslim population, who did not figure in any European plan for the region, except in references to their brutality against their Christian neighbors, and who viewed the European agents in the region as an occupation force engaged in the final preparations for the secession of the country from the Ottoman Empire. Consequently, local Muslims also started to take up arms and form bands.

More important, the Ottoman Committee of Progress and Union (CPU),[112] which had merged with the Macedonian-based Ottoman Freedom Society in 1907, used this atmosphere to boost its recruitment and networking efforts in the region, connecting the independent and scattered bands to form a single organization.[113] Rumors of an impending Macedonian autonomy, which peaked after the meeting of the Russian tsar Nicolas II and the British monarch Edward VII in Reval, served as a catalyst the CPU agitation plans.[114] The affiliated Ottoman officers and clandestine agents were the organizational backbone of the CPU in the region, but its final plan of action also depended on an elaborate network that involved local notables, former brigands, and the neutralization, if not cooption, of the fighting bands in the region.[115] Their subsequent success in the revolution of 1908 put an end to

---

111. Hanioğlu, *Preparation for a Revolution*, 235.

112. Although CUP (Ottoman Committee of Union and Progress) is the better-known acronym and commonly used in reference both to the coaliton of opposition organizations against the regime of Abdülhamid II and the political party that dominated the Ottoman Empire after the 1908 constituional revolution, I have opted for CPU here which is the more accurate term: this was the specific organization active in Macedonia at the time; for the fragmentation in the Young Turk opposition movement and the emergence of the CPU see Hanioğlu, *Preparation for a Revolution*.

113. Mehmet Hacisalioğlu, *Die Jungtürken und die Makedonische Frage (1890–1918)* (Munich, 2003).

114. Hanioğlu, *Preparation for a Revolution*, 236.

115. IMRO, despite its split into two enemy factions, was still the most important presence in the region. The CPU leaders never managed to convince its right wing (under control of the Supremists) to form a collaboration, but Jane Sandansky and the Serres group under his command agreed to a tactical alliance shortly before the revolution. Greek and Serbian bands were under the central command of their respective governments, and they opposed CPU overtures to join forces. For a full account of this network and the CPU tactical maneuvers to establish this base, see Hanioğlu, *Preparation for a Revolution*.

the European reform program and brought about a fleeting sense of peace in the region. The restoration of the constitution was celebrated across Macedonia, where people rejoiced together on the streets regardless of their differences and where armed bands, even though they held on to their arms, came out from hiding. One of the most dramatic scenes was the legendary Sandansky's arrival in Salonika, where he was welcomed like a comrade in arms by Enver Pasha, one of the CPU leaders who had planned the revolution. The euphoria, alas, would prove to be another Macedonian illusion.

CHAPTER TWO

Education and the Creation of National Space

ΕΛΛΗΝΕΣ ΚΑΛΟΥΝΤΑΙ ΟΙ ΤΗΣ ΠΑΙΔΕΥΣΕΩΣ ΤΗΣ ΗΜΕΤΕΡΑΣ ΜΕΤΕΧΟΝΤΕΣ
[Greeks they are called those who assume our education.]
—Isocrates, *Panegyricus,* inscribed across the façade of Gennadius Library in Athens

The Museum of Macedonian Struggle in Salonika occupies an elegant neoclassical building that used to be the Consulate of the Hellenic Kingdom in Ottoman Selânik. The street in which the museum is located is named after Consul Koromilas, who was one of the most illustrious residents of the building and a chief facilitator of the Greek nationalist movement in Macedonia. Material and personal belongings of the heroes of the Greek struggle for Macedonia are kept and displayed here, much like relics in a shrine, as is an impressive collection of photographs from the era. Before a recent upgrade, the basement was dedicated to a permanent exhibition behind glass screens of dioramas that represented important scenes from the struggle. The combination of dimmed lights and the musty smell in the hall gave the place an eerie and bizarre feel, one reminiscent more of a taxidermy exhibit than a museum of national history, but this also contributed an unexpected charm to the somber atmosphere. As far as one can tell from the information website for the museum, the dioramas still stand, but the museum has acquired a more contemporary outlook with new lighting, flooring, and impressive photo-essays about the protagonists of the Greek struggle for Macedonia.

Except for a few stray foreign tourists who happen to stumble on the place by mistake, the Museum visitors are almost exclusively Greek, and a significant portion is under ten years of age. They are schoolchildren, some kindergarteners, whose teachers are presenting what is likely to be their earliest lesson in national history. One of the scenes they observe represents the classroom in village school in Macedonia. The keen interest with which the pupils appear to listen to their teacher suggests a degree of wishful projection. The effect, nevertheless, is quite impressive. The children staring into this time capsule may be too young to be subject to some of the more sophisticated tools of national indoctrination; they are years away from the draft, hardly able to read newspapers, and placed in a playground of sorts. But, prompted by their teacher, they are able to make a connection between themselves and the figures in the box, just like other groups of kindergarteners and elementary schoolchildren before and after them. The diorama establishes a visible link between the schoolchildren and their predecessors a century earlier while enshrining the classroom in a special place in the collective memory of the nation. The dioramas represent critical moments during the national struggle for its rightful territory, and just like the legendary "secret schools" of the Greek revolution, the classroom in Macedonia symbolizes resistance against foreign domination and assimilation—a beacon of light showing the way to those who would follow it.

The schools that became the scene of violent opposition between the Greek Orthodox and Exarchist communities in the countryside carried little resemblance to the institution that the word *school* elicits in contemporary minds. They occupied either a small building or a few rooms of a relatively bigger structure, and they were each run by a couple of teachers—ideally one each for boys and girls—and enrolled ten to fifty students.[1] In fact, even the diorama in the museum, which idealize the humble resources the Greek scholastic establishment had at its disposal—present a rather sterilized version of what an actual classroom in the Macedonian countryside would have looked like circa 1900. George F Abbott, who toured the region around that time, had a Greek schoolmaster as one of his travel companions. The schoolmaster, after having been removed from several positions due to his "arrogance," was desperately looking for a new outlet for his nationalist fervor. They finally reached Tachino (district of Serres), where he had secured a position. Here, Abbott describes the idealist teacher's post in his trademark sardonic style: "The school was in harmony with the sty aspect of the village. Repeated outpourings of ink had lent to the floor the appearance of a map of the world on a large scale, while the walls bore evidence of the *cacoethes scribendi,* the characteristic malady of youthful scholars the world over. The schoolroom contained a dozen rows of decayed desks covered with initials carved deeply into them. I should not have been at all surprised had I found a class of young pigs ranged behind them. Above the master's desk there hung an icon of Christ, and in the desk lay a register. ...."[2]

This register contained names of students, all boys, who had had to abandon their studies for various reasons, including, their parents' whim. This was hardly the school environment that some nationalist visionaries yearned for, which would have been clean and orderly, with a map hanging beside (if not in lieu of) the icon of Christ, a refuge where all peasants' children would be initiated into the national community by learning about its glorious past

---

1. *Carte des Écoles Chrétiennes de la Macédoine* (Paris, 1905).
2. Abbott, *Tale of a Tour in Macedonia,* 244.

4. Priest, teacher, and schoolchildren. From Leonidas Papazoglou, "Photographic Portraits from Kastoria and Its Vicinity at the Time of the Macedonian Struggle," George Golobias Collection, Museum of Photography, Thessaloniki. Used with permission. (Credit applies to figures 4–13.)

and heroic present and, more important, by learning how to write and speak its language.

If language is the most important indicator of cultural affiliation, the Greeks certainly started with a clear advantage in the Ottoman Balkans. Greek was the language of the Enlightenment in the Balkans in the late eighteenth century and continued to be so for most of the nineteenth. It was also the lingua franca of the "conquering Orthodox merchant" and the language of the high clergy and other learned classes.[3] Regardless of the language that one spoke at home, becoming a member of the nascent bourgeoisie meant learning to speak Greek in public.[4] This was in large part a result of the domination of the Greek establishment over education in the Ottoman

---

3. Traian Stoianovich, "The Conquering Balkan Orthodox Merchant," *Journal of Economic History* 20, no. 2 (1960): 234–313.

4. By contrast, among the Greek bourgeoisie outside the Balkans (in Alexandria, for instance), no refined Greek would consider a language other than French to be the utmost indication of civilization.

5. Gymnasium, teacher and students.

Balkans, where it reached non-Greek ethnic groups such as the Vlachs and Slavs, and even non-Orthodox groups such as the Catholic Albanians.[5]

By the first decade of the twentieth century, Greek had lost its cultural monopoly. Education, and especially education in parish schools, had traditionally been under the control of the Patriarchate, which appointed the teachers and also provided the curriculum and instructional materials. After the 1850s, however, the demand for Bulgarian schools—or at least schools where instruction was in Bulgarian—started to increase in the Macedonian provinces, and the trend was bolstered by the gains made in the north, in the Danube Province, during the *Tanzimat*. Vlach and Serbian schools constituted the secondary tier of competition to Greek Orthodox schools. Although the representatives of Greek national interests were vexed by the proliferation of Vlach schools, functioning almost exclusively courtesy of Romanian subsidies, they presented a negligible disturbance compared to the effects of the Bulgarian schools. The majority of Vlachs, either out of choice or exigency, still continued to identify as Greek Orthodox.[6] Moreover,

---

5. Selçuk Akşin Somel, *Modernization of Public Education, 1839–1908* (Leiden, 2001), 213.

6. A Vlach teacher reportedly insisted on teaching Slavic-speaking children Greek to, in his words, "open up their eyes." PRO, FO 195/1849, Samokov, December 11, 1894.

Vlach speakers were more scattered and less numerous than the Slavic speakers of the area. As for Serbian schools, they were more a nuisance for Bulgarian nationalists than for their Greek counterparts because they concentrated their propaganda efforts not in eastern and south-central Macedonia but in the northwest, a region in which Greeks did not have strong claims.

In November 1886, the French consul in Salonika called the proliferation of "Bulgarian schools" a "scholarly awakening" that checked the hegemony of the Greeks, who were used to a position of superiority in cultural matters thanks to their schools and the influence of the Greek Orthodox clergy. "Seeing reappear in Macedonia an element, which we would hardly pay any attention to in Athens fifteen years ago, would not be the least interesting spectacle of our times," he wrote to the minister of foreign affairs. "[B]y this awakening, which did not surprise the literati, the Greeks were stopped in the tracks of an ethnic assimilation that promised to take Cineas as its guide."[7] Less than two decades later, the Bulgarian side was so confident in the success of its challenge to Greek cultural hegemony that a pundit declared, "The century of Pericles marked the apogee of the Greek genius. Immediately after that was the decline. The Greek genius abandoned Athens. It made a few short appearances again in Byzantium. Then, it fell into lethargy ... and since then, its slumber has rarely been interrupted."[8]

The Greek and Bulgarian educational establishments resembled each other in their reliance on the religious establishment, rather than secular institutions of learning, to reach the masses. In this respect, the rivalry between the two closely paralleled the uneasy relationship between the Exarchate and the Patriarchate that resulted in the schism in 1872, only two years after the establishment of the Bulgarian Exarchate by imperial decree. Years later, the leading cadres of the Revolutionary Organization, founded in Salonika in 1893 with independence for Macedonia and Thrace as its aim, would come from among the products of the Bulgarian higher-educational establishment and would use their credentials as teachers to reach deep into the remote corners of the Macedonian countryside and enlist volunteers for their cause. The Greek side, for its part, enlisted the help of an Athens-based organization, the Society for the Dissemination of Greek Letters, to counter the efforts of Bulgarian activists and adopt the Patriarchate-dominated schooling system into its irredentist agenda.

---

7. MAE, vol. 7, Consul to the Minister of Foreign Affairs, Salonika, November 30, 1886.
8. D. M. Brancoff, [Dimitar Mishev] *La Macédoine et sa Population Chrétienne* (Paris, 1905), 62.

The Establishment of the Bulgarian Exarchate

On September 16, 1872, the Local Synod, convened in Constantinople at the behest of Patriarch Anthimos VI (Koutalianos) declared the newly formed Bulgarian Exarchate to be schismatic by reason of committing the heresy of ethnophyletism[9] despite the ongoing efforts by several clergymen, diplomats, and politicians to forge a reconciliation of the dispute between the Ecumenical Patriarchate and the Bulgarian Exarchate.[10] The decision was a turning point not only in terms of the relationship between the Ecumenical Patriarchate and the Exarchate but also the intercommunal relations of Christian Orthodox communities in the Ottoman Balkans. We could also argue that the Church schism indirectly—but profoundly— affected the evolution of Greek nationalism by compounding its emphasis on a collective consciousness defined and reinforced by membership in the Greek Orthodox Church.[11]

An imperial *ferman* issued on March 12, 1870, had recognized the establishment of a semi-autonomous Bulgarian Church in Constantinople, with an Exarch, a rank that fell somewhere between Archbishop and Patriarch in the ecclesiastical hierarchy. The *ferman* was the culmination of a protracted struggle that had started in the late eighteenth century, led by influential lay members of the Bulgarian community in Istanbul and by clergy frustrated by what they perceived to be an openly Greek bias and domination in the church organization. This particular cause of discontent with the Patriarchate was also duly noticed and exploited by Catholic and Protestant missionaries, who played a significant role in the evolution of Bulgarian nationalism throughout the nineteenth century.[12] These missionaries recruited increasing numbers of converts by taking advantage of Ottoman Bulgarians' desire for an independent church.[13] Encouraged and financed in large part by France

---

9. This is a specific form of nationalism based on race, declared heretical in 1872.

10. The Ecumenical Patriarch had convened in Constantinople the patriarchs of Jerusalem, Antioch, and Alexandria; the archbishop of Cyprus; and several bishops; A. Ischirkoff [Anastas Ishirkov], *La Macédoine et la Constitution de l'Exarchat bulgare* (Lausanne, 1918), 28; Thomas A. Meininger, *Ignatiev and the Establishment of the Bulgarian Exarchate, 1864–1872* (Madison, 1970), 181–89.

11. Paschalis Kitromilides argues that it was in the "symbolic universe of the Great Idea" that the Church and the nation could finally come together. "'Imagined Communities' and the Origins of the National Question in the Balkans," in *Modern Greece: Nationalism and Nationality*, edited by Martin Blinkhorn and Thanos Veremis (Athens, 1990), 60. For a general discussion of the Greek historiographic treatment of religion as an element of Greek nationalism, see Effi Gazi, "Revisiting Religion and Nationalism in Nineteenth-Century Greece," in *Making of Modern Greece: Nationalism, Romanticism, and the Uses of the Past (1797–1896)*, edited by Roderick Beaton and David Ricks (Aldershot, 2009), 95–106.

12. Victor Roudometof, *Nationalism, Globalization, and Orthodoxy, the Social Origins of Ethnic Conflict in the Balkans* (Westport, 2001); 133.

13. James F. Clarke, *The Pen and the Sword*, edited by Dennis P. Hupchick (Boulder, 1988), 328–30.

and also supported by Austria, the Uniate movement, which professed canonical communion with the Roman Apostolic See, started to make modest but considerable headway in the Ottoman Balkans.[14] In fact, conversion to Catholicism of the Eastern rite continued to be a viable option for some Bulgarian communities wanting to sever their ties with the Patriarchate even after the establishment of the Exarchate, despite the growing antagonism of local clergy and civil administrators, but this option lost momentum after the church struggle spread into and concentrated in Macedonia during the first decade of the twentieth century.[15]

Protestant missionaries, on the other hand, who were relatively late additions to the religious rivalry in the Balkans, created an alternative to the Uniate movement by emphasizing the reformation of preexisting beliefs and practices.[16] Although the Evangelical Alliance faced an uphill battle in spreading the gospel and "reforming" the Slavic-speaking Orthodox into a Protestant Church, the Bulgarian nationalists made apt use of the missionaries' presence when mustering up diplomatic support for their cause, especially from Britain and later from the United States.[17] Even though a proponent of the Bulgarian national movement has given credit to U.S. missionaries for contributing more directly—if unintentionally—to the creation of an independent Bulgarian Church by publishing the first bible in modern Bulgarian (Eastern dialect) in Istanbul in 1871, the Exarchate preferred Old Church Slavonic for the liturgy.[18]

The establishment of the Exarchate is viewed, with good reason, as the outcome of the Bulgarian community's frustration with its subjugation by the Patriarchate and with Bulgarian clergy's inability to participate in the higher church hierarchy. The Bulgarian community, constrained by the "double yoke" of the Patriarchate and the sultan, followed through with its plans for independence by, first, throwing off the former in preparation for throwing off the latter. The Exarchate, briefly put, is considered a

---

14. MAE, vol. 7, Salonika, May 23, 1885, Consul to the Minister of Foreign Affairs.
15. MAE, vol. 7, Salonika, September 14, 1881, Consul to the Minister of Foreign Affairs, Barthélemy Saint-Hilaire, concerning the activities of Lazarists and the conversion of the Bulgarian community of Goumendje (in Yenice-Vardar) into Catholicism, and threats from the Ottoman police and bishop of Vodena.
16. They actively pursued the mission of "reforming" the Greek Orthodox Christians of Asia Minor; Gerasimos Augustinos, "'Enlightened Christians and 'Oriental' Churches: Protestant Missions to the Greeks in Asia Minor, 1820–1860," *Journal of Modern Greek Studies* 4, no. 2 (1986): 129–42.
17. James Baker, who resided in Macedonia in the 1870s claimed that "In 1874 the Bulgarians in Macedonia, in their religious struggles, actually petitioned the British embassy to interfere in their behalf, and to have them placed under the ecclesiastical rule of the Bulgarian Exarch! They even went so far as to ask whether, in the event of their becoming Protestants, the British Government would watch over their interests!" *Turkey in Europe* (London, 1877), 57.
18. Clarke, *Pen and the Sword*, 290.

direct product of the culmination of Bulgarian nationhood.[19] Although this statement is largely accurate, at least as far as the Bulgarian clergy and intelligentsia of the late-nineteenth and early twentieth centuries are concerned, the events and personalities involved in the establishment of the Exarchate were so complex that this proposed linear connection between Bulgarian nationhood and the formation of the Exarchate as its utmost expression is inadequate. In fact, the most recent revision of this consensus argues that the establishment of the Exarchate should be seen as part of a broader process of secularization that transformed the Patriarchate in the second half of the nineteenth century; that the movement for the Exarchate was a product of the same process; and that the Exarchate cannot be viewed as an entity entirely separate from and antagonistic to the Patriarchate, even after the Schism of 1872.[20] This, I must add, speaks more to the motivations of the Greek clergy and lay elite in finally coming to terms with the establishment of an autocephalous church than to the desire of the Bulgarian side to undermine the influence of the Patriarchate (and, by implication, Greek cultural hegemony) over what they viewed as their own turf.[21]

During the second half of the nineteenth century the Ottoman imperial capital, rather than areas with large Bulgarian-speaking populations in the Balkans, hosted the most influential elements of Bulgarian nationalism.[22] The first concession that the Bulgarian community obtained from the Sublime Porte was the right to build a church in Istanbul in 1848 that would still be ecclesiastically subject to the Patriarchate but also serve as an "advisory body for Bulgarian communities everywhere in the Empire."[23] The lay elite of the Bulgarian community of Istanbul assumed most of the responsibility in the church struggle, and their leadership would greatly influence the

---

19. See, for instance, Ishirkov, *La Macédoine et la Constitution*. The classic work on the formation of the Bulgarian Exarchate published in Bulgarian is Zina Markova, *Bŭlgarskata Ekzarhiya, 1870–1879* (Sofia, 1989). An early classic, first published in German, is Richard von Mach, *Der Machtbereich des bulgarischen exarchats in der Türkei* (Leipzig, 1906); this was published in English: *The Bulgarian Exarchate: Its History and the Extent of Its Authority in Turkey* (London, 1907).

20. Dēmētrios Stamatopoulos, *Metarrythmisē kai Ekkosmikeusē: Pros mia Anasynthesē tēs Istorias tou Oikoumenikou Patriarcheiou tou 19o Aiōna* (Athens, 2003).

21. In fact, the first instance of an autocephalous church sparking tensions within Greek Orthodoxy was the formation of the National Church of Greece; Paraskevas Matalas, *Ethnos kai Orthodoxia: Oi Peripeties mias Schesēs apo to "Elladiko" sto Voulgariko Schisma* (Irakleio, 2002).

22. Ishirkov notes that, although there were highly educated Bulgarians in the service of the governments in Russia, Romania, Greece and Turkey, one of the most striking elements of the "Bulgarian renaissance" was the sheer number of Bulgarian periodicals appearing in Constantinople in the mid-nineteenth century; *La Macédoine et la Constitution*, 8–13.

23. Roudometof, *Nationalism, Globalization, and Orthodoxy*, 133. According to Ishirkov, Sultan Abdülmecid, after listening to the complaints of his Bulgarian subjects during his tour of the "Bulgarian provinces" (presumably referring to his tour of Rumeli in 1846), asked the Patriarch to defer to their wishes, again to no avail; *La Macédoine et la Constitution*, 10–11.

unfolding of this bitter quarrel within the Orthodox hierarchy. The Patriarchate agreed to a few more concessions in 1858 and 1859, such as the permission to use Slavonic in liturgy in certain regions and to name Ilarion of Macariopolis "Bishop *in partibus* (without seat) of the Bulgarian Church" in Constantinople.[24] The council convened by the Patriarchate deemed these concessions sufficient for the time being, and after deliberations that continued from October 1858 to February 1860, the council refused further concessions, including a proposal to grant parishioners the right to elect their bishop and to require bishops to speak the language of their congregations.[25]

It is important to note, first, that this council, which was known, somewhat anachronistically, as the first Ethnosyneleusē (National Assembly), was a response to the demand of the Sublime Porte, from the heads of the *millets*, in accordance with the 1856 *Islahat Fermânı*, to form representative councils.[26] More important, the work of this assembly between 1858 and 1860 resulted in instituting the participation of lay representatives in the election of Patriarchs and the establishment of a permanent *Diarko Ethniko Symvoulio* (Mixed Council), whose members included lay elements and had control over the Patriarchate's administration.[27] This council later played a great role in curbing the powers of the Holy Synod and became instrumental in unseating Patriarchs who did not agree with the influential members' agendas, bringing the networks between powerful members of the lay community, called the Neophanariots; representatives of foreign powers; and the clergy directly into ecclesiastical politics. The Mixed Council, according to Anastas Ishirkov, included only four Bulgarian members, three of whom, in protest over the council refusal to take up the issue of administrative changes in dioceses with Bulgarian populations, did not participate in the final sessions of the council. When Stephanos Karatheodori, a prominent Phanariot and the sultan's physician, issued an angry statement concerning Bulgarian demands, it triggered a response, composed in Greek, from Gâvril Krastevič.[28] Krastevič was a protégé of Stephan Vogoridis, a prominent

---

24. Tozer notes that in certain districts "as for instance, in the neighborhood of Ochrida, permission has been given within the last few years to introduce the Slavonic tongue ... but these are quite exceptions." Henry F. Tozer, *Researches in the Highlands of Turkey* (London, 1869), Vol. 1: 182. It seems that the use of Slavonic, although not officially condoned by the Patriarchate, had made its way into a few churches, at least for nonliturgical purposes out of local exigencies, much earlier than the 1860s; Cousinéry, for instance, notes that all the archbishops in Vodena had to learn Bulgarian even if they were of Greek descent if they wanted a good level of donations to the church in their diocese; E. M. Couisinéry, *Voyage dans la Macédoine, contenant les recherches sur l'histoire, la géographie et les antiquités de ce pays* (Paris, 1831), 77.
25. Roudometof, *Nationalism, Globalization, and Orthodoxy*, 138.
26. Stamatopulos, *Metarrythmisē kai Ekkosmikeusē*, 77.
27. Ibid., 121.
28. The response was presented under the name of Hatzi Nikolas Mintzoglou, the Bulgarian representative from Tirnovo, according to Ishirkov, *La Macédoine et la Constitution*, 15.

Phanariot who was, just like Krastevič, of Bulgarian origin. Although Krastevič, unlike his patron, was quite far from being entirely Hellenized, his close relations with other Phanariot families even after the establishment of the Exarchate, in which he had played an important part, is one among many examples that underscore the important role played by extremely complicated power, social, and political networks that had nothing to do with nationalism in shaping the relationship between the two rival Orthodox churches.[29]

On Easter Sunday 1860, Ilarion of Macariopolis performed a highly symbolic act of protest by omitting the name of the Patriarch from the liturgy, which earned him his excommunication from the Church and established him as one of the bravest voices against the hegemony of the Church elders.[30] Four years later, Nikolai Ignatiev, arguably the most influential Russian ambassador to the Sublime Porte in the nineteenth century, arrived to take up his post. After 1872 Ignatiev directed his energies to the mending of the division in the Orthodox *oikoumene,* to which he felt he had partially and unwittingly contributed.

Although the separation of the Exarchate had been in the works long before Ignatiev set foot in the Ottoman capital, his meddling in the affairs of the Church, including the election of Patriarchs, and the ties he cultivated with Ottoman statesmen that allowed him to exert just the right amount of pressure both on the Patriarchate and the Bulgarians, did contribute to the schism that occurred in 1872. The initiative he took to reconcile the two churches had to strike a very fine balance between catering to the desires of Bulgarians on the one hand and not alienating the Patriarchate on the other—and it was doomed to failure for the same reason. Ignatiev could not have lived to see the schism eliminated, which happened only in 1945.

The *ferman* that established the Exarchate was promulgated on March 12. The text was based loosely on an earlier blueprint drawn up by a Bulgarian council consisting of lay notables as well the clergy. It granted the Exarchate complete autonomy in administrative matters while preserving its ecclesiastical subordination to the Patriarchate. The Exarchate, in other words, was neither independent nor autocephalous but was granted fifteen dioceses, almost all of which were in Danubian Bulgaria. In this form, it far from satisfied the demands of the more ambitious nationalists in the Bulgarian

---

29. For a summary of Krastevič's career and other examples of such complicated networks, see Demetrios Stamatopoulos, "The Splitting of the Orthodox Millet as a Secularizing Process," in *Griechische Kultur in Südosteuropa in der Neuzeit,* edited by Maria A. Stassinopoulou und Ioannis Zelepos (Vienna, 2008), 243–70. The competing influences of Russia and Britain should not be overlooked in determining the outcome of power struggles within the Patriarchate; Christine Philliou, *Biography of an Empire: Governing Ottomans in an Age of Revolution* (Los Angeles, 2010), 143–44.

30. Ishirkov, *La Macédoine et la Constitution,* 17.

side but it was acceptable to the moderates and — with reservations — even to the Patriarchate. There were two major "time bombs" planted in the text, however, and these two issues would thwart all future actions taken to lift the schism. The first one was the location of the Exarch's seat in Constantinople, which was a disturbing but not extremely egregious decision to the Greek side when there was as yet no Bulgaria in existence. Yet many Greeks wondered why the Exarchate had not been located in Tirnovo, where Tsar Ivan Asen II had revived the Bulgarian Patriarchate in 1235. The second issue was even more menacing in terms of its long-term consequences: this was the clause sanctioning that, after a plebiscite, if two-thirds or more of the population of a given district voted in favor of it, the Exarchate could establish a diocese in that district.[31]

Immediately after the promulgation of the *ferman*, the Bulgarian community started to organize its own council of lay and clerical leaders to finalize a governing statute. Among the delegates who arrived in Constantinople for the occasion were those from Macedonian provinces, none of which was included in the jurisdiction of the Exarchate. A new demand emerged, namely, the official recognition of Bulgarian dioceses in Macedonia. This was not a matter that could simply be brought before the Ottoman government because the *ferman* clearly stated that the Exarch had to be recognized by the Patriarch. The efforts of Ambassador Ignatiev, Greek Ambassador Alexandros Rizos Rangavis, and the moderates on both sides to find a compromise seemed within reach, but the extremists on the Bulgarian side, such as Stoian Chomakov, who were not willing to settle for a solution that left out Phillippopoli, Strumnitza, Moglena, and Monastir (Bitola), went against the instructions of the Patriarch and celebrated Epiphany on January 6, 1872, with a ceremony conducted by the bishops of Makariopolis, Phillippopoli, and Loftzo. As a result, the last two bishops were dismissed from their duties, whereas Ilarion of Makariopolis, having already received this distinction, was excommunicated.[32] The Ottoman government tried to placate the Bulgarian side by approving the election of an Exarch, and Bishop Anthimos of Vidin received the title after the other four candidates were eliminated. He was presented to the sultan during a ceremony in Dolmabahçe Palace on April 12 — but without the approval of the Patriarch.[33] Subsequent attempts by Anthimos, who, unlike the other candidates to the position, had kept his ties to the Patriarchate,[34] to earn the Patriarch's endorsement were all turned down. The weakening ties between the Patriarchate and the new

---

31. A. Schopoff, *Les Reformes et la Protection des Chrétiens en Turquie* (Paris, 1904), 134–37.
32. Ilarion (Stoianov Michailovski) and Stoian Chomakov had both trained at the school of Theophilos Kaïris, the Greek theologian. Matalas, *Ethnos kai Orthodoxia*, 89–193.
33. Ibid., 297–99.
34. Anthimos had remained as the director of the Theological Seminary in Halki; ibid., 298.

autocephalous church finally broke completely after the Exarch, along with the three (by now notorious) bishops, Panaretos, Ilarion of Loftza, and Ilarion of Makariopolis, celebrated mass on the day of saints Cyrill and Methodios, and declared the independence of the Bulgarian Church on May 11, 1872. On May 13, the general synod convened by the Patriarchate defrocked the former bishop of Vidin, excommunicated Panaretos and Ilarion of Loftza, and anathemized Ilarion of Makariopolis, condemning him to eternal hell.[35] The Local Synod convened in Constantinople officially declared the Bulgarian Church schismatic on September 16.

At first, it seemed that the schism was not final; lay and clerical actors on both sides of the split worked for a reconciliation until well into the first years of the twentieth century. After the settlement in 1878, all the dioceses originally recognized by the *ferman* of 1870 within the jurisdiction of the Exarchate fell outside the borders of the Ottoman Empire. Between the schism and 1876, when insurrectionary activity in the Danubian provinces soured the relations between the Sublime Porte and the Exarchate, the Bulgarian Church had secured several concessions and expanded its jurisdictional reach to include Skopje and Ohrida. The Russo-Ottoman War reversed these gains and left the Bulgarians in a precarious position until the 1890s, when the Sublime Porte finally approved the *berats* (licenses), first for the dioceses of Ohrida and Skopje and then for Veles (Köprülü) and Nevrekop.

Patriarch Ioachim III, who ascended the throne for the first time in 1878 (his second term was from 1901–1912), now faced the daunting task of preserving the Orthodox *oikoumene* that remained in the Ottoman lands. Maintaining the schism and further antagonizing Slavophone Christians, Exarchist or Patriarchist, against the Patriarchate would not be conducive to this end. Ioachim's conciliatory attitude toward the Exarchate was inspired by this concern. However, the loss of territory also resulted in a sudden loss of revenue, which forced the Patriarchate to accept financial assistance from the Greek government, weakening its institutional position and establishing an external dependency.[36] Financial support from the Greek government compromised the Patriarch's credibility vis-à-vis his goal of mending the schism and reasserting his role as the head of the imperial Orthodox community. He astutely tried to circumvent this problem by enlisting the help of wealthy Greek Orthodox families in Istanbul, which did not sit well with the Greek government.[37] In the end, Patriarch Ioachim III's efforts proved

---

35. Ishirkov, *La Macédoine et la Constitution*, 28.
36. Evangelos Kofos, "Patriarch Joachim (1878–1884) and the Irredentist Policy of the Greek State," *Journal of Modern Greek Studies* 4 no. 2 (1986): 107–20.
37. Another source of conflict between Ioachim III and the Greek government was the increasing Russian influence in Mount Athos, which the Greek nationalists viewed as a bulwark against Slav encroachment on Macedonia. Ioachim III's views on how to deal with this issue were again conciliatory, which the Greek side took as "anti-national." Ibid., 115–16.

insufficient to, on the one hand, counteract the divergent positions of the Patriarchate and the Greek irredentists and, on the other, reconcile the differences between the Patriarchate's and the Exarchate's visions for the future of Macedonia.

The seat of the Exarchate in Istanbul became an extremely important bone of contention, especially after the formation of the Bulgarian principality in 1878 and the unification of the principality with Eastern Rumelia in 1885. The Exarchate was not the first Orthodox Church to become independent of the Patriarchate without the Patriarchate's approval; even the Church of Greece, which was established in 1833 and actually had served as a model for the Exarchate, had not been recognized by the Patriarchate until 1850. The Exarchate was exceptional, however, in the sense that church autonomy had preceded political independence from the Ottoman Empire.[38] This meant that the rival Church in Istanbul challenged the Patriarchate's authority *within* the Empire. After the formation of Bulgaria under Russian patronage, the Exarchate could not be marginalized outside the borders of the Empire, despite efforts to do so, because the Bulgarians were unwilling to give up the central position of the Exarch's seat in the imperial capital and the rights grandfathered in with the plebiscite clause. As the influence of nationalists on both sides drowned out the dissenting voices of the moderates, the schism was gradually accepted as a permanent situation. Even as late as 1901, when Ioachim III came into his second term as Patriarch, the views of the Patriarchate on the issue of an autonomous Bulgarian Church were not definitive, and they clearly acknowledged the need for special arrangements for "Bulgarian" speakers in Macedonia.[39] This is in striking contrast to the attitude and actions of the representatives of the Great Church in Macedonia only a few years later, including Ioachim III himself, when refusing peasant demands for priests who could understand their language became a matter of course. Even though the dominant opinion among lay and clerical members of the leadership in Istanbul seemed to favor the possibility of a reconciliation with the Exarchate, this opinion lost its relevance as the struggle for Macedonian dioceses transformed from ecclesiastical rivalry into armed warfare. It seemed that the ties between the two churches were now cut off for good. By this time, the schism was no longer an issue originating and contained within the capital, but had spread and mutated into a relentless struggle that claimed the lives of Macedonian peasants by the thousands.

---

38. The Serbian Church, which was restored in 1557, was abolished again in 1766.
39. Evangelos Kofos, "Attempts at Mending the Greek-Bulgarian Ecclesiastical Schism (1875–1902)," *Balkan Studies* 25 (1984), 365–66.

The Growth of Bulgarian Schools

Köprülü (Veles), Kukliş (Koukoush), and Cuma-i Bâlâ (Gorna Djoumaya) were the earliest among the districts of Macedonia to acquire Bulgarian schools.[40] The Bulgarian nationalist intelligentsia of Constantinople viewed the new schools with enthusiasm and raised funds for their support and maintenance. In May 1858, for instance, an article in *Bulgarski Knizhitsi* reported the introduction of Bulgarian into the churches and schools in Koukoush, replete with allegories of awakening and quenching the thirst for hearing "the word of God in their native tongue" following a period of sadness. The author warned the readers that a sorry state of affairs was still the case in many dioceses: "Ohrid, Bitola, Kostur, Moglena, Voden, Stroumnitza, Polyanino (Doyran), Melnik, Serres, Drama, and a few more, where the inhabitants intermingle with Greeks."[41] Not surprisingly, this list overlapped with the dioceses, where the "interests of Hellenism" should be protected through schools, according to the Athens-based Society for the Dissemination of Greek Letters (*Syllogos pros Diadosin tōn Ellinēkōn Grammatōn;* henceforth, Syllogos).[42] We must note, however, that some of the schools described as "Bulgarian" were officially under the control of the Patriarchate, and in many cases Bulgarian was taught or used in church services (Slavonic, in this case) without the knowledge of the local Greek Orthodox bishop.[43] After the establishment of the Bulgarian Exarchate in 1870, the number of communities demanding instruction in Bulgarian started to increase. In 1895, an *irâde* placed Bulgarian schools under the authority of the Exarchate, following the existing model for Greek Orthodox (*Rum*) schools. According to this, teachers would be appointed directly by the Exarchate, subject to the approval of local authorities.[44] As the conflict in Macedonia crystallized around the Exarchist-Patriarchist division, schools, like church buildings, came to represent entities much larger than themselves.

The *irâde* of 1895 that placed Bulgarian schools officially under the authority of the Exarchate was in accordance with established imperial procedure and required a protocol of scrutiny over their activities. The Exarchate would present a list of appointed teachers to the local civilian authorities,

---

40. See *Macedonia, Documents and Material* (Sofia, 1978), 142–51.
41. "Report from Koukoush," *Bulgarski Knizhitsi,* no. 10 (May 1858), cited in ibid., 149. (All citations from this source are transliterated as in the original.)
42. Mavrokordatos and Pantazidis to Kontostaulos, Athens, December 11, 1875 (Ta archeia tou Ypourgeiou Exoterikōn, Archives of the Foreign Ministry, [henceforth AYE]), a.a.k. 1876–77/3, in Sophia Vouri, *Pēges gia tēn Istoria tēs Makedonias: Politikē kai Ekpaideuse* [Sources for the History of Macedonia: Politics and Education] (Athens, 1994), 30–33.
43. Russian Consul in Manastir, M. A. Hitrovo to Ignatiev, August 6, 1864, cited in *Macedonia, Documents and Material,* 212–14.
44. MAE. vol. 39, Consul to the Minister of Foreign Affairs, Salonika, February 6, 1904.

who would then perform a background check to see if the teachers were "trustworthy" individuals.[45] Textbooks were subject to inspection by an office specifically created for this purpose, namely, the inspector of Bulgarian schools. After the Ilinden Uprising, the level of surveillance increased significantly. The inspector kept detailed registers of Bulgarian teachers, including their names, places of birth, past appointments, and any information on their ties to the "Committee," which were then presented to the Inspectorate.[46] If the administrative council of a village could not vouch for the character of a teacher and report his or her whereabouts, the teacher would be denied permission to work and confined to his or her place of birth.

During the early stages of the Bulgarian educational project in Macedonia, a mix of local communal support and donations from wealthy patrons elsewhere financed the schools. The latter category included members of the Bulgarian bourgeoisie in the imperial capital, who established nationalist civil organizations such as the Macedonian Society of Constantinople. Support from Russia, which the Greeks found so irritating, did not come until later, in the 1860s, along with support for the Church movement in response to the increasing influence of the Uniate movement, which the Patriarch of Moscow perceived as a threat to Eastern Orthodoxy.[47] The Russian consuls in Macedonia actively sought information on the state of the Bulgarian schools in the area and reported on their need for support by the Russian government.[48] Another important link to Russia at the time was the Russian-educated nationalists of Macedonian origin. Many of them had completed their education thanks to scholarships provided by the Moscow Benevolent Society and by the Russian Embassy in Istanbul. They replaced the earlier generation that had studied in Greece, and they usually returned to Macedonia as teachers and to raise consciousness for the Bulgarian national cause.[49] Finally, commercial guilds made important contributions to the educational effort in the region.[50] Funding Bulgarian education was a mark of social distinction, and failing to do so might cause considerable damage to one's social capital; periodicals announced the names not only of the benefactors but also of their less generous compatriots to the community.

---

45. Ibid.; BOA, TFR.I. SL 14/1381, Director of Educational Affairs [Maarif Müdürlüğü] to the Inspectorate, Salonika, July 12, 1903.

46. BOA, TFR.I.SL 144/14331, Inspector of Bulgarian Schools, Salonika, May 19, 1907.

47. Jelavich and Jelavich, *Establishment of the Balkan National States*, 133; *Macedonia, Documents and Material*, 186.

48. Consul Hitrovo to Novikov, Manastir, January 16, 1864 and July 1864, cited in *Macedonia, Documents and Material*, 209, 211-14.

49. All but one of the six teachers cited in the Russian consul's report on Bulgarian education in Macedonia had been trained in Russia; *Macedonia, Documents and Material*, 298.

50. The first Bulgarian schools were founded in commercial centers. Some of the communities that later sent financial contributions to Bulgarian schools in Macedonia were also important trade towns such as Plovdiv, Pazardjik, and Kalofer; "Report from Nevrokop," *Turtsia*, June 20, 1865, cited in ibid., 219.

An article published in the newspaper *Turtsiia*, January 8, 1866, praised the kindness of those notables who were participating in the efforts to provide Bitola (Monastir) with a Bulgarian school and berated those "who still tarry and keep aloof," identifying the members of this category by name in the hopes that "God will enlighten and strengthen them."[51]

The Greek state was actively interested in raising national consciousness in the "enslaved lands," including Macedonia, even before the Exarchate's sphere of influence had started to spread through the few dioceses it was originally granted. As early as 1871, the Ministry of Foreign Affairs had identified, in a circular to the consulates, the need for more schools because nothing would "support Hellenism and national sentiment like Greek education and language."[52] After the Greek state and literary societies started to appreciate the significance of the scholastic rivalry and the influx of funds from Russia and independent Bulgaria into Macedonia, they increased their financial assistance to the Macedonian schools and sought further funds. Syllogos, after 1869, and the Committee for Support of Greek Church and Education, after 1886, were the two proxies through which the Greek state lent support for the cause of Hellenism in the "enslaved lands." By the 1900s, when the struggle with the Exarchate reached its zenith, the efforts of these organizations were combined with those of the Patriarchate, and a full counteroffensive was launched against the proliferation of Bulgarian schools. According to Captain Leon Falconetti, who was with the French gendarmerie in Serres, the Greek government had spent 1.5 million drachmas in 1906 from its meager budget just for this purpose.[53] In this later part of the counteroffensive, the Patriarchate and Greek learned societies (which, despite having joined forces tactically, were at odds with each other more often than not) benefited from the Ottoman authorities' somewhat justified distrust of the Bulgarian educational establishment.

When a community could not agree on the medium of instruction, disputes arose regarding the use of the school building, very similar to those arising regarding the use of church buildings. In fact, in many cases, the disputes involved both the church building and the school building, if there was one, because the latter was seen more or less as an extension of the other. Just as in the disputes concerning the use of church buildings and newly appointed priests, in solving problems relating to the schools the authorities usually sided with the Greek Orthodox Metropolitan. Problems did occur frequently, especially when communities that were at least nominally under

---

51. "Report from Bitola," *Turtsiia*, Constantinople, no. 27, January 8, 1866, cited in ibid., 221–22.

52. Eleni D. Belia, "Ē Ekpaideutikē Politikē tou Ellinikou Kratous pros tēn Makedonia kai o Makedonikos Agōn" [The Educational Policy of the Greek State toward Macedonia and the Macedonian Struggle], in *O Makedonikos Agōnas: Symposio*, [Macedonian Struggle, Symposium Proceedings] (Thessaloniki, 1987), 30.

53. MAE, vol. 416, Report by Captain Falconetti, March 19, 1906.

the jurisdiction of the Patriarchate demanded Bulgarian-speaking teachers. Even though authorities usually attributed this "extraordinary" demand to the pressures of armed bands in the area, it was equally, if not more, likely that the demand for a Bulgarian-speaking teacher was motivated by more practical concerns, such as the desire to have the children learn to read and write in their native tongue or, more precisely, in an idiom closer to it than Constantinople-approved Greek. Note that these communities were not exclusively those that wanted to sever their ties with the Patriarchate. In April 1883, a scandalized Greek consul in Monastir reported to the president of the Syllogos in Athens that not only the "schismatic but also some Bulgarophone Orthodox communities" supported Bulgarian schools with "monies from the church fund and monastic revenues." He blamed the bishops for this outrage because, although it was actually within their authority to forbid the use of church money for such purposes, they did not do so for fear of alienating the population that they depended on for their own living.[54]

Some clergymen's tendency to accommodate and appease the locals, as opposed to the "take-no-prisoners" approach of action-minded consuls and other representatives of the Greek national intelligentsia, was a recurring source of tension. The conflict between the lower clergy in Macedonia and the Greek national elites in the Hellenic kingdom as well as the Ottoman Empire became more pronounced, particularly with regard to the language of instruction in parish schools during the last two decades of the nineteenth century, when there still seemed to be a chance to mend the schism. The Ecumenical Patriarch Ioachim III (who had ancestral roots in Macedonia), for instance, was in constant conflict with Athens, specifically with representatives of the Syllogos, during his first term as Patriarch between 1878 and 1884 over the need to reconcile with the Exarchate. Leaders such as Konstantinos Paparrigopoulos viewed the schism as beneficial for the interests of Hellenism in Macedonia, whereas Ioachim III was convinced otherwise.[55] Likewise, even a Patriarch such as Anthimos VII (1895–1897), who was thought to be much less lenient toward Bulgarian demands for ecclesiastical authority, criticized the actions of the Greek government during a visit to the Hellenic embassy in Constantinople and defended a policy of appeasement toward the "fellow Orthodox," especially the Serbs, to overcome the "isolation" that the Greek Orthodox were mired in. The views of His All Holiness were not welcome by Mr. Zalokostas, the secretary of the Syllogos, who rebutted that as long as the Serbs did not limit themselves to their logical "ethnological boundaries" there would be no use in a reconciliation, and

---

54. AYE, fak. 1883, Consul Dokos to President of the Society for the Dissemination of Greek Letters, Monastir, April 1883, in Vouri, *Pēges gia tēn Istoria tēs Makedonias*, 46.

55. Kofos, "Attempts at Mending," 357.

that they were trying to overthrow a status quo in the church, which it was in the interests of the Greek nation to preserve.[56]

The most common method of resistance that Slavic-speaking villages displayed against Greek-speaking teachers was to prevent the newly appointed teachers from taking up residence. An angry Metropolitan of Vodine wrote to the Inspectorate in September 1904 that this was exactly what was going on in several villages under his jurisdiction. According to the Metropolitan, the behavior of the villagers was the result of threats by "Bulgarian brigands" who had been circulating the vicinity, telling people "you are Bulgarians, you will read Bulgarian, don't accept the *Rum* teachers sent to your villages."[57] On receiving the letter, the Inspectorate warned the local authorities about the Metropolitan's concerns and ordered that they provide the *Rum* teachers with all the protection they needed to assume their positions because such "harassment" and the intervention of Bulgarian priests and teachers in these villages were utterly "inappropriate." The village councils were duly warned to properly welcome the new appointees because they would be held personally responsible for the safety and well-being of the teachers.[58] When the Inspectorate was flooded with angry petitions from Greek Orthodox bishops in the area about similar cases of resistance, as happened often, they routinely demanded from local authorities that the Greek Orthodox Metropolitans' concerns be fully addressed. Some officials carried out their assignment with exceptional zeal, not only giving a warning to the village heads and notables but also ensuring that they were detained and duly reprimanded by the Greek Metropolitan himself.[59] Having been berated by the Metropolitan and roughed up by the gendarmes, it was then the villagers' turn to send protest telegrams to the authorities.[60] It is hard to tell whether the children received any schooling at all in either language after such heated exchanges among their parents, the Metropolitan, the insurgents, and the government.

Higher Education for Higher Classes

Schools of higher learning, the gymnasia and secondary schools that served the important mission of training teachers, proliferated in Macedonia

---

56. AYE, fak. 1895, Ambassador Mavrokordatos to Minister Deliyianni, Istanbul, March 11, 1895, in Vouri, *Pēges gia tēn Istoria tēs Makedonias*, 269–70.
57. BOA, TFR.I.SL 53/5289, Metropolitan of Vodine to the Inspectorate, September 4, 1904.
58. BOA, TFR.I.SL 53/5289, Inspectorate to the Kaymakamlık (Prefecture) of Yenice Vardar and Vodine, September 6, 1904.
59. BOA, TFR.I.SL 53/5204, Inspectorate to the Prefecture of Vodine, September 26, 1904.
60. BOA, TFR.I.SL 52/5186, Telegram to the Inspector, September 1904.

after the 1890s. The graduates of these schools spread the national gospel to their less unenlightened brethren in the countryside. By 1905, according to D. M. Brancoff (Dimitar Mishev) there were thirty-seven Bulgarian (and one Bulgarian Uniate) and twenty-three Greek secondary schools in the province of Salonika; the numbers of these schools in Monastir were sixteen and twelve and in Kosovo eighteen and two. Although there were, in fact, only a couple of large gymnasia in centers such as Salonika, Serres, and Monastir, and Mishev's numbers included any institution slightly more sophisticated than a parish school with one or two teachers, he was correct in noting a trend to augment the capacity of national schools in Macedonia belonging not only to Greeks and Bulgarians but also to Vlachs and Serbs.

The town of Salonika hosted the best-known gymnasia, while a majority of provincial centers had at least one, and as many as five, secondary schools by 1905.[61] In 1882, however, according to a report of the French consul in Salonika, the Bulgarian community had one high school and the Greek community one *école normale,* both exclusively for boys.[62] Higher education for girls was not offered. The consul noted the great importance for Greek national interests of the *école normale,* which trained the teachers that were to staff the village schools in Macedonia, a task that had become even more critical in the face of growing competition from the schools of other groups. All students enrolled in the school received a monthly stipend for food and lodging, but the school did not have boarding facilities.

The curriculum of the Greek *école normale* concentrated on history, mathematics, and philosophy. It was among the best, according to the consul, except for language instruction, which was limited to ancient and modern Greek. The duration of studies was six years, and there were six classes. The consul also noted that Greeks were exceptionally quiet about the activities of the school, especially concerning its finances. The annual costs were estimated at 70,000 French francs; instruction was free in principle, except for a small entry fee, so most of this amount was covered by donations from well-to-do families and other philanthropic benefactors.

According to the same report, the Bulgarian high school in Salonika was the top such institution in Macedonia in terms of its quality of instruction, and the administration had plans to turn it into a gymnasium.[63] There were three classes, and all students learned Bulgarian, French, and Turkish. Most

---

61. Unlike the primary schools, which were scattered around the countryside and consisted of a room, a teacher, and a few students, it was more difficult to manipulate number of secondary schools. For this reason, the "Greek" and "Bulgarian" sets of statistics published by Mishev concur on the number of secondary schools in the *vilâyet* (province) of Salonika; *La, Macédoine et sa Population Chrétienne,* 240–41, 260–61.

62. MAE. vol. 6, Consul to the Minister of Foreign Affairs, Salonika, May 30, 1882.

63. Bernard Lory notes that the school was founded in 1880; "Soloun, Ville Slave?" in *Salonique, 1850–1918: La "Ville des Juifs" et le Réveil des Balkans,* edited by Gilles Veinstein (Paris, 1993), 133. However, there had been a Bulgarian school in Salonika since 1870, which had operational difficulties because it did not have a stable residence. The Vuzrozdeni (Revival)

of them came from the interior of the province, and the demand for enrollment was so high that the school was forced to turn down some of the candidates. The student body was all boarding, and they also received a yearly stipend of 345 French francs. Fifteen of the students were on scholarships from the Exarchate.[64] The state-of-the-art facilities included, among other things, fully equipped chemistry and physics laboratories and a biology hall (complete with a grand taxidermy collection), which apparently served double duty as an entertainment center for the town.[65]

The Ottoman authorities and members of the rival sects alike loathed secondary schools of this kind because they were seen as indoctrination centers dispensing hatred rather than enlightenment to young minds.[66] The Bulgarian school in the town of Serres, for instance, was continuously the target of the wrath of the Serres Greek community. In July 1873, final exams in the school were interrupted by a Greek mob that stormed into the building, cried "Damnation to all Bulgarians," and ran away. They were followed by Greek students, who "noisily climbing the stairs ... began stamping with their feet and hooting at those present." Following this incident, local Greeks reportedly harassed the schoolteacher and his wife whenever they walked about town, swearing and throwing stones at them.[67] This was not the only instance in town when the Greek community creatively used schools and their pupils to stage a protest against their Bulgarian neighbors. In November 1905, students of the Greek Orthodox gymnasium in Serres marched around the Bulgarian establishments in the town, loudly singing songs that seemed to have been written precisely for the purpose. The lyrics, far more graphic in their violence than the usual marching song, a genre not known for its subtlety, were:

It is my duty to declare
the Bulgarians schismatics
arsonists and murderers
as well as savage and bloodthirsty
Being merciful to murderers
is not philanthropy
it is an outrage

Society of Salonika was raising funds for a new school building in May 1873; *Macedonia, Documents and Material*, 292.

64. MAE. vol. 6, Consul to the Minister of Foreign Affairs, Salonika, May 30, 1882.

65. Lory, "Soloun, Ville Slave?" 143.

66. The contribution of schools to intercommunal violence was undeniable. For an overview of the situation in Monastir, see Bernard Lory, "Schools for the Destruction of Society: School Propaganda," in *Conflicting Loyalties in the Balkans: The Great Powers, the Ottoman Empire and Nation-Building*, edited by Hannes Grandits, Natalie Clayer, and Robert Pichler (New York, 2011), 46–63.

67. "Report from Serres," *Pravo*, July 30, 1873, cited in *Macedonia, Documents and Material*, 299.

and a crime against God
For the vile and cruel enemies
of the glory and honor of my country
for the arsonists and authors of all our troubles
a bitter hatred is a hard thing
Divine punishment and the world's opprobrium
will be the bloodthirsty savages' punishment
and if ever the history of this country is written
a dark page will open for them[68]

Another marching song of Greek schoolchildren recorded by a French gendarmerie officer in Serres suggested "setting the Bulgar on fire,"[69] and apparently this is exactly what some Greek activists in the town attempted to do to the Serres Bulgarian gymnasium in May 1907 before their plans were foiled.[70] The Greek family renting a building to the Bulgarian school was not spared either; Colonel Vérand seized a threatening letter sent to the family by "the Invisible Macedonian Committee."[71]

Regardless of the background of a pupil who attended one of the distinguished secondary schools, such as the gymnasia in Salonika and Serres, by the time of graduation he would have taken the first steps in joining the national elite of his community, instilled with a sense of distinction that set him apart not only from the members of the other community but also from the uneducated youths of his own, who, in their backwardness occupied a different temporal space. This notion continued to hold sway in much later accounts of national awakening. James Clarke, for instance, denies the peasants "coevalness," to paraphrase Fabian,[72] even as he notes that the educated few and the peasants both carried nationality, albeit in different ways: "At almost any time in the last two centuries the educated few were closer to Europe than to their own simple peasant, whether he was Albanian, Bulgarian, Greek, Romanian or Serb. Conversely, the peasants remained in the Turkish era ... long after political Europeanization."[73]

That there was a conceived difference between the elite and the peasants in terms of their intellectual proximity to Europe and, hence, national consciousness hardly needs an explanation. What is more interesting is how some of the national elites applied this principle to their ambitious enterprise of spreading national sentiment through schools, for what we see here

---

68. MAE, vol. 147, Serres, November 29, 1905.
69. Ibid.
70. PRO, FO 195/2263, Vice Consul Bosanquet to Consul Graves, Serres, May 30, 1907.
71. MAE, Turquie, Question de Macédoine, Gendarmerie Internationale, vol. 416, Colonel Vérand's report, Paris, July 2, 1907.
72. Johannes Fabian, *Time and the Other: How Anthropology Makes Its Object* (New York, 1983).
73. Clarke, *Pen and the Sword*, 52.

is entirely different than the educational policy of the modern nation-state, whereby the ideal is to create a common denominator for the model citizen that goes across class lines, at least in principle, if not in practice. On the contrary, the scholastic mission of nationalist visionaries in Macedonia was a two-tiered process that aimed, through village schools, to recruit foot soldiers for the struggle from among the peasantry and, through institutions of higher learning, to train the children of the middle and upper classes, who would lead the way for their underprivileged co-nationals.

It is important to note that the Greek government under Trikoupis had signed an agreement with the Syllogos, essentially outsourcing the application and oversight of Greek educational policy in Macedonia to this organization. The Syllogos was extremely active and influential in furthering the Greek claim on Macedonia through cultural, ethnographic, and educational channels. While the Patriarchate had no serious disagreements with the Syllogos educational agenda, relations at the local level seem to have been less than harmonious. The representatives of the Syllogos were unhappy with what they perceived to be an unwillingness to cooperate with the national mission, and they demanded more direct Greek government control over the religious establishment in the Ottoman Empire while the local bishops, in their letters to the Patriarch, revealed what Evangelos Kofos describes as a patriotism "imbued with the ethnarchic mission of the church."[74] The subtlety in this patriotism was apparently lost on the more zealous members of the Syllogos.

In a report addressed to the Greek minister of foreign affairs in 1883, Paparrigopoulos and G. I. Zolotas, the president and secretary, respectively, of the Syllogos, discussed the relative advantages of the *dimotika* (primary schools) and gymnasia for the national cause to determine how limited funds could be allocated most efficiently. The former category targeted a larger segment of the population and required more modest resources, whereas the latter demanded more investment, both human and financial, from the Greek state through the agency of the Syllogos. While the ministry was in favor of more impact with less immediate investment, favoring the proliferation of the *dimotika* instead of the dedication of precious resources to the gymnasia, Paparrigopoulos and Zolotas insisted on striking a balance because, they argued, "however extensive and well-organized our primary education became, if this primary education did not get refined both in heart and in spirit via the establishments where the youth of the middle classes, who in fact, hold the future of external Hellenism in their hands, study, this [primary] education would not only collide with the centuries-old national tradition, it would also become leaderless."[75]

---

74. Kofos, "Patriarch Joachim," 111.
75. AYE, fak. 1883, K. Paparrigopoulos and G. I. Zolotas to Kontostaulos, Athens, October 13, 1883, in Vouri, *Pēges gia tēn Istoria tēs Makedonias,* 88.

Like the Ministry of Foreign Affairs, Patriarch Ioachim III was also of the opinion that small grammar schools rather than extravagant high schools in urban centers were more appropriate for the educational mission of the Church in Macedonia.[76] At this point, there seemed to be a consensus among the Greek national elite that the elementary schools in the Macedonian countryside and their pupils had special needs that could not be met through curricula or material appropriate for schools in Greece or even other parts of the "enslaved lands." Most of these needs stemmed from the facts that, in large parts of the area where they sought to Hellenize the population, demotic Greek was not the spoken language and that there was little, if any, familiarity with *kathareusa* (the version of Greek that was taught in secondary schools), even among the priests and teachers serving these regions. Some of the schoolteachers had only a rudimentary knowledge of Greek in any form.[77] This was recognized by some of the Greek consuls in Macedonia, who argued that establishing schools in rural areas inhabited by Bulgarophone communities, although having potential in the long run, was not an efficient policy for the time being. Unlike their more urbane neighbors, who traveled around for commerce — and hence appreciated the importance of speaking Greek — these communities consisted of "peasants who cultivate the land and never move around."[78] The only feasible method for coopting these communities, then, was not through education but with the help of "zealous and influential priests."[79] What James Clarke defines as "remaining in the Turkish era" was seen to be the lot of the peasants, who were to be included in the national community not through modernizing institutions such as schools but through more traditional means found appropriate for their standing, such as the village church.

The logistical difficulties of convincing Slavic-speaking peasants to send their children to Greek schools notwithstanding, there was also an element of *bon pour l'orient* in the Greek intelligentsia's attitude concerning the rural masses. In their opinion, given the insularity and backwardness of these communities, it sufficed to instill only an elemental sense of nationhood in their children rather than aiming for full-scale socialization. At this point, they differed from the Patriachate's educational ideals. For instance, Ion Dragoumis, reporting to Athens in his capacity as a member of the Committee for the Support of Greek Church and Education (Epitropē pros Enischysēn tēs

---

76. Kofos, "Patriarch Joachim," 115.

77. Abbott, *Tale of a Tour in Macedonia,* 104. Similar questions about the linguistic capabilities of teachers appointed by the Exarchate were also current; Alexandar Trajanovski, "L'Activité Politico-Educatrice de l'Exarchat en Macédoine dans les Premieres Années avant et après la fondation de l'Organisation Revolutionnaire Macedo-Adrinienne Secrète," *Macedonian Review* 1 (1981), 191.

78. AYE, fak. 1883, Consul Dokos to President of the Society for the Dissemination of Greek Letters, Monastir, April 1883, in Vouri, *Pēges gia tēn Istoria tēs Makedonias,* 48.

79. Vouri, *Pēges gia tēn Istoria tēs Makedonias,* 59.

Ellēnikēs Ekklēsias kai Paideias; EEEP), complained about the hopeless situation in the schools, not because the teaching departed from the centralized curriculum, as we might expect, but because it did not. In his complaint was also a frustration with the old-fashioned and Orthodox-centered methods of the Patriarchate, which sent the same primers to all the schools, but his real concern was that peasants' children needed more "simple" material. "Very rarely do teachers understand what they should not teach," he wrote, and, "they try to infuse the peasants' children hard-to-digest and useless or even redundant courses in syntax and [make them] parrot analytical grammar always in accordance with the curricula from Constantinople instead of teaching them how to more fluently use Greek in a simple form. ... The primers in use are rarely well-chosen and they usually contain material that is useless or very heavy for villagers' kids and they are written in a difficult and scholarly language."[80]

In other words, sophisticated articulations of what it meant to be "Greek" were neither necessary nor useful for the peasant masses. This and the other consul's remarks reveal that socialization into the national community was seen to require a different process for peasants' children than for middle- and upper-class urbanites; the former were expected to contribute to the cause as its human weight, or "in bulk," whereas the latter were to distinguish themselves as the leaders of the crowd.[81]

In Bulgarian institutions of higher learning such as the gymnasium in Salonika, the student body came from geographically diverse areas in the countryside, and it consisted not only of the children of the Bulgarian-speaking middle and upper classes but also youths of more modest means. But what we might today celebrate as diversity was not a quality that impressed the (pro-Greek) anonymous author of *The Population of Macedonia, Evidence of the Christian Schools,* who held that Greek schools were genuine centers of learning, whereas Bulgarian schools were simply propaganda tools. The fact that they offered tuition waivers and free food and lodging was proof of this according to the author: "the place of origin of the pupils is important, not only from an ethnological point of view, but also from the point of view of its social consequences. The fact of filling the colleges with lads who attend them only because they find material advantages there, has really created an intellectual laboring class, which has become a charge on

---

80. AYE, a.a.k. K' 1907, Vice Consul Ion Dragoumis to EEEP, Dedeagaç, July 1906, in Belia, "Ē Ekpaideutikē Politikē tou Ellinikou Kratous," 39. Dragoumis made a similar point in relating a conversation with a school teacher in Iōnos Dragoumis, *Ta Tetradia tou Ilinten,* edited by Giōrgos Petsivas (Athens, 2000), 435–37.
81. Greek high schools were not entirely inaccessible to children of the lower classes. Many of the philanthropic organizations in Greece and the Ottoman Empire, such as the Ellēnikos Philologikos Syllogos Kōntantinoupoleōs [Greek Literary Society of Constantinople] ensured that scholarships were provided to needy children; Chares Exertzoglou, *Ethnikē Tautotita stēn Kōnstantinoupolē tou 19o Aiōna: O Ellēnikos Syllogos Kōnstantinoupoleōs, 1861–1912* (Athens, 1996).

the government that has encouraged it. ... The case of Greek schools is quite different. There, only young men in comfortable circumstances and those who feel themselves really capable of carrying on superior studies become bachelors."[82]

Even though Dragoumis's, Dokos's, or the anonymous author's hardly concealed condescension and patronizing attitudes may appear cynical, we should not lose sight of the fact that they were not only idealists, who presumably subscribed to notions of national brotherhood, but also realists, actively working to attain results for a cause with an uncertain outcome. The transition to nationhood could not occur as the result of a uniformly applicable process under the prevailing circumstances. In the absence of the resources that a modern state could mobilize to ensure attendance, ideological content, and centralized curriculum and method in schooling, a one-size-fits-all education policy was impossible to sustain, and even counterproductive as far as the elite leadership was concerned.

For the Slavic-speaking community, the relationship of higher education to class differentiation was more complicated, given the historical role that Greek educational institutions played as the vehicle for upward social mobility for Greek and non-Greek speakers alike. Traditionally, acceptance into the upper classes implied a certain degree of (if not complete) assimilation into the Greek linguistic community and culture, but with the establishment of Bulgarian high schools that could easily rival their Greek counterparts with their modern facilities, young and energetic faculty, and European-inspired curricula, refinement and enlightenment were no longer the exclusive domain of Greek institutions. The establishment of these schools and the spread of literacy among Slavic speakers in the Macedonian countryside were the culmination of a process that had started to bear fruit, as we have seen, in the mid-nineteenth century. This process naturally required the material support of a rising middle class, which it had, but the sense of distinction between the rural and urban, and the upper and lower classes, in terms of their contribution to the national cause was not as keen among the Bulgarian intelligentsia as it was among their Greek counterparts. We may attribute this to a number of factors, principal among them the definition of Bulgarian nationalism from its beginning as the fight of the doubly oppressed people (by the "Turks" and the "Phanariots") and its championing of the simple but hard-working peasant as the real and deserving owners of Macedonia.

The pursuit of knowledge despite all obstacles was a sentiment proudly espoused by the Bulgarian national intelligentsia, such as Grigor Purlichev, or the Miladinov brothers, the pioneers and heroes of Bulgarian education in Macedonia. Purlichev and the Miladinov brothers had been educated in

---

82. *The Population of Macedonia, Evidence of the Christian Schools* (London, 1905).

Greece, and they had utmost facility with literary Greek, which was not atypical of young Bulgarian nationalists in mid-nineteenth-century Macedonia.[83] Instead of Hellenizing the Miladinovs and Purlichev however, the Athens experience had actually aroused a more conscious sense of being Bulgarian—and different—in them. Purlichev wrote in his autobiography that he had worked hard to raise the money necessary for his training in Greece. He had enrolled as a medical student but continued to compose poetry, which was his real passion. In fact, his poem "Amartōlos" won first place in 1860 at a poetry contest in Athens, where he competed against acclaimed poets and philology professors. Purlichev's reminiscence of his victory exuded not so much of elation as bitter redemption:

> We, Bulgarians, have been so abused and despised by other nationalities that it is high time we regained our dignity. When one reads our folk songs, in which every beauty is called a Greek woman, then one will instinctively conclude that wretched self-contempt is a national characteristic of the Bulgarian. It is high time we prove ourselves men among men. Bulgarian industriousness is rarely to be found among other nationalities; it has ennobled us, and it will be our salvation. ... Having listened to the abuses heaped upon all the Bulgarians, I have lived all my life with the idea that I was a nonentity. The same thought has kept me away from the highest circles of society without which no one has ever become a famous citizen, or a man of letters. It is true that a proud man comes to no good, but it is also true that he who despises himself is a suicide [sic].[84]

Purlichev, in describing his encounter with Rangavis, the head of the organizing committee and renowned man of letters, emphasized Rangavis's apparent scorn for his decision to donate only half, not the entire amount, of the monetary prize he received. When he told Rangavis "the other half I need for myself, I am not rich," Rangavis was clearly displeased with his answer, or so Purlichev reported. In either case, we can sense the assumption, likely but not necessarily on Rangavis's part, but certainly on Purlichev's, that composition of fine poetry was a vocation normally reserved for the well-off and not for poor students from the Macedonian countryside.

Despite the Bulgarian intelligentsia's vehement desire to teach their national brethren to celebrate their differences from the Greeks, we can wonder to what extent they had subconsciously internalized philhellene notions about the superiority of certain cultural traits and were competing with

---

83. Dimitar Miladinov penned his opinions about the need to educate children in their mother tongue (i.e., Bulgarian) entirely in Greek; Miladinov to Alexander Exarch, Bitola, August 20, 1852, [The Miladinov Brothers Correspondence] (Sofia, 1964), cited in *Macedonia, Documents and Material*, 145–47.

84. Grigor Purlichev, [Selected Works] (Sofia, 1939), cited in *Macedonia, Documents and Material*, 401–2.

Greek nationalism within these accepted, externally set parameters.[85] Bulgarian nationalists often complained about the lack of enlightenment among their co-nationals in Macedonia, which also happened to be a favorite theme of Greek propagandists. For instance, a notable from Prilep, trying to convince a teacher to accept a post in his town, wrote in June 1865 that "Here, as almost all over Macedonia, learning, as well as national consciousness, are still in their infancy. Therefore, a good and capable educator is needed to bring up the new generation properly. But such educators are scarce and costly, and our compatriots, apart from the fact that they do not know where to search for such, what is worse, they are not yet used to offering what they would describe as huge salaries.... They are not, however, against learning or slow in understanding, but only ignorant, and at first they find it strange to offer a high salary."[86]

That most people did not appreciate the importance of training in their mother tongue and the need to provide financial support to that end was a common source of grief among the Bulgarian intelligentsia during the formative years of Bulgarian nationhood in Macedonia.[87] This point is significant because of the disputes between the two communities concerning how the schools were to be financed. The nature of that support presumably determined which movement was "authentic," and because this was understood to be a winner-take-all situation, the possibility that both could be "authentic" was not one that was entertained often. Despite both parties' insistence that theirs were the "authentic" educational institutions, functioning due to great sacrifices on the part of their respective communities, both sets of schools were assisted by extra-communal benefactors.

Education and Cultural Superiority

Not surprisingly, each side claimed that its schools were better institutions of academic excellence. In addition to sources of funding, which presumably constituted a measure of "authenticity," the location of schools, the numbers enrolled, and the teachers were all taken as indications of one movement's dominance over the other. Even more striking were the comparisons made on the basis of the methods of teaching, which revealed the self-image

---

85. Desislava Lilova argues that European cultural superiority was internalized by the Bulgarian intelligentsia, who also saw themselves at a disadvantage in terms of the Europeans' regard for their culture as opposed to that of Greeks, which was considered part of a universal cultural heritage; "Barbarians, Civilized People and Bulgarians: Definition of Identity in Textbooks and the Press (1830–1878)," in *We, the People: Politics of National Peculiarity in Southeastern Europe*, edited by Diana Mishkova (Budapest, 2009), 181–206.

86. Kouzman Shapkarev to Georgi Ikonomov, Prilep, June 8, 1865, cited in *Macedonia, Documents and Material*, 217.

87. See also "Report from Veles," *Tsarigradski Vestnik* [Constantinople Newspaper], no. 7, October 28, 1850, cited in *Macedonia, Documents and Material*, 142–43.

as a nation of each side. These self-images were clearly influenced by accepted and generalized notions of each nation's characteristics—characteristics originally observed by a western gaze, articulated in a rich literature of travel writing and fiction as well as ethnographic and geographical works. The characteristics then found their way into the national elites' definitions of their own community and perceptions of what made that community different from the other.

In Greek-Bulgarian polemics concerning schools and learning, the vestiges of these deeply engrained notions are hardly disguised. Bulgarians emphasized the industrious and humble nature of their nation, in line with the commonly accepted stereotype of the Bulgarian as a simple, honest peasant, and based their arguments of scholastic superiority not only on having successfully taught peasants how to read and write in their "mother tongue" but also on having raised a new generation through a rigorous but practical system of education. On the opposite side, Greek nationalists invoked their special connection to the heritage of antiquity, the very source of western civilization and higher culture as the world knew it. It was not sheer quantity but quality that mattered, and the Greeks were the sole bearers of that quality.

The first modern Bulgarian schools were the result of the efforts of Vasil Aprilov, who founded a school in Gabrovo in 1835.[88] Aprilov's school followed the Lancaster model. Its popularity aside, the Lancaster model was a perfect fit for the Bulgarian scholastic movement, which was defined against the hegemony of the Patriarchate, just as Joseph Lancaster had been driven by his isolation from the English educational establishment because of his Quaker faith. The model was emulated by many small schools opening up in Macedonia, and Bulgarian schools came to be known for their emphasis on practical knowledge such as language and vocational training, whereas the majority of their Greek counterparts continued to teach a classical curriculum.[89] The relative merits of these two approaches differed considerably, depending on the referee's subjective notions of what constituted superior national education.[90] Not everyone agreed, for instance, on the principle of

---

88. Jelavich and Jelavich, *Establishment of the Balkan States*, 131. Mishev dates the first school to 1821; Brancoff [Mishev], *La Macédoine et sa Population Chrétienne*, 53.

89. This was also mentioned in the French consul's report in 1882; MAE, vol. 6, Consul to the Minister of Foreign Affairs, Salonika, May 30, 1882. The Bell-Lancaster method was originally not used solely by the Bulgarian community. In 1830, before the emergence of a scholastic rivalry between Greeks and Bulgarians, the first school was established for the Christian community of Monastir, Greek was the medium of instruction, using the Bell-Lancaster method; Lory, "Schools for the Destruction of Society," 50. The heyday of the method was the beginning of the nineteenth century in Europe, and the Greeks in Chios, the Ionian islands, and Jassy were among the early adopters, even though the Church viewed the method with suspicion; Christina Koulouri, *Dimensions Idéologiques de l'Historicité en Grèce, 1834–1914: Les Manuels Scolaires d'Histoire et de Géographie* (Frankurt, 1991), 38–41.

90. See, for instance, Victor Bérard's evaluation of Bulgarian and Greek schools in Macedonia, cited in Brancoff [Mishev], *La Macédoine et sa Population Chrétienne*, 77.

functional education favored by the Bulgarian gymnasia. For the defenders of the Greek educational establishment, institutions of higher education were not simply vocational training centers; they were representative bodies of a national cultural heritage and civilization. Greek nationalist discourse adopted and nurtured this position, eventually integrating it into the official historiography of the era as exemplified by Douglas Dakin: "Greek communities and wealthy Greeks of Macedonian origin had built up a relatively large educational system. Greek education, however, did not altogether meet the requirements of a modern age, and in some respects Bulgarian education which, though of poorer quality, emphasized languages and useful knowledge, had in some quarters the stronger appeal: nevertheless Greek education had social standing and maintained in vigorous existence that culture, that ecclesiastical rule and that way of life which we call Hellenism."[91]

Going back to the period in which this discourse was being established, we must also note the importance placed on the way Hellenism was represented outside the Hellenic world. In this respect, educational institutions, and especially those of higher learning, were yet another indicator of the superiority of that culture. In the words of Paparrigopoulos and Zolotas, the president and secretary of the Syllogos: "to those from abroad who study the national struggles in the East, institutions of such caliber inspire a belief in the vital powers and the superiority of the nation that sustains them."[92]

This belief in the ultimate role of schools as the face of Greek civilization to the rest of the world was a corollary to the elite discourse on the hierarchical order of nations and Greek superiority within that hierarchy. Less conspicuous within that discourse was also a conviction that some kind of "civilizing mission" was accorded to the Greek nation, which it was to perform through institutions of learning and culture. One of the instances when that conviction revealed itself was a July 14 celebration performed by Greek schoolchildren in Serres. According to a Piraeus newspaper, a student of the gymnasium delivered a speech in French that compared the civilizing missions of the Greek and French nations. The lecture was meant to make an impression on Captain Lamouche, chief of the French gendarmerie in the Serres sector, who had been invited to the school for the occassion. Alas, Lamouche (whom the newspaper repeatedly referred to as 'M. Mouche') proved to be a complete disappointment and disgrace to the finest Gallic tradition of discourse, according to the paper, and delivered "a few banalities, such as saying that France cares about the people of the Orient and has their interests in mind." He did not "even deign to take to his bulgarophile lips a statement of courtesy with regard to the Greeks."[93] The Greek elite of the

---

91. Dakin, *Greek Struggle in Macedonia*, 19.

92. AYE, fak. 1883, K. Paparrigopoulos and G. I. Zolotas to Kontostaulos, Athens, October 13, 1883, in Vouri, *Pēges gia tēn Istoria tēs Makedonias*, 88.

93. MAE, vol. 416, August 4, 1904.

town were apparently offended but also bemused by Captain Lamouche's behavior. A representative of French civilization, who, by definition, should have appreciated Greek culture and been favorably disposed to the Greek position in Macedonia, had completely let them down by his indifference.

The Greek side was quite correct in suspecting that Captain Lamouche's aloofness was a result of his personal sympathy for the Bulgarian side; Lamouche was later appointed "honorary consul" of Bulgaria because of his conduct during the Macedonian conflict, and he later wrote a book that narrated the events in Macedonia from a pro-Bulgarian viewpoint.[94] It seems that the captain, adding insult to injury, not only displayed a blatant indifference toward the July 14 celebration of this Greek school but made a point of paying special attention to the Bulgarian schools in the area. Greek protests against Captain Lamouche were not limited to this newspaper article. Minister Theodoros Deliyannis's office expressed the discontent of the Greek side through higher diplomatic means, such as notes to Paris. According to anonymous reports, Lamouche was not happy when Greek teachers paid him a visit and told him that they spoke Greek at home and at school in those parts. Nor did he express any interest when the teachers explained to him that Romanian and Vlach were different languages and that the Vlachs declared themselves to be, and therefore were, Greeks. Finally, during a visit to a Greek school, he greeted the students in the "Bulgar manner," and even though his salutation was reciprocated in Greek, he continued to speak in Bulgarian. He insistently asked what language was spoken "within families," and without waiting for a response, he continued to talk to the students in Bulgarian. The teacher told him that the students were Greek but they also spoke Bulgarian. "So they are Bulgarians," he commented, and the teacher said, no, "they are not schismatic Bulgars, they call themselves Greeks, go to Greek Church and follow the Patriarchate." The captain's response, apparently, was "an ironic smile."[95]

Lamouche's own recollection of these events was naturally quite different: "The Greeks in Serres as in all of Macedonia, were extremely fanatical and intolerant," he wrote in his book. "From the time we arrived, they claimed monopoly over our relations and were offended by the slightest interest that we might offer to anyone other than themselves. Even though I always tried hard to maintain the impartiality that my position required, I could not sacrifice the causes that years of study had already had proven just to me, for the friendship of Greeks."[96]

The French captain's conduct, which made no secret of his sympathy for the Bulgarian side, was not atypical of the foreign officers sent to Macedonia, who were viewed by the local population as representatives of the

---

94. Lamouche, *Quinze Ans d'Histoire Balkanique*.
95. MAE, vol. 416, Confidential Note, November 9, 1904.
96. Lamouche, *Quinze Ans d'Histoire Balkanique*, 56.

Great Powers sent to save them from their misery. They were also seen as the potential arbiters of an ultimate resolution of the "Macedonian problem," which made it important to appeal to their personal opinions. As the case of Captain Lamouche demonstrates, such opinions were often formed before the officers' arrival at their posts and were a result of the ways that Europeans conceived of peoples of the Ottoman Empire since the "discovery" of Eastern Europe.[97] Winning the fight required not only numerical superiority but also, and arguably more important, the establishment of a morally superior position that would win foreign public opinion. The assertion of cultural superiority, therefore, was not a supplementary but a fundamental component of this competition. In a pamphlet intended for a francophone audience, Ioanna Stephanopoli asked, "Is it to this rebellious, factional, barbarian minority [i.e., Bulgarians] that we are to sacrifice a race that is counted among the greatest contributors of European civilization?"[98] The question was meant to convey the message that not only were the Bulgarians a numerical minority but that they were also qualitatively dwarfed compared to the great civilization they were up against.

The distance covered by Bulgarian academic institutions in the second half of the nineteenth century was impressive. The new schools directly contributed to the emergence of a political movement demanding the independence of Macedonia from the Ottomans by training the leadership cadres of IMRO, an outcome not necessarily foreseen by the Bulgarian upper classes who pioneered the scholastic leap forward. IMRO would become one of the principal political forces leading the insurgency against the Ottoman Empire and would maintain its influence (and retain its violent tactics) during the interwar years. Nearly all the founders of IMRO—Damian Gruev, Andon Dimitrov, Ivan Hadzi Nikolov, Hristo Batandzhiev, and Petûr Poparsov—were schoolteachers, trained either in Bulgaria or Macedonia. Duncan Perry, in his work on the early years of the Macedonian liberation organizations, argues that the sociological base for the revolutionary movement evolved because as "schools flourished, graduates multiplied and became teachers, little changed on the socio-economic front, and thus restlessness and dissatisfaction with the status quo ultimately fed a steady stream of students, graduates and teachers into revolutionary circles and later into guerrilla bands."[99] Although the IMRO ideological direction and strategic planning did come from its educated leadership, the movement also blended the well-established *haidut* (bandit) tradition into its organization, enlisting the aid of several "social bandits" in the region.

---

97. By his own account in 1928, Colonel Lamouche had been interested in "the life of the Bulgarian nation" for forty years. He had been a student of Louis Léger, the Slavist, and had taken his Russian class at L'Ecole des Langues Orientales. Later his interest became more focused on Bulgaria and Bulgarians; ibid., 7–8.
98. Ioanna Z. Stephanopoli, *Macédoine et Macédoniens* (Athens, 1903), 7.
99. Perry, *Politics of Terror*, 30.

CHAPTER THREE

Territoriality and Its Discontents

Maps are too important to be left to cartographers alone.
—J. Brian Harley, "Deconstructing the Map," 1992

"*Roumeli* is not to be found on maps of present-day Greece," wrote Patrick Leigh Fermor at the start of his eponymous account of travels in northern Greece, published in 1966, which has since become a classic and required reading for students of anthropology. Fremor explained that he was "perhaps seduced by the strangeness and the beauty of the name."[1] The meaning of *Roumeli* is of course more obvious to those familiar with the history of the Byzantine and Ottoman empires, yet it is not one that can easily be attributed to a fixed entity. The simplest definition of *Roumeli* (*Rumeli* in its Turkish spelling) is the land of the *Rum*, or Romans. It does not, however, include Asia Minor or the Peloponnese or Thessaly. The term Fermor picked to describe what was essentially northern Greece was the name Ottomans gave to the province that was formed by their first major conquests in the Balkan Peninsula, which they also referred to as Rumeli. As the Ottoman territories expanded, so did the area of the province, including not only northern Greece but also parts of present-day Bulgaria and Macedonia.[2] As a geographical term, *Rumeli* did not have clearly demarcated boundaries. The elasticity and nostalgic ring of the term were precisely why Fremor found it so fitting for his "random journeys." It was also proper for a book that described peoples and ways of life that sit uneasily within the strict confines of a nation-state, such as the transhumant Sarakatsani and the fiercely localist Cretans. In one passage a Sarakatsan lamented about the times when they could pasture their flocks

---

1. Patrick Leigh Fermor, *Roumeli: Travels in Northern Greece* (New York, 2006).
2. The province of Rumeli was divided into smaller provinces after the *Tanzimat* reforms and became practically a geographical name after the *vilayet* law of 1864. After the conclusion of the 1877–1878 Russo-Ottoman war and the Berlin Treaty, an autonomous province of Şarkî Rumeli (Eastern Rumelia) was established in part of the territory that had earlier been promised to Bulgaria under the San Stefano Treaty. Şarkî Rumeli united with the principality of Bulgaria in 1885, which was nominally under Ottoman suzerainty until 1908. In 1902, the Inspectorate of Rumeli was founded, which functioned as a special administrative unit directly under the Grand Vezirate.

as far as Bithynia and the "caiques sailing past in the Sea of Marmara could hear my bells."[3] Now that the national boundaries had been drawn, those pasture lands were out of reach.

Empires, of course, do not have boundaries but frontiers. Frontiers are elastic and porous; they are zones of transition, not demarcation lines. People, animals, and commodities move more or less freely (if clandestinely) within and across frontiers, whereas boundaries contain, regulate, and restrict all such motion. Frontiers are defined primarily in military terms; they are zones where sovereignty is not stable and are always subject to change with the movement of armies.[4] They cannot, however, be defined exclusively as zones of perpetual conflict; frontiers are also places of synthesis and syncretism, of heterogeneity and mingling, in contrast to boundaries, which exist precisely to correct or prevent such uncertainty. Rumeli was such a frontier zone for the early Ottomans; they were extending their realms in Europe through military conquest, often in coalition with the locals who were subsequently coopted into the ranks of the Ottoman "frontier lords."[5] Physical reminders of that period are scattered across the Balkans, despite generations of benign neglect and deliberate eradication, in the vast inventory of architectural monuments (or remains thereof) endowed during the first centuries of Ottoman rule in the area by people, many of whom were recent, not to say nominal, converts to Islam.[6] Rumeli, then, became the center of gravity of the empire as it continued its expansion west. After 1453, the capital of the Ottoman state moved east from Edirne to Constantinople, but the governor of the province of Rumeli preserved his prestigious position in the military/administrative hierarchy of the empire. As the commander of the forces of Rumeli, he was part of the imperial council directly below the Grand Vezir, and sometimes the governor of Rumeli and the Grand Vezir were one and the same person. Anadolu was Rumeli's counterpart on the Asian side of the Bosphorus, and these two provinces, with Istanbul in

---

3. Fermor, *Roumeli*, 18.

4. The terms meaning "frontier" and "boundary" in Turkish are *serhad* and *hudud*, respectively, with further distinction for those regions at the very edge of the zone of military venture, *uc*, which literally means "edge" and fell from use after the first wave of Ottoman expansion into Europe. By the twentieth century, *hudud* and *serhad* had largely been fused; the former was used more often in describing state boundaries, but *serhad* still better carried the meaning of "military frontier." For the historical evolution of the term *frontière*, see Lucien Febvre, "*Frontière*: The Word and the Concept," in *A New Kind of History from the Writings of Febvre*, edited by Peter Burke, translated by K. Folca (London, 1973), 208–17.

5. On early Ottomans and their frontier society see Cemal Kafadar, *Between Two Worlds: The Construction of the Ottoman State* (Berkeley, 1995). Heath Lowry portrays these frontier lords as a "coalition of marauders"; *The Nature of the Early Ottoman State* (Albany, 2003).

6. The vast number of public edifices endowed by Gazi Evrenos, almost certainly a Christian convert and the conqueror of almost the entire region of northern Greece for the Ottomans, is a good case in point; Heath Lowry, *The Shaping of the Ottoman Balkans, 1350–1550* (Istanbul, 2008).

the center, formed the heartland of the empire until Rumeli was lost by the Ottomans after the Balkan Wars in 1912–1913.

As Fremor's account reveals, *Rumeli* was not a household name among the western audience in the twentieth century. Nor was it ever the term of choice in describing the Balkan Peninsula among the learned in Europe. European cartographic imagery of the sixteenth- and seventeenth-century maps and atlases depicted the Ottoman Empire as a whole, under various iterations of the name *Turkish Empire*, although the Ottomans themselves never used either term in reference to their territories until the nineteenth century when the Ottoman diplomatic service started using the terms "Turquie" to refer to the Ottoman empire and "sa Majesté Impériale le Sultan" in reference to the sultan. By the middle of the eighteenth century, however, European cartographers had started to divide the Ottoman realms into "estates," and the term *Turkey in Europe*, which took hold then and stayed the norm until the early twentieth century, covered the area the Ottomans called Rumeli. The invention of Turkey in Europe was partly an outcome of the Ottomans' declining military might in the eyes of Europeans, but more important, it was directly related to the post-Enlightenment idea of Europe, which defined itself in civilizational opposition to the Oriental/Turkish Other.[7]

Most, if not all, maps of the Ottoman Empire drawn by European cartographers in the sixteenth and seventeenth centuries denoted classical names for regions such as Macedonia but did not ascribe boundaries to these regions, and the way the inscriptions were printed implied an overlap among these designations. In Pierre du Val's "Carte de l'Empire des Turcs et de les Contins," dated 1664, for instance, "Grèce" and "Macédoine" overlapped, as did "Turcomanie" and "Arménie."[8] By contrast, Nicolas Sanson, whose 1692 "Les Estats de l'Empire des Turques en Europe [et en Asie]" was an early harbinger of the practice of representing the Ottoman Empire in separate sheets for Europe and Asia and Africa, also drew boundaries within the "Beylerbeglic de Roumelie," demarcating "Bulgarie," "Romanie," "Macédoine," "Albanie," "Thessalie," "Epire," and "Achaia." Needless to say, none of these designations corresponded to Ottoman administrative divisions, which were not, in any case, conceptualized through cartographic imagery at the time. Interestingly enough, the only inscription mentioning "Grèce" on Sanson's map denoted the "Mer Ionienne ou Mer de Grèce."

Ascribing boundaries to a specific region would turn into an extremely important and ideologically fraught practice in the nineteenth century as those regions became increasingly considered the exclusive domain of a certain

---

7. Larry Wolff, *Inventing Eastern Europe: The Map of Civilization on the Mind of the Enlightenment* (Stanford, 1994), 144–94.

8. Pierre du Val, "Carte de l'Empire des Turcs et de les Contins," in *Le Monde, ou la Geographie Universelle Contenent les Descriptions, les Cartes & le Blazon de Principaux Pays du Monde* (Paris, 1664), in Ian Manners, *European Cartographers and the Ottoman World, 1500–1750* (Chicago, 2007), 42.

"racial" group, or as they became territorialized. For the seventeenth-century cartographer, however, boundaries simply served as approximations, devices meant to divide up an unknown entity into chunks that would more easily evoke some sort of geographical order in European minds that were familiar with Ottoman lands only through the classics and a limited number of travelers' accounts. This state of affairs changed dramatically in the nineteenth century when the domain of the "Grand Turc" became more accessible and developments in the disciplines of geography and ethnography introduced novel methods of map-making, classification, and cartographic representation. In the late nineteenth century, when the enduring presence of the Ottoman Empire in Europe was increasingly seen by liberal Europeans and local irredentists as an anomaly that needed immediate rectification, the maps of Turkey in Europe acquired an even more pronounced political weight. After 1878, that map was at the center of diplomatic debates concerning the Eastern Question, or how the corpse of the "Sick Man of Europe" would be disposed of when the time came. Rumeli was now prize territory for the small Balkan nation-states desperate to expand their borders and a zone of influence to be partitioned among the Great Powers. Macedonia happened to be at the center of this territory.

The school of geopolitics founded in the early twentieth century by Friedrich Ratzel, German political scientist and geographer of Leipzig University, and his followers described the relation among political power, geography, and territory in Darwinian terms, as a struggle for survival.[9] Even though Ratzel himself did not place states at the center of his analysis, focused as he was on the role of the environment, similar ideas about geopolitics defined the way western European geographers and politicians discussed the future of Rumeli, which was also adopted by the Balkan national elites. The idea of Macedonia as a distinct geographical region and as a potentially independent country came into being in this context of Darwinian geopolitics. Neither of these projects survived the struggle that ensued (until they were revived in the post–World War II period); the dream of "Macedonia for Macedonians" was shattered, but the attempts to define Macedonia and its inhabitants had a lasting effect on the way the nation-states that claimed it as their own conceptualized their territory and on the relationship of the land to the people that inhabited it. This was a process that was largely carried out through the medium of maps, and as such, it was a product of the epistemological shifts in the discipline of geography and its principal visual technique, cartography. These shifts reflected current notions concerning the supremacy of science; the expanding boundaries of knowledge; and

---

9. Jeremy Black, *Maps and History* (New Haven, 1997), 83. For an early critique of Ratzel and other geographical determinists, see Lucien Febvre, *A Geographical Introduction to History*, translated by E. G. Mountford and J. H. Paxton (New York, 1925).

the possibility of knowing, indexing, calculating, and mapping not only the physical world but also the "moral" attributes of people.

My starting point for this chapter was a collection of ethnographic maps of "Turkey in Europe" published from the mid-nineteenth to the early twentieth century. I did not quite understand what these maps were trying to say when I first came across them as I was browsing the stacks at the Gennadion Library in Athens, but I soon realized that they were not merely images to "illustrate the Macedonian Question" to (dis)interested parties. They represented, instead, their authors' visions of what the landscape, both physical and human, *should* look like; they were projections of the reality they claimed to represent. They were, in other words, political statements. They could not be read without our first understanding the context of their production and dissemination. This chapter therefore builds that context to show that these maps were essentially a grid imposed on the populations that inhabited the depicted terrain and were an essential tool in projecting the territoriality of a nation and its discontents. This is not to say that their power was hegemonic. J. B. Harley saw maps as "preeminently a language of power, not of protest."[10] The same language of power, however, also generated resistance, effectively allowing a language of protest to use the same medium of the map.

The contextualization of ethnographic maps (or any cartographic representation for that matter) requires that we first recognize that maps are more "than the territory they represent," to paraphrase Alfred Korzybski.[11] The notion of an objective map, especially one that claims to represent ethnic groups *in situ*, is pure fiction even today after the invention of sophisticated imaging techniques and access to detailed census reports; in the early twentieth century, it was fantasy dressed up as "science." The maps we discuss here are, first and foremost, depictions and, by implication, assertions of territoriality. Territoriality, according to David Sack, signifies something far more complicated than spatial relationships drawn on a plane. It is, above all, "the key geographical component in understanding how society and space are interconnected." A given delimited area is not "territory" in and of itself; it becomes so "only when its boundaries are used to affect behavior by controlling access."[12]

The primary apparatus of territoriality is cartography, and when applied to the principle of national determination, it created nothing less than the spatial definition of a nation—not necessarily its current shape but the territory

---

10. J. Brian Harley, "Maps, Knowledge, and Power," in *The Iconography of Landscape: Essays on the Symbolic Representation, Design and Use of Past Environments,"* edited by Denis Cosgrove and Stephen Daniels (Cambridge, 1988), 300–301.

11. Alfred Korzybski, *Science and Sanity: An Introduction to Non-Aristotelian Systems and General Semantics* (Englewood, 1994).

12. Robert David Sack, *Human Territoriality: Its Theory and History* (Cambridge, 1986), 3–11.

it *should* occupy. In *Siam Mapped,* Tongchai Winichakul persuasively argues that maps do not follow the social reality of a nation dispersed across delimited domains; they are not depictions of something that already exists but *predictions* of it. He presents this process as resulting from a confrontation between indigenous definitions of the realm and its modern geographical interpretations, and he calls the resulting novel concept of the territoriality of a nation its "geo-body," which he argues, "is merely an effect of modern geographical discourse whose prime technology is a map."[13]

Much of the discussion in this chapter takes its cue from Tongchai's conception of the emergence of nationhood and the field of critical geography, represented in the writings of J. B. Harley, Denis Cosgrove, Jeremy Black, Denis Wood, and Robert David Sack, among others. It does not, however, single out any one method favored by these authors and apply it to the maps of Turkey in Europe. What it borrows from this field is the notion that cartography is not, and never was, a disinterested scientific discipline but a technique of power and a perfect tool in the service of Darwinian geopolitics. The dizzying colors on maps of Turkey in Europe makes sense only when read against this background.

Geographical Knowledge and Governmentality

In eighteenth-century Europe, as the definition of geographical subjects of inquiry sharpened, detailed topographical surveys uprooted astronomic observation and traveler reports as the gold standard of cartography. A novel technique called geodetic survey was introduced—a technique still used today with different measuring implements. The principal method of geodetic surveys was triangulation, which can roughly be described as the application of trigonometric principles to the measurement of distance to "triangulate," or fine-tune, the contours of Earth as they were depicted on a map and to increase the resolution of a map to the greatest possible extent.[14] French geographers were the leaders in the practice of geodetic surveys in the eighteenth century. The survey of France carried out between 1744 and 1789 by the Cassinis, a family of astronomers, and financed by the king, resulted in the 182-sheet *Carte de France,* which depicted the entire country in a uniform manner. The *Carte de France* became a model to be emulated as other European countries followed suit.[15]

---

13. Winichakul Tongchai, *Siam Mapped: A History of the Geo-body of a Nation* (Honolulu, 1994), 17.

14. Matthew H. Edney, *Mapping an Empire: The Geographical Construction of British India, 1765–1843* (Chicago, 1997), 106.

15. Matthew H. Edney, "Mapping Parts of the World," in *Maps: Finding our Place in the World,* edited by James R. Akerman and Robert W. Karrow Jr. (Chicago, 2007), 151.

It is not an exaggeration to say that the Cassinis' project was a turning point in the history of geography. The *Carte de France* was not only groundbreaking in its implementation of a complex survey technique over a vast territory, but it also signified a new application of geographical knowledge in the service of "governmentality," providing the state and its expanding edifice of bureaucracy a novel technique of calculation, of control over territory. Not surprisingly, this type of survey was also perfectly suited for the purposes of the colonialist enterprise, and it was put into use in Egypt by the French and in Ireland and India by the British, to mention a few prominent examples.[16] That the bar for scientific precision had been set too high by geodetic surveys did not prevent the popularization of the idea that all maps had to rely on the latest instruments and techniques. As a result, even those maps that did not rely on surveys boasted the method in their titles, and graticules (the grid formed by parallels and meridians) on a map became the minimum requirement for a claim to mapping precision and authority—never mind the fact that the graticules were often added to maps post-production in a completely haphazard manner.

It is important to take note of this new-found confidence in the superiority of cutting-edge scientific methods, as faulty and fraudulent as they might be, because this transformation took place during the period when European geographers had also set their eyes on the task of mapping the "lost lands" of Europe, which meant Eastern Europe.[17] The Russians seemed amenable to reform by "enlightened" Europeans, and created their own cartographic office in collaboration with the French as early as 1719,[18] but the project of redeeming the lost lands through cartographic knowledge met a serious roadblock at the western frontier of the Ottoman realms. The Ottomans' reluctance to aid (and possibly their sheer neglect) of European cartographers in their quest to survey their territory became the source of much resentment and frustration among scholarly circles in Europe. Here is an excerpt from the *Atlas Universel* of 1757:

> If in the detail of the different parts of Europe that one has traveled through to the present, we have had satisfaction of receiving aid from the savants who have worked on their countries, we can not say that we have enjoyed such an advantage in the description that we have to make of the states submitted to

---

16. This should not, however, lead us to the conclusion that trigonometric surveys became a common tool at the hands of an omnipotent state or colonial power. To start with, they were simply too expensive and laborious to be implemented widely. Furthermore, even in the presence of the resources and the political will to undertake such detailed surveys, they were quite limited and riddled with inaccuracies; Edney, *Mapping an Empire*, esp. 325–31.

17. Wolff, *Inventing Eastern Europe*, 144, Wolff's reference to "lost lands" was taken from Voltaire's *Charles XII*.

18. This is not to say that the Russians had been incapable of, or did not care to, represent their domains through cartography; Valerie A. Kivelson, *Cartographies of Tsardom: The Land and Its Meanings in Seventeenth-Century Russia* (Ithaca, 2006).

Ottoman domination. We would have wished to be able to conclude (*terminer*) European geography with more success; but the approach to these states is difficult for enlightened people (*gens éclairés*), and does not permit on ever to hope for sufficient lights (*lumières*) to give something satisfying in geography; for the relations that voyagers give us are not of sufficient help to confirm the topographical detail of the lands that they have traveled through. It would be necessary for these voyagers to be instructed in mathematics.[19]

This excerpt is an early reminder of a specific rhetoric that was better articulated and more pervasive among scholarly circles in the second half of the nineteenth century in their discussions about the deplorable state of sciences such as geography and ethnography in the Ottoman Empire. The contrast between light and darkness, symbolizing the contrast between reason and superstition, between science and ignorance and calling for the illumination of the dark corners of "states submitted to Ottoman domination" for the scientific gaze of the Europeans were common elements of this rhetoric. What distinguishes it from later expressions of similar sentiments is the tone that hinted at the notion that "Turks" did not belong in Europe, and it was precisely their presence there that made the "terminus" of the continent so dark. For the sixteenth- and seventeenth-century geographers, the presence of Ottomans in the eastern Mediterranean was not an anomaly that needed explanation.[20] In the nineteenth century, this rather subtle discourse was replaced by explicit calls to chase the Turks out of Europe once and for all. It is important to note that the sudden interest in surveying the lands at the edge of Europe was taking place in the context of Habsburg-Ottoman rivalry in Eastern Europe and of the Russian expansion to the south at the expense of Ottoman territory. In the words of Larry Wolff, "the lands that the Habsburg and Russian statesmen coveted were precisely those that geographers sought to study; the two ambitions were inevitably related and arguably interdependent."[21] The inextricable link between geographical knowledge and imperial ambition became even more pronounced in the nineteenth century as European colonial projects not only charted and measured their overseas acquisitions but also created and named entire regions according to their interests.[22]

It is important to bear in mind that geography is a culturally constructed realm and geographical knowledge reflects the particular intellectual milieu in which it is produced. The eighteenth-century developments outlined here

---

19. Robert de Vaugondy, *Atlas Universel* (Paris, 1757), Vol. 1: 22, cited in Wolff, *Inventing Eastern Europe*, 148–49.
20. Manners, *European Cartographers and the Ottoman World*, 36–37.
21. Wolff, *Inventing Eastern Europe*, 169.
22. On the invention of India, for instance, see Edney, *Mapping an Empire*. The power of naming through geographical exploration was so persuasive that a colonial invention could later be embraced by anti-colonial nationalist elites as the definition of a homeland they would liberate.

all had a role in determining the shape of cartographic representations of the Ottoman Empire and its inhabitants, and the lengthy notes that accompanied them. A final element we should mention in this regard is the Enlightenment establishment of ancient Greece as the source of "Western Civilization." The centrality of ancient Greece in Enlightenment thought directly and indirectly influenced the production of knowledge about the European "lost lands" in the nineteenth century. For one thing, ancient Greece, as Enlightenment philosophers reconstructed it, was a largely sterilized and stylized version, completely stripped off its elements of African and Asian origin.[23] Although we might disagree with Martin Bernal's assertion that the "Aryan" model of ancient Greece later dominated the field of classics, it is indisputable that the Enlightenment, by defining "Civilization" as the product of an exclusive Greco-Roman lineage, not only branded the peoples that fell outside the confines of that intellectual heritage as inferior but also created a foil for the submission of the same peoples to European colonial power.[24] Turks were definitely on the other side of this civilization divide, but Eastern Europeans were not entirely part of the inner circle either, stranded as they were between the darkness of the Orient and the light of the Occident. This notion is clearly noticeable in the writings of European travelers in the region and in the way that "scientific" works of ethnography recorded, classified, and ranked the same people.

Moreover, the notion of ancient Greece as the source of Western Civilization fueled an interest in Classical Geography, which became a curricular requirement for the educated classes. In the mid-nineteenth century, "maps of the classical world dominated other atlases," notes Jeremy Black.[25] The increased demand for these atlases meant that more research was needed to bring the classical world to homes and classrooms. The same quest for the ancient world for their own eyes motivated travelers, who started to explore these as yet uncharted lands in increasing numbers in the nineteenth century.

The Marriage of Cartography to Statistics and the Rise of Ethnography

The emergence of a dominant discourse among the European literati and illuminati that established the peoples beyond the ambiguous European

---

23. Martin Bernal, *Black Athena: The Afroasiatic Roots of Classical Civilization* (New Brunswick, 1991).
24. This notion still resurfaces in European establishments of high culture, despite all pretenses about its eradication. We need only visit the Musée du Quai Branly in Paris, which opened in 2006 but has curatorial choices and an exhibition style that would not have been out of place in 1906. In fact, most the artifacts in the museum were transferred from the old museum of ethnography.
25. Black, *Maps and History*, 30.

borders in the east and the north as fundamentally different and inferior to the white Europeans was rooted in post-Enlightenment notions of scientific knowledge and civilization.[26] The same discourse reached its peak through the course of the nineteenth century as it penetrated not only elite institutes of knowledge production but popular conceptions of the Orient in the growing domain of European public opinion. As far as cartography of Turkey in Europe is concerned, one of the crucial developments that took place in the nineteenth century was the combination of geography with statistics and the appearance of statistical tables on maps. All forms of basic data graphics that we readily recognize today, such as bar and pie charts, histograms, and line graphs, were invented during the first half of the nineteenth century.[27] Familiar as they may seem to the modern eye, this technique was quite unheard of at the beginning of the nineteenth century. Combined with the heightened interest in the "distribution of races" across the globe, especially in the second half of the nineteenth century, the marriage of cartography to statistics gave birth to the ethnographic maps that we are familiar with.

Ethnographic maps essentially constitute a subgroup of "thematic maps," or maps that "[display] the occurrence, spatial pattern, or variation of one or a small number of phenomena in the physical, biological, social, or economic world, such as climate, natural resources, population characteristics and commerce."[28] Even though their origins can be traced back to the seventeenth century, it was only in the nineteenth century—after the introduction of new graphical representation methods and the transformation of geography as a discipline into a branch of natural sciences that covered physical elements of Earth in its entirety, including its atmosphere, climate, flora, fauna, and geological layers—that thematic maps became widely used tools of cartographic representation. Carl Ritter and Alexander von Humboldt, the pioneers of this transformation, introduced the cartography of physical phenomena into the discipline. Von Humboldt was also extremely influential in popularizing the use of new graphic methods among geographers; among his disciples was Heinrich Berghaus, whose *Physicalischer Atlas* was widely copied and plagiarized.[29] Superficially, the new techniques were indeed the accomplishment of "pure" science, untainted by any sort of measuring error or bias because they represented physical phenomena as accurately as possible and served the purpose of expanding humankind's knowledge of the globe it inhabited. The mapmaker's curatorial authority and choices, however, were never a simple exercise of a "purely scientific"

---

26. For European ambiguity about the eastern borders of the continent, see Wolff, *Inventing Eastern Europe*.

27. Michael Friendly and Gilles Palsky, "Visualizing Nature and Society," in *Maps: Finding our Place in the World*, edited by James R. Akerman and Robert W. Karrow Jr. (Chicago, 2007), 231.

28. Ibid., 212.

29. Ibid., 222–23.

method but a reflection of the dominant weltanschauung. Consider, for instance, the folio in Berghaus's *Atlas* depicting the "Geographical Distribution of the Human Races": a Mercatorial projection of the globe occupies the center, while the margins are packed full of information with the aid of graphical charts and an inset map showing how population density correlates with dietary patterns.[30] The most striking illustrations are scattered on the top and sides of the map; they are portraits representing the different human races—some rendered grotesquely ugly—and the corresponding skull shapes.[31] The distinctions based on physiognomy (which looks even uglier than it sounds) lent the author's racial classification the aura of scientific knowledge; it asserted the notion (accepted as fact at the time) that race was something that could *positively* be identified, although the criteria used for determining race still oscillated between definitions based on physical traits (such as the color of skin) and what we would consider cultural elements today (such as costumes). In any case, the purely physiognomic conception of race was not entirely dominant, and *race* was mostly used as a term that might correspond to *ethnicity* today, with the notable distinction that it was understood to be essentially fixed.

Berghaus's map was an early example of cartographic representations of ethnographic knowledge, and it made use of tables and illustrations external to the map to explicate its subject matter. It certainly had a significant visual impact, but another technique, known as "choropleths" was an even more potent medium for communicating knowledge about the distribution of "measurable" phenomena in space. The earliest known example of the choropleth technique is "Figurative Map of Popular Education in France" ("Carte figurative de l'instruction populaire de la France") by Baron Charles Dupin, published in 1826. Dupin's stated purpose for his map was to illustrate the effects of public education on prosperity in France.[32] He shaded the map such that the coloring became darker as the number of pupils in school in a given department decreased. A better proxy for representing "enlightenment" could not be found, and in fact, the map became a reference for dividing France into "obscure" and "eclairé" regions. Choropleths became a widely used tool in the depiction of social problems, such as crime and disease, and their correlation with schooling, region, and social class.

By the middle of the nineteenth century, the toolbox was complete for those who wanted to undertake the ambitious project of writing up the

---

30. *Geographische Verbreitung der Menschen-Ranssen* (Gotha, 1848).
31. For a critical commentary on this map and Berghaus's intellectual connection to von Humboldt, see Denis Cosgrove, "Tropic and Tropicality," in *Tropical Visions in an Age of Empire*, edited by Felix Driver and Luciana Martins (Chicago, 2005), 197–216.
32. Charles Dupin, *Effets de l'enseignement populaire de la lecture, de l'écriture et de l'arithmétique, de la géométrie et de la mécanique appliquées aux arts, sur les prospérités de la France* (Paris, 1826), quoted in Friendly and Palsky, "Visualizing Nature and Society," 240.

cartography of the human race. The rise of ethnography as a scientific discipline during the same period contributed to the proliferation of maps of European Turkey and its "races." The discipline of ethnography (which many academic institutions housed in the same general department of geography), despite its claim to objective and empiricist foundations, was at the time dominated by theories that classified humans and cultures along a sliding scale that placed white Europeans at the top. The superiority of Europeans was not just an extreme position implicitly present in the sister disciplines of geography and ethnography; it was one of the premises of their methodology. The other premise was the teleology of the European model of nations. These two premises were in place well into the twentieth century, and combining forces with the concept of "natural frontiers" (another nineteenth-century invention), they helped shape geopolitics around the globe. Consider, for instance, the definition of *ethnology* and *ethnography* in the 1910 edition of *Encyclopædia Britannica*: "sciences which in their narrowest sense deal respectively with man as a racial unit (*mankind*), i.e. his development through the family and tribal stages into national life, and with the distribution over the earth of the races and nations thus formed. Though the etymology of the word permits in theory of this line of division between ethnology and ethnography, in practice they form and indivisible study of man's progress from the point at which anthropology leaves him."[33] The assumption that human races go through an evolutionary process, the ultimate result of which is organization into nations, is the central idea of this definition. We should also note that anthropology, ethnology, and ethnography constituted a continuum under the general rubric of "natural history" and that the study of the different races was determined according to their location on that continuum: anthropology for the "savages," ethnology and ethnography for the more familiar and literate "other," and finally national history for those who had reached the culmination point.[34] It is interesting to note that the Balkan national elites, whose ethnic kin was the subject matter of European ethnographers, imported and internalized similar assumptions about the relative qualities of different ethnic groups and their potential for "civilization," as we will see later. This was not a bizarre form of self-regard but a carefully strategized method used to substantiate one ethnic group's claim to territory over another's because the European Powers understood the principles of popular sovereignty and national self-determination in terms of natural frontiers and "national maturity."

---

33. "Ethnology and Ethnography," *Encyclopæaedia Britannica* (New York, 1910), vol. 9: 849.
34. Bernard Cohn calls the ethnography of this period "the description of 'primitives,'" which entailed "a theory of history which is based on the idea of a chronological ordering of types of societies interpretable as a sequence of cultural or biological evolution." Bernard Cohn, "History and Anthropology: The State of Play," in *An Anthropologist among the Historians and Other Essays* (Delhi and Oxford, 1987), 24.

Mapping Macedonia and Its Races

The reinvention of the term *Macedonia* owed much to the early travelers in the area, who came in search of ruins and, following cartographic custom, referred to these little-known parts of the Ottoman Empire by their ancient names, as if they were visiting Roman provinces.[35] The most significant among the earlier explorers was E. M. Cousinéry, whose topographical descriptions are still used as a reference by archaeologists.[36] The explorers were writing not only about geography and the ruins, of course, but also about the inhabitants of those lands or the "human geography," influenced by assumptions about their ancestors and their geographical origins based on the classics and the earlier deliberations of historical atlases. The author of the first significant work on the ethnography of the region was Amie Boué, who published the results of his research in 1840, a decade after Cuisinéry's *Voyage dans la Macédoine*. An ethnographic map that indicated a large presence of "Bulgarians" in the area accompanied his work. The map introduced, for the first time, the notion that Bulgarians constituted the largest "racial" group in Macedonia.[37] Ethnographic research on European Turkey became more popular during the late nineteenth and early twentieth centuries, and even the nonspecialist visitors made sure to note ethnographical peculiarities in their travel accounts as they saw fit.

Maps based on the findings of these researches also started to appear in the middle of the nineteenth century. Some of these were published as separate works, and some were included in prestigious annals and journals of geography such as Berghaus's *Atlas* or *Petermann's Mittheilungen*. Henry R. Wilkinson, in his 1951 book on maps of Macedonia, which is still considered a classic reference source, notes that the map published in 1842 by Pavel Schafarik, pan-Slavist scholar and an Austro-Hungarian subject of Czech descent,

---

35. The reinvention of Macedonia by nineteenth-century travelers and geographers was not something identified by deconstructionist historians in the late twentieth century. For instance, in 1920 Jordan Ivanoff, professor and member of the Bulgarian academy of sciences, wrote, "The passionate desire of those from the Balkans [les Balkaniques] to resuscitate the name Macedonia is stimulated by the publications of Europeans about the Balkan peninsula, especially since the beginning of the 19th century. We shall cite only the names that are most frequently seen: Félis de Beaujour, Cousinéry, Pouqueville, Urquhart, Viquesnel, Boué, Grisebach, Grigorovitch, etc. In their research on the Balkans, they consider Macedonia as a geographic unity." *La Question Macédonienne au Point de Vue Historique, Ethnographique et Statistique* (Paris, 1920), 5.

36. Cousinéry had served as consul general for France in Salonika; Cousinéry, *Voyage dans la Macédoine*. Pouqueville is cited among the earlier travelers, but according to a later explorer, he did not actually go to Macedonia; see Charles Édouard Guys, *Le Guide de la Macédoine* (Paris, 1857), vi.

37. Amie Boué, *La Turquie d'Europe, ou Observations sur la Géographie, la Géologie, l'Histoire Naturelle, la Statistique, les Moeurs, les Coutumes, l'Archéologie, l'Agriculture, l'Industrie, le Commerce, les Gouvernements divers, le Clergé, l'Histoire, et l'état Politique de cet Empire* (Paris, 1840): see also Amie Boué, *Receuil d'Itinéraires dans la Turquie d'Europe, Détails Géographiques, Topographiques, et Statistiques cur cet Empire* (Vienne, 1854).

"virtually revolutionized the prevailing ideas on the distribution and character of the peoples of south-eastern Europe" and "set the fashion for nearly all ethnographic maps of this area."[38] As thorough as Wilkinson was, we take this assertion with a grain of salt because Jovan Cvijić, Serbian scholar and another contributor to the ethnographic geography of southeastern Europe, remarked that, having been published in Czech, Schafarik's *Slovansky Národopis* "remained unknown to other cultured nations."[39] Nevertheless, Cvijić also noted that the map was ground-breaking in its classification and labeling of six major groups currently inhabiting the Balkan Peninsula: Albanians, Turks, Serbo-Croats, Greeks, Bulgarians, and Romanians. The more likely person to be credited with familiarizing the "cultured nations" of Europe with the racial riches of European Turkey for the first time was Amie Boué, who published an ethnographic map in Berghaus's *Atlas* in 1847, seven years after the appearance of *La Turquie d'Europe*. Boué attributed an even larger territory to the Bulgarians than Schafarik had and denoted Turks only in a few major cities. When read in the context of his other writings about the Ottoman Empire, however, this should not necessarily lead us to conclude that he was making a visual statement, questioning the legitimacy of Ottoman rule in the Balkans, as the majority of European geographers did. His writings suggest that Boué was more interested in presenting policies to bring the Ottomans on par with other European states than in supporting an ethnic basis for challenging their presence in Europe.[40] His suggestions did not involve the replacement of an imperial source of authority with a national one defined by language but, instead, called for the reform of the existing structure. Boué had unfaltering confidence in the potential of modernity to change everything within the reach of railroads.

Yet Boué's map made such a good case for the Bulgarians as the dominant element in Macedonia that it was reproduced during the first decades of the twentieth century several times in other ethnographic works and atlases used as propaganda material by the Bulgarians; the scholar's reputation no doubt provided the stamp of scientific objectivity to these publications.[41] In 1861, another map that would later become a frequent reference work for the Bulgarian propagandists was published in *Petermann's Mittheilungen*,

---

38. Wilkinson, *Maps and Politics*.
39. Jovan Cvijić, *Remarks on the Ethnography of the Macedonian Slavs* (London, 1906), 19. This article was originally published in French and was also translated into Serbian and Russian. It immediately drew a reaction from Anastas Ishirkov, who argued that this was a transparent attempt to prove that the Bulgarians of the Morova valley and Macedonia were in fact Serbs; *Études Ethnographiques sur les Slaves de Macédoine* (Paris, 1908).
40. Boué considered the Ottoman Empire a European state rather than an aberration in the continent, in contrast to, for instance, Bianconi. It is worth noting that he mostly compared it to Spain, sometimes to England and France, and occasionally did so in a favorable manner. See, for instance, Boué, *Turquie d'Europe*, Vol. 2: 158.
41. According to Cvijić, Vasil Kûnchov's *Makedonia: Ethnographia i Statistika* (Sofia, 1900) was one such example; Cvijić, *Remarks*, 30–31.

a map by Guillaume Marie Lejean, a former consul of France in the Ottoman Empire.⁴² The map was based on data that Lejean had collected during two trips made in 1857 and 1858. Lejean noted in the introduction to his work that the "ethnographic study of the Ottoman Empire" was no longer an "object of purely scientific curiosity." He separated himself from earlier ethnogeographers with his position that language could not be used as a criterion to determine nationality in "Turkey" since "religious hatred and political inequality" had caused people to adopt languages that did not correspond to their races.⁴³ Instead, he argued, the criterion of history should be used to determine nationality. Despite the change in the criterion for measuring nationality, the coloring of the map still favored the Bulgarians in Macedonia. The most striking feature of his map, in contrast with earlier examples, was a great block of Turkish settlement in northeastern Bulgaria, covering regions that were more usually attributed to the Romanians.

James F. Clarke argues in his book *The Pen and the Sword,* one of the formative texts of Bulgarian history in the English language, that "the persistence of classical cartographic conventions—the dead hand of Ptolemy— together with the *terra incognita* nature of the Turkish Balkans which prevailed up to the second half of the nineteenth century" contributed to the "cartographical misfortune" of Bulgarians, who, "in addition to re-educating themselves ... had the task of educating Europe."⁴⁴ European cartographic material from 1842 to 1877, however, tells an entirely different story. Far from suffering from a "cartographic misfortune," Bulgarians were represented abundantly in these maps. In 1869, August Heinrich Petermann, the esteemed editor of *Petermann's Geographische Mittheilungen,* published a map titled *Die Ausdehnung der Slaven in der Türkei und der angrenzenden Gebieten.* The work claimed to represent the epitome of the previous three decades of work on the ethnogeography of Turkey-in Europe.⁴⁵ The map showed uniform Bulgarian dominance over the entire Balkan Peninsula with the exception of the coastal regions, where the Greeks were indicated, and towns, which were marked Turkish (or Muslim.)

After 1877, as ethnographic maps of European Turkey proliferated, the coloring style of the maps, the criteria used to determine nationality, and the nationality of the authors of the maps began to diversify. Even the "Bulgarianness" of Macedonian Slavs, which had been accepted as more or less self-evident, came to be questioned by new works. Although maps favoring

---

42. It was later appended, for instance, to A. Ofeicoff, *La Macédoine au Point de Vue Ethnographique, Historique, et Philologique* (Constantinople, 1887). Ofeicoff was a pseudonym used by A. Shopov, the Bulgarian commercial agent in Salonika and a frequent contributor to polemics about the ethnographic composition of Macedonia.

43. Guillaume Lejean, "Ethnographie de la Turquie d'Europe" in *Peterman's Geographische Mittheilungen* (Gotha, 1861), 1–2.

44. Clarke, *Pen and the Sword,* 34.

45. Wilkinson, *Maps and Politics,* 55.

one particular group continued to be the norm, a few exceptions appeared that questioned the homogeneity of choropleths and used hybrid color combinations to account for ethnic variety.

In the latter half of the nineteenth century, the name Heinrich Kiepert came to the fore as one of the best-known cartographers of the time. A prolific professor of geography at the University of Berlin, Kiepert counted among his many talents expertise in the geography of European and Asian Turkey, and Bismarck among his many admirers.[46] Kiepert published his *Ethnographische Übersicht des Europäischen Orients* in 1876. In this map, Thrace was colored as half Turkish and half Greek, and further north, a more or less similar proportion was observed between Turks and Bulgarians. This map had had such a good reception in Europe that it was used as a reference at the Congress of Berlin—presumably a testament to its objectivity.[47]

It was not long before this apparent status quo was challenged by maps that favored Greek claims over Macedonia. Two significant examples published in 1877 were the Stanford Map and a map drafted by F. Bianconi, French engineer and geographer.[48] The same year, A. Synvet, a French philhellene and a teacher of geography at *Galatasaray Lisesi* (also known as Lycée de Galatasaray, a prestigious public school in Istanbul that produced a large proportion of the Ottoman bureaucratic and literary elite) published another map that was considered pro-Greek and received considerable publicity in Europe. Synvet's map was relatively modest in its claims about Greek territory; it did not directly negate the earlier maps showing sizable Bulgarian populations, but by stressing the existence of dense "Turkish" settlements all over the Balkan Peninsula, it showed that the Greek population of the Ottoman Empire had been grossly underestimated.[49] His figures were largely based on the results of a two-year-old survey commissioned by the Patriarchate to determine the number of Greek Orthodox households that would be liable for a tithe for the support of bishoprics. A year later, Synvet

---

46. V. Colocotronis, *La Macédoine et l'Hellenisme, Étude Historique et Ethnologique* (Paris, 1919), 484; Wilkinson, *Maps and Politics*, 67.

47. Wilkinson notes Bismarck's high regard for Kiepert and mentions that his map was used at the Congress of Berlin and "was regarded as part of Bismarck's 'honest brokerage.'" *Maps and Politics*, 67–68. It must be noted however, that Kiepert's maps that were used at the Congress of Berlin had been prepared under Russian sponsorship; Karpat, *Ottoman Population*, 26. They were first published in Russian, and according to Paparrigopoulos, had been translated into French on Bismarck's orders to be used at the Congress; Paparrigopoulos's correspondence with P. Argiropoulo, in K. Th. Dimara, *Kōnstantinos Paparrēgopoulos, ē epochē tou, ē Zōē tou, to ergo tou* (Athens, 1986), 348.

48. F. Bianconi, *Ethnographie et Statistique de la Turquie d'Europe et de la Grèce* (Paris, 1877).

49. A. Synvet, *La Carte Ethnographique de la Turquie d'Europe et Denombrement de l'Empire Ottoman* (Paris, 1877). He adjusted the numbers produced by community registers by referring to the records of *syllogues*. Kemal Karpat notes that the figures he calculated proved to be exaggerated "when the Ottoman census of 1881/82–1893 gave the first truly comprehensive account of the Greek population." *Ottoman Population*, 49.

published *Les Grecs de L'Empire Ottoman,* where he supplemented these figures using those provided by membership registers of *syllogues* (Greek cultural organizations), which, he argued, gave a more accurate picture. Using this method, the Greek population of Macedonia, which he had estimated at 474,000 the year before, was now reported as 587,860.[50] It is important to note that as the fight over Macedonia shifted into one carried out using guns rather than maps, the Greek side still recognized the weight of ethnography to be as significant as the guerrillas wielding weapons. So, when a crowd gathered in Piraeus to protest the events in Macedonia in August 1903 and present a memorandum to the government and the diplomatic delegations in Athens, one of the six resolutions of the memorandum was against the "false statistics published by Slavists to mislead European public opinion to the detriment of the Hellenic nationality."[51]

In 1878, two new maps covering Macedonia appeared: one by Carl Sax and a new map by Heinrich Kiepert. Compared to other ethnographic maps of the era, which usually displayed different ethnic groups by clearly delineated blocks of color on the map because of their reliance on the graphic principle that favored a "preponderance" of a given "race," Sax's map looked like a painting by his fellow countryman, Oskar Kokoschka. Jovan Cvijić later remarked that, although there was some merit to Sax's work, "the well-known, peculiarly Austrian, bureaucratic methods made him tear nations into atoms."[52] Perhaps we should concede that Cvijić did have a point, for Sax cited no fewer than twenty-one groups in his classification and his concern with justifying Austrian intervention in the region did not go unnoticed. We might even go as far as to suggest that this was the first pro-Austrian map of the Balkans. On the other hand, Sax's "peculiar" method was the first to question the raciolinguistic criteria that had hitherto been the norm. He pointed out that the importance of religion had been neglected and that what he called a sense of "group consciousness," or the sum of elements that keep a community together, had not been taken into account.[53] It is very likely that Sax's method was an application of the theories of Karl von Czörnig and his pupil, Adolf Ficker, who "were opposed both to the language criterion constituting the sole marker of nationality, as well as to the principle of enquiry into the nationality of individuals. They argued that any enquiry into nationality should be directed at discovering the national identity of communities, rather than the language used by individuals. They in addition regarded history, geography, anthropology and ethnography as the essential correctives of the language criterion."[54]

---

50. A. Synvet, *Les Grecs de L'Empire Ottoman: Étude Statistique* (Constantinople, 1878).
51. Quoted in Paillarès, *Imbroglio Macédonien,* 22.
52. Cvijić, *Remarks,* 24.
53. Wilkinson, *Maps and Politics,* 77.
54. Z. A. B. Zeman "Four Austrian Censuses and Their Political Consequences," in *The Last Years of Austria-Hungary,* edited by Mark Cornwall (Exeter, 1990), 32.

What seems to be a curious absence during this period, considering the Russian interest in the region, and the "protection" it offered to its Slav brethren, are ethnographic maps prepared by Russian geographers. It is difficult to attribute this to a lack of know-how or sufficient resources because the St. Petersburg–based Imperial Russian Geographical Society had been active since 1845, when it was established under the tutelage of German geographers, most notably Karl Baer, who passed the mantle on to such Russian colleagues as the influential K. I. Arsenyev [Arsenieff] (1789–1865) and P. P. Semënov [Semenoff] (1827–1914).[55] In fact, during the tense period preceding the Constantinople Conference in December 1876, which concluded yet another Balkan crisis between the Ottoman Empire and Serbia — and by implication Russia — the Russian Embassy in London, according to a report by Ioannis Gennadius, displayed an ethnographic map of the Balkan Peninsula drawn not by one of its own but by the famous G. M. Lejean.[56]

According to Jovan Cvijić, there were only three Russian maps that had any influence among the Slavs (even though they were not noted by European intellectuals), all published by the Slav Union based in St. Petersburg. The first, published in 1887, by Marković and Rittich, was almost entirely a copy of Lejean's map, with certain notable exceptions, such as the island of Thasos improbably marked as containing an "oasis of Bulgarians."[57] The second, published by N. C. Zarjanko and V. V. Komarov in 1890, was based on Kiepert's map and marked as dominated by "Bulgarians" an area found to be "exaggerated even by the Bulgarians themselves."[58] The same year, Komarov published another map that used a neutral color for Macedonian Slavs, marking them as neither Serb nor Bulgarian.[59] This shift is not hard to explain: having assumed the patronage of all Slavs, Russia had to strike a delicate balance in appeasing the Serbs and the Bulgarians, whose southern Slavic fraternity reached its limits somewhere between Niš and Skoplje and fell short of preventing the war in 1885. The earlier work of Serbian scholars, such as Stefan Verković, on the ethnography of Macedonian Slavs apparently did not have any reservations about attributing the term *Bulgarian* to their language, yet toward the end of the nineteenth century this attitude had made a complete turn in the other

---

55. Semënov (also known as Tian-Shanskiy, in tribute to his expedition of Tien Shan) was also involved in the preparation of the first Russian census of 1897; David J. M. Hosoon, "The Development of Geography in Pre-Soviet Russia," *Annals of the Association of American Geographers* 58 (1968), 259.

56. S. Karavas, "Oi Ethnografikes Peripeteies tou Ellēnismou, "*Ta Istorika* 19 (2002), 34.

57. Jovan Cvijić, "Remarques sur l'Ethnographie de la Macédoine," *Annales de Géographie* 15, no. 81 (1906), 256.

58. Ibid. As noted previously, Cvijić was referring to Kûnchov's work when he referred to "Bulgarians" finding Zarjanko and Komarov's work exaggerated.

59. Another Russian map worth mentioning is T. D. Florinski's *Etnografska Karta na Slavyanstvovo v Europa*, published in 1908, which counted Macedonian Slavs as "Bulgarians"; Wilkinson, *Maps and Politics*, 153.

direction.⁶⁰ The reaction against the "Greater Bulgaria" of St. Stefano seems to have had a sobering effect not only on Serbian authors but on their Russian counterparts, who became more circumspect about using the term *Bulgarian* in reference to Macedonian Slavs.⁶¹

Russian geographers' relative lack of interest in the Macedonian Slavs also had to do with their more pressing projects at the time. The outreaches of the Russian Empire were still in the process of "discovery" by strongly motivated Russian explorers, watched closely with approval by European geographers. When the Russian Geographical Society published a compendium summarizing the work it had done between 1845 and 1895 in celebration of its fiftieth anniversary, the highly condensed accounts of its explorations filled·up some 1,378 pages in three volumes.⁶² The surveys stretched from the Kirghiz steppes to the Siberian tundra, from the Black Sea shores to the slopes of the Urals, and passed borders into territories within the confines of neighboring states. Russians were by no means indifferent to the geographical distribution of their Slavic brethren in Macedonia, but their geographers had bigger fish to fry elsewhere, and they were stretched thin over a vast territory that needed to be properly measured, counted, and recorded to be fully incorporated into the empire.

Spiridon Gopčević published the first significant study by a Serbian scholar to make a claim about Macedonian Slavs in 1889. This was an impressive volume of ethnographic work, illustrated with fine drawings and photographs and accompanied by an ethnographic map.⁶³ Nevertheless, it was largely viewed as a "propaganda piece."⁶⁴ Strictly speaking, Gopčević was

---

60. Anastas Ishirkov, *Le Nom de Bulgare: Eclaircissement d'Histoire et d'Ethnographie* (Lausanne, 1918), 3–4. Verković was the author of *Narodne Pesme Makedonski Bugara* [Folk Songs of Macedonian Bulgars] (Belgrade, 1860).

61. Compare the work, for instance, of Victor Grigorović on the ethnography of Turkey in Europe, first published in 1848 and frequently cited by Bulgarian authors (such as Ishirkov, *Nom de Bulgare,* 35) as proof that the Macedonian Slavs were recognized as "Bulgarians" by scholars writing well before the establishment of the Exarchate. See also the writings of Iastrebov, published in 1886, which considered Macedonian Slavs to be "Serbs"; Cvijić, "Remarques," 257, n. 1.

62. P. P. Semenoff, *History of a Half Century of Activity of the Russian Geographical Society, 1845–1895,* with the collaboration of A.A. Dostoiyevsky (St. Petersburg, 1896) [in Russian], cited in Peter Kropotkin, "The Fifty Years' History of the Russian Geographical Society," *Geographical Journal* 10 (July 1897): 53–56. The compendium included "a map showing the process of geographical exploration of the Russian Empire, and the neighbouring countries within the last fifty years" (53). For activities of the society during this period, see also "Recent Russian Geographical Literature," *Geographical Journal* 6 (December 1895): 554–58; E. Delmar Morgan, "Russian Geographical Work in 1886 from Russian Sources," *Proceedings of the Royal Geographical Society and Monthly Record of Geography* 9 (July 1887): 423–37.

63. Spiridon Gopčević, *Makedonien und Alt-Serbien* (Vienna, 1889).

64. Wilkinson notes that "it is a firm axiom of the propagandist ... that an initial failure may be turned into an ultimate success by the simple process of reiteration," and that Gopčević "provided the Serbs with their initial failure." *Maps and Politics,* 103. To be fair to Gopčević, the volume that the map accompanied was a remarkably crafted book, full of interesting

not the first cartographer to place Serbians in the region, his most important predecessors being M. S. Miloyevitch (1873), Colonel Dragashevitch (1885), and M. Veselinovitch (1886), but it seems that he earned this reputation because his work became widely available to European scholars after its publication in *Petermann's Mittheilungen*.[65] This map was also the first one among those mentioned so far to use the term *Macedonia* in its title. Ten years later, C. Nicolaides, the Greek scholar, published another ethnographic and linguistic map of Macedonia, and maps dedicated to Macedonia, as opposed to Turkey in Europe, started to appear as the political rivalry became more concentrated in this region. The Serbians had now firmly entered the cartographic contest. An anonymously prepared "Serbian University Map" was published in 1891.

Other maps of the period worth mentioning were those of Gustave Weigand (1895); Richard von Mach (1899), who based his ethnographic representation on the distribution of Serbian, Bulgarian, and Greek schools; a map published anonymously in Sofia in 1901;[66] another anonymous map showing Christian schools in Macedonia (1905); and Brancoff's maps showing the Christian population and Christian schools of Macedonia (1905). Another significant example of maps prepared with school data is the anonymous "Carte des Écoles Chrétiennes de la Macédoine," published in Paris in 1905.[67] Brancoff's map of Christian schools, in rebuttal, claimed that Greek schools were protected by the Ottoman government and that, in contrast, Bulgarians could not get even a permit to open up a school in areas where the population had joined the Exarchate but given sufficient time, Bulgarian schools would prevail because they offered better education.[68]

This new trend of ethnographic maps based on school data was largely the invention of Greek nationalists, who were despairing at the notion, which was gaining firmer ground in western Europe, that Macedonia was largely inhabited by a Slav population. Needless to say, the sizable Muslim population (Turkish, Albanian, and Slavic speakers) of the region was entirely neglected owing to the perception that these people were "aliens" who did not belong there in the first place.[69] As we have noted, this is a notion that can

---

ethnographic information, including the author's research on folklore, and definitely warrants more than a dismissive label.

65. Cvijić, *Remarks*, 29.

66. According to Cvijić, there was "no doubt that this edition belongs to the Bulgarian Ministry of War." Ibid., 31.

67. Cvijić notes, "there is nothing which represents better than this chart the gigantic efforts of the Greeks to Hellenise these two vilayets." Ibid., 32. School statistics in favor of the Greeks were initially published in the form of statistical tables, but the visual impact of a map was certainly stronger. For the statistics see, *Population of Macedonia*; Ioanna Z. Stephanopoli, *Grecs et Bulgares en Macédoine* (Athens, 1903).

68. Brancoff [Mishev], *La Macédoine et sa Population Chrétienne*, 77–79.

69. Even in a mainstream source of general information such as *Encyclopædia Britannica* (11th ed.), the population of Macedonia was described as follows: "The greater part of Macedonia is inhabited by a Slavonic population, mainly Bulgarian in its characteristics; the

be traced back as far as the eighteenth century, when post-Enlightenment philosophers were in the process of "inventing Eastern Europe," a transition zone within the vaguely defined borders of Europe with dangerously close proximity to the anomaly of Turkey in Europe. Lacking a proper vocabulary to describe the exotic inhabitants of these "lost lands," scholars borrowed familiar names from ancient history; Scythians served as a generic name for these people in the eighteenth century, until, as Larry Wolff observes, "Herder appropriated another identification from among the barbarians of ancient history, and gave Eastern Europe its modern identity as the domain of the Slavs."[70] The first generation of ethnographic maps claiming Macedonia as Greek, however painstakingly prepared, failed to undo this perception. The school criterion was introduced as a new basis for identifying ethnic groups because it provided the mapmakers with numbers that they could compile with relative ease and that had a reliability that was harder to challenge. These figures also happened to favor Greek schools, which, despite the relatively recent rivalry of Bulgarian and, to a lesser extent, Serbian schools benefited from the authority of the Patriarchate as well as the material and personnel support of the Greek state and the Greek bourgeoisie. More important, this criterion combined consciousness and culture as the main determinants of national identity rather than racial or linguistic factors, thereby emphasizing the element of free will and invoking the charisma for liberal European public opinion of Greek culture and its classical heritage.

Three ethnographic maps published during the first decades of the twentieth century were distinguished by the influence they had over their audiences. The first was a book of population statistics compiled by Vasil Kûnchov, a former inspector of Bulgarian elementary schools in Macedonia. Kûnchov's book, published in 1900, also contained maps based on his figures and instantly became a respected reference source not only in Bulgaria but also in France. The book was not translated into French or English, but its statistical tables were used by the popular press and geography journals.[71] The second, Karl Peucker's *Karte von Makedonien, Altserbien und Albanien*, published in 1903 was, as its subtitle notes, drawn to illustrate the Macedonian Question, but it did not used choropleths. In fact, compared to the base maps of the other examples mentioned so far, Peucker's map was the most sophisticated. Instead of choropleths, the map addressed questions of history, language, religion, and culture with two insets that included summary

---

coast-line and the southern districts west of the Gulf of Salonica by Greeks, while Turkish, Vlach and Albanian settlements exist sporadically, or in groups, in many parts of the country." "Macedonia," 216.

70. Wolff, *Inventing Eastern Europe*, 11.

71. Vasil Kûnchov, *Makedonia: Ethnographia i Statistika* (Sofia, 1900). Kûnchov's statistics were considered among the best and were reproduced in European-language publications. See, for instance, Routier, *Macédoine et les Puissances*, 267.

statistical tables and a color key to indicate "language zones." It was topographically and toponymically extremely detailed. The map did not indicate a source for the topographic survey it was based on (the cultural groups were reportedly listed according to Cvijić's classification), but it was likely the work of Austrian engineers. The Ottoman map office had also obtained a copy of this map.[72]

Peucker's reference to Jovan Cvijić is a testament to the respect the Serbian geographer had garnered during this period. If Kiepert had been the pop geographer of Europe in the 1870s, that title belonged to Cvijić during the first two decades of the twentieth century.[73] His demographic research and ethnographic maps were considered a benchmark for other works on the populations of the Balkans, much to the chagrin of Bulgarian scholars and activists. Until the 1880s, the assumption that the Macedonian Slavs were Bulgarian had not really been questioned because this was more or less the position of the European geographical establishment. As we have seen, worries about the revival of St. Stefano Bulgaria fueled the initial reaction against this status quo, and the Bulgarian side was quick to take note and answer in kind.[74] Cvijić's intervention, on the other hand, was a game changer. He put forth the notion that *Bulgarian* was not a term that denoted nationality among the Macedonian Slavs, who in any case lacked any such consciousness until well after the formation of the Bulgarian Exarchate.[75] He challenged the work of early European scholars and travelers, including François C. H. L. Pouqueville, Cousinéry, Boué, August Heinrich Rudolf Griesebach, Lejean, Georgina Mary Muir Mackenzie and Adeline Paulina Irby, and even Kiepert, who all, he pointed out, lacked the necessary linguistic skills to write authoritatively about the ethnography of the Macedonian Slavs and who therefore relied on the interpretation of their Greek and Turkish guides and ended up repeating the same errors. He held Joseph Müller, who had worked as a physician for the Ottoman army, to be the only exception and considered his book to be the most reliable among the earlier works. Müller, not surprisingly, had classified the Macedonian Slavs in the regions he traveled as "Serbs."[76]

---

72. BOA, HRT 251.
73. It helped that Cvijić wrote in an academic, seemingly objective style; published his prolific output in several European languages, including English; and was good at marketing his work. I could not but notice that all the reprints of his articles held at the Bibliothèque Nationale de France were gifts of the author.
74. See, for instance, Ofeicoff [Shopov]'s polemic *Macédoine au Point de Vue Ethnographique*, in which he argues, using current political events, toponyms, historical figures, and grammar (while conceding the distinctiveness of the Macedonian dialect and its common traits with Serbian), that the Macedonian Slavs are Bulgarian.
75. Jovan Cvijić, *Questions Balkaniques* (Neuchâtel, 1916).
76. Joseph Müller, *Albanien, Rumelien und die österreichisch-montenegrische Grenze.* Nebst einer Karte von Albanien. Mit einer Vorrede von Dr. P. J. Šafařík (Prague, 1844), 103, cited in Cvijić "Remarques," 251. The region that Müller wrote about did not include "Aegean Macedonia" but was limited to the province of Monastir, parts of Albania, and Old Serbia.

Even more egregious, as far as the Bulgarian intellectuals were concerned, was Cvijić's insistence that the adjective *Bulgar* was widely used in the Balkans simply with the meaning "country bumpkin [*rustaud*]" and "before the establishment of the Exarchate and the establishment of present-day Bulgaria, the word Bulgar did not signify anything other than this pejorative sense [used by] the Greek people and Turkish functionaries."[77] Therefore, the travelers in the Balkans saw Bulgarians everywhere because this was what their Greek and Turkish guides called the peasant populations of the Balkans. What worried the Bulgarian establishment more than Cvijić's publications was his target audience (European scholars) and how they evaluated his writings (with respect). This anxiety was palpable in a pamphlet written by Anastas Ishirkov as a response to Cvijić: "Had Mr. Cvijić published his study on Balkan questions in no language other than Serbian, I certainly would not spend my time on the question of the name Bulgar [*la question du nom de Bulgare*], since, for the Serbs, this question is not a scientific question, but a question of nationalist politics." This, alas, was not the case; Mr. Cvijić had targeted "the educated people of the whole world" by writing in French, and "since the readers of this new book on Balkan questions are not familiar with the literature on the Balkans," they might be misled by the author, especially because he was "well known in scholarly circles as a geographer and a geologist."[78]

Ishirkov's worries were not baseless. The manuscript map of Cvijić's *La Peninsule Balkanique* on the geographical distribution of "races" in the Balkan Peninsula, published in 1918, turned out to be arguably the most influential of the time, demonstrated by the fact that it served as a blueprint for marking national boundaries during the Paris Peace Conference of 1919, much as Kiepert's map had been used at the Berlin Congress.[79] Cvijić's rise to such prominence among geographers of the Balkan Peninsula represented a clear shift within three decades in western perceptions about the ethnic make-up of the region and underscored a major defeat for the Bulgarian side in the fight for supremacy in Macedonia.[80]

---

77. Cvijić, *Questions Balkaniques*, 22, cited in Ishirkov, *Nom de Bulgare*, 47.
78. Ishirkov, *Nom de Bulgare*, 5.
79. A critical analysis of the way the map served the U.S. delegation at the conference can be found in Jeremy Crampton, "The Cartographic Calculation of Space: Race Mapping and the Balkans at the Paris Peace Conference of 1919," *Social & Cultural Geography* 7, no. 5 (October 2006): 731–52.
80. The attempts to distance Bulgaria from Germany in the hopes of influencing U.S. public opinion in favor of Bulgaria at the end of World War I did not really pay off. Pamphlets published in English emphasized the role played by U.S. missionaries in the liberation struggle of the Bulgarian people, the commitment of Bulgarian people to democracy, and, predictably, the majority of Bulgarians in regions claimed by Bulgaria. See, for instance, Dimitur Mishew [Dimitar Mishev], *America and Bulgaria and Their Moral Bonds* (Bern, 1918); Radoslav Andrea Tsanoff [Tsanov], "Bulgaria's Case," *Journal of Race Development* 8, no. 3 (1918): 296–317.

Ottoman Maps, or Their Conspicuous Absence

What was the Ottoman response to this cartographic activity? Did they answer back with their own ethnographic maps? The answer is an emphatic no, but before concluding that the Ottomans were woefully behind in the game of ethnographic cartography (which is true), it is useful to consider, in broad strokes, the developments that Ottoman cartography and Ottoman imagery of their world went through after the eighteenth century. Benjamin Fortna, in *The Imperial Classroom,* his book on public education in the Hamidian era (1877–1908), argues that the translation of European works of cartography by military officials for use in schools in the nineteenth century represented a continuity with earlier Ottoman traditions of state patronage of cartography and "of incorporating the cartographic developments of other lands."[81] This, I think, is a position that needs to be qualified. Fortna samples school maps and atlases used in the 1890s, which were typically organized by continents and did not have political boundaries or topographical detail except for the area in focus (e.g., Asia, Europe). He argues that this practice was, again, due to the influence of European mapmakers, for whom "the continental approach ma[de] more sense," as opposed to a more global outlook. According to Fortna, the explanation had three parts: "geographical, political, and philosophical." Geographically, it served the "[artificial] claim [of Europe] to be a continent," and politically it was influenced by the interests of the colonial powers in overseas territories. Finally, "the rational, positivist mode of thinking so prominent in Europe in the nineteenth century ... was bent on dividing up the things of the world, the better to analyze them."[82] While Fortna is right in all three counts, none of this actually implies that there was a general trend in Europe in the nineteenth century that favored the production and export of continental maps. In fact, cartographic production in Europe was prolific and covered a wide range and scale of representation in the late nineteenth century.[83] Maps of the globe were certainly represented among these in significant numbers, and it was precisely this Eurocentrism, the desire to project the power of Europe, and the belief in the superiority of rational knowledge that made "Great Globes" a popular item. This was the intended effect of the global (usually Mercatorial) maps in historical atlases and of the public display of outsized globes.[84] Elisée Reclus, anarchist and arguably the most antiestablishment of the French geographical establishment of the late nineteenth

---

81. Benjamin Fortna, *The Imperial Classroom: Islam, the State, and Education in the Late Ottoman Empire* (Oxford, 2002), 173.
82. Ibid., 182–83.
83. Cf. Black, *Maps and History,* esp. 51–101.
84. For a critical approach to images of the globe from the Renaissance to the recent past, see Denis Cosgrove, "Contested Global Visions: One-World, Whole Earth, and the Apollo Space Photographs," *Annals of the Association of American Geographers* 84, no. 2: 270–94.

century, "proposed that an enormous terrestrial globe be displayed at the Paris Exposition Universelle in 1900."[85]

A more likely explanation for "truncated" images of Ottoman domains was that these maps were not inspired by but were exclusively based on translations of maps produced in Europe, where representing the Ottoman Empire in separate sheets and continents had been the norm since the eighteenth century, as we have already seen. While it is true that there was some continuity in the European influence on Ottoman cartography since the early modern era, a distinct divergence occurred in the eighteenth century. The exchange of comparable technical knowledge was no longer the case after this time, and the Ottoman world gradually became bereft of advanced cartographic techniques. It is difficult to explain the origins of this divergence in the eighteenth century, but by the nineteenth century, as the Ottomans endeavored to adopt these techniques, they were already in the position of "translating" rather than incorporating, or even imitating. One possible reason for this has to do with the way "governmentality" was the impetus behind technical innovation in Europe, espousing ever more sophisticated methods of knowing the land to strengthen the control of the central state over territory and human and physical resources in the eighteenth century, exactly when the Ottoman state was delegating more control over administrative practice to its provincial lords. For the Ottomans, incorporating geographical knowledge into local administration became a concern and a possibility only in the late nineteenth century.[86] Even then, the main motivation for expanding cartographic knowledge continued to be the military, rather than provincial administration.[87] In fact, Ottoman cartographers were trained exclusively by the military, by the Fifth Department of Science of the General Staff (Erkân-ı Harbiye-i Umumiye Dairesi Beşinci Fen Şubesi), to be precise.

The Fifth Department decided to start a geodetic survey of the Protected Imperial Domains in 1896.[88] Two French engineers, M. M. Defarges and Barisain, were commissioned with the task and accorded military rank as

---

85. Morag Bell, Robin Butlin, and Michael Heffernan, eds. *Geography and Imperialism, 1820–1940* (Manchester, 1995), 5, cited in Black, *Maps and History*, 63.

86. Ensuring the accuracy of the changing and newly established borders with Bulgaria, Russia, and Greece and their protection seems to have been the primary motive in the quest for detailed topographic knowledge; BOA, BEO 1011/75822, September 9, 1897; BEO 1164/87254, July 25, 1898; BEO 1501/112536, June 12, 1900.

87. This is not to suggest that the Ottomans did not appreciate the usefulness of graphic or cartographic representations of statistical data at the service of imperial administration. The first significant example of these novel methods of visual representation applied to statistical data by an Ottoman official was the 1895 Ottoman Social Survey compiled by Mehmet Behiç; for more details about this survey see Fatma Müge Göçek and Şükrü Hanioğlu, "Western Knowledge, Imperial Control and the Use of Statistics in the Ottoman Empire," CRSO Working Paper no. 500, Ann Arbor, 1993.

88. BOA, BEO 783/58682, May 20, 1896.

colonel and lieutenant colonel, respectively.[89] The survey started in Anatolia, in Eskişehir, but it was plagued with financial difficulties from the start. The salaries of the French engineers and other commission members were in arrears, and the 200,000 guruş estimated to cover the first stage of operations turned out to be an impossible amount to raise.[90] When the Finance Ministry refused to foot the bill, the officials sought to obtain the funds from the military budget, which also failed. Finally, the military suggested that the sum be taken from the Salonika provincial budget.[91] We do not know the response of the officials in Salonika, but in all likelihood, the money failed to materialize because the project was all but abandoned by 1899. When the Royal Geographic Society of London requested a copy of the resulting map, they were told that it was "incomplete" at the moment.[92] There is no indication that it ever existed. The general staff published a map of Rumeli that year, which seems to have been drawn on the basis of another topographic map. The title did not mention an author, but it indicated that it had been "edited and drawn" by the Fifth Department (of Science). The prime meridian of the map was noted as Paris, which strongly suggests French origins.[93]

In 1909, a separate map commission was established under the general staff's Fourth Department, which was presumably to take on the task of surveying the empire. An army colonel was sent to Paris to purchase the necessary equipment. It is hard to tell how far this project went, but even after the Balkan Wars, the maps used by the Ottoman military were translations of European maps—ironically, it is not clear how reliable these maps could be, given the Ottomans' determination to prevent foreigners from carrying out topographic surveys in the empire or around its borders.[94]

Throughout the late nineteenth century, Ottoman officials continued to subscribe to European geographical publications, import and translate maps produced by European geographers (including Kiepert), and use them in classrooms of public schools as well as the army college.[95] What they lacked in technique, the Hamidian bureaucracy tried to make up with practical ingenuity. Benjamin Fortna demonstrates that Ottoman officials, growing

---

89. Their exact names may be different; my guess is based on the Ottoman spelling as "Döfarj" and "Barazin," and I was not able to locate these two individuals in French sources. The timely payment of their monthly salaries seems to have been a continuous source of trouble; BOA, BEO 997/74754, August 24, 1897; BEO 1139/85420, June 10, 1898. M. Barisain was also later promoted to the rank of colonel; BOA, I.TAL 151/1316, October 10, 1898.

90. BOA, BEO 993/74404, August 8, 1897; BEO, 1011/75822, September 22, 1897.

91. BOA, BEO 1232/92377, November 27, 1898.

92. BOA, BEO 1348/101064, July 31, 1899; BEO 1355/101582, August 30, 1899.

93. *Rumeli-i Şâhâne Haritası*, 1899, scale 1: 310,000 km (from the personal collection of Heath Lowry; many thanks to Prof. Lowry for sharing this map with me).

94. See, for instance, the reaction to the discovery that some Russian cartographers were in the process of taking geodetic measurements around the Euphrates River; BOA, I.DH 881/70280, April 11, 1883.

95. BOA, BEO 9/606, May 24, 1892; BEO 1662/124647, May 5, 1901; BEO 1710/128181, August 27, 1901.

Territoriality and Its Discontents → 105

sensitive about the pedagogical limitations of maps displaying the Ottoman realms in series of separate sheets, commissioned different maps that displayed the entire territories of the empire on one unbroken sheet. He notes that this was the "most striking change to be observed in Hamidian cartography."[96] Not surprisingly, these maps colored regions that had ceased to be "Ottoman," or were only nominally so, with the same colors assigned to the Ottoman Empire.[97] Commissioning maps from Europe that would supposedly project Ottoman grandeur and educate young Ottoman minds could lead to certain unforeseen "accidents," such as the case when the global maps ordered for use in public schools turned out to carry the legend "Armenia" in eastern Anatolia, causing embarrassment for the Education Department, which was forced to pull the maps out of circulation.[98] Even as late as 1914, a private publishing house in Istanbul used Peucker's 1903 map as the base map for one showing "the Borders of the Balkans after the Balkan War." In the direct translation of place names into Ottoman Turkish, the map introduced a term that would never have been used by the Ottomans to refer to Rumeli: "Avrupa-i Osmani," or "Ottoman Europe," which was actually an inversion of "European Turkey." Ironically, at this instance, "Avrupa-i Osmani" was limited to eastern Thrace, only a tiny portion of what Rumeli had been.[99]

As for ethnographic maps, they were not part of the vocabulary of Ottoman statecraft. The Ottomans did count and classify the population according to state-defined criteria, which had the unintended result of reinforcing ethnic differences (see chapter 4), but they were not interested in picturing those numbers on maps as a countermeasure to the ones circulating in Europe and the Balkans. They did not make a case for territoriality through ethnic graphics because ethnic unity had never defined the boundaries of the Ottoman realm; on the contrary, just like any other imperial structure, the Ottomans had a lot to fear from an organization of their territory according to administrative divisions favoring ethnic homogeneity. Interestingly enough, the Hamidian bureaucracy, which attentively watched all publishing activity in Europe for the handiwork of "evil-doers" and did its best to prevent the circulation of "harmful" material, was surprisingly reticent when it came to ethnographic maps. The bureaucracy was, however, much more sensitive to another kind of map: maps that distorted the boundaries of the well-protected domains or inscribed "inappropriate" terms such as "Armenia"

---

96. Fortna, *Imperial Classroom*, 187.
97. Ibid., 190. Note that the Ottomans were not the only ones suffering from delusional cartography; we only need to look at French maps that annex Alsace-Loraine when it was definitely not part of France; Black, *Maps and History*, 57.
98. BOA, BEO 397/ 29760, May 3, 1894.
99. BOA, HRT 159, 1914.

over parts of them.¹⁰⁰ These were to be kept from view, or better yet, eradicated. After all, Abdülhamid II did not have any desire to transform the empire into a nation-state; that would be the agenda of the Young Turks.

The Logic of Geography and Natural Borders

Before we move on to a discussion of the various criteria in determining "race" among the inhabitants of the Balkans, it is instructive to first consider the issue of geographical boundaries because it was often evoked to substantiate the link between the land and the people, an important element of territoriality. The discipline of geography had already established in the eighteenth century that the surface of Earth could be observed to have certain zones, regions, and subregions based on a variety of physical criteria such as climate, latitude, and topographical characteristics and the correlation of these criteria, which then could also be linked with the cultural practices or physical traits of the populations indigenous to these regions. There was an obvious logic to this kind of geographical organization; in other words, geography had a purpose. Some geographers argued, however, that such logic was entirely lacking in Ottoman Europe, whose geography seemed to be conspiring against logic and order. Élisée Reclus, the French anarchist geographer, had strong opinions on this issue:

> Their [travelers and geographers] task was by no means an easy one, for the mountain masses and mountain chains of the peninsula [Haemus or Balkan] do not constitute a regular, well-defined system. There is no central range, with spurs running out on both sides, and gradually decreasing in height as they approach the plains. Nor is the center of the peninsula its most elevated portion, for the culminating summits are dispersed over the country apparently without order. The mountain ranges run in all directions of the compass, and we can only say, in a general way, that those of Western Turkey run parallel with the Adriatic and Ionian coasts, whilst those in the east meet the coasts of the Black Sea and the Aegean at right angles. The relief of the soil and the water-sheds make it appear *almost as if Turkey turned her back upon continental Europe*. Its highest mountains, its most extensive table-lands, and its most inaccessible forests lie towards the west and the north-west, *as if they were intended to cut it off from the shores of the Adriatic and the plains of Hungary*, whilst all its rivers, whether they run to the north, east, or south, finally find their way into the Black Sea or the Aegean, whose *shores face those of Asia*.¹⁰¹

---

100. These maps were confiscated at customs and post offices; BOA, BEO 397/ 29760, May 6, 1894; BEO 430/32238, July 4, 1894; BEO 471/35273, September 19, 1899.

101. Elisée Reclus, *The Earth and Its Inhabitants*, Vol. 1, *Greece, Turkey in Europe, Rumania, Servia, Montenegro, Italy, Spain and Portugal*, edited by Ernst G. Ravenstein (New York, 1882), 89. (Emphasis added.)

The Balkan Peninsula, as Reclus saw it, was an impossibly complex, unfriendly terrain that lacked normal contours that might give it some order. More interestingly, the geography of (European) Turkey was so strange that one might even wonder if it was in Europe at all: Turkey had physically "turned its back" on Europe, while the Adriatic and Hungary had embraced it with their pleasant shores and wide open plains. But there was more, the chaotic geography accompanied (or fostered, we are invited to think) chaos of a different order, one that had yet to be sorted out:

> This irregularity in the distribution of the mountains has its analogue in the distribution of the various races which inhabit the peninsula. The invaders or peaceful colonists, whether they came across the straits from Asia Minor, or along the valley of the Danube from Scythia, soon found themselves scattered in numerous valleys, or stopped by amphitheatres having no outlet. They failed to find their way in this labyrinth of mountains, and members of the most diverse races settled down in proximity to each other, and frequently came into conflict. The most numerous, the most warlike, or the most industrious races gradually extended their power at the expense of their neighbours; and the latter, defeated in the struggle for existence, have been scattered into innumerable fragments, between which there is no longer any cohesion. Hungary has a homogenous population, if we compare it with that of Turkey; for in the latter country there are districts where eight or ten different nationalities live side by side within a radius of a few miles.[102]

Clearly, the anomalous geography was instrumental in creating yet another anomaly with regard to the distribution of the inhabitants. Reclus showed his readers, on the one hand, how physical elements of geography could determine the moral character of the people tied to the land, and on the other, he warned about the difficult consequences that might arise when geography was simply not a cooperative partner. In this case, it had helped the warlike peoples to dominate the land, leaving the others to occupy small scattered pockets. Hungary was, again, the contrasting example. Compared to Turkey, it emerged as a country with a homogenous population that had not blocked itself from the continent of Europe and presumably its civilizing influence; Turkey was a harder (if not impossible) case for redemption.

It is interesting to note that Reclus's characterization of Turkey as a place that was not really European, even though it was in Europe, and his use of Hungary as a contrasting example are highly reminiscent of the process Larry Wolff so eloquently describes in *The Invention of Eastern Europe*. This is a process that took place in the eighteenth century, when the eastern borders of Europe were still not fixed and there was room for ambiguity, intellectual and geographical, in these vaguely defined lands that did not

---

102. Ibid.

quite belong to Asia but were certainly not within Europe either. The need to define what we might call a zone of transition between the Orient and the Occident inspired an intellectual project that invented the idea of Eastern Europe while defining Europe itself. Wolff notes that the "paradox of 'Turqie d'Europe,' in Europe yet of the Orient, was essential to the emerging idea of Eastern Europe."[103] As the *philosophes* were articulating this process, Hungary went from being classified as Asiatic and associated with Bulgaria and Wallachia to being that liminal area between the Orient and the Occident. Reclus's remarks are an encapsulation of this process, which was complete by the end of the eighteenth century. As Sir Charles Eliot summed up the general feeling about Turkish presence in Europe at the end of the nineteenth century, "The Turks are an Asiatic people who have settled but not taken root in our continent, and their presence there is a question which may be treated by itself and quite independently of their existence in Anatolia and elsewhere."[104] The Englishman had not a hint of irony in calling Europe "our continent."

Even more than identifying continental borders, identifying borders of a different kind preoccupied the geographers as well as laypeople touring the Balkans in the late nineteenth and early twentieth centuries and frustrated them with their absence — namely, "natural borders" that should replace the current irrational ones. At the time, natural borders were almost exclusively associated with national territory and were mentioned often in notes accompanying ethnographic maps of Macedonia. The *Carte Ethnocratique des Pays Hellèniques, Slaves, Albanais, et Roumains*, dated 1878 and attributed to Kiepert, for instance, came with a note that claimed that it used a new method, which separated "South-Eastern Europe according to divisions or groups of race, and, to the possible extent, *natural frontiers,* historical requirements, traditional affinities, and to assign to each division or group a single color. This color would not claim rigidly that the constituent parts of each section are occupied exclusively by a single race, it would only indicate the race that would be preponderant."[105] (This happened to be the Greeks in this case.)

Even though there was nothing natural about the way the population of a certain area was identified, measured, and captured in color on a map depending on the "scientific criteria" applied by the author, the assumption was that natural boundaries did exist. This basic assumption was not challenged by the fact that the social reality rarely fit within the confines of those natural boundaries. The real challenge was turning those natural boundaries into actual political ones. It was only "natural" that a map be drawn for better communicating those demarcation lines.

---

103. Wolff, *Invention of Eastern Europe,* 165.
104. Sir Charles Eliot, *Turkey in Europe* (New York, 1907), 1–2.
105. Henri Kiepert, *Notice Explicative sur la Carte Ethnogratique des pays Helleniques, Slaves, Albanais et Roumains* (Berlin, 1878), 5. (Emphasis added.)

Consider this description by H. N. Brailsford, British journalist and member of the Relief Mission that arrived to assist the survivors of the 1903 Uprising: "Macedonia lies confounded within three *vilayets* (i.e., provinces), which correspond to no *natural* division either racial or geographical. ... The result is that no race attains a predominance, and no province acquires a national character. The *natural* arrangement would have been to place Greeks, Servians, and Albanians in *compartments of their own,* leaving the Bulgarians to occupy the center and the East."[106] How could we determine "natural" divisions and restore order given the current situation of unnatural mixing? Obviously, an intervention by an expert was needed, and in fact, in the obligatory ethnographic map that Brailsford appended to his book, *Macedonia, Its Races and Their Future,* he performed this necessary task. What he called "Bulgarians" occupied the center and east of the peninsula, whereas Chalkidiki was marked as Greek territory. Other ethnic groups recognized by the author were assigned symbols rather than colors. Not counting the random disturbances on the map, it more or less conformed to what Brailsford argued was the "natural" arrangement of races.

Natural frontiers or, more precisely, the lack thereof, in Ottoman Macedonia was an important theme in an earlier publication written in response to the British Blue Book of 1889. Its anonymous author criticized the British consul in Salonika in his failure to acknowledge their existence:

> Mr. Blunt [the consul] ought to have admitted that the administrative division of Turkey is not scientific, that is to say, that is has not as a basis *natural boundaries,* nor is it stable, and at the same time to have recorded one at least of the many arbitrary changes in the boundaries, such as that of the department of Velisso, which eight years ago did not belong to the Vilayet of Salonica, and was annexed to it later on upon the demand of the Russian Embassy in Constantinople, in order to fictitiously strengthen the Bulgarian element in the vilayet of Salonica, which would in consequence thus acquire different geographical boundaries and another ethnological character.

The author then presented an alternative, more "scientific" approach to the boundary problem:

> I confine myself to the following remarks 1) that it is both just and practicable to give to these three Macedonian vilayets such geographical boundaries as to be separated from each other by lines, parallel to the Macedonian coast on the Aegean 2) that the delimitation of the geographical boundaries of the vilayet of Salonica on such a scientific basis would include about as much Christian population as Mr. Blunt records in treating of the present vilayet of Macedonia 3)

---

106. Brailsford, *Macedonia, Its Races and Their Future,* 7. (Emphasis added.)

that the principal and most heroic method for the attainment of tranquility in Macedonia, in which Mr. Blunt is interested, and, moreover, for the removal of the intricacies of the Macedonian question, for which Lord Salisbury is justly concerned, would be the scientific administrative division of Macedonia upon the basis of its natural boundaries.[107]

It is difficult to imagine how and why "parallel lines" would be any more "natural" than the existing boundaries of the Macedonian provinces.[108] A glance at a topographic map of Macedonia makes us realize that there are no unyielding mountain chains, unsurpassable rivers, and impossibly isolated plains in the geography. Assuming geographical formations would determine the demarcation lines, or natural boundaries, it is extremely difficult to argue in favor of one division as opposed to the other. But topography was not even the issue here; these natural boundaries amounted in effect to what we might today call "ethnic gerrymandering." It was a way of imagining the geo-body of a nation on paper, sterilized and not obfuscated by blurry visions of ethnic ambiguity.

As unconvincing as it may seem, this was a project worth pursuing by the interested parties, as hindsight tells us—and not because they would finally settle on a unanimously agreed "natural" division. Obviously, the conflicting contours of natural boundaries created by European observers of the geographical and ethnic chaos that was Ottoman Macedonia was not the simple outcome of the extreme difficulty of the puzzle they were trying to solve or of the lack of reliable demographic data. The conflict was in the very premises that these projections of boundaries were built on. We have already noted the importance of the underlying ideological framework that essentially saw the construct of "Turkey in Europe" as a freakish geographical accident and proposed to replace it with a more rational spatial arrangement. We have also noted the primacy of the notion that nation-states were the only legitimate and meaningful form of human political organization. It is not a surprise that the logical conclusion emerging from the fusion of these two theses would be the projection of a new geographical order based on *national* boundaries, also conceived as one and the same as *natural* boundaries.

There were, however, two immense and interrelated problems with this position. The first and obvious one is the disagreement about who belonged in the nation, and by implication in its territory. The second is the less visible but no less significant issue of who was to define the shape and contents of the natural boundaries and how. We should not ignore the fact that what

---

107. *The English Blue Book Regarding Macedonia, Comments by A.K.* (Athens 1891), 7. (Blue Book No. 3 1889, Turkey, Official Correspondence on Eastern Affairs.)

108. It is interesting to note that the boundaries of counties (*nomoi*) in contemporary Greek Macedonia are informed by the boundaries of Ottoman-era *sancaks*.

constituted natural borders was hardly something that the entire political and intellectual establishment of Europe could agree on, as the two world wars have made painfully clear. Natural borders, or the assumption that the territorial divisions between states are justified based on their conforming to certain geophysical markers such as rivers or mountains, was current in the nineteenth century.[109] This was an idea that can be traced back to the "natural frontiers" doctrine of seventeenth-century France, which was formulated by Richelieu and remained a staple of French history textbooks until quite recently.[110]

An important intervention to this notion came from Friedrich Ratzel in the late nineteenth century.[111] In Ratzel's treatment, the "natural" element of the relationship between states and territory was not to be found in the contours of rivers or mountains. Instead, he argued, it was the nation, an *organic* entity, that determined the boundaries of the state and not the other way around.[112] He also introduced the concept of *Lebensraum,* which was based on the same idea, that the nation, the state, and the land were organically connected and that the borders of the state would change depending on the physical needs of the growing state. Geographical constraints and the need to overcome them were also determinants of culture: "A state, for example, was simply the result of a particular people's adaptation to an environment. The form that a state or an entire culture took was therefore shaped by the relationship to Lebensraum and the struggle for it."[113] Ratzel understood the struggle for *Lebensraum* to be driven by Darwinian principles. It is well known how these specific elements of his work were embraced first by German conservatives and later by the Nazis as the justification for territorial expansion. There was also something quite appealing in his theory for those who saw the nation as a linguistically homogeneous entity — a

---

109. The assumption that natural borders do indeed exist continues to inform research in social science, popular culture, and journalistic approaches to border conflicts. For a critique of this pervasive myth, see, Juliet J. Fall, "Artificial States? On the Enduring Myth of Natural Borders," *Political Geography* 29, no. 3 (2010): 140–47.

110. Daniel Nordman argues that the conceptualization of a national border emerged in France even earlier than Richelieu's time and that we need to distinguish between the fluctuation of actual geographical borders and the concept of borders as clear and precise demarcation lines; "From the Boundaries of the State to National Borders," in *Rethinking France: Les Lieux de Mémoire,* Vol. 1, *The State,* edited by Pierre Nora, translated by Mary Trouille (Chicago, 2001), 105–32. Cf. Peter Sahlins, "Natural Frontiers Revisited: France's Boundaries since the Seventeenth Century," *American Historical Review* 95, no. 5 (1990): 1423–51. The meanings of the terms *frontière* and *limites* overlapped in the nineteenth century; see Febvre, "Frontière," 213.

111. For a critique of Ratzel and the idea of natural borders, see Febvre, *Geographical Introduction to History,* 296–315. Gaston Zeller was an even more vocal critique of the notion; Sahlins, "Natural Frontiers Revisited."

112. Robert Kaiser, "Geography," in *The Encyclopedia of Nationalism,* edited by Alexander Motyl, 315–33 (San Diego, 2000).

113. Woodruff D. Smith, "Friedrich Ratzel and the Origins of Lebensraum," *German Studies Review* 3, no. 1 (1980), 53.

dominant notion in the early part of the nineteenth century—as opposed to one determined by common culture, interests, and goals. This distinction also roughly corresponded to the changing conceptions of nationhood and territory in France and Germany; the French had largely abandoned the principle of linguistic unity, whereas it was still paramount for the Germans.[114] The shifting criteria for what constituted the nation and its natural borders obviously correlated with the political interests of those making the observation, which was also true for the ethnographers trying to establish those boundaries in the Balkans. It is important to note that the double standards of their methods, as well as the idea that territorial expansion could be necessary (and justified) to ensure the coherence of the national and spatial units, informed the way Balkan national elites drew their own versions of natural borders on map.

How to Diagnose Different Races

Today there is more or less a consensus that nationalities are social constructs, with much of the academic debate and disagreement centering on the how and when of that construction process; in the nineteenth century the self-evident issue was that nationalities were objectively identifiable categories, with the academic differences stemming from alternative methodologies of "diagnosis." Would it be language? Religion? Historical consciousness? All these elements and more figured in the ways European ethnographers defined the criteria for sorting out the population of Macedonia into "racial" groups. Some candidly noted that what worked in civilized parts of the continent was sadly irrelevant in these lands, which had essentially been cut off from their enlightened distant neighbors and forced to sustain an anomalous intermingling of races. It is interesting to note that while this degree of intermingling reportedly made the ethnographer's task impossible, everyone except for the inhabitants of Macedonia seemed to be able to assign a race/nationality to each community—some even assigned nationalities to dogs.[115] Although the terms *race* and *nationality* were often confounded, *race* as we have already noted, was akin to what we might call ethnicity today, and it was the term more commonly used to refer to the population of Macedonia; however, *nationality* also appeared in various texts, especially after the turn of the twentieth century.

The beliefs in the intrinsic character of national identity and in the nation as the ultimate evolutionary stage of social organization were pervasive in late-nineteenth-century Europe. Nationality was conceived as a code inscribed on every human community, and whether they were "evolved"

---

114. Nordman, "From the Boundaries of the State," 127.
115. Mary Adelaide Walker, *Through Macedonia to the Albanian Lakes* (London, 1864).

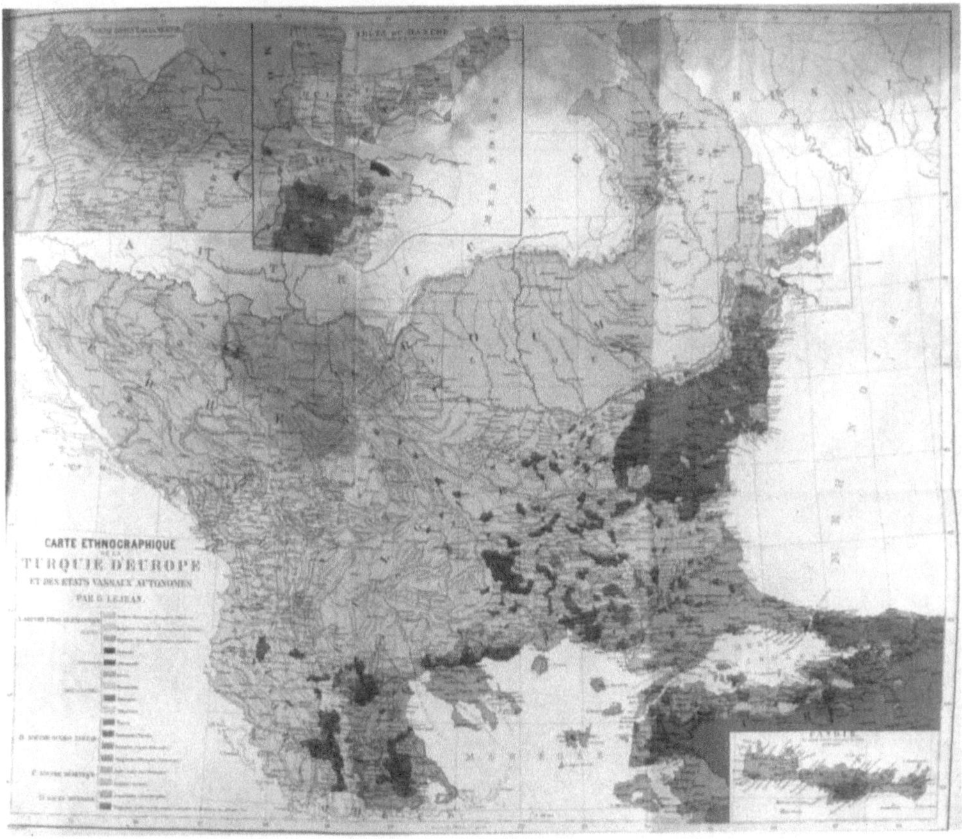

Plate 1: Map, G. Lejean. 1861, Gennadius Library, Athens.

Plate 2: Map, Heinrich Kiepert. 1876, Gennadius Library, Athens.

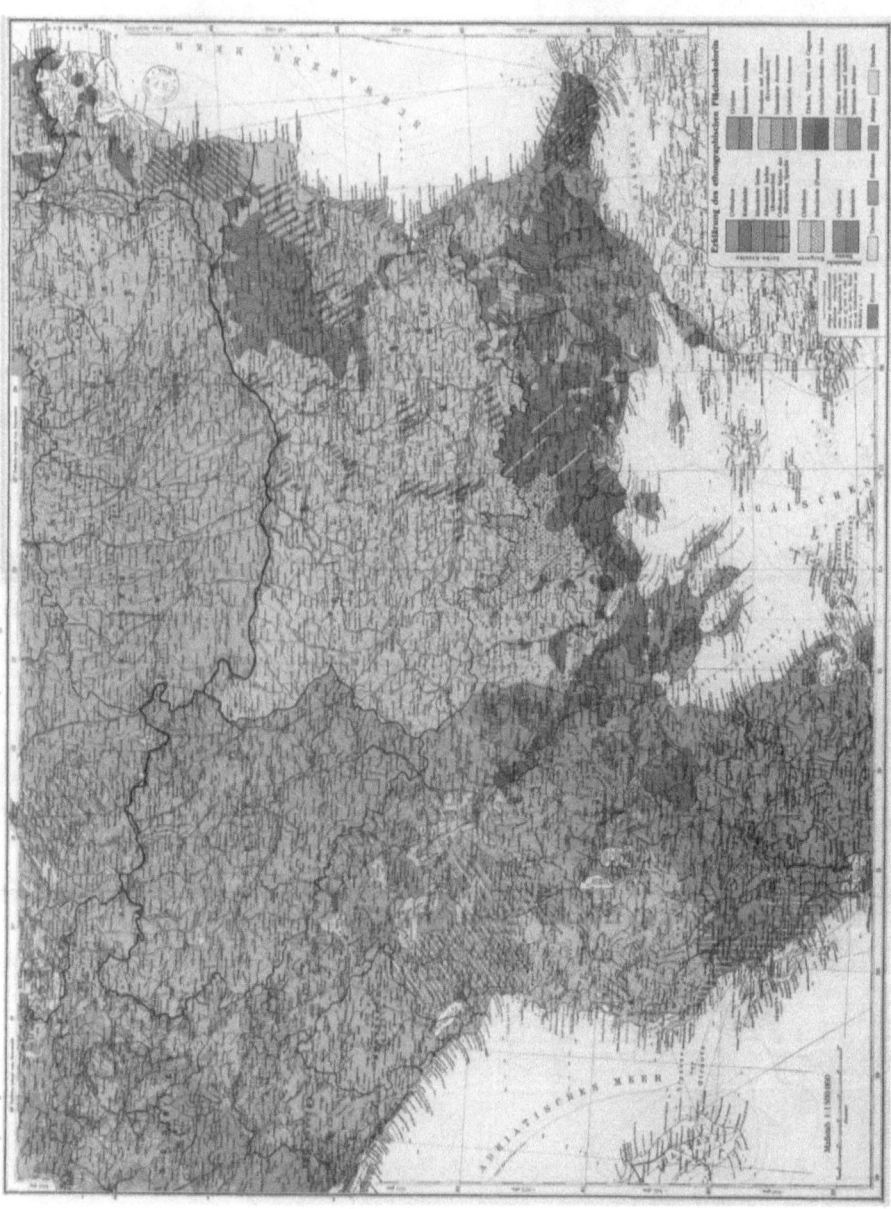

Plate 3: Map, Jovan Cvijić, 1913. Bibliothèque Nationale de France.

enough to be conscious of it or not, it could be identified and decoded through the authoritative knowledge at the disposal of the trained observer. This also implied that it was possible, at least in principle, to access and restore the original code no matter what had been written over it through acculturation, submission, or corruption.[116] Thus, communities could be "restored" and the original code "retrieved." For instance, M. E. Picot, in *Les Roumains de la Macédoine,* in which he traced back a common genealogy for the Koutzo-Vlachs or Tzinzars of Macedonia and the Roumanians of the Carpathian Mountains, lamented that a good part of the Koutzo-Vlachs had been Hellenized but pointed out that it was not clear in "what proportion" they were Hellenized and whether this "Hellenization was final,"[117] thus invoking a whole world of opportunities for the redemption of "Hellenized Vlach" peasants as "Roumanians." In similar vein, a note accompanying the *Tableau Ethnocratique* could foresee a time when the layers obstructing the inner and intact consciousness of the "Musulmans" would be lifted to reveal the shining core of their original nationality because they were not racially Turks; they were renegades: "When Christian rule prevails in the Orient, when there are no longer masters and slaves[,] ... the Muslim renegades no longer having an interest in separating themselves from their own stock [*congénères*],[118] the feeling of race will take over among them its natural force."[119]

Ethnographers and geographers working in European Turkey might have different criteria for determining nationality, but they were united in their attachment to the ideas that nations were the only legitimate and viable form of collective identity and that the nation-state was the manifest destiny of any meaningful communal organization. In addition, they were not immune to the idea, dominant in the tomes of the period's natural history, that racial groups were marked by innate characteristics that not only made them distinct from each other but also allowed for their ranking in a hierarchy. Consider, for instance, the observations of Auguste Viquesnel, companion to the famous explorer and geographer Amie Boué during his travels in European Turkey. Viquesnel's main thesis in his 1868 book was that the borders of Europe ended at Dnieper based on racial categorization. In his introduction to the book, Henry Martin asserted that Viquesnel had studied "these people" with the "same scientific independence and the same investigation procedures that he used for the study of geological layers or of

---

116. This principle also informed policies in Europe much later in the twentieth century, such as the "re-Slovakization" of self-identifying Magyars in Slovakia after World War II, the assimilation of Macedonians into Bulgarians, the attempt to "restore" Turks in Bulgaria to their Bulgarian origins, and the redefinition of Kurds as "mountain Turks" in Turkey in 1980s.
117. M. E. Picot, *Les Roumaines de la Macédoine* (Paris, 1875), 41.
118. *Congénères:* "of the same genus."
119. K. Paparrigopoulos, note in Heinrich Kiepert, *Tableau Ethnocratique des pays du sud-est de l'Europe* (Berlin, 1878).

114 → *Chapter 3*

hydrographical basins." He summarized the findings of the scientist's "long and rigorous research":

> the Aryan and the Touranian families tend to express their respective spirits in two completely different types of societies. The principle of individuality and moral and political liberty dominates in the Aryan race. ... In the Touranians, by contrast ... people do not have but a weak sentiment of personal liberty. ... These people [Touranians] who do not have a feeling of personal liberty have an instinct for liberty of movement which results in a taste for nomadic life. They only attach themselves to the land despite themselves and leave whenever they can. The Aryan, by contrast, loves the land and [is] wedded to it, so to say. It is the agricultural race *par excellence* and the spirit of ownership allies itself closely with the spirit of liberty with them whereas the spirit of community and that of patriarchal authority, easily degenerating into autocracy, dominates the Touranians.[120]

Extreme as it may seem, ethnographic studies on the distinct qualities of the Touranian and Aryan races, demonstrating the superiority of the latter, were quite common and had been received as well-respected works of science since the eighteenth century, and they were inextricably linked to the post-Enlightenment definition of Europe through the denigration of the Oriental. The analytical categories used to rank different races were not exclusively based on those relating to political organization such as the capacity for settled life, complex political organization, and love of liberty. They also included costume, language, religious practices, and superstitious beliefs. Nevertheless, even these categories could then be checked to determine a given race's potential for evolution, culminating in the nation form. The inferiority of the "Touranian" race, which included Turks, Tartars, Mongolians, Huns, and Bulgars, had not prevented them from penetrating into Europe during darker times, which made their expulsion from where they did not belong all the more urgent. Historical atlases published in the mid-nineteenth century tinted the "tribes of particular races" with different colors to demonstrate their movements "from their former localities to their present possessions."[121] This practical graphic tool also had the effect of giving visual emphasis to the alienness of certain races in Europe. In his *Encyclopédie* article on the Tartars, Louis de Jaucourt wrote, "Goths, who conquered the Roman Empire brought monarchy and liberty, the Tartars, wherever they conquered, brought only servitude and despotism [It was]

---

120. Henry Martin, introduction to Auguste Viquesnel, *Voyage dans la Turquie d'Europe* (Paris, 1868), xix–xx.
121. Edward Gover, *Historic Geographical Atlas of the Middle and Modern Ages* (London, 1853), cited in Black, *Maps and History*, 79.

humiliating for human nature that these barbaric peoples should have subjugated almost all of our hemisphere."[122]

The consensus on the inferiority of the Touranian race was not something that served only to justify the necessity of throwing the Turks out of Europe.[123] Despite the good press they received in Europe from liberal politicians, journalists, and, apparently, ethnographers, the Bulgarians found themselves in a disadvantaged "racial" position because of their ancestry. In addition to all the positive stereotypes depicting Bulgarians as a peaceful, agrarian, hard-working folk, there were a few other, less flattering ones painting them as slow (both mentally and physically), uncouth, and uninspired. Among those peddling the latter stereotypes was G. F. Abbot, Cambridge ethnographer, and author of several works on Macedonian folklore published by the same university.[124] The following is a typical excerpt from his books; here he is recording a participant-observation in Petritch (village in the province of Serres) of the villagers dancing at the festival of the *panageia* (festival commemorating the Dormition of the Mother of God):

> Notwithstanding this weight of wool and metal, they danced with great perseverance and an air of truly Christian resignation. Bagpipes—the favorite instrument of the Bulgarian—supplied the local equivalent for music. Round this squealing band a wide circle footed it slowly and exceedingly stupidly. ... The dance consisted of a one step forward, one backward, and one to the side, without any variation whatsoever. A melancholy refrain Sospita Yanno, Sospita Yanno [sic], drawled out in sleepy and sleep-begetting tones, accompanied the sad measure.[125]

Not surprisingly, the non-Aryan roots of the Bulgars were a favorite topic of authors who wanted to give credence to Greek claims in the Balkan Peninsula. Eduard Driault, journalist, wrote effusively of the Greeks at the dawn of the Balkan Wars, "The Greeks know that they have formidable enemies, that the Turk is still strong, that the Slavs are more numerous in Macedonia. But Hellenism is not a simple question of races; it is an idea, an intellectual and moral force, made by the rational support of free men to principles that established the grandeur of ancient Greece and that are the essential sources

---

122. Louis de Jaucourt, "Tartares," in *Encyclopédie: Ou Dictionnaire Raisonné des sciences, des arts et des métiers,* nouvelle impression en facsimilé de la première édition de 1751–1780 (Stuttgart, 1967), Vol. 15: 921–23, cited in Wolff, *Inventing Eastern Europe,* 192.

123. The title of an article that Leon Dominian published just as the Turks had finally been removed from Europe sums up the general sentiment about the presence of this "race" in Europe: "The Turk, Casual of Geography," *Journal of Geography* 18, no. 1 (1919): 3–13. Dominian's concluding remarks were written not without a certain degree of relief: "The history of this great race of conquerors is drawing to a dishonored close before the gaze of the whole civilized world. The casual of Asiatic geography has become the outcast of Europe" (13).

124. George F. Abbott, *Macedonian Folklore* (Cambridge, 1903). He was also the author of *Songs of Modern Greece* (Cambridge, 1900).

125. Abbot, *Tale of a Tour,* 174.

of European civilization."[126] A few pages later, as he was writing about Bulgarians, he remarked that they were "not pure Slavs, they seem to be Slavicized Tartars."[127] Slavs, who used to be considered only slightly above the Tartars in the racial hierarchy, were now counted among the "Caucasian and Greco-Roman" types.[128] Too bad for Bulgarians that they had to keep proving their Slavic credentials, most notably through references to saints Cyril and Methodios.

In another example of attempts to rectify the racial stock of Bulgarians, Henry F. Tozer used every single physiognomic proof and detailed the various "infusions of blood" they received to dispel the notion that contemporary Bulgarians might in any way be related to the barbarian "Bulgars." This was by no means possible because:

> The Bulgarians, who form the largest element in the Christian population from Salonica to the confines of Albania, are a very interesting people, and are highly spoken of for industry and honesty. They are the most numerous of all the nationalities inhabiting European Turkey, and are estimated between five and six millions. There can be no doubt that the original Bulgarians were of Turanian descent, and near relations, if not actual descendants, of Attila's Huns; but after they became so intermingled with the Slavonian inhabitants of that country that they adopted their language. A large number of them seem to have emigrated into Western Macedonia before the ninth century, and there, in all probability, received a further infusion of Slavonic blood. The traces of this are very evident in the present appearance of the people; for the Tartar type of face, which generally is remarkable for its permanence, has here for the most part disappeared. Notwithstanding this, you will not often find a people with such well-marked characteristics. They have straight noses, high cheekbones, flat cheeks, and very commonly light eyes; their complexions are frequently almost swarthy from exposure to the sun, but the children are generally fair.[129]

The possible non-Aryan roots of the Bulgarians continued to pose a problem for advocates of the Slav side in the Struggle for Macedonia well into the turn of the century. H. N. Brailsford, for instance, the well-known champion of Macedonian Slavs, had to come up with the following apologetic

---

126. Edouard Driault, *La Question d'Orient depuis ses Origines jusqu'a nos Jours* (Paris, 1912), 282.
127. Ibid., 286.
128. This notion inevitably affected general perceptions about the different ethnic groups of Ottoman Europe and consequently their entitlement to political sovereignty. Ravenstein, for instance, argued in a paper presented to the Statistical Society in London in June 1877 that the critical difference that legitimized the Russian Empire and disqualified that of the "Turks" was the fact that Russians were "intellectually superior to the races they govern, while the opposite is true of the Turkish Empire." E. G. (Ernest George) Ravenstein, "The Population of Russia and Turkey," *Journal of the Statistical Society* 40 (September, 1877), 438).
129. Tozer, *Researches in the Highlands of Turkey,* 176.

explanation about their racial purity, distinguishing them, quite unusually, from the Bulgarians in this instance:

> They [Macedonian Slavs] are not Serbs, for their blood can hardly be purely Slavonic. There must be in it some admixture of Bulgarian and other non-Aryan stock. ... On the other hand, they can hardly be Bulgarians, for quite clearly the Servian immigrations and conquests must have left much Servian blood in their veins, and the admixture of non-Aryan blood can scarcely be so considerable as it is in Bulgaria. They are probably very much what they were before either a Bulgarian and or a Servian Empire existed—a Slav people derived from rather various stocks, who invaded the peninsula at different periods.[130]

It was not long until the Balkan national elites internalized this discourse of racial inferiority and civilizational capacity, and started to produce their own versions of natural boundaries based on the same premises. Pamphlets and propaganda material were the obvious outlets for this rivalry, but some intellectuals went so far as to usurp the very same scientific authority of the European cartographers to support their case. The Balkan elites were late arrivals in the game of geopolitics through ethnographic maps, but they proved to be a quick study. They mastered the principles, the rules, and, more important, the shortcomings of this technique of power to project their own agendas of ethnic superiority. Even the association of Bulgarians with an Asiatic tribe of questionable provenance could be given a positive spin at the hands of a talented propagandist. Note, for instance, how Anastas Ishirkov, after naming this tribe the "Prebulgars," not to be confused with "Bulgars," embraced their contribution to the early Bulgarian political formation: "The nomadic prebulgars, who had cleared a path, sword in hand, from central Asia to the Balkans, distinguished themselves with their bellicose spirit, their robust discipline and their talent for organization, characteristic traits of all the nomadic peoples of the steppes." These nomadic peoples had important redeeming qualities after all, but the way they were absorbed by the Slavs they had come to conquer would leave no doubt that their union had actually resulted in a synergy that bolstered the Bulgarian state and national character:

> They [the Prebulgars] placed under their rule, either through these traits or through force, the Slavs, [who were] agriculturalists more numerous and more civilized, but less organized. During the creation of the Bulgarian state the two peoples, different with respect to their way of life and their organization mutually completed each other in a happy manner. The prebulgars, less numerous, became the ruling class thanks to their military organization in the Slavic state,

---

130. Brailsford, *Macedonia, Its Races and Their Future*, 101.

but in return lost their language and adopted Slavic, which became the official language of the state and the national church.[131]

In other words, the Prebulgars served their genealogical mission as the neutral nucleus of the Bulgarian nation that took its essential racial characteristics from the Slavs. The Prebulgars had injected qualities of political and military organization into, but had not changed, the true Slavic stock that the Bulgarians were made out of; they were Slavs, only better. Lest the point was not clear enough, Ishirkov also emphasized the role of the early Bulgarian state in establishing a national church for the Slavs and in giving them the language in which they still worshipped.[132]

Questioning Cartographic Authority and Projections of Nation Space

Ethnographic maps were primarily tools of territorial hegemony, a point not lost on the Balkan national elites. Let us now return to two maps mentioned at the beginning of the chapter—the Stanford Map and Kieper's *Tableau Ethnocratique*—and take a closer look at the circumstances surrounding their production to expose the ideological currents that found an ideal environment in the medium of ethnographic maps.

The map known as the Stanford Map was published in 1877. Even though luminaries such as Carl Sax and Heinrich Kiepert dismissed the map as utter nonsense, it did acquire a certain degree of attention in Britain, having been published by a respectable institution. It was translated into various languages and circulated among European geographical institutions.[133] The map was often incorrectly attributed to Stanford himself, but the author was anonymous and was listed as such even in Henry Wilkinson's widely referred 1951 book.[134] There were rumors, however, that the real author was a member of the Greek intellectual elite. As a matter of fact, the anonymous author was none other than Ioannis Gennadius, who at the time of

---

131. Ishirkov, *Nom de Bulgare*, 14–15.
132. Ibid., 15.
133. Wilkinson, *Maps and Politics*, 75. Carl Sax's verdict on this map was that "it cannot even be mentioned seriously," whereas Kiepert said that it "extended Greek pretensions to the utmost limits possible to man." Cvijić, *Remarks*, 23.
134. It seems that even Kiepert was not able to figure out the identity of the author; the only answer to his inquiries about this was the information that the author was Greek. See Letter from Kiepert to Paparrigopoulos, published in K. Svolopoulos, "O Kōnstantinos Paparrēgopoulos kai ē Chartografēsē tēn Chersonēsou tou Aimou apo ton Heinrich Kiepert," in *Afierōma eis ton Kōnstantinon Vavouskon* (Thessaloniki, 1992), 366. In 1906, Cvijić did disclose Ioannis Gennadius as the author; *Remarks*, 22. But the knowledge must have remained obscure because Wilkinson in 1951 cited the author as "anonymous"; *Maps and Politics*, 71.

the publication of the map held the post of Greek chargé d'affairs in London and who later served as the minister to London and to The Hague.[135]

In the pamphlet that accompanied the map, Gennadius argued that "the different nations and races inhabiting European Turkey and the western portion of Asia Minor ... are all more or less marked by a confusing diversity of origin, language, national character, political condition, social status, intellectual development and religious persuasion." Because these categories could not be matched to religious or linguistic principles either, it was, in his words "an abortive, not to say an impossible, undertaking to establish in a graphic representation the distribution and intermixture of race, language, and creed in Turkey." Instead, Gennadius suggested that "a practically useful ethnological map" would "explain and represent the actual relations in which those nations stand toward one another."[136] These relations were revealed in Gennadius's work through a method that employed a hybrid of historical and cultural claims, religious influence, and occasional references to statistical data. He insisted that the area north of the Balkans was characterized by long-time Bulgarian settlement, whereas the south had remained purely Greek and that even the "Bulgarians" of northern Macedonia and Thrace were Greek. In his own words:

> During a period of darkness, internal convulsions and administrative prostration, the mixed Greek and Bulgarian populations of those regions were gradually merged into a new and common body, neither purely Bulgarian, nor purely Greek, but appertaining to both races. This mixed people may be appropriately designated as "Bulgarophone Greeks," for it is easily proved that Greek is the prevalent element in its constitution. The outward features of this race differ considerably from those of the Bulgarians north of the Balkans; the latter are clearly of the Mongolian type, whereas South of the Balkans we find the Caucasian, and very frequently the purely Greek type. Their dress is identical with that of the Greeks whereas a Bulgarian is always distinguished by the unavoidable pootoor—breeches large and full to the knee and tight around the leg to the ankle—and the characteristic cylindrical-shaped cap, or calpak of black sheep skin. Their language is not only more smooth and much softer than that of the Northern Bulgarians, but it contains an immense admixture of Greek words, wholly incomprehensible to a pure Bulgarian. ... In their churches, their schools, and their correspondence they always use the Greek language, which they understand and study.[137]

---

135. Today Gennadius is remembered more as a bibliophile than a diplomat. He donated his impressive collection of books and manuscripts to the American School of Classical Studies in Athens, which keeps the collection in a separate library building that carries his name.

136. [Ioannis Gennadius], *Ethnological Map of European Turkey and Greece with Introductory Remarks on the Distribution of Races in the Illyrian Peninsula and Statistical Tables of Population* (London, 1877), 2.

137. Ibid., 13.

Gennadius, posing as an anonymous British scholar, managed to cover all the important elements an ethnographer should employ to establish a racial ranking: the difference in costume, the Bulgarians favoring a decidedly more "alien" or folkloric kind that required a detailed description and the definition of a foreign word; the difference in language, the Bulgarians speaking a rough-sounding language; the propensity to use Greek, which helped to identify one as a member of the bourgeois (or more refined) classes in the Balkans; and finally, the M-word—the identification of Bulgarians as a member of the larger Mongol family, those hordes whose descent on Eastern Europe was considered an aberration of history and geography.[138] The references to costume as a distinguishing feature of the Bulgarian "race" was not at all strange because language, customs, habits, and religious beliefs were often counted among the "mental" factors that distinguished one racial group from another at the time.[139]

Even assuming that the Stanford Map was not taken very seriously by educated circles in Europe, the pamphlet that accompanied it was quite significant in the sense that it demonstrated a mechanism through which the European rhetoric about superior and inferior qualities of races could find their way back into the discourses of self-perception generated by the subject cultures. The map may have been a flop in Europe, but that was only one part of Gennadius's intended audience. The other, more important part was the Greek elite, and the example Gennadius set showed the Greek elite how to fight against the claims of romantic Slavophiles: by wielding the weapon of cultural and racial superiority, by invoking the powers of ancient Greece over the European elites, who considered its legacy their own source of civilization. Most of the output following this line of attack was published in Greece, suggesting it was Greek propaganda aimed at Greeks, but short pamphlets making the same point in different iterations also appeared in English and French at the beginning of the twentieth century. In one such pamphlet on the populations of Macedonia, Ioanna Stephanopoli, one of the most vocal supporters of the Greek cause in Macedonia, who also had the distinction of being the first female student of Athens University School

---

138. More specifically, he described them as "a mixed people formed by the fusion of Mongolian and Hunnish tribes, with much Tartaric blood in their veins. ... It is true that owing to a close contact with Slav races the Bulgarians, during their descent upon the Balkan peninsula, absorbed into a widely different dialect a large proportion of Slavonic words. But the Bulgarian language contains also a considerable Turkish element; and by a similar process the Slavs of Turkey have adopted many Bulgarian words, the roots of which are not to be found in Slavonic." Ibid., 11. The Bulgarians had been classified among the Southern Slavs by A. Balbi in 1828 in his *Atlas Ethnographique de Globe ou Classification des Peuples Anciens et Modernes d'après leurs Langues*, cited by Wilkinson, *Maps and Politics*, 29. This classification was more or less the norm, especially among ethnographers who gave precedence to linguistic affiliation.

139. See, for instance, *Illustrations of the Principal Varieties of the Human Race, arranged according to the system of Dr. Latham*, descriptive notes by Ernest Ravenstein (London, ca. 1850), 2.

of Philosophy, wrote, "Bulgarians are not Macedonians, and Macedonians are not Bulgarians," and continued, "if they are proud of belonging to the Family of Aristotle, of Alexander, of the Diadochoi, they [the inhabitants of Macedonia] would find it demeaning in their own eyes to be confused with the 'peoples without glory' who have not added even the smallest stone to the edifice of civilization that humanity has been erecting for centuries."[140]

It is interesting to note that the rhetoric of racial and cultural superiority was not in the exclusive purview of the educated Greek national elite by the beginning of the twentieth century. The same sense of civilizational distinction could be detected in the discourse of Greek Orthodox notables in Macedonia when they pleaded with Ottoman authorities for protection against Bulgarian encroachments on their community. For instance, when the Greek notables and bishop of Salonika petitioned the Ottoman governor in March 1904 demanding that Bulgarian insurgents be punished more severely, they made extensive allusions to the superiority of *Rumlar* (Greeks), who "have acquired an exalted place in international opinion as well that of the Ottoman state thanks to their accomplishments in civilization and learning from time immemorial" and to the inferiority of the Bulgarians, who were "a 'nation' that has not benefited from the grace of civilization and learning."[141] Complaints about Bulgarian bands' transgressions emphasized the attacks on teachers and schools, underscoring the point that precisely this progress in education and civilization was targeted.

The second map is the bizarrely titled 1878 map attributed to the famous Kiepert, *Tableau Ethnocratique des pays du sud-est de l'Europe*. This map and the conditions surrounding its publication constitute a truly impressive example of how a clever member of the Greek national elite could employ ethnographic cartography to assert Greek territoriality while turning the authority wielded by those same maps on its head. The title, *Tableau Ethnocratique*, is the first and obvious clue that this map was not claiming any false pretense of representing a scientifically based (and objective, by implication) ethnographic picture of southeastern Europe. The intermediate step was completely done away with—the author of this map was not interested in displaying natural boundaries between ethnic groups as determined by population count and geographical distribution; instead, he directly addressed what other ethnographic maps only alluded to, natural boundaries between ethnic groups as determined by their relative "fitness to rule."

If we place this map right next to Kiepert's well-known *Ethnographsiche Übersichtskarte*, published only two years earlier, it becomes clear that they

---

140. Stephanopoli, *Macédoine et Macédoniens*, 7.
141. The Ottoman word for "nation" used here was *kavm* (from Arabic *qaum*), which may mean both "nation" and "race"; BOA, TFR.I.SL 33/3228, Greek Community of Salonika to the Inspectorate, March 6, 1904.

are the complete opposite of each other.[142] Had the famous cartographer had a change of heart? Was he trying to shake up the establishment by espousing a controversial new method of determining the graphic distribution of races based on "preponderance" as the accompanying note suggested? Was it publicity he was after? The professor's lengthy correspondence with a certain gentleman named Konstantinos Paparrigopulos reveals that his motivations were entirely different and casts a shadow over the famous geographer's professional integrity.[143]

Konstantinos Paparrigopoulos (1815–1891) may not be instantly recognizable among a non-Greek audience, but he is in fact one of the greatest names of Greek national historiography, whose magnum opus, *History of the Greek Nation,* has been called "the most important intellectual achievement of nineteenth-century Greece."[144] At the time of his correspondence with Kiepert, he was among the members of Society for the Dissemination of Greek Letters (Syllogos), which took an active interest in ethnographic maps of European Turkey.[145] Feeling the need to counter the alarming prestige Bulgarians seemed to have with ethnographic cartographers—confirmed by the recent recruitment of Kiepert, the best of Europe, to their side—Paparrigopoulos took it upon himself to persuade Kiepert to draw a new and remarkably different map sponsored by the Syllogos.[146] The historian left for Berlin in July 1877 with this goal.

During his stay in Berlin, Paparrigopoulos apparently convinced Kiepert to draw a new map of the region comprising roughly the Peloponnese, Thessaly, Epirus, Macedonia, Thrace, and Eastern Rumelia. At this first meeting, Paparrigopoulos provided certain specifications about the borders of the map and how it would be "colored." During the year that passed between this meeting and the publication of the final version of the map, Kiepert and Paparrigopoulos maintained a correspondence, over the course of which the German cartographer changed his earlier depiction of the region almost entirely, in line with Greek claims, despite his initial reservations concerning

---

142. Heinrich Kiepert, *Ethnographische Übersichtskarte des Europäischen Orients* (Berlin, 1876); Kiepert, *Tableau Ethnocratique.*

143. The correspondence is in MAE, A.A.E.; C.P, Grèce, 106: Tissot (Athènes) à Waddington, March 6, 1878; March 25, 1878, Annexe à la Dépêche Politique d'Athènes, No. 35 March 25, 1878, cited in Svolopoulos, "Kōnstantinos Paparrēgopoulos," 361–70.

144. Paschalis Kitromilides, "On the Intellectual Content of Greek Nationalism: Paparrigopoulos, Byzantium and the Great Idea," in *Byzantium and the Modern Greek Identity,* edited by David Ricks and Paul Magdalino (Hampshire, 1998), 28, In this article, Kitromilides provides a brief yet instructive analysis of the historiographical significance of the work (25–34). See also, Antonis Liakos, "The Construction of National Time: The Making of the Modern Greek Historical Imagination," *Mediterranean Historical Review* 16 (2001), 27–42, esp. 33.

145. Dimara, *Kōnstantinos Paparrēgopoulos,* 336; Svolopoulos, "Kōnstantinos Paparrēgopoulos," 358.

146. Dimara, *Kōnstantinos Paparrēgopoulos,* 343 (based on Alexander Rizos Rangavis's memoirs).

the coloring of certain regions and the name(s) to be printed on the map. The first disagreement regarded two "transition zones," the first one around Karaca Dağ and Orta Dağ (Meson Oros or Strednagora), and the second the upper valleys of the Strymon and Vardar (Struma/Strimonas and Axios). Kiepert was in favor of drawing the line demarcating the Greek "ethnocracy" from that of the Bulgarians a little further south than Paparrigopoulos wanted it. The first region was, Kiepert asserted, "exclusively inhabited by Bulgarians," and as for the second region: "I made it extend in a way that may seem exaggerated to you, though it is justified by the fact that we don't find any Greeks there (except for merchants and teachers at schools established here and there in some towns) and finally because Bulgarians constitute the large majority also in the southern part of Macedonia, which is indicated as Greek territory."[147]

Kiepert asked to be informed if any alterations were made to the borders he had proposed, in which case, he further demanded, Paparrigopoulos's or another committee member's name should be cited as the "coloring author." A later correspondence of Kiepert from Naples on October 9, 1877, reveals that the modifications he proposed had been rejected. Kiepert was surprisingly accommodating in his response; he stated that he "perfectly appreciated the reasons and the facts" presented by Paparrigopoulos to prove that the southern part of Macedonia was more than half Greek. Concerning a revised version of the map, he pointed out it was impossible to draw an exact line from memory and suggested that Paparrigopoulos send a "sample of the entire map" colored in correspondence with his corrections.

But when he found out the title that Paparrigopoulos had picked for the map, "Chart of Greek Lands," Kiepert's patience apparently ran out and he made it known that he drew the proverbial line right there. Finally putting his foot down, the professor wrote to Paparrigopoulos, "I have nothing to object to *Pinax tōn Ellēnikōn Chōrōn* [Chart of Greek Lands], except for the fact that at least half of the area represented on the map includes lands that were never either Hellenic or Hellenized, like Serbia, Wallachia, Danubian Bulgaria, Montenegro, Northern Albania."[148]

Paparrigopoulos's letter to Kiepert, dated February 16, 1878, from Athens, reveals that the letter and the latest color proof of the map sent by the cartographer had not settled the differences concerning the limits of Greek dominance in the regions of Thrace, Macedonia, and Epirus. Paparrigopoulos was also upset about Kiepert's objection to the title of the map and pointed out that it was enough to take a look at Kiepert's own proof to see that "these lands [Hellenic or Hellenized] fill up more than three quarters

---

147. Svolopoulos, "Kōnstantinos Paparrēgopoulos," 365.
148. Ibid., 366.

of the whole map."¹⁴⁹ Moreover, the cartographer had repeated his demand that someone else's name be published on the map as the "coloring author." Finally, despite their previous conversations, the Kingdom of Greece had been given "a color different than other Hellenic lands." This last "mistake" was the straw that broke the camel's back. This time Paparrigopoulos was indignant:

> As you see, Professor, your last work is far from corresponding to the first arrangements, to which you had kindly given your complete consent. It goes without saying that it is impossible to accept these modifications. We cannot but attribute them to a simple misunderstanding; we also have the firm hope that after the considerations we hereby present to you, you will kindly give M. Reimer the necessary instructions to place the different colors conforming to the basis established by you, and that we hastened to accept. We have sent a telegram to M. Reimer in order to stop all further work on the map, until an agreement can be reached between us.¹⁵⁰

It is not clear what the "considerations hereby presented" were, but Paparrigopoulos's bluff evidently had the desired effect because Kiepert's final letter, dated February 25, 1878, from Berlin, was almost apologetic in its acceptance of the terms suggested by Paparrigopoulos:

> I did not, in any manner want to anticipate by this temporary sketch (which, as M. Reimer told me should not represent anything other than a sample of the style of coloring) the definitive decision about the frontier lines to adopt. I had thought instead with M. Reimer that the printing of the map (the corrections of which are at the moment on lithography stones) should be deferred for a short term, from what it seems, when it will be possible to present in it the new frontiers of Bulgaria, Serbia, and Montenegro established by the peace [Treaty of San Stefano]. ... However, if you absolutely want to be in possession of a certain number of samples of the map, intended for the needs of the moment, we can print and color them, according to the instructions and corrections that you would like to send.¹⁵¹

In the same letter Kiepert implored, yet again, that another name along with his be published as the coloring author, afraid that he would be found accountable by critics who would not know, in his words, to "distinguish between the very different trends of this map, and the ethnographic maps" that he had published earlier.

---

149. Ibid., 368. The title of the final and published version of the map suggests that this was the only compromise Kiepert could obtain from Paparrigopoulos.
150. Ibid., 369.
151. Ibid., 370.

In the end, it was Paparrigopoulos who prevailed, even though it seems to have taken another three to four months for him to persuade the geographer with his persistence and what no doubt must have been compelling (dis)incentives—unfortunately not documented. We do learn from a letter by Paparrigopoulos to his protégé Argiropoulos that the final agreement was reached around June. In the same letter, it is hard to miss a certain element of sarcasm in Paparrigopoulos's style when he uses of the title "the eminent geographer" [*o epiphanēs geographos*] repeatedly when referring to Kiepert: "The eminent geographer (who nowadays is busy with the translation of his Russian maps of Asian borders into French for the conference [of Berlin] on Bismarck's commission), the eminent, well, geographer, was persuaded to color our chart the way we wanted it to be from the beginning; and even better, *under his name.*"[152]

These letters clearly show Paparrigopoulos's determination to get a geographer who had been named the best of Europe by none other than Bismarck to publish a map supporting Greek claims. It was not good enough to obtain a map simply *drawn* by Kiepert; the map also had to have his seal of authority—and so the key issues that surfaced many times in the correspondence were "coloring" and "authorship," which brought the project to a standstill at least twice because of Kiepert's understandable reluctance to paint a huge chunk of southeastern Europe in Greek colors. But Paparrigopoulos's persuasion tactics, covering the range from flattery to bribery, from criticism to outright threats, ultimately resolved the disagreements.

Paparrigopoulos's talent in manipulating ethnographic maps surpassed that of Gennadius because he did not just deploy that map as an apparatus of power, a visual tool with which the rights of the Greek nation over an expanse of territory were asserted. He also highlighted the holes in the presumably scientific premises of the whole process and questioned the *authority* of ethnographic maps in principle. The literal issue of authorship was the most important symbolic element of the map, communicating to the public the *scientific authority* embodied in the geographer's name. Gennadius had claimed that authority by remaining anonymous and giving the impression that the map had been prepared by a British author.[153] By contrast, Paparrigopoulos usurped the already existing and unquestionable authority of Kiepert by making sure that Kiepert's name was the only one printed on the map and on the text that accompanied it (written, however, by Paparrigopoulos himself), deliberately misleading the reader. The result was so convincing that even the otherwise meticulous and thorough Wilkinson did

---

152. Paparrigopoulos's letter to Argiropoulo, in Dimara, *Kōnstantinos Paparrēgopoulos*, 348. (Emphasis added.) Colocotronis also made a sarcastic remark about the geographer's willingness to publish a map negating his previous work: "Certainly M. Kiepert did not want to disappoint anyone." Colocotronis, *Macédoine et l'Hellenisme*, 484.

153. The confusion created was enough that Dimara, as recently as 1986, cited "the famous English Edward Stanford" as the author of the map. *Kōnstantinos Paparrēgopoulos*, 343.

not doubt its authenticity when he wrote in his 1951 book, "In the explanation accompanying the map Kiepert outlined the difficulties inherent in the production of an ethnographic map and he maintained that the use of such maps for drawing up political boundaries was a malpractice which no geographer ought to countenance."[154]

It is difficult to gauge the exact magnitude of the impact that the Kiepert-Paparrigopoulos map had in western Europe. It is likely that it remained somewhat obscure in comparison to Kiepert's previous work,[155] but Paparrigopoulos's persistent efforts had helped him kill two birds with one stone. Paradoxical as it may sound, the first of these goals was demonstrating that ethnography was not an exact science. He did this by making his correspondence with Kiepert public and disclosing it to representatives of European Powers in Athens months before he had guaranteed the publication of the map under his terms.[156] To the letters he attached a memo in which he argued that, although no one would dispute the merits of Kiepert's geographical work, the same certainty could not be sustained for its ethnographic component because Kiepert himself was "far from believing in the absolute value of the data we have on the population of the diverse races of the Orient."[157] Questioning the criteria whereby the ethnographic component of a map was determined meant that one could introduce alternative methods that would result in different outcomes. This did not detract from the power of such maps, however. To the contrary, it underscored their importance in visualizing a political objective without naming it as such and making it available in its simplest form to the observers, which was the second, and more conventional, goal of Paparrigopoulos's map. The map thus conceived was not intended for the audience of the geographers of Europe, for whom it was probably too crude, but for classrooms in Macedonian schools that the Syllogos provided with textbooks, teachers, and, apparently, maps. "At the level of mass culture, lies and propaganda are submerged in a sea of cultural expectations and beliefs," observes Matthew Edney; "propaganda maps are not so much arguments as cultural and social reaffirmations."[158] Likewise, Paparrigopoulos's "Chart of Greek Lands" gave the Greek public a means to transform the faith they had in their stake in Macedonia and the much needed assurance that, if maps were to be drawn to "display the races of the Orient," the heritage of Greek civilization was a more justifiable principle than mere numbers in determining their colors.[159]

---

154. Wilkinson, *Maps and Politics*, 75.

155. Cvijić does not mention the original map, but he does refer to Nicolaides's rendering of it (1899) and notes that he was "astonished to see Kiepert's name on this map." *Remarks*, 32.

156. This is why we do not know how exactly he convinced Kiepert to publish the map under his name; Svolopoulos, "Kōnstantinos Paparrēgopoulos," 360.

157. Ibid., 361.

158. Edney, *Mapping an Empire*, 338.

159. As N. Kasasis, president of the University of Athens and the society *Hellenisme*, wrote, "But it is not through numerical significance that Greeks maintain their incontestable

Maps as Fiction

In an article published in the *Bulletin of the American Geographical Society* in 1913, W. L. G. Joerg compared the recent political map of the Balkans, following the conclusion of the second Balkan War, with Jovan Cvijić's ethnographic map, which was considered the gold standard for ethnographic maps at the time. According to Joerg, "despite minor discrepancies," this comparison showed that "at last the guiding principle of European history since the beginning of the nineteenth century, the establishment of coincident racial and political boundaries, has made itself felt in Balkan affairs." The celebratory tone of the article and hopeful words for the future of the Balkan peoples rang hollow, and nowhere more poignantly than in the concluding remarks: "the reapportionment of Balkan territory on broad lines *does* satisfy the requirements of the principle of nationalities. In this lies the significance of the recent conflicts; in this, too, lies the hope of the future. Given the opportunity to work out their own destinies, the Balkan peoples, we may hope, will enter upon a new era of progress and development."[160]

Joerg, if he lived long enough, would learn differently. Only five years after the publication of this article, boundaries were being redrawn in the Balkans, and they would be revised several more times throughout the century, at an immensely tragic human cost. Jovan Cvijić, whose expertise on the ethnic groups of the Balkans and their geographic distribution had by now acquired near-cult status, was once again influential; his work was adopted as a reference by a group known as the Inquiry, convened by Woodrow Wilson in September 1917 "to collect data, compare competing claims to territory and to map out possible future political boundaries."[161] Thanks to Jeremy Crampton's work, we now know how the members of the Inquiry used a combination of maps and statistical data from a variety of sources to draw the map they would support and how these maps were also used by President Wilson as he was drafting the Fourteen Points. A report they prepared made the following recommendations: "i) Make a racial map of Europe, Asiatic Turkey, etc., showing boundaries and mixed and doubtful zones. ii) On basis of i) draw racial boundary lines where possible, i.e. when authorities agree; when they disagree select those *we* had best follow; when *these* disagree map the zone of their disagreement; study density and distribution of peoples in these zones."[162]

This excerpt summarizes in one concise paragraph all the main themes of Denis Wood's monograph, *The Power of Maps,* which has chapter titles

---

superiority over other races; it is also through the influence of their intellectual culture, their commercial and economic activity, briefly, through the triple privilege of seniority *[l'ancienneté]*, intelligence and money." Néoclès Kasasis, *L'Hellenisme et la Macédoine* (Paris, 1903), 63–64.
    160. W. L. G. Joerg, "The New Boundaries of the Balkan States and Their Significance," *Bulletin of the American Geographical Society* 45 (1913), 829–30.
    161. Crampton, "Cartographic Calculation of Space," 731.
    162. Quoted in ibid., 739.

such as "Maps Are Embedded in a History They Help Construct," "Every Map Shows This ... but Not That," and "The Interest the Map Serves Is Masked," ending with "The Interest the Map Serves Can Be Yours."[163] Incredible as it may seem, this was how boundaries were drawn in 1917, and still are to a large extent. What is even more disturbing than the hardly disguised motive of self-interest is the conviction that it was in fact possible, with the aid of comparative statistics and geographical knowledge, and the guidance from experts with a "conscientious and scientific attitude" such as Jovan Cvijić, to separate propaganda from legitimate claims and draw a map that would reflect the "real" ethnic boundaries.[164] Once this task was complete, attaining a fair peace agreement would be just a matter of drawing lines that best conformed to those boundaries—and too bad if some outliers could not be accommodated.

This, in brief, is the fiction that conflict will be permanently resolved once the demarcation lines between groups of people coincide with their respective political entities, and it is not a thing of the distant past, when naïve politicians collaborated with ethnographers to "determine racial boundaries." In fact, this fiction is held in high esteem to this day and surfaces time and again in commentaries on conflicts in those strangely heterogeneous zones of the world, such as contemporary Macedonia. During the late 1990s, when the (western) world observed the mounting tension in the Republic with anxiety, the two authors of an op-ed piece in the *New York Times*, "Redraw the Map, Stop the Killing," argued that violence was "inevitable" given the reluctance of the Slavs to work with the Albanians. They proposed a plebiscite that would determine whether the Albanians wanted to stay or leave, and then would "partition" the Republic of Macedonia.[165] We do not know if the authors were (pleasantly, we hope) surprised that the apocalyptic violence they foresaw has not materialized despite the lack of partition. Redrawing maps and partitioning territory, far from preventing violence, usher it in. Population "exchanges," the oppression of newly created minorities, killings, the uprooting of countless lives, and, at the very least, assimilation follow partitions, not peaceful exchanges of land. The lines drawn on a map are hardly just an academic exercise; they are constitutive of the reality they purportedly represent and tear through human lives in the process.

I am not arguing that the ethnographic map is a "fiction" because of my distrust in the data collected by ethnographers such as Cvijić. Nor am I

---

163. Denis Wood, *The Power of Maps* (New York, 1992).
164. Not surprisingly, the Bulgarian side would beg to differ with the general opinion concerning Cvijić's "scientific attitude." Radoslav Tsanov, a Bulgarian émigré who acquired recognition as a professor of philosophy in the United States, called the geographer "shameless." Tsanoff, *Bulgaria's Case*, 305.
165. John J. Mearsheimer and Stephen Van Evera, "Redraw the Map, Stop the Killing," *New York Times*, April 19, 1999.

suggesting that ethnographers and cartographers were all motivated by nefarious motives of territorial domination. H. R. Wilkinson's 1951 book on ethnographic maps of Macedonia, for example, presents them in sequence, standardized to the same scale and fully demonstrating their inconsistencies in representation, which makes it a great work of reference half a century after its publication.[166] Nevertheless, it seems as though Wilkinson also subscribed to the assumption common to all these maps and their creators—the assumption that there is a better way to draw an ethnographic map, that ethnicity can be objectively identified, enumerated, and depicted in two dimensions. The wishful assumption seems to be: if only we had a miraculous ethno-meter that could measure and record a standardized national allegiance index for each person, and chart his or her exact location with satellite imagery, then we would have the perfect ethnographic map. And until then, we should keep trying.

To believe in the possibility—even theoretical—of the perfect ethnographic map is to ignore how people live, think, and act. "Maps collapse both space and time"; that is, the information that has been measured is captured and remains fixed on the map.[167] Ethnographic maps and the statistical data they are based on "flatten and enclose" people.[168] This is hardly the ideal medium to capture the essence of a concept as fluid, as contingent, and as changing as ethnicity—especially ethnicity in Ottoman Macedonia at the turn of the twentieth century. The static depictions of essentialized ethnicities on the unsophisticated base maps of southeastern Europe did not simply suffer from shoddy scholarship; they entirely masked the complexity of human experience.

Maps are practical cognitive tools that help us organize complex spatial relations in a readable format. It is precisely this feature of the map medium, translating complexity into two dimensions, that lends it so easily to ideological manipulation, and nowhere is this manipulation more consequential than in ethnographic maps. Ethnographic maps, through the dictum that national will is the ultimate principle of political legitimacy, reflect the nation-space, its reach and its boundaries, which may or may not coincide with actual political boundaries. The important point here is that these maps are drawn not only to reflect but to will that space into existence.[169] They are, above all, iconographic representations of territoriality.

---

166. Wilkinson, *Maps and Politics*.
167. Christine Boyer, *The City of Collective Memory* (Cambridge, 1994), 209.
168. Arjun Appadurai, "Number in the Colonial Imagination," in *Orientalism and the Postcolonial Predicament: Perspectives on South Asia*, edited by Carol A. Breckenridge and Peter van der Veer (Philadelphia, 1993), 329.
169. A telling example of how these maps can be used to popularize the idea of border changes is the depiction of conflict zones, such as Kosovo or, now more recently, Iraq and Syria in widely read magazines such as *The Atlantic Monthly* and *Vanity Fair*, which have published alternatives to the current map of Iraq with no self-conscious examination of the inextricable links to colonialism of this kind of exercise.

The power of the map medium to create, predict, and enforce the territoriality of a nation is one of the most important political expressions of cartography. We should, finally, note the flip side of that expression—namely, its social consequences. Cartography helps to disinvest the process of nation-state formation of moral concerns by presenting map-making as an entirely scientific, benign exercise. The mapmaker drawing lines on a map, no matter how much "research" s/he puts into their drawing, cannot foresee the human cost of new boundaries. The importance of the choices available to the mapmaker and of the decisions that he or she makes is underscored by the fact that the product of these decisions does not represent merely a topographical image but a very potent suggestion as to how the territory that Harley called "a socially empty space" is to be filled: "The abstract quality of the map, embodied as much in the lines of a fifteenth-century Ptolemaic projection as in the contemporary images of computer cartography, lessens the burden of conscience about people in the landscape. Decisions about the exercise of power are removed from the realm of immediate face-to-face contacts."[170]

Colorful blocks on an ethnographic map do not only demonstrate how different ethnic groups "stand with respect to one another," as Gennadius suggested, but also make a powerful statement about the discontents of those clearly demarcated territories, namely the people who did not "fit the scale." This statement is not as loud and clear as that voiced by the guerrillas. It is not, at least at first instance, physically violent. It does, however, serve the same process thorough which homogeneity as an ideal becomes homogeneity in practice within the (imagined) boundaries of a nation.

---

170. Harley, "Maps, Knowledge, and Power," 303.

CHAPTER FOUR

Fear of Small Margins

> I certainly should never expect Turkey to survive unless she consented to become statistical like the rest of Europe.
> —William Farr, address to the Statistical Society in London, 1877

When he made this declaration, Dr. William Farr, later called the "Father-in-Law of the British Census," was voicing an opinion prevalent among western European geographers.[1] That is, the Ottomans were different than the rest of Europe in yet another matter: they refused to procure and publish detailed statistics that were considered to be among the very basic tools of effective administration, such as population figures, import and export values, and distribution of natural resources. This was a deficiency that was both an indication and the cause of their backwardness. It certainly did not bode well for the future of "Turkey, the lowest and apparently the most irreclaimable of European countries."[2]

The lack of useful statistics was only one side of the serious demographic problem of the Ottoman Empire; there was also the issue of population decline. Notwithstanding the apparent lack of statistics on the imperial population, it was commonly assumed by statisticians in Europe that the number of Turks, the dominant element of the Ottoman Empire, was in steep decline due to such practices as widespread abortion, moral vice, overindulgence of children, and bad hygiene. Although not as indulgent of their children as the Turks, Jews were threatened by the same calamity because of their squalid living quarters. The Christian population, by contrast, was believed to be on the rise.[3] Alas, the implicit hope that Turks (and Ottoman Jews) might become extinct, disappearing from Europe by an auspicious kind of attrition, was not based on any substantial empirical study; rather, it was based

---

1. Athelstane Baines, "The Census of the Empire, 1911," *Journal of the Royal Statistical Society* 77 (1914), 381.
2. James E. Thorold, "Opening Address of the President of Section F (Economic Science and Statistics) of the British Association for the Advancement of Science," *Journal of the Statistical Society*, v. 29, no. 4 (December 1866), 502.
3. Hyde Clarke, "On the Supposed Extinction of the Turks and Increase of the Christians in Turkey," *Journal of the Statistical Society* 28, no. 2 (1865): 261–93.

on the observations of foreign travelers, most notably those of Pouqueville, who, in his three-volume travel account published in 1805, wrote that the fertility rate was much lower among the Muslim women than among Christians. He claimed that the scourges afflicting the Muslim population of the Peloponnese and decimating their numbers were abortion and polygamy, both of which were not practiced by the Christians.[4]

The bulk of population statistics of the Ottoman Empire published in European journals of statistics and geography were based on a similar method. Despite the proclaimed difficulties of compiling any sort of data from Turkey, the observations of travelers, occasionally adjusted by figures obtained from European consuls, were deemed good enough to provide an educated guess, which would then be published and join the tomes of knowledge about the globe. These writings repeatedly complained that there was not even a single census of the Ottoman Empire they could consult. As E. G. Ravenstein, a noted geographer of the times, put it, "Some statistical information on the populations of that part of Eastern Europe which is now devastated by the Turkish hordes will prove acceptable at the present time. It is scarcely necessary to state that no regular census of the population has ever been taken."[5]

Ravenstein, in a more dispassionate paper read before the Statistical Society of London on June 19, 1877, acknowledged that the Ottoman authorities did collect data and published them periodically. They did not, however, meet the geographer's exacting standards: "The data collected by the local authorities and occasionally published in the Salmanes [sic], or official almanacs of the vilayets, are not deserving of much confidence, and there exists no properly organized statistical office to check the returns."[6] These shortcomings did not prevent Ravenstein from compiling his own figures. He explained that he had consulted the work of authorities such as Carl Sax and Major Zur Helle, who had "devoted special attention to Turkish population statistics." He added that he had availed himself of "wherever additional information was procurable, from consular reports or otherwise."[7]

---

4. F. C. H. L. Pouqueville, *Voyage en Morée, à Constantinople, en Albanie, et dans Plusieurs Parties de l'Empire Ottoman, pendant les Années 1798, 1799, 1800 et 1801* (Paris, 1805). There may have been some degree of truth to the difference in fertility rates among Christians and Muslims. Kemal Karpat also argues that the rate was higher among the Christians until the mid-nineteenth century, but he attributes this to the Muslim males' spending their peak reproductive years in the army; *Ottoman Population*, 11.

5. E. G. Ravenstein, "Distribution of the Population in the Part of Europe Overrun by Turks," *Geographical Magazine* 3 (October, 1876): 259–61. Ravenstein was a prolific scholar better known for his research on Africa, more particularly on demographic issues concerning the colonization of the continent by Europeans. He was the author of many articles on the subject, such as E. G. Ravenstein, "Lands of the Globe Still Available for European Settlement," *Proceedings of the Royal Geographic Society and Monthly Record of Geography* 13, no. 1 (January 1891): 27–35.

6. Ravenstein "Population of Russia and Turkey," 433.

7. Ibid, 434.

"Consular reports or otherwise" indicates a conveniently vague range of sources for Ravenstein's statistical tables. Just like maps, the reliability of statistics rested on the compiler's reputation as much as anything else. The unreliability or complete lack of Turkish statistics was a predictable, formulaic preamble to works that presented alternative figures that claimed to represent the latest and most accurate knowledge about the population of the Ottoman Empire. Even though the Ottoman Empire had possessed a flawed but serviceable census system since the 1830s, the insistence on its inaccuracy, if not complete absence, served as a perfect foil against the scientific authority of the compiler. In fact, certain "authoritative" sources on Ottoman population were simply fabricated by copying a previous work and declaring it as the most "reliable" one without providing any tangible proof of the superiority of these figures over any others. After a source had been quoted once and, in turn, quoted by another author, a third party could comfortably declare the numbers "reliable," apparently without bothering to trace the chain of transmission. For instance, Bianconi's figures relied largely on those provided by the Stanford Map, supplemented by a few British consular reports and the author's own observations from the time when he worked in the region as an engineer for the French railroad company that built the Jonction Salonique-Constantinople.[8] And the Stanford tables (which, as we have seen in the last chapter, were actually published by I. Gennadius) were again "estimates," but the author was comfortable in publishing them because they were attributed to the most reliable "authority" on the issue. This reliable and objective source that Gennadius quoted for his own work was Henri Mathieu's *La Turquie et ses Différents Peuples*. Nor surprisingly, Mathieu himself stated that, although he had made every effort to approach the "truth," he still did not pretend to be giving exact figures.[9]

We have seen in the last chapter how, as the notion of popular sovereignty based on national will gained hold in Europe and among the Balkan national elites, ethnographic map-making turned into an open contest about projecting territoriality. Population statistics were an inextricable part of this practice because they endowed the choropleth maps with a numerical basis. Most of these maps, and the accompanying plans for territorial hegemony, obviously privileged homogeneity rather than complexity, making demographic rivalry among different groups a high-stakes game of numbers.

---

8. Bianconi, *Ethnographie et statistique*, 22–26; Stanford [Gennadius], *Ethnological Map*, 16.

9. Henri Mathieu, *La Turquie et ses Différents Peuples* (Paris, ca. 1857), 44. It is interesting to note that Salahaddin Bey, an Ottoman official apparently followed the same method for the statistical tables he presented at the Exposition Universelle of 1867. Ernest Dottain claimed that his figures were taken from Viquesnel's *Voyage dans la Turquie d'Europe*, which, in turn, were taken from the Ubicini statistics; Dottain, "La Turquie d'Asie d'après la Traité de Berlin," *Revue de Géographie*, no. 3 (1878), 209, cited in Karpat, *Ottoman Population*, 25 n. 32. Remember that Ubicini's numbers were presumably based on Ottoman official statistics.

Gaining the upper hand in a certain region required the establishment of population statistics that clearly favored the preponderance of one group. After the implementation of the Mürzsteg Reform Program, which called for a future reorganization of the Macedonian provinces according to "racial" criteria, the urgency of producing proof of demographic superiority became even more acute among the leaders of the various nationalist movements that sought the same territory for expansion.

In this chapter, I view population statistics and census practices from the perspective of the participants in the process, both the counters and the counted. I first review the methods of enumeration and comparison available to the parties fighting for demographic supremacy in Macedonia. There were obviously enormous political stakes involved in the production of these statistics, which makes them quite suspect, but my purpose here is to underscore how statistical knowledge came to be understood as the basis for formulating a legitimate territorial claim rather than to evaluate the soundness of these figures. Then I shift the focus to an actual census survey as it was experienced on the ground. This is the Ottoman "Census of 1903," which acted as a force of mobilization in making people aware of a radically new understanding of their collective identity.[10]

When the Ottoman government decided to proceed with its own plans of enumeration in the middle of an already tense situation, the rivalry among the different camps was no longer limited to duels on the pages of books, propaganda material, or respected geography journals; it had spread to the countryside. The body count of the census now included the bodies of those who were killed in this fight for demographic superiority. The census became yet another step in the hardening of communal boundaries. It was not a snapshot of the population divided into different confessional groups; it was a mechanism through which those very same categories that it presumably enumerated were, in fact, created. It directly involved (nearly) every member of a largely illiterate and rural population in a process that it otherwise would have stayed indifferent to—the process of nationalization. For the same reason, looking at the implementation of the census in the countryside gives us a glimpse into the meaning of nationalist movements, not as defined by the elite who spearheaded them but by the people who were swept into the movement by the trickle-down effects of nationalist ideology.

---

10. Perhaps a more appropriate title would be the "Census of 1903–1907" because, although the regulations concerning a new population count were issued in 1903, the count was not completed until 1907. The choice of the word *census* itself deserves an explanation here. Justin McCarthy has argued that the term is inappropriate because the count was not a survey taken on a given day throughout the empire and therefore not a *census* in the strictly modern sense;, *Population History of the Middle East and the Balkans* (Istanbul, 2002), 118, 136. Nevertheless, I have chosen to follow the more established practice of calling the Ottoman population counts of 1831, 1881/82–1893, and 1903–1907 censuses not only for the sake of convenience but also to distinguish them from earlier attempts and routine upgrades of registers.

Methods of Counting

How could the Ottomans "know" their population if they were so ignorant of methods that would allow them to "read" it? Thanks to the work of social and economic historians, we know that the Ottomans were actually not as hapless as these European geographers would have us believe when it came to gathering information about the population of the empire.[11] Sources of demographic data for the fifteenth through nineteenth centuries range from information revealed by *tahrir* registers and *salnâmes* (Ottoman state almanacs) to the results of more targeted surveys such as the population counts of the empire after the 1830s, which have been deemed fairly reliable, if imperfect, estimates of Ottoman population.[12] Figures such as the value of exports and imports from major ports, the population of cities, and the population density of the empire by region were provided by the *salnâmes* and were also republished in consular reports and in various compilations by European scholars.[13] The first detailed population count of the empire was taken in 1831–1838 and repeated in 1844.[14] Another European

---

11. The attempts by the Ottoman state to gather and record information about its population have attracted a considerable amount of scholarly attention from social and economic historians of the Ottoman Empire. Ömer Lütfi Barkan pioneered the field of demographic studies in Ottoman historiography; his works include "Türkiye'de İmparatorluk devirlerinin büyük nüfus ve arazi tahrirleri," *İktisat Fakültesi Mecmuası* 1–2 (1940): 1–40; "Tarihi demografi araştırmaları ve Osmanlı tarihi, *Türkiyat Mecmuası* 10 (1953): 1–26; "Essai sur les Données Statistiques des Registres de Recensement dans l'Empire Ottoman aux XVème et XVIème Siècles," *Journal of the Economic and Social History of the Orient* 1 (1957): 9–36. For a detailed bibliography of Ottoman population studies, refer to Daniel Panzac, *La Population de l'Empire Ottoman* (Aix-en-Provence, 1993).

12. *Tahrir* registers were kept for fiscal purposes and not as population registers; more specifically, they listed taxable revenue sources assigned to *timar (prebend)* holders, and their reliability as a source for demographical information should not be overestimated; Heath Lowry, "The Ottoman Tahrir Defterleri as a Source for Social and Economic History: Pitfalls and Limitations," in *Studies in Defterology* (Istanbul, 1992), 3–18. For the nineteenth-century surveys, see Karpat, *Ottoman Population*; Kemal Karpat, "Ottoman Population Records and the Census of 1881/1882–1893," *International Journal of Middle East Studies* 9 (1978): 237–74; Stanford Shaw, "The Ottoman Census System and Population 1831–1914," *International Journal of Middle East Studies* 9 (1978): 325–38; McCarthy, *Population History*; Justin McCarthy, *Muslims and Minorities: The Population of Ottoman Anatolia and the End of the Empire* (New York, 1983).

13. For a detailed list of contemporary European sources see Karpat, *Ottoman Population*. Ottoman sources were routinely disregarded by most European scholars, who claimed they were not reliable. Ravenstein provided his own population statistics of the Ottoman Empire, Ravenstein "Population of Russia and Turkey."

14. Justin McCarthy claims that there is no record of the 1844 count, but the well-known Ubicini statistics published in 1851 have later been attributed to this count; "Factors in the Analysis of the Population of Anatolia, 1800–1878" in McCarthy, *Population History*, 87. Enver Ziya Karal called the 1831 count the "first census" of the empire. *Osmanlı İmparatorluğu'nda ilk Nüfus Sayımı* (Ankara, 1943). The Ubicini statistics were published in A. Ubicini, *Lettres sur la Turquie* (Paris, 1853). Göçek and Hanioğlu mention another count that was carried out in 1866–1873, but little is known about its results; Göçek and Hanioğlu, "Western Knowledge."

scholar who apparently had access to these figures was Eugene Boré, French Orientalist, who published them in *Almanach de l'Empire Ottoman pour l'Année 1849/1850*.[15] In 1866, a detailed census of the *Tuna Vilayeti*, the model province for administrative reforms, was taken. In 1877–1878, the Ottoman government published, for the first time, the population estimate for the entire empire (as opposed to the tax and conscription base, i.e., number of male adults) in the imperial *salnâme*. These numbers, however, were not based on an actual count but on figures provided in the provincial *salnâmes*, supplemented by information gathered by provincial administrators.[16]

Abdülhamid II was interested in census surveys as a tool of government policy, and the first comprehensive survey, which required census clerks to cover all regions of the empire and to indicate when they used estimates rather than an actual count (such as areas with a nomadic population), was taken during his reign, between 1881/1882 and 1893.[17] This survey anticipated the census of 1903 in an important way: compliance with registration was enforced through the introduction of *nüfus cüzdanları* (identity cards) issued according to the information in the census register. Lacking an identity card, which was now required for the completion of any official transaction, was an offence punishable by jail time. Those who avoided registry to escape from the military draft would "be immediately conscripted."[18] Kemal Karpat notes that the results of this survey, presented to the sultan by the Grand Vezir Cevat Paşa in 1893 "represent the most complete and reliable Ottoman population figures complied in the nineteenth century."[19] In fact, these results also served as the main reference for the 1903 census, as we will see shortly.

Between these population counts, census clerks tracked demographic changes, such as the number of males who were liable for draft and paying taxes, through entries made into separate registers called *yoklama* and *vukuat defterleri*.[20] In 1905–1907, the 1903 census, which classified the population according to sectarian affiliation, was carried out. The final population count of the empire took place in 1914, after the immense

---

15. Eugene Boré, *Almanach de l'Empire Ottoman pour l'Année 1849/1850* (Constantinople, 1849/50), cited in Karpat, *Ottoman Population*, 23.

16. Karpat, *Ottoman Population*, 25.

17. The tenth U.S. census of 1880 served as an important model for Abdülhamid II. Samuel Sullivan Cox, who was appointed as the U.S. representative to the Ottoman court in 1885 had chaired the Census Commission of the House of Representatives. The sultan was very impressed with the summaries of the U.S. census results presented by Cox and remarked that "with such data for administrative policies, [the United States] could not be other than prosperous." Samuel S. Cox, *Diversions of a Diplomat in Turkey* (New York, 1893), 43, cited in Göçek and Hanioğlu, "Western Knowledge," 2.

18. Karpat, *Ottoman Population*, 32.

19. He also notes that it is difficult to determine the ending date for this census process, "if it ended at all," but that the results were presented to Sultan Abdülhamid II in 1893. Ibid., 33.

20. McCarthy, *Population History*, 86.

demographic changes brought about by the Balkan Wars.²¹ This last count classified the population into twenty-two categories but did not distinguish the numbers of men and women, nor did it provide any information about age. These population counts were taken not for the benefit of European geographers but to meet specific administrative needs of the state, and they therefore were not widely published.²² As for their reliability, Daniel Panzac points out that, precisely because they were collected for internal use, there is no reason to assume that the Ottomans would want to commit any errors in their aggregation.²³

The reliability of sheer aggregates, however, was not the only the concern of nineteenth-century critiques of Ottoman census practices. As we have seen in the previous chapter, what the statisticians in London, Berlin, and Paris wanted to capture, enumerate, and map were the different "races" of the Ottoman Empire. The Ottoman statistical sources, even if they had been widely available, would not have assisted with this quest because they did not classify the population into "racial" or "national" groups. The Ottoman imperial government felt no pressing need for such a classification; the information was gathered mainly for the purposes of estimating potential tax revenue and the number of soldiers to be recruited, for which wealth and religion—and not ethnicity—were the only two relevant categories.²⁴ There was, however, a significant change with the 1903 census, which classified the population not only with regard to simple religious distinction but also divided the Christian population according to sectarian and "national" affiliation. But this principle was not applied uniformly; the entire Muslim

---

21. This population count should not be considered a census because no survey was actually taken. The numbers were based on the results of the 1903 census, adjusted according to the registered births and deaths; Karpat, *Ottoman Population,* 189. Panzac, even though he uses the term *recensement* for the published population statistics of 1914, notes that this was more "a count rather than census." D. Panzac, "L'Enjeu du Nombre: La Population de la Turquie de 1914 à 1927," *Revue de l'Occident Musulman et de la Méditerranée* 50, no. 4 (1988), 48.

22. One of the most important internal uses of these statistics was as a basis for calculating the proportions by which non-Muslim communities would be represented in the bureaucracy and other official capacities. Fuat Dündar notes that these numbers also helped to determine the number of non-Muslims in provincial administrative councils and the number of parliamentary representatives during the short-lived experience of representative government, pointing out that the state logic of representation was not based on individuals but communities; Fuat Dündar, *Modern Türkiye'nin Şifresi: İttihad ve Terakki'nin Etnisite Mühendisliği, 1913–1918* (Istanbul, 2008), 85–107.

23. Panzac, "L'Enjeu du Nombre," 48. Justin McCarthy has also been extremely vocal in emphasizing the reliability of Ottoman population statistics and argues that their shortcomings were comparable to those of modern censuses in the developing world; *Population History.* Fuat Dündar, on the other hand, thinks that these statistics may not be as reliable as Karpat, McCarthy, and Panzac suggest, but he also discredits the claims that Ottoman statistics were entirely baseless as being purely political, Dündar, *Modern Türkiye'nin Şifresi,* 107.

24. For statistical data on the Macedonian population, see Daniel Panzac, "La Population de la Macédoine au XIXe Siècle," *La Revue du Monde Musulman et de la Méditerranée* 66 (1992): 113–29; Cem Behar, *Osmanlı İmparatorluğu'nun ve Türkiye'nin Nüfusu, 1500–1927* (Ankara, 1996).

population was counted under one category, with the exception of the *kıpti* (Roma), as was the usual practice. On the other hand, the Vlachs constituted an exceptional case in that they were assigned a separate category even though they did not have an autonomous, national church.

In 1905, the statistical data available to the Ottoman administration were derived largely from the results of the 1881/1882 census, which were periodically updated by the census authorities, but the numbers were largely underestimations. Muslim and non-Muslim alike, the population had ample incentive to hide away from the census clerks, such as evading the tax collector and dodging the army.[25] According to a report of the French consul in Salonika in March 1904, the rural population could not easily avoid registry because these small communities were easier to monitor and it was in the interest of Muslims that everyone was conscripted. The situation differed in larger centers, however, where *muhtars* (communal leaders) managed to hide some of the (Christian) population in exchange for a share from the spoils rescued from the tax collector.[26] Although the consul's remark that the Muslim population did not have an incentive to avoid registry is off the mark in the sense that the military tax was not the only personal liability of the population, it is true that the *salnâme* of 1903 that he referred to, like other compilations of Ottoman official population statistics, was in all likelihood an underestimation; this was a general problem that the state was trying to overcome through the implementation of new measures.

Reliable or not, the statistics complied by the Ottomans did not serve the purposes of propaganda groups nervous about their co-nationals' numbers in disputed regions coveted by multiple parties (how they determined who the "co-nationals" were was an entirely different matter, as we will see shortly). For one thing, Ottoman statistics did count Muslims, a significantly large group scattered across the land just like the other confessional groups but also the dominant element in certain areas. This was not necessarily useful information for the propaganda groups, whose statistics usually did not even mention the Muslim population, as if they did not exist. And for the purposes of propagandists, they just might as well not exist because

---

25. The categories for the 1881/1882–1893 census were Muslims, Greeks, Armenians, Bulgarians, Catholics, Jews, Protestants, Latins, Monophysites (Syriacs), non-Muslim Gypsies, and Foreigners. In 1906/1907, to these categories were added Cossacks, Wallachians, Greek Catholics, Armenian Catholics, Maronites, Chaldeans, Jaconites, Samaritans, Yezidis, and Gypsies (without religious distinction); See Karpat, *Ottoman Population*, tables I.8.A (132–33) through I.16.A (166–67). According to the 1905 census, the total population of the three provinces of Monastir, Salonika, and Kosovo was 2,417,840, of which 1,127,775 were recorded as Muslim, 628,253 as Bulgarian, 564,067 as Greek, 59,552 as Jewish, and 26,042 as Vlach. According to the same figures, in Monastir Muslims constituted 40 percent of the total population, Greeks 35 percent, and Bulgarians 24 percent. In Salonika, these percentages were 45.5, 28.6, and 17.2; and in Kosova, 56.5, 2, and 40, respectively (calculations based on the data published by Karpat, *Ottoman Population*.

26. MAE, vol. 40, report "Population du Vilayet du Salonique," Salonika, March 1904.

it was understood that the Muslim population's "self-consciousness" would not factor into the calculations that would partition the area into distinct nation-states when the imminent death of the Ottoman Empire occurred.[27] In a memo to the French Foreign Ministry, dated October 15, 1901, a member of the French diplomatic corps made the following observation: "The inhabitants [of Macedonia] belong to four different races: the Greek race, the Serbian race, the Bulgarian race, the Roumanian race." Nevertheless, he conceded, a couple of paragraphs after this, the presence of "a population entirely different than the four others mentioned, namely the Albanians." This alien population, he further noted, "if they are Muslims, exercise a kind of dominance which truly is oppression, thanks to the Sultan." The "difference" of the Albanians from the others and, more important, the Muslim contingent of this large ethnic group, apparently disqualified them from membership among the indigenous inhabitants of Macedonia. Nowhere in this memo was there a mention of the presence of other Muslim groups.[28]

According to another observer, H. N. Brailsford, British journalist, the important issue to be addressed in Macedonia to ensure peace and prosperity was determining the proportions of various *Christian* groups with respect to one another. Brailsford's recommendations for meaningful reform in Macedonia did not explicitly call for an expulsion of Muslims, but it was understood that national homogeneity should be the goal and that, when it came to the "future of Macedonia's races," the Muslims, whatever their numbers might be, would either be absorbed into the nation-state they found themselves in or, as it was implicitly assumed, follow their Ottoman overlords into Asia. Brailsford's plan had it all worked out:

> It would obviate much injustice, and help to disentangle the present confusion of races, if a Land Commission were instituted to facilitate exchanges. All the Balkan races, save the Bulgarians, have the migratory habit. Albanians dissatisfied with the new *régime* might prefer to return to Albania. Slavs left stranded in an unreformed Albania would certainly wish to emigrate to Macedonia. Within Macedonia itself, and even within the Bulgarian principality, there are,

---

27. It would become clear after World War I that the right to self-determination was a principle applied selectively and did not necessarily include the Muslims' rights to express any such political will; nor did it reflect a politically sound consensus for those who presumably exercised this right. Commenting on this principle as it was applied at the Paris Conference, the Paul Ignotus, journalist, remarked cynically, "Self-determination ... meant that a few gentlemen in and around Paris told the peoples concerned what to 'determine' about their future." P. Ignotus, "Czechs, Magyars, Slovaks," *Political Quarterly* 40, no. 2 (1969), 188.

28. MAE, vol. 26 Série B, Carton 77, Dossier 1, October 15, 1901. According to A. d'Anvil, the diplomat who wrote the memo, these four races were not "scattered and mixed higgledy-piggledy all over Macedonia: whatever they say, each have their own territory." He appended an ethnographic map illustrating this point. The Bulgarians covered a large area of the center of the map, with smaller areas of Greeks along the Aegean coast, Serbians and Albanians in the periphery, and even smaller islands of Vlachs and Turks.

doubtless, Greeks who would like to leave a Slav district and settle in an area where they could speak their own tongue and be governed by men of their own race. The more such exchanges were encouraged the less risk would there be of racial friction. There is certain to be a stampede of the worse type of Turks from a reformed Macedonia. It is important to save them from selling out at an unjust price, and at the same time fill their places with immigrants whose case will be bettered by transference.

Brailsford was so confident of his plan that he cheerily recommended its application in "the whole of European Turkey, and—for that matter, [in] the more advanced regions of Asia Minor as well, more particularly the provinces where Armenians are numerous."[29] His recommendations would not sound so chilling if we did not know that these "exchanges" were indeed put in practice, with horrible consequences for the people Brailsford had relocated on the map with strikes of his pen.[30]

Racial fiction was the apparent antidote to racial friction, and Ottoman sources of statistics did not provide suitable material for such plans. They had been produced by Ottoman officials, for Ottoman officials—and certainly not to validate the wished-for demographic superiority of any one group in a certain region. No wonder they were consulted only when they happened to support a claim and were discounted otherwise.

School Enrollment: A Better Way of Counting?

As we have seen in the last chapter, the prevalent public opinion in Europe viewed southeastern Europe, including Macedonia, as a place where Slavic peoples constituted the original and dominant racial group. Naturally, this was a cause of concern for the national elites of the Hellenic Kingdom, who believed they had legitimate claims to the same region. They were joined by the Greek Orthodox of the Ottoman Empire in their worries that Macedonian Greeks might be absorbed into a hostile Slavic mass. By 1884, long before the demographic struggle took a physically violent turn, it was common knowledge and an immense concern also among the Ottoman Greek elites that statistics favoring the Slavs were being published and circulated in Europe. The Greek Orthodox community of Salonika voiced its discontent in December 1884 in a letter to the French consul in

---

29. Brailsford, *Macedonia*, 333.
30. Not to mention that, despite his predictions of people "self deporting," people preferred to stay in the lands they knew as home despite all the hardships brought on them by this choice. For instance, the Greek communities in Bulgaria that had escaped from the violence anti-Greek movement of 1906 to safety in Greece clamored to return as soon as the dust settled; Dragostinova, *Between Two Motherlands*, 57–61.

Salonika signed by Archbishop Constantinos, protesting the circulation of these statistics.[31]

As the battle of numbers started with a clear advantage on the Slav side, the Greek defense against these claims came out of the same elites' deep-seated belief in the superiority of Greek culture and civilization—and what could represent that culture better than schools?[32] Therefore the idea of publishing statistics based on school enrollment numbers was born. The Greek educational establishment indeed had a longer history and larger enrollment numbers in Macedonia than their Bulgarian counterparts. It did not take long, however, for Bulgarian pundits to answer with scholastic statistics of their own, statistics that emphasized quality" over quantity. The widespread notion that population statistics, whether based on Ottoman officials' or European consuls' and travelers' reports, were not to be trusted lent support to the popularity of school enrollment numbers as a more accurate source of data that could be verified with relative ease.[33] Moreover, school statistics presumably offered a less tangible but politically not insignificant advantage: they were in harmony with a liberal conception of nationhood that favored choice over racial predeterminism. The anonymous (Greek) author of a critical commentary on the 1889 British Blue Book on Macedonia argued that ethnology should take into account four fundamental elements in defining national affiliation: "consciousness, language, religion, and shared aspirations." There was, however, an equally important but often overlooked "fifth ethnological feature" — "school enrollment." He admonished Consul John Elijah Blunt, who had contributed the report on populations statistics to the Blue Book for not giving this important feature due consideration.[34] Another anonymous (again Greek) author wrote, "In Turkey the father of a Christian family in sending his children to a particular school declares, not only the language which he wishes them to learn, but also the nation with which he is connected, and of which he shares the memories and hopes. In short he declares which is his mother country."[35]

Unfortunately for the Greek national elites, making school enrollment numbers a valid measure of national consciousness was largely wishful thinking on their part, at least as far as the European audience that these statistics were aimed at was concerned. As we have seen, when it came to categorizing the people of Macedonia, most European observers trusted their own judgment, which favored a more "organic" understanding of nationality, based on mother tongue or historical anthropology, rather than self-declared

---

31. MAE, vol. 7, January 9, 1885. (The date of the petition was December 28, 1884.)
32. See, for instance, Kasasis, *Hellénisme et la Macédoine.*
33. *Population of Macedonia;* Stephanopoli, *Grecs et Bulgares en Macédoine.*
34. *English Blue Book,* 14.
35. *Population of Macedonia,* 10. The pamphlet was also published in French under the title *Les Écoles Chrétiennes de Macédoine* (Paris, 1905).

affiliation, no matter how vehemently defended.³⁶ Furthermore, there were serious problems with the school statistics presented as beyond reproach by both sides. First, the numbers did not quite rise to the task, and second, and more important, even assuming that every schoolchild in Ottoman Macedonia had been properly counted and classified according to the community that provided his or her education, the act of choosing a school by the parents was by no means an autonomous, individual expression of preference for a certain national culture.

Regarding the published figures and their inconsistencies, it is instructive to take a look at some of the widely available statistics on school enrollment at the time. In 1903, according to Ottoman official records, of the total of 706 schools run by the Greek Orthodox and Bulgarian communities within the province of Salonika, 400 belonged to the Greek community and the rest to the Bulgarians. The overwhelming majority of the 306 schools run by the Bulgarian community was under the control of the Exarchate, but 12 of them were in the Catholic rite. Greek schools employed 766 teachers and enrolled 34,044 students, whereas the Bulgarian schools employed 452 teachers an enrolled 15,339 students.³⁷ These figures are not at extreme variance with another set of statistics that originated from a publication of the Greek Patriarchate in 1902, subsequently published by the Syllogue Macédonien of Athens in fall 1903 and by the *Bulletin d'Orient* in November 1904, making them available to a wider audience.³⁸

Although this set of statistics circulated in consular reports as well as publications in Europe as the main frame of reference, it is likely that the number

---

36. Colonel Vérand wrote in a report to the French Embassy in Constantinople, "It is fairly difficult to determine exactly which race the inhabitants belong to. Only the spoken language might be a reliable [*sérieuse*] indicator, which, however, cannot be considered absolutely accurate." MAE, Constantinople, Série E, Colonel Vérand to Amabassador, Serres, July 10, 1904.

37. Numbers for the other communities were Muslim, 988 schools, 1,305 teachers, and 36,843 students; Serbian, 17 schools, 60 teachers, and 798 students; and Vlach, 13 schools, 30 teachers, and 606 students. The totals are for male and female teachers and pupils; BOA, TFR.I.SL 14/1345-1, July 6, 1903. The seemingly high number of schools for Muslim children should not lead us to the assume that the Muslim educational establishment was the best organized and funded in the region. During the Hamidian period (1878–1908), there was indeed a visible commitment to public education for the (Muslim) masses, and the number of primary and secondary schools increased proportionately with this policy; Somel, *Modernization of Public Education*; Fortna, *Imperial Classroom*. At the same time, however, inspectors often complained about the deplorable state of Muslim schools, especially compared to the schools of other communities; see, for instance, BOA, TFR.I.AS 54/5355, Report prepared by Erkân-ı Harb Binbaşısı Ahmed Nuri for the Inspector General, December 12, 1907; TFR.I.SL 1/59-2, *Maarif Encümeni* (Education Council) official Mehmed Tahir to the Inspectorate, December 1902.

38. The Patriarchate's publication, entitled *Tableau Comparatif des Écoles Helléniques et Bulgares dans les Vilayets de Monastir, de Salonique et d'Adrianople*, also included, as the title suggests, the province of Edirne; *La Macédoine et les Reformes, Mémoire du Syllogue Macédonien* (Athènes, 1903).

of Bulgarian schools were indeed higher than these statistics suggested.[39] The Ottoman statistical attribution of an even smaller number to Bulgarian schools does not really corroborate these figures, given the Ottoman authorities' alignment with the Patriarchate on any issue concerning Bulgarians, and more important, of the presence of Bulgarian schools that operated without license from the government. Moreover, at least according to the claims of the acting British consul in Salonika, these figures included only the Bulgarian students who had passed their examinations, rather than the original enrollment at the start of the school year, thereby giving the Greek statistics an unfair edge.[40] Even this point, however, was a cause for dispute.: The French, who were hardly proponents of the Greek cause, reported the same numbers with the caveat that the numbers referred to students who were "present at the time of exams," obviously duplicating the note in the Syllogue publication that the total number of students attending Bulgarian schools also included 19,348 who "reported" only during exams.[41] It appears that the Bulgarian schoolchildren's drop-out rates were put to different uses with contradictory implications. For instance, the anonymous author of *The Population of Macedonia* asserted that most students of Bulgarian schools quit before the end of the semester to demonstrate the failure of these schools to keep their students committed.[42] But the claim also lent credence to the British acting consul's argument that there were actually more students who enrolled in Bulgarian schools than the statistics suggested.

It is hard not to notice that the number of Greek schools, although based on the same source, had a mysterious way of creeping up in each reproduction. By the count of the Syllogue, published in 1903, there were 968 Greek schools attended by 57,681 students. In Kasasis's book, published in the same year, the figures were 989 and 59,043 respectively. Only a year later, when the *Bulletin d'Orient* came out in November, the numbers had climbed up to 998 and 59,640. Other sources kept the number of students the same, but estimated the number of schools at 1,041.[43] Douglas Dakin noted the most phenomenal increase in his 1966 book; according to his source, "in or about 1902 there were just over 1,000 Greek schools in Macedonia with close to 70,000 pupils." His source was a Greek pamphlet published in 1904 that was based on the *Bulletin d'Orient* statistics, which,

---

39. MAE, Turquie, Correspondence Politique et Commerciale, vol. 410, November 17, 1904. The British acting consul general in Salonika, in referring to the same set of figures, noted problems with the Greek statistics; PRO, FO 195/2183, Du Vallon to Embassy, Salonika, December 2, 1904. In addition to British and French diplomatic sources, other works reproducing the statistics of the Syllogue Macédonien include Kasasis, *Hellénisme et la Macédoine*; *Population of Macedonia*; Frédéric Boissonnas, *La Macédoine Occidentale* (Genève, 1921).

40. PRO, FO 195/2183, Du Vallon to the Embassy, Salonika, December 2, 1904.

41. MAE, Turquie, vol. 410, Correspondence Politique et Commerciale, November 17, 1904; *Macédoine et les Reformes*, 16.

42. *Population of Macedonia*, 11.

43. Belia, "Ē Ekpaideutikē Politikē tou Ellinikou Kratous," 33.

in turn were, derived from the Patriarchate's figures.[44] Despite claims of verifiable soundness, school statistics were no different than general population statistics in the way they were deployed for the demographic war effort.

Not surprisingly, the figures for Bulgarian schools also fluctuated enormously depending on the source. For instance, the number of Bulgarian schools in the *sancak* of Serres, according to the *Bulletin d'Orient* statistics, was 129. According to the same source, 3,783 students were enrolled in these schools. According to Mishev's figures however, which were based on the records of the Exarchate and dated 1902, in this same *sancak* there were 184 Bulgarian schools with 7,718 students.[45] Strangely enough, the most generous figures concerning Bulgarian schools were reported in April 1894 by the British Vice Consul in Serres, a Greek Orthodox. Vice Consul Constantine Capety reported that the number of Bulgarian schools had steadily been increasing. The data he provided placed the number of schools at 172 and the number of students at 9,426. Capety's seemingly strange generosity with the numbers of Bulgarian schools in Serres is more easily explained in the broader context and the timing of the report he was penning. He was taking issue with those who claimed that the Ottoman government was partial to the Greek side; as the school numbers made clear, the imperial government did not "impede Bulgarian instruction." At this instance, demographic one-upmanship was not the real issue, which may explain the vice-consul's unusual viewpoint.[46] Capety's report was corroborated by the French Consul in Salonika, who reported that despite their complaints against local authorities, the Bulgarians had opened up a large number of schools in the area within the past few years. The number of schools just in the "*sancaks* of Selânik and Serres" (presumably including the *merkez*, or center of Salonika, and all the *kazas*, or subdivisions of Serres) was estimated to be "more than 300, with approximately 17,000 students of both genders."[47]

A final point to consider about the Bulgarian school statistics is the Ottoman authorities' attitude toward these institutions, which went from suspicion to hostility after the Ilinden Uprising of 1903. After the involvement of Bulgarian schoolteachers in the Macedonian revolutionary movement became undeniably clear, the Ottoman authorities started to view the schools as breeding grounds for potential "brigands." As a result many of them were closed down, their teachers were incarcerated and the schools left functioning were placed under the close (but hardly infallible) scrutiny of the government.[48]

---

44. Dakin, *Greek Struggle in Macedonia*, 19. His reference was A. T Spiliotopoulos, *La Macédoine et l'Hellénisme* (Athens, 1904).
45. Brancoff [Mishev], *La Macédoine et sa Population Chrétienne*.
46. PRO, FO 195/1849, Serres, Vice Consul Capety to Consul Blunt, April 24, 1894.
47. MAE, vol. 9, Consulate General of France in Salonika to Casimir Perier, president of the council, May 9, 1894.
48. MAE vol. 36, Annexed to the political dispatch dated August 16, 1903 (report by the Bulgarian commercial agent).

More important than the reliability of school enrollment numbers, the way they were counted, or the underestimated size of the "subversive" community schools was the way in which schoolchildren were essentially turned into numbers on statistical tables. Contrary to the assertion of the anonymous author of *Schools of Macedonia,* the school where parents sent their children was not necessarily a statement about nationality. For one thing, as we have seen, even the nationalist elites had widely different opinions on what schooling should involve to mold young minds into national unity. Moreover, the final decision to choose a particular school was determined by factors that were not indicative of national identity, whether defined linguistically, religiously, or as a matter of individual preference borne out of a composite consciousness of history, customs, class, and aspirations. National affiliation was not simply a matter of choice in Ottoman Macedonia at the turn of the century, and school choice did not follow that choice in logical sequence. Nor was national affiliation a relic of "innate racial qualities." The school and population statistics that presumably quantified nation-ness were, in fact, reflections of its contingent and contested nature.

What Censuses Count

Studies on Ottoman census practices have so far concentrated more on the numbers recorded in the registers after these population counts, on their accuracy and comparative advantages over contemporaneous European sources on Ottoman demography.[49] Census registers have mostly been valued as a source for Ottoman social history only to the extent that they help shed light on the structural composition of society, be it vocational, ethnic, or religious. In other words, the assumption that censuses reflect a social reality has remained current, and not much attention has been paid to the role that the census could potentially play in the construction of the reality that it purportedly represents. This is partly because of a general tendency in the field to take at face value the thesis that the nation-states that emerged out of the Ottoman Empire consisted of peoples previously caught in a time warp as *millets,* immobilized but otherwise untouched and pure until their "national awakening" in the nineteenth century. Another reason for this tendency is that the reification of collective identities through what seems like a routine statistical exercise of the bureaucracy is a concept more readily demonstrated in contemporary population counts, and it is only (relatively) recently that we have come to realize the significance of this phenomenon for identity construction.

---

49. See, for instance, Halil İnalcık's "Review of Kemal H. Karpat 'Ottoman Population: Demographic and Social Characteristics.'" *International Journal of Middle East Studies* 21, no. 3 (1989), 424.

The census is the ultimate tool used by the modern state to classify and enumerate, or simply to know, its population. In other words, the census brings meaning and order into what is an amorphous, indistinguishable mass, rendering it, in James Scott's words, "legible" to the state.[50] Conversely, the census is an opportunity for the people being counted to define themselves and make that definition count. The origin of the census, however, is not necessarily located in the tradition of liberal politics and citizenship rights. Many scholars have theorized on the emergence of census practices from the colonial versus subject viewpoint, and as a result much of the theoretical literature on the census tends to coalesce in two groups: studies of contemporary population counts and of colonial census practices in the past.

Bernard Cohn's classic work on British colonial administration in India and its classificatory practices inspired many scholars to further analyze these practices and their role in redefining caste differences as the principal reference for social differentiation and in the reification of collective identities and their subsequent relationship to one another.[51] Benedict Anderson, for instance, draws a distinction between earlier attributions of group identity and the practice, after the 1850s, of not only actively constructing these identities but enumerating them according to "a maze of grids which had no immediate financial and military purpose."[52] Arjun Appadurai, writing on British colonial practices in India, diagnoses a similar distinction for what he names the "colonial body count."[53] Anderson's and Appadurai's conclusions embody a general consensus in the scholarship that colonial population counts represented a clear break from earlier surveys, which were never concerned with the entire population, only with those who mattered for fiscal or military purposes. The preexistence of locally formulated identity categories did not mitigate this break because they did not inform the new taxonomies as much as the colonizers' imagination did. Moreover, the very introduction of those taxonomies and, more important, their quantification, undermined the relevance of preexisting norms.

David Kertzer and Dominique Arel underline the disjuncture between the categories imposed on a local population by colonial administrators and the locals' self-perceptions. In fact, they consider this to be the distinguishing mark of the colonial census: "the formulation of categories in the colonies was unilaterally done by the ruling officials, while European categories of cultural nationality and language were already being negotiated, to some extent, with social groups."[54] The distinction may seem too clear-cut;

---

50. James Scott, *Seeing like a State* (New Haven, 1998), 2–3.
51. Bernard Cohn, "The Census, Social Structure and Objectification in South Asia," in *An Anthropologist among the Historians and Other Essays*, 224–54 (Delhi and Oxford, 1987).
52. Anderson, *Imagined Communities*, 169.
53. Appadurai, "Number in the Colonial Imagination," 329.
54. David Kertzer and Dominique Arel, "Censuses, Identity Formation, and the Struggle for Political Power," in *Census and Identity*, edited by David Kertzer and Dominique Arel (Cambridge, 2002), 10.

Fear of Small Margins → 147

however, and it is not without its detractors. Norbert Peabody and Sumit Guha, among others, have critiqued this view of the colonial census as an isolated and pure exercise of colonial power and have documented different aspects of the negotiation that went on in colonial contexts, especially during earlier stages of census design, including the mediation of the locals or their attempts to make the population more intelligible to colonial administrators.[55]

The distinction expressed by Kertzer and Arel is still a point that needs consideration, however, not only because of its sheer importance as a widely held opinion but also because colonial census categories were increasingly designed with more attention to ethnographical data. The growing prestige of ethnography brought about an increasing reliance on "racial" categories (however defined by Western ethnographers) as opposed to the earlier principles that took into account, at least theoretically, preexisting markers such as religion.[56] After this point, the authority, determined by the "objective" rules of ethnography, was in the hands of colonial administrators, which significantly reduced the space for negotiation and more clearly separated the ruler from the ruled.

To what extent can we analyze the census experience of a dynastic empire that ceased to exist at the end of the First World War against the background of colonial population counts? It is tempting to argue that the Ottoman census of 1903 in Macedonia can be seen as an incident of (re)colonization, the imperial center taking stock of its subjects. After all, recent exceptions notwithstanding, the bulk of extant historiography on the "rise of nationalism in the Balkans views the Ottoman period as one of alien rule and a rupture, much like the rupture of colonialism, which makes parallels between the Ottoman and British census practices apropos. According to this view, the census was a population count carried out by alien bureaucrats according to criteria the population did not have much agency in generating—which was true to a certain extent, but due to reasons completely different than what the national-lineage histories would have us believe. Even more relevant is the recent turn in Ottoman historiography, especially of the Arab provinces, that reframes the administrative reforms of the nineteenth century as internal colonialism and their language as "Ottoman Orientalism." The principal theme that such works converge on is the *mission civilisatrice* implicit in the discourse of the Ottoman bureaucracy in their description of the "natives," and their role in bringing them into the civilized imperial fold.[57]

---

55. The literature on the role of colonial censuses in reifying the caste structure in India has generally accepted the assumption that this process was defined solely by colonial administrators and their (mis)perceptions of the system. For a literature review and critique of this approach, see Norbert Peabody, "Cents, Sense, Census: Human Inventories in Late Precolonial and Early Colonial India," *Comparative Studies in Society and History* 43 (2001): 819–50; Sumit Guha, "The Politics of Identity and Enumeration in India c. 1600–1990," *Comparative Studies in Society and History* 45 (2003): 148–67.

56. Anderson, *Imagined Communities*, 164.

57. Although I do not entirely agree with the premises and conclusions of this scholarship, especially with regard to the early period of reforms, I do find it to be an analytically richer

According to Selim Deringil, who makes the most convincing case for an Ottoman *mission civilisatrice,* the Ottoman elite's view of the imperial periphery as a "colonial setting" was, much like that of late imperial Russia, a "borrowed colonialism."[58] As accurate a term as *Ottoman colonialism* may be in describing a certain segment of the Ottoman elite's internalization of notions of a hierarchy of civilizations propagated by colonial powers to legitimize their continued exploitation of a large part of the world's physical and human resources, it still is one that needs to be qualified, not least because the epistemological foundations that supported the European colonial project were almost entirely absent in the Ottoman case. Moreover, the production of knowledge for governing peripheral and less-known areas and peoples differed widely in the Ottoman from the European colonial context, and even from imperial Russia. I think that a more proper rationale for drawing comparisons between colonial census categories and the Ottoman experience is not located so much in the source and nature of power but the impetus for quantification, which in both cases was ushered in by modernity—and by this I do not mean a modernity that was sourced from Europe by definition but a modernity defined by indigenous exigencies.

Common Hazards of the Census

On the evening of August 20, 1905, a shepherd was grazing his sheep on a hill outside Negorçe/Negortzi (Negorci), when he was approached by four men he did not recognize. The men, all of whom were armed, ran away after one of them handed the shepherd a letter written in Bulgarian addressed to the inhabitants of Negorçe. A day later, the police had reported the incident to the prefecture, which had the letter translated and sent to the General Inspectorate of Rumeli. The letter, written by a certain Vlad Vasil, apparently one of the local guerrilla leaders, read as follows:

> I greet you all. The census clerks who will be coming to your village will give you new identification cards (*nüfus tezkereleri*), and ask you which denomination you belong to. Tell them "we are not Rum, we are Bulgars" and that you are of Bulgar denomination because you speak Bulgarian. And don't be afraid of

---

framework for understanding the *Tanzimat* than the one provided by the tired modernization paradigm. See, for instance, Ussama Makdisi, "Ottoman Orientalism," *American Historical Review* 107, no. 3 (2002): 768–96; Ussama Makdisi, "Rethinking Ottoman Imperialism: Modernity, Violence, and the Cultural Logic of Ottoman Reform," in *Empire in the City: Arab Provincial Capitals in the Late Ottoman Empire*, edited by Jens Hanssen, Thomas Philippe and Stefan Weber (Wörzburg, 2002), 29–48; Jens Hanssen, *Fin de Siècle Beirut: The Making of an Ottoman Provincial Capital* (Oxford, 2005).

58. Selim Deringil, "They Live in a State of Nomadism and Savagery: The Late Ottoman Empire and the Post Colonial Debate," *Comparative Studies in Society and History* 45, no. 2 (2003): 318.

anyone. You will answer, "we want Bulgar identification cards."' Villagers, look, open up your beautiful eyes. Don't have yourselves registered Rum, because then no good will come to your children, your goods and your animals, you will [have to] go up the mountains. Until today we somehow forgave your mistakes, but you could lose your well-being. Know that it is thanks to me that you have stayed alive.... Don't imagine that you will stay in Negortzi, escape to Gevgili and be saved. There was a man like you in Cuma-i Bâlâ, a Rum, he escaped to America; we also have men over there; they killed him, keep that in mind.[59]

Although some of the subtleties may have been lost in the awkward translation into Turkish (and further into English), the message of the letter was clear enough: declare yourselves Bulgarians or die. The threat, a typical incident for the region at the time, also makes it clear that as far as the inhabitants of Macedonia were concerned this census was no ordinary population count. Establishing demographic supremacy—through whatever means necessary—had become part of the struggle for Macedonia, and the competition would have a horrible impact on the people claimed by both sides.

When the central administration dispatched census clerks to the Macedonian countryside in spring 1905, the struggle for Macedonia had already entered its most violent phase. Like its predecessor from 1881/1882–1893, the new census questionnaire was to register the population according to membership in a given religious denomination, such as Exarchist or Patriarchist (i.e., followers of the Exarchate or the Ecumenical Patriarchate). Unfortunately, this seemingly straightforward principle proved to be a recipe for disaster. In November 1905, the British consul in Salonika reported to his superior, "the Italian adjoint, Colonel Albera told me that it was his belief that the acuteness of the struggle between Greeks and Bulgarians was largely due to the senseless manner in which the census operations were being conducted. Nothing could have been more untimely than the attempt to revise the ethnological statistics of Macedonia during the present crisis, as both parties were anxious to establish the preponderance of their own element, and equally unscrupulous as to the means they employed to that end."[60] What the consul failed to explain was how the local population had come to understand the census as "ethnological statistics" and why the reaction was so strong. The violent propaganda tactics of the guerrilla bands were surely effective in this regard, but if the census itself was the trigger for the tensions, why had the earlier census not caused similar problems? The key issue here was the popularization of the idea that collective consciousness, once identified and quantified, could serve as the legitimizing principle for territorial claims. Given the active role the European Powers played in

---

59. BOA, TFR.I.SL, 81/8053, Prefecture of Gevgili to the Inspectorate, August 21, 1905.
60. PRO, FO 195/2208, Graves to O'Connor, November 18, 1905.

reaffirming this principle, it is difficult to understand the incredulousness of the consuls at the way the census polarized the population.

The point was not lost on Hüseyin Hilmi Pasha, who countered the criticisms by pointing out that the decision for a general census had been made long before the Mürzsteg Reform Program came into existence. The Reform Program carried a clause stipulating the reorganization of the region according to ethnic lines in the future, and according to Hilmi Pasha, it was this clause, and not the census itself, that had exacerbated the situation in the provinces. In a communiqué to the Grand Vezirate, he protested, "[the decision for a general census was made] during a time when the provision of the Mürzsteg Program that the region shall be reorganized according to ethnic lines in time of peace did not exit, and the bands formed with the encouragement and support of great powers and certain small states and especially the Bulgarian evil-doers did not attempt or dare to menace the population in order to force them to change their denomination [*mezheb*]."[61]

Hüseyin Hilmi Pasha was not alone in protesting the "third provision" of the Mürzsteg Program calling for the regularization of ethnic groups; the French consul also criticized it in a report to the embassy, where he dismissed it as an already abandoned plan. Whatever the relevance of the clause may have been, propaganda-related violence did escalate in the region in anticipation of the census. In the meantime, confusion concerning the "national affiliations" of the population continued to occupy all sides, including the representatives of European Powers, who could not decide which figures to believe and what terms to use, and the Ottoman administration, which could not fix a uniform census questionnaire. Although the operation was already in full swing, the British consul was not even aware of the categories in the census questionnaire. In the same letter where he complained about the inopportune timing of the census, he was also relieved to report that "the attempt to register the Christian population as Bulgarians, Greeks, Vlachs, Serbs, etc." had been "abandoned, and [that] orders [had been] issued to the Census Commissions to confine themselves for the present to the broad lines of Mussulman [*sic*], Christian and Jew."[62] Graves was clearly unaware that the category "Serb" had never been recognized as a separate entry and that other denominations, rather than the three general categories, were being reported.

While the census survey continued, the pressure exerted by propaganda groups was not the only grievance of the local population. Certain Ottoman officials, who viewed the third provision and the European presence in the region as the first steps toward annexation into a Greater Bulgaria, took it upon themselves to protect the interests of the Patriarchate. Complaints of abuses inflicted by Ottoman soldiers in Exarchist villages were frequently reported to Hüseyin Hilmi Pasha and to the military and civil representatives

---

61. BOA, TFR.I.A. 24/2387, June 3, 1905.
62. PRO, FO 195/2208, Graves to O'Connor, November 18, 1905.

of European Powers. One such letter of complaint, written by a certain Ivan Madjaroff to Colonel Vérand, the commander of the French gendarmerie stationed in Serres, reached the desk of the French chargé d'affairs in Istanbul. The letter suggested that abuses took place with the full awareness of high-ranking provincial officials. According to Madjaroff, one of the census commissions headed by a certain "Silamsiz Ali Pasha" was demonstrating "a lot of zeal" in registering the villages they were assigned as Rum. The commission had told villagers they would be chased out of their farms, and it threatened one of the communal leaders that his farm would be burnt down unless the village all registered as Rum. Costandine Tantcheff, who apparently was encouraging the villagers to take up Exarchist identity cards (*nüfus tezkeresi*), had been taken by gendarmes to the subgovernor of Serres, who "after expressing his dissatisfaction, told him: you know that Bulgarians are malicious people, and yet you teach the villagers to call themselves 'Bulgarians.'" Tantcheff was then informed that he would have to go live in another village if he insisted on calling himself a Bulgarian. The villagers, terrorized and threatened as they were, still refused to take up identity cards as *Rum,* defying the government decree at the cost of being deprived of these documents. The same Ali Pasha had also told the inhabitants of Kakaraska (Agia Eleni) that "the government assigns the *tezkere* it desires."

The letter continued to recount similar incidents, such as one that took place in the small village of Melnikich (Melenikitsi), where the inhabitants were told by the owner of the *çiftlik,* a "Greek by the name of Mikail Pasha," that people "who declared themselves Bulgarians would have to leave the village." On June 22, a different census commission went to Prosenik (Skotoussa) and started registering the population as Greek without asking their opinion. Ninety among the villagers refused to take their *tezkere*s in protest. The last case reported was Elsan (Karperi), which was visited by the same census commission on June 28. The commission, the letter claimed, "did everything to register all the villagers as Greeks, but could not do it except for four Vlach households, all the rest of the village refused to take the Greek *nüfus.*" The census commissions, he continued, always had a Greek member, but never a Bulgarian one, and they had soldiers assigned to their service, who beat up villagers if they refused to register as Greek.[63]

According to the allegations of another letter, submitted anonymously to an ambassador in Constantinople, some census commission members even resorted to outright torture. The letter reported an incident in Zihna (Palia Zichni), where every head of a family was summoned by Lieutenant (Mülâzım) Hüseyin Efendi, rounded up into a pigsty, and forced to "crawl on bare knees on stones for three hours."[64] Village notables were tortured further by soldiers who "sat on their heads and clubbed them." They were

---

63. MAE, Constantinople, vol. 147, Série E Macédoine, July 27, 1905.
64. The same report mentions that Mülazim Hüseyin had committed similar acts in Eğri Dere and Gorentzi.

then forced to take oaths that they would register as *Rum* because, they were told, they would "otherwise be killed." The next morning, the Mülâzım "brought them in front of the head of the census commission, where the unfortunates had the courage to declare 'given that the census is done by blows of sticks, we can register not only as Rums, but gypsies as well, if that will please the commission.'" The angry official reportedly registered them as neither.[65]

It is no coincidence that all the mentioned villages in these two reports were cited in the statistical tables of Mishev's pro-Bulgarian study, published in 1905, as "Hellenizing Bulgarian Patriarchist, where the important adjective, naturally, was "Bulgarian."[66] Mishev's figures should not be taken at face value, especially because he, among other things, could cite the same "Bulgarian" village twice and disregarded the Muslim population altogether—which was estimated to constitute at least half the population of Macedonia even by pro-Russian and pro-Greek sources, not to mention Ottoman population statistics.[67] The figures do, however, support the hypothesis that all these problem cases were locations inhabited mostly by Slavic-speaking followers of the Patriarchate, whose loyalties could go either way. Even though allegations about a systematic policy directed from the Imperial center aiming to register all Christians as *Rum* is impossible to document (and similar allegations were made by the Greek side as well), there is ample evidence that a significant number of Ottoman provincial administrators were at least in tacit collaboration with the Patriarchate to bring the unruly Christian subjects back into the grip of an established imperial institution.[68] In addition, there is enough extant evidence to suggest that Hüseyin Pasha had a pro-Patriarchist bias.[69] For instance, a communiqué sent by the Inspectorate to the prefecture of Vodine [Edessa] on September 28, 1904, reveals that months before the commencement of the census process, provincial administrators were called on to be on the defense against the "Bulgarian evil-doers," who, it was understood, "had the idea of bringing Bulgarians to the majority in the latest census."[70] Months later, an encrypted message from the Inspectorate to the Sublime Porte stated

---

65. MAE, Constantinople, vol. 147, Série E Macédoine, September 7, 1905.
66. Brancoff [Mishev], *La Macédoine et sa Population Chrétienne*, 198–201.
67. MAE. vol. 40, report "Population du Vilayet du Salonique," Salonika, March 1904.
68. After stating that Colonel Vérand would ask for the resignation of the mentioned Mülâzım who was harassing the villagers, the report continues, "but this resignation would serve nothing, since it is Constantinople where the orders to transform the Bulgars into Greeks by all means possible come from." MAE, vol. 147, Série E Macédoine, September 7, 1905.
69. It was a common notion among the French mission that Hüseyin Hilmi Pasha was partial to the Patriarchists and would do anything within his power to increase their numbers. On the other hand, the Greek Consulate was disturbed by what it perceived to be a "Bulgarian bias" among most of the French gendarmerie; MAE, Turquie, Gendarmerie Internationale, vol. 415, August 4, 1904.
70. BOA, TFR.I.SL 53/5221, September 28, 1904.

the necessity of minimizing the problems related to the census and urged explicitly that officials should prevent "the registry of the Christian population's majority that have long been members of the Patriarchate among Bulgarians."[71] It may be difficult to comprehend the Ottoman establishment support of the Patriarchate if we look through the lens of nationalist teleology, but at the time, this was a rational choice for both parties involved — the Patriarchate constituted "the lesser of two evils," and the Sublime Porte wished to reestablish the authority of an imperial institution. This attitude gradually started to change as the activities of "action-minded" priests in the Patriarchate drowned out the dissenting voices of their more moderate colleagues and as diverging tendencies within Greece and the Patriarchate coalesced and then clashed with their Young Turk counterparts in Macedonia.

The Greek side was far from content about the timing and implementation of the census. The Syllogue Macédonien of Athens, the semi-official advocate of the Greek cause in Macedonia, delivered a memorandum to the representatives of the Great Powers on June 26, 1905, about the "ethnographic census," protesting its rationale and the way it was being carried out. The memo alleged that the census was being taken in preparation for the implementation of the Mürzsteg Reform Program's third article. The picture that the Syllogue Macédonien informants drew was one that was in complete contrast with the reports and complaints already mentioned. According to them, far from forcing the population to refuse Bulgarian identity cards, the census agents, "often under occult influences," did quite the opposite. They "[distorted] the will of the local populations by all means to extort declarations from them contrary to the national faith they profess with conviction." It was not the Bulgarians who were undercounted by the census clerks, the Syllogue informants averred: "despite their formal declarations claiming the right to be registered in the lists of the Greek community, there were a good number of Macedonians [listed] among the Bulgarians and others." The resolution demanded by the Syllogue Macédonien was nothing less than a halt to the census process, which it recommended be postponed until "a more favorable time when the work conducted under conditions of tranquility, trust and individual liberty could result in the production of a picture faithful to the Macedonian populations and to the national sentiment that dominates in this or that part of the region within the reach of the project of reforms."[72] There is no reason to doubt the veracity of Hüseyin Hilmi Pa-

---

71. BOA, TFR.I.SL 24/2387, Inspectorate to the Sadâret and Başkitâbet, June 3, 1905. Another common complaint about the partiality of Ottoman officials was that they always visited villages accompanied by *Rums* but never Bulgars; MAE, Constantinople, vol. 147, Série E Macédoine, July 27, 1905.

72. MAE, Constantinople, Correspondance Générale, M. d'Ormesson, Ministère de France à Athènes to M. Rouvier, Prèsident du Conseil, June 30, 1905.

sha's statement that the decision to conduct a general census had nothing to do with the Mürzsteg Reform Program. The record confirms his statement, and the claim that the Ottomans were carrying out a census to confirm to an ill-defined clause of a Reform Program that they considered an affront to Ottoman sovereignty, and detested by all accounts, does not make much sense. Moreover, the parties fighting over the timing of the census were so focused on the demographic fight over Macedonia that they completely ignored that this exercise was meant to be a population count of the empire as a whole, including Macedonia, which, despite all efforts to the contrary, was still part of the Ottoman Empire. As the reforms continued, and the disappointment of the Greek side with the actions of the representatives of the European Powers in the region grew, so did their protests, not to mention the armed activity supported by the Hellenic Kingdom. The head of the French mission, Colonel Vérand, noted what was becoming more obvious in a report written on July 2, 1907: "They [Greeks] completely forget that Macedonia is TURKISH, they assume that Europe will treat Turkey as a negligible entity and will dispossess it for their advantage. The example of Crete gives them confirmation of this idea."[73] The Greek side was not the only one drawing lessons from Eastern Rumelia, the Bulgarian Principality, and Crete; the writing was clear for the other Balkan nation-states desperately trying to extend their boundaries. More important, Colonel Vérand's admonishment of the Greeks ignored the fact that it was European Powers, and not Greek politicians, that had been supporting the notion that Turkey in Europe was an anomaly that had outlived its historical relevance. Obviously there was not a chance that a demographic picture of the European provinces of the Ottoman Empire would make any of the interested parties happy, no matter how and when it was carried out, and the real burden of the census fell not on the protesting elites but on the people being counted.

Taking the Nation out of Denomination

Fights over who would be called what on the census register had begun before the census itself. It seems that the Ottoman administration had entertained the idea of dropping the denomination or *millet* question altogether in favor of proceeding with the three benignly general categories of Muslim, Jewish, and Christian.[74] This idea was abandoned after Hüseyin Hilmi Pasha pointed out that, because the military exemption tax (*bedel-i askeriye*) was paid separately by each *millet,* based on the total number of men eligible for military service, it could not be collected effectively under

---

73. MAE, Politique Intérieure, Turquie, Colonel Vérand's report, July 2, 1907.
74. PRO, FO 195/2208, Graves to O'Connor, November 18, 1905.

such a classification.⁷⁵ It is not clear, however, whether this was really the reason for the inspector's insistence on registering denominational affiliations. The 1881/1882–1893 census (henceforth, 1893 census) included denominational affiliations, but the principal register (*esas defter*) of 1893 contained only one entry for the Greek Orthodox population, which, although more specific than a general religious category such as "Christian," was not as specific as denominational affiliation. That distinction (for tax purposes) was made in separate registers called *Bulgar* and *Rum defterleri*, where the Greek Orthodox population was recorded as Exarchist or Patriarchist. It seems that in the 1903 census the desire of the central state to obtain an accurate count of its population, vertically ordered, and to preserve a common census policy across the empire, overrode concerns about the potential problems that might arise from this distinction in a politically volatile area. The government attempted a compromise solution whereby denominational affiliation would be recorded in the main census register but the identity cards handed to individuals would display only religious affiliation. But this too was ineffective in quelling attacks by propaganda groups, who knew all too well that it was the denominational aggregates that mattered in the end.⁷⁶

Perhaps more problematic were continuously confused administration efforts at "rectifying" terminology, which neither confirmed traditional markers of identity nor devised new ones that would comfortably accommodate the sensibilities of the population. After the official recognition of the Vlachs as a *millet* that would be acknowledged in the census register in 1905, the term *millet* no longer corresponded strictly to denominational affiliation. This raised questions about the naming of other ethnically differentiated members of the Ecumenical Patriarchate.⁷⁷ For instance, when some villagers petitioned the Inspectorate to be registered as belonging to the Serbian denomination *(Sırb mezhebi)*, the administrator of their subprefecture felt the need to elaborate, in his response to the Inspectorate inquiry, that "Serbness is not a denomination but a nationality (*Sırblık bir mezheb olmayub milliyet bulunduğuna*)." Therefore, he argued, any demands to change census records on this basis should be rejected.⁷⁸ *Milliyet* ("nationality")—confusingly, derived from the word *millet*—was an entirely

---

75. BOA, TFR.I.A 24/2392, June 10, 1905; Stanford J. Shaw, "The Nineteenth-Century Ottoman Tax Reforms and Revenue System," *International Journal of Middle East Studies* 6, no. 4 (1975), 456.
76. PRO, FO 195/2232, Monahan to O'Connor, January 5, 1906; Karpat, *Ottoman Population*, 162–63.
77. The Vlachs spoke a Romance language and constituted a separate sociolinguistic group but were followers of the Ecumenical Patriarchate. During this period, Romania emerged as their patron state, claiming kinship based on language and with an eye toward establishing a base in an area that would soon be partitioned among Balkan nation-states.
78. BOA, TFR.I.SL 80/7938, Doyran Prefecture to the Inspectorate, August 10, 1905.

new term, recognized but not completely understood by the Ottoman bureaucracy. Even though this particular administrator noted the distinction between *mezheb* and *milliyet* and recognized only the relevance of the former for census categories, there were many cases in which local officials were faced with even more perplexing choices, especially concerning the registry of people who identified themselves as Albanian, Serb, or Greek, categories that did not necessarily correspond to one specific denomination. Another concept, *cinsiyet* (which more or less corresponded to "race" in its nonbiological, turn-of-the-century meaning or to "national affiliation" in this context), was thrown into the mix to differentiate such people.[79]

This perpetually shifting terminology reflected the problems of a new order that was short of words to express the nuances of preexisting norms of social organization and local differences. The problem, it is important to note, should be attributed to a lack of expertise or fluency in the new categories of collective identity. It is true that the census clerks' apparent lack of training made worse an already dire situation. There is no reason to expect, however, that better training based on expert knowledge would have produced indisputable results. The issue was not that the criteria (or lack thereof) by which the state measured and classified the population or its faulty transmission to the people who implemented the census but, instead, that the very act of taking a census that would tie people into a single category of identification, which, uneducated as they were, the peasants understood to have important and tangible ramifications for their lives.

About a decade earlier, during the all-Russian census of 1897, the Russian officials had had a similar experience when trying to register and classify the population of the empire according to their "nationalities." Unlike the Ottoman Empire, the Russian Empire had more extensive resources, know-how, and, more important, newly colonized territories that should be rendered "legible" to the state. The Russian Imperial Geographical Society had a special Ethnography Division whose research directly informed how the subjects of the empire would be registered and classified.[80] Yet even the expert members of the division had no clear consensus on how *narodnost* or *nationalnost*, two terms for "nationality" that were used interchangeably at the time, would be established.[81] In the end, a compromise was found that considered "native language as the 'primary category' of *narodnost.*" Even though the census questionnaire did not include a direct question on nationality, the information gathered on religion and confessional affiliation was later used to compose a list of the *narodnosti* of the empire.[82] The

---

79. In modern Turkish, *millet* and *milliyet* still refer to concepts akin to their turn-of-the-century meanings, but *cinsiyet* has changed meaning to denote gender.
80. Francine Hirsch, *Empire of Nations: Ethnographic Knowledge and the Making of the Soviet Union* (Ithaca, 2005), 35–51.
81. Ibid., 39.
82. Ibid., 38.

implementation of this compromise, however, was quite uneven across the vast territories of the Russian Empire, and especially in regions where the questions of religion and language were considered politically sensitive, the "self-declaration" principle was largely ignored.[83] Moreover, nationality, in its conception as either *narodnost* or *nationalnost*, did not make much headway among the populations of the rural periphery of the Russian Empire. Even decades later, when the first all-union census of the Soviets was taken in 1924, despite the highly centralized and organized structure of the census and the number of analytical tools at the disposal of the census takers, local and religious identities in Europe and Asia, respectively, continued to be the dominant references for self-identification among the peasants.[84]

Nevertheless, imposing a certain degree of control on the chaos that prevailed over the census categories was an urgent necessity in the Macedonian countryside, and in the absence of a similar panel of experts on ethnography, the task fell to Inspector General Hüseyin Hilmi Pasha, who issued some general guidelines that would be followed in the registration of the Christian population. He first of all decreed that August 1903, that is, the date of the Ilinden Uprising, be legally instituted as a cut-off date for official recognition of conversions to and from the Patriarchate. Conversions after this date would be declared void to minimize the incentives the bands might have in coercing the population during the census. The census clerks were instructed to follow four general principles with regard to disputable cases:

- Those who were followers of the Exarchate or the Patriarchate before August 1903 should be registered according to their old church affiliation.
- Those who claim to be Rum or Serb now, even though they have been followers of the Exarchate for a long time, should be registered as "Orthodox, member of the Exarchate" until their nationalities (*cinsiyetleri*) are determined after the disturbances are over.
- Those Christians who have long been followers of the Patriarchate and who clearly will insist on having their nationalities as well as their denominations spelled out [*mezhebleriyle beraber cinsiyetlerinin dahi tasrihini mussirren iddia edecekleri derkâr olan*] such as Serbs, Vlachs, and Albanians who reside in *vilâyets* (provinces) of Monastir and Kosovo should be registered as "Serb, Vlach or Albanian, member of the Patriarchate."
- Those who are followers of the Patriarchate and claim to be Serb, Vlach, Albanian, and Bulgarian although their nationalities are disputable [*mes'ele-yi*

---

83. David W. Darrow, "Census as a Technology of Empire," *Ab Imperio* 4 (2002): 145–76.

84. It took another two decades of Soviet social engineering to consolidate those peasants into nations inhabiting geographically delimited territories. For a concise account see Francine Hirsch, "The Soviet Union as Work-in-Progress: Ethnographers and the Category Nationality in the 1926, 1937 and 1939 Censuses," *Slavic Review* 56 (1997): 251–78.

cinsiyetleri taht-ı itirâz ve ihtilâfda kalacaklar] should be registered, as in the second clause, "Orthodox, member of the Patriarchate."[85]

These guidelines did little in practice to solve the problems. In fact, they aggravated them by adding more variables and jargon to an already muddled system of classification. One of the direct effects was to increase the already high volume of correspondence generated by lower-level provincial officials, who sought the approval of their superiors regarding their decisions in situations that might constitute exceptions or failed to fit any category. It was only a couple of days after the Inspectorate had communicated these regulations to all the departments that the subgovernor of Serres asked for approval from the inspector general to register "Bulgarians who are attached to the Patriarchate as 'Bulgarian, member of the Patriarchate' (*Rum Patrikhanesine mensub Bulgar*)," given that "according to the general orders, Albanians, Bosnians etc. attached to the Greek Patriarchate will be registered as 'Albanian or Bosnian, member of the Greek Patriarchate.'"[86]

The subgovernor's inquiry is interesting for two reasons. First, it highlights the careful omission of the Inspectorate of the word *Bulgar* from the final registers in favor of the more ambiguous "Orthodox member of the Exarchate," reinforcing the perception that the Patriarchists enjoyed a privileged position vis-à-vis their Exarchist brethren, especially given that the subgovernor's request to acknowledge the *Bulgar cinsiyeti* (albeit with a qualifier) in the register seems not to have been granted. Second, it illustrates a common problem faced by local administrators in following regulations sent from the center. Their decisions, as in the case of the subgovernor of Serres, were often at odds with their superiors mostly because of the contradictory imperatives to take the initiative in settling a dispute and to ensure that the decision would comply with the vague guidelines of the central administration. Another example in this regard is the *kaymakam* (prefect) of Doyran (Kilkis and Nov Dojran), who did not find it appropriate to follow the entries in the 1893 register for three villages under his jurisdiction but still forwarded the matter to the Inspectorate, seeking approval for his course of action.[87] The first of the villages was Valandova (Valandovo), which consisted of twenty households that had been "claiming to be Bulgarians for the last five years," even though the 1893 register cited them as *Rum*. "In order to prevent the complaints and hardships that will probably emerge," the prefect found it appropriate to register them as Exarchists. The other two cases concerned Fourka (Furka) and Vladya (Akritas). Apparently, the residents of Fourka had somehow been registered in the *Bulgar*

---

85. BOA, TFR.I.A. 24/2387, June 3, 1905.
86. BOA, TFR.I.SL 74/7367, Siroz (Serres) Mutasarrıfı (Subgovernorate) to the Inspectorate, June 8, 1905.
87. BOA, TFR.I.SL 74/7301, Doyran Prefecture to the Inspectorate, 21 Mayıs 1321 [June 3, 1905].

defteri during the past census even though they had been attached to the Patriarchate for a long time, a mistake they had petitioned to have corrected on March 28, 1901. On August 30, 1904, they petitioned again, but this time to change their denomination to the Exarchate. They also demanded a Bulgarian teacher on the grounds that their children did not speak Greek. This final petition, however, was not accepted. The prefect expected that they would complain and try to be registered as "Bulgars" again, but his decision, pending approval, was to refuse their request because, he noted, they had been "Rum by origin and for generations." The case of Vladya, on the other hand, was the complete opposite. The residents of this village had been registered in the *Rum defteri,* but because a majority of them had been "Bulgarians for the last ten years and their church and school belonged to the Bulgarians" the prefect's counsel was to register them among "Bulgars" without regard to the old register.

The criterion used by the prefect to justify his decisions, namely that of "church and school belonging to one community and not the other," underscores another complication with the census process. In fact, the proprietorship of churches and schools was itself an often disputed issue among communities. Therefore the use of the church and school building by a community was subject to the same problems as the original question. In other words, the prefect's logic, however well-intentioned, confused the basis of the problem with its solution and did not address the fundamental problem of recording the villagers' "true identity," which, according to the Inspectorate, was to be found in the 1893 register—at least until further notice. The process seemed completely to exclude the wishes of the counted. It did not mean, however, they were incapable of finding ways to resist.

Resisting the Count

In 1903, the Ottoman government (re)issued a law requiring that a *nüfus tezkeresi* (personal identity card) be produced for the completion of any official transaction. This was one of the major instruments of the state for coaxing or coercing the peasants to participate in the count.[88] Identity cards were to be handed to every individual in conjunction with the census survey. The requirement was a novel concept in state surveillance but remained ineffective against a sizable segment of the population.[89] Even though the

---

88. Cem Behar, "Qui Compte? 'Recensement' et Statistiques Démographiques dans L'Empire Ottoman, du XVIe au XXe Siècle," *Histoire et Mesure* 13, no. 1–2 (1998), 142–43. This requirement was introduced with the 1881/82 count.

89. The *mürur tezkeresi* was another document that contained similar information, but it was required only for travel; in other words, it was an internal passport.

government was adamant about completing the census, many villagers slowed the process down by simply refusing to obtain their *tezkeres*.[90]

In Negovan (Xiloupoli), for instance, the peasants were called in for an interview by the authorities to settle the dispute about their denomination. They did not respond to the summons, however, and as a result no *tezkeres* were assigned. According to the correspondence between the prefecture of Langaza (Lagadas) and its administrative superior, the province of Salonika, the inhabitants of Negovan had converted twice: they were originally *Rum*, then they had converted to the Exarchate "under threats from the brigands," and finally they had converted back to the Patriarchate. According to the tax and census bureaus, they were still listed in the Bulgarian register, and the province demanded that this be corrected.[91] This order was evidently carried out, and the village was transferred to the *Rum* register. The issue, however, was not resolved here. The Exarchist archbishop of Salonika sent a petition requesting the transfer of their records back to the Bulgarian register. The general census administrator took the petition seriously enough to advise the census bureau of Langaza to carry out an inquiry. The commission was to inspect military tax-exemption records and find out whether the community had employed Bulgarian priests and teachers and so determine the "proper" denomination of Negovan residents.[92] The village notables, the community leader, and the priest had presumably been called in to settle this last issue, but they had not presented themselves even two weeks after they had been called in. As a result, the matter remained unresolved.[93]

It is not clear from the correspondence of the local Ottoman authorities why the village elders failed to attend the interview. The exchange, back and forth, of conflicting petitions suggests a certain hesitation among the inhabitants to register one way or the other. This incident is also remarkable in that it was the Exarchist archbishop of Salonika who requested a transfer of records, not the villagers themselves, as was the normal procedure. The villagers' unwillingness to come forth under these circumstances strongly implies that they had been threatened by one or both of the parties of propagandists in the area, who employed equally brutal methods to enforce their rules.

Another case that testifies to the kind of objections the peasants raised against the census process occurred in Kavaklı (Leukonas]) a village located right outside of Serres.[94] The inhabitants complained to the Inspectorate in

---

90. PRO, FO, Monahan to O'Connor, January 5, 1906; MAE, Constantinople, vol. 147, Série E, October 7, 1905, and July 27, 1905.
91. BOA, TFR.I.M 11/1088-1, Governor of Salonika to Prefecture February 22, 1906.
92. BOA, TFR.I.M. 11/1088-1, Nüfus Nâzırı to Langaza Nüfus Müdürlüğü, February 25, 1906.
93. BOA, TFR.I.M 11/1088-1, Governorship of Salonika to Prefecture, March 11, 1906.
94. The entire correspondence concerning this village is located in BOA, TFR.I.SL 74/7395.

a telegram dated May 31, 1905, that despite their objections they had been registered as Exarchists, and they returned their *tezkeres*. This telegram, coupled with the Greek Consul Lambros Koromilas's personal intervention, apparently precipitated a full investigation of the church and ethnic affiliation of the village, which, it seems, could not simply be determined by asking the villagers which church they attended. Even the telegram itself reveals why Kavaklı was a controversial case; most of the names signed at the end of the petition stating they had been "*Rum* since old times" and that would "remain so until eternity" were Slavic rather than Greek versions of popular Orthodox Christian names—Yovan Yorgi, Mitye Renya, Simyo Yuvan [*sic*].[95] It is also interesting to note that this village had been cited in two ethnographic maps published by Bulgarians in 1901 and 1905 as Exarchist and Patriarchist, respectively, whereas Mishev listed it as a "Hellenizing Bulgarian Patriarchist" village with a population of 328.[96] Kavaklı, it seems, preserved its "confessional ambiguity" even in the eyes of the propagandists.

It is instructive to recall the 1897 census experience in Russia as a comparison here. The nexus of the problems there, as in the Ottoman case, lay with the emerging notion that demographic superiority could be translated into political gain and with the dissemination of this notion among a population precisely through the statistical exercise that was designed to measure it. Naturally, regions with a highly "mixed" population, such as Macedonia and Galicia, were particularly prone to manipulation, if not violence, as population statistics turned into a political battleground. For both the Ottomans and the Russians, the question amounted to one of political legitimacy, albeit for slightly different reasons. The Ottomans were in a bind not because of the number of Muslims in the region, which, even by the accounts of propagandists, made up about half the total population. These lands had been part of the Ottoman Empire since medieval times. Nevertheless, the Ottomans were aware of the precariousness of their hold on sovereignty in a region where they were considered an anomaly not only by the neighboring Balkan states yearning to redeem their brethren along with the territories they inhabited but also by European statesmen, liberal and conservative alike, who viewed the sincerity of the Ottoman reforms with suspicion if not cynicism. The various political purposes the results of the census could serve, and the consequences of establishing one non-Muslim group as the dominant demographic element among the others were clear. The Russian anxieties, on the other hand, were more acute in areas whose Russian pedigree was questionable because they were relatively more recent additions to the imperial territories and where the number of Russians was not securely

---

95. BOA, TFR.I.SL 74/7395, Kavaklı residents to the Inspectorate, May 31, 1905.
96. *Cartes Ethnographiques des Vilayets Salonique, Cossovo, Monastir* (Sofia, 1901); *Carte des Ecoles Chrétiennes;* Brancoff [Mishev], *La Macédoine et sa Population Chrétienne,* 198.

high to serve as an indisputable basis for political legitimacy, such as acquisitions from the partition of Poland and Austrian Galicia.

Unlike their Ottoman counterparts, the Russian census clerks had been given clear instructions to fill out the census questionnaire based on "self-identification." In practice, however, these instructions were overridden by orders from provincial governors. The enumeration of the population of Galicia, with its large Uniate population, turned out to be particularly problematic. David W. Darrow notes that "petitions from Uniate families and—in most cases—from entire villages" poured in, asking to be registered as Uniate; "to emphasize that their complaint was not based on any fickleness of faith connected to the census, many villages emphasized the fact that they had been practicing Roman Catholics for nearly thirty years," not unlike their counterparts in Ottoman Macedonia who had produced records to prove the longevity, and hence the sincerity, of their sectarian affiliation. In the Russian case, that the petitions supposedly coming from "Russian" peasants were written "in Polish" did not help their case, and the category "Uniate" simply disappeared from the final tally of the census, even though it was present in the "initial drafts of proposed tables on the population's religious composition."[97]

Only a few years before Uniate peasants were trying to convince the Russian census authorities not to register them as "Orthodox," another government official in the Ottoman Empire had registered the inhabitants of the village of Kavaklı (mentioned previously) as "Exarchist," not because they had declared themselves so but because—at least according to the local governor—they had been heard speaking Bulgarian.[98] As it turns out, Kavaklı residents had never petitioned to join the Exarchate between 1893 and 1905; instead, the census commission had simply copied the previous register of 1893, repeating the mistake of the earlier commission. The governor had an all-too-bureaucratic explanation for why the registry could not be amended: "[in 1893] according to the orders of the Ministry of the Interior, part of them [Kavaklı residents] had been given Bulgarian, and later 'Christian and Orthodox' *tezkeres*. Besides, since the principle register does not contain *millet* affiliation, and the inhabitants obviously spoke in Bulgarian, they were written down in the register called *Bulgar sicili*, [and later] they were registered as *Bulgars* in compliance with the order that former records would not be changed."[99]

There is no doubt that the inhabitants of Kavaklı were Slavic-speaking. Even Greek Consul Koromilas, in his letter to Hüseyin Hilmi Pasha, did not dispute this. What he disputed was whether the language spoken could be considered enough indication of the ethnic affiliation of a village. Obviously

---

97. Darrow, "Census as a Technology of Empire," 168–70.
98. BOA, TFR.I.SL 74/7395, Governorship of Salonika to the Inspectorate, June 1, 1905.
99. BOA, TFR.I.SL 74/7395, Governorship of Salonika to the Inspectorate, June 3, 1905.

the consul's sentiments were not based on an attachment to the liberal principle of self-determination. In fact, Koromilas would hardly have advocated the distribution of *tezkeres* based solely on the choices of peasants in Macedonia. His point of view was encapsulated in his words: "As for the language spoken [in the village], I am amazed that the commission has the right to state it without the inhabitants' consent. I admit that this census is complicated since we must *not* conform to the statements of the inhabitants except up to a certain extent."[100]

We can draw a number of conclusions from the case of Kavaklı. First of all, it demonstrates once again the ambivalence that those in the region possessed toward ethnic affiliation, not only the villagers themselves but also the Ottoman local administrators and the Greek consul. Second, as the consul's words revealed, the people's own perceptions of their identity, even when explicitly stated, were often considered irrelevant. This was not specific to Kavaklı, or even to Ottoman Macedonia, because state officials and bureaucrats had a bias against rural populations, inhabitants of regions deemed "backward," or with lifestyles that did not conform to the rules of civilized society. Undercounting and top-down reporting should be attributed to this bias. In the case of Kavaklı, the consul and the local administrators, even though they were well aware of the dubious definitions in the census questionnaire, were less interested in questioning the usefulness, under such conditions, of such a census than they were in neutralizing those very same conditions to obtain what they considered to be the "appropriate" results. The governor, in seeking the inspector general's approval, argued that the principle of preserving the old records had to be applied consistently to all cases for the sake of preventing other villagers from demanding changes in the census records for similar reasons—and therefore Kavaklı residents should tolerate *Bulgar tezkeres* for the time being, even if they were justified in their claims.[101] Hüseyin Hilmi Pasha, in contrast, advised that the village be registered as "Patriarchist" despite apparent concerns about "inconsistency."

Finally, it is revealing that the peasants, who had apparently been paying their military tax as Exarchists, had not objected to their status until 1905, when they were to receive their new *tezkeres*. This could be either because they were not aware of the previous situation or, if they were, because they did not care to object. Both possibilities underscore the sheer novelty of the issue for the party it affected most. And, finally, the fact that the Kavaklı inhabitants—who claimed that they were *Rum* and would "remain so for eternity"—actually conversed with one another in a Slavic idiom demonstrates the complexity and resilience of traditional and, in this case, religious loyalties.

---

100. BOA, TFR.I.SL 74/7395, Greek Consul General Koromilas to Inspector General Hilmi Pasha, June 1, 1905. (Emphasis added.)

101. BOA, TFR.I.SL 74/7395, Governorship of Salonika to the Inspectorate, June 4, 1905.

Counting from the Bottom Up

In October 1905, census authorities dispatched an inquiry commission to the small village of Zervi (Zervi), to establish under which denomination the villagers should be registered. They suspected that the residents of Zervi were Exarchists even though they were registered as Patriarchists in the 1893 register. When the commission members reached their destination and started to question the villagers, the response they received was not what they expected. "We are neither Rum nor Bulgarian," insisted the villagers, "we are Christians."[102] The term *Rum,* which had denoted a religious affiliation in the past, namely (Greek) Orthodox Christian, no longer meant the same thing. Nevertheless, some obviously still held on to that religious identity.

The response of the peasants of Zervi to the Ottoman census commission should not come as a surprise. When modernizing states came into contact with rural communities and attempted to integrate them into new sociopolitical structures, they often found out that these communities did not give up their long-established references for social differentiation on demand. Religious identity was one of the strongest such anchors. To say that peasants had a propensity to identify as members of a religious group is not to privilege religion as a "pure" marker of identity as opposed to an "alien ethnic grid" imposed on the population. We must keep in mind that religion was also used to inform the "racial" enumeration categories and, more important, that religion itself was a marker produced socially and deployed in dynamic forms. Nor am I suggesting that peasant communities inhabited a magically peaceful world of undifferentiated and coherent units before they were nationalized. Just as caste was "not a figment of the British political imagination," religious and linguistic differences in Macedonia were not invented by the Ottoman administration or the European patron states.[103] But their politicization was. To see the ways in which those differences were socially articulated before and after the onset of the process of nationalization, we first need to divest that process of its assumed teleology. From this perspective, it is useful to remember that the two conflicting communities described here had, until recently, been living side by side, baptizing their children in the same churches, sending their children to the same schools, and burying their dead in the same cemeteries. Even the church schism did not erase these practices overnight; the two denominations often took turns using a

---

102. BOA, TFR.I.SL 87/8623, Vodine Prefecture to the Inspectorate, October 26, 1905.
103. Appadurai, "Number in the Colonial Imagination," 319. It is also important to remember how British experts on race and caste, such as H. H. Risley, the commissioner for the 1891 census, and the director of ethnography for India, relied on "Brahmanical measures, and opinions, concerning caste rank." Nicholas Dirks, *Castes of Mind: Colonialism and the Making of Modern India* (Princeton, 2001), 213.

church building or held mass together.[104] Boundaries and divisions occupied a much smaller place in the collective memory of these communities until normalization and enumeration linked those same divisions with the politics of representation. In other words, the sectarian division within the Orthodox Church, which had been a very narrowly defined difference, was transformed into a general principle on which the society was divided and represented—not just locally but in the eyes of an international audience.

The unyielding, rigid classificatory practices of the modern state, such as the census, were a galvanizing force in creating national identity in the imperial and colonial contexts I have mentioned here (and ironically facilitated their own destruction). Nevertheless, there are limits to the parallels we can draw between these contexts. The most obvious limit is that many of the peculiarities of the colonial census can be gleaned not from what it counted in the colonies but from how that count contrasted with its metropolitan counterpart. One important feature that distinguishes the dynastic empires in this regard is the singular relationship the state had already established and kept in place with its subjects through its bureaucracy. Even though there were variations in local practices, these were not of the same nature as those that separated colonial and metropolitan administration principles. The distance that separated the census clerk from the people he was counting was much smaller than the distance between the British surveyors and the colonial subjects they were classifying and counting.

When we look at the implementation of the 1903 census, for instance, we clearly see that the census takers did not start with a *tabula rasa* on which they sketched a system of classification that they had conjured up based on an ethnographic study of local customs. Instead, they had to work within an organic system that preceded the modern notions and categories of collective identity—a "system" that included gendarmes torturing villagers to make them accept their identity cards, local administrators relentlessly reporting protests to their superiors (some of whom did not know if "Serb" was a religious or national category), and peasants who kept insisting that they were simply Christians. The census takers, as unwelcome and alien as they may have been in the villages they visited, represented an authority with which the population was accustomed to communicating. This culture of negotiation was especially significant because it allowed the voices of the peasants to be heard. Their position was expressed through protests, petitions, and, failing that, outright refusal to participate, suggesting that the census was not simply an operation executed in a top-down manner and that the population itself significantly affected the way it was implemented.

Another element that distinguishes the Ottoman census of 1903 from colonial body counts, as well as from previous methods of enumeration, was

---

104. BOA, TFR.I.SL 67/6606. See also Brailsford, *Macedonia, Its Races and Their Future,* 72.

the tension generated by the inherent contradiction between a new practice, which presumably relied on information at the level of the individual, and the preexisting relationship between the peasants and the state, which defined the peasants solely in terms of their communities. Even though the peasants were given individual identity cards, the choices they made in accepting those cards were not individual ones. It is remarkable that most petitions were signed by representatives of an entire village and processed by the administration under the name of the village, not of the individuals. We should also recall that disputes concerning allegiance to the Patriarchate and the Exarchate required lengthy investigations into the community church attendance by the census commission instead of a simple question addressed to the individuals during the census. The inhabitants' own statements were not to be taken at face value, and this was a point on which the Greek consul and Ottoman administrators agreed, albeit for different reasons.

Beshara Doumani's analysis of a population count in Nablus in the mid-nineteenth century helps us see the census functioning as a domain staked out between the center and the periphery. The negotiations that went on between the state and the local notables in Palestine may seem reminiscent of the negotiations we saw in early-twentieth-century Macedonia, but in fact there was a significant difference, which Doumani hints at in his final remark: "By the end of that [nineteenth] century all individuals regardless of sex and age would become the basic unit of counting, further facilitating the integration of the local population into new administrative, cultural, and legal categories aimed at undermining local affiliation and creating loyal Ottoman 'citizens.'"[105] The difference, in other words, concerned the politics of counting, which was no longer concentrated within an elite domain but diffused across a much wider segment of society.

The degree of the success of the state in carrying out its ideological objective of creating "loyal Ottoman citizens" through modern population counts is another matter. According to Cem Behar, the vocabulary of the last two censuses of the Ottoman Empire went even further than erasing local affiliations; it sought to substitute national identity with an Ottoman one.[106] The way in which the classificatory logic of the census was imposed on the population in Macedonia suggests that there was indeed a concern with placing people in categories designated by the state, but the same agenda, as we have seen, did not always trickle down to the lower echelons of provincial administration. In any case, under the circumstances that prevailed in Macedonia—and in other regions of the empire—the executors of the 1903 census had neither the means nor the will to inject a sense of "Ottomanness"

---

105. Beshara Doumani, "The Political Economy of Population Counts in Ottoman Palestine: Nablus, circa 1850,"*International Journal of Middle East Studies* 26, no. 1 (1994), 14.
106. Behar, "Qui Compte?" 143.

in the society. On the contrary, it was more effective in the "minoritization" of the confessional categories in the empire than in their Ottomanization.[107]

It is obvious that, when there are political incentives involved, a census can never be a purely statistical exercise. A less obvious fact, but equally important, is that no census is without a political motive. But the assumption remains that it is possible to separate those incentives from the census process by introducing categories that can be "objectively" determined—and this assumption was a widely accepted principle among European ethnographers and geographers at the turn of the twentieth century. In practice, however, these "objective" categories engendered a different set of problems. Take, for instance, the censuses of the Habsburg Empire between 1880 and 1910, whose scientific sophistication and efficient implementation, unlike the condemned efforts of the Ottoman Empire, were not disputed by any self-respecting statistician in Europe. Because of a question concerning language, nationality became an issue in the census questionnaire of the Habsburg Empire.[108] Language was understood simply as the medium of daily communication in the Austrian half of the empire, whereas the Hungarian half defined it as "mother tongue," apparently with no clear consensus on what "mother tongue" meant, and, despite officials' vehement assertions to the contrary, inextricably linked the language question with nationality, at least in the minds of the national elites.[109] Any bilingual person can testify that language is an ideologically charged subject, and there were thousands of bilingual people in the Habsburg Empire.[110] The Austrian census commission did not consider bilingualism as an available option, despite the fact that including it might have resolved a good deal of controversy over the question. This is not surprising, given that not more than one language, one religion, or any other marker—however defined—can be associated with an individual if a register is to serve the classificatory purpose it is designed for: the translation of complex social relations into raw data that can be organized in columns and aggregates. In other words, fluidity of and overlap in social identity have no place in census registers (nor in maps based on those registers, as we have seen, which complete the job of "flattening" and "enclosing"), despite the testimonials of resistance to rigid classification such as were buried among the lengthy notes and explanations scribbled on the margins of endless bureaucratic exchanges.

---

107. I use the term *minoritization* here to underline the contradiction and tension inherent in the state's modernizing efforts to classify the population. An action that is presumably meant to assimilate a group essentially creates a minority out of a confessional community by objectivizing the membership and compounding the sense of distinctiveness and subjugation.

108. It must be noted that Adolf Ficker, who was in charge of the surveys, did not agree that nationality could be equated with language alone, or even that it had a place in the census questionnaire at all; Zeman, "Four Austrian Censuses," 31.

109. King, *Budweisers into Chechs and Germans*.

110. Pieter Judson, *Guardians of the Nation: Activists on the Language Frontiers of Imperial Austria* (Cambridge, 2006).

Kertzer and Arel emphasize an extremely important function of the census, namely, that it "does much more than simply reflect social reality; rather, it plays a key role in the construction of that reality."[111] In the examples cited in this chapter, it is easy to see that a one-to-one correspondence between census categories and the social reality of the groups they purportedly represented is difficult to achieve. What is not equally self-evident, and what Kertzer and Arel mean when they speak of the "construction of that reality," is that the introduction of those categories is a mechanism through which are created the social groups and their collective identities that fill in those columns. Their social reality does not precede the entries in the census registry. To the contrary, those very categories name, and thereby bring into existence, what we perceive as social reality; the two mutually shape and reinforce one another. We must note, however, that the experience of the Ottoman census of 1903 in Macedonia demonstrates that this mechanism worked through more than the power of naming. The census, by deepening and reifying vertical divisions within the population, contributed to a general consciousness of being one thing and not the other, and the violence that accompanied that consciousness turned a piece of paper—the identity card—into the difference between life and death.

---

111. Kertzer and Arel, "Censuses, Identity Formation," 2.

CHAPTER FIVE

A Leap of Faith: Disputes over Sacred Space

The stupidest peasant sighed for a life of quiet and the departure of the Turks. But the means, the courage, the instinct of mutual help had first to be trained. The leaders had to inspire the peasants with the same courage and faith which the schools of the Exarchate had already created in the minds of the educated class. They had to weld the isolated Macedonian villages, which regard the district beyond their own valley as a foreign land, into a conscious nation.
—Henry N. Brailsford, *Macedonia, Its Races and Their Future*, 1906

Until recently, the historiography of the Balkans viewed the relationship between religion and nationalism as straightforward and even self-evident, and mostly treated it as such. The *millet* system and the endurance of the Orthodox Church were seen as the saving grace of Balkan nations, which kept them "free for their national awakening, in which Orthodox affiliations, linked up with the medieval background, played a very conspicuous part."[1] Likewise, textbook explanations attributed the emergence of the national churches in the nineteenth century simply to the resuscitation of their forbears, which "were historically national churches and symbols of a nation's sovereignty."[2] Although there was certainly a connection between the forging of national identities and religion, this connection was historically determined as the result of a process too complicated to be reduced merely to an equation of church membership or declared church affiliation with national identity.[3] More

---

1. George Arnakis, "The Role of Religion in the Development of Balkan Nationalism," in *The Balkans in Transition,* edited by Charles Jelavich and Barbara Jelavich (Berkeley, 1963), 133. See also Nikolaos J. Pantazopoulos, *Church and Law in the Balkan Peninsula during the Ottoman Rule* (Thessaloniki, 1967); Zina Markova, "Bulgarian Exarchate 1870–1879," *Bulgarian Historical Review* 16, no. 4 (1988):, 39–55.
2. Peter F. Sugar, *Nationalism and Religion in the Balkans since the 19th Century* (Seattle, 1996), 9. See also, Peter F. Sugar, "External and Domestic Roots of Eastern European Nationalism," in *Nationalism in Eastern Europe,* edited by Peter F. Sugar and Ivo J. Lederer (Seattle, 1969), 28–33.
3. Paschalis Kitromilides asserts that "religion came last in the struggle to forge new national identities and did not become a functional element in national definition until the nation-states had nationalized their churches." Kitromilides, "'Imagined Communities,'" 59.

169

recent interpretations of this link have cautioned against accepting a binary opposition between "religious and secular values" and call particular attention to the cross-hybridization of religious and post-Enlightenment secular notions of collective belonging.[4] In this chapter, I look at the link between religion as a marker of national identity and an enabler of nationhood from a different perspective, which suggests that the most important element that consolidated this connection in popular conception, specifically among the rural populations, was the politicization of religion and religious identity after they became inextricably linked with violence.

In the previous chapter, we saw that religion still played a major role as a reference for people's conceptions of collective identity and that, for many of them, this was something that differentiated them not from other Orthodox Christians in their vicinity but from Muslims. When H. N. Brailsford took a few local boys from a village near Ohrid to the "ruins of the Bulgarian Tsar's castle," the boys, proving right every prejudice the journalist entertained about them, failed to give the correct answer to the question, "Who built this castle?" Despite repeated prodding and hints by Brailsford, including the words "Serbs, Bulgarians, Greeks," the boys' final answer was: "They weren't Turks, they were Christians."[5] Brailsford, not quite as frustrated as the Ottoman census clerk who had to register people who insisted on being "Christian" as one of the official categories, nevertheless attributed the boys' (and, more generally, the Bulgarians') lack of historical and national consciousness to the fact that "[t]heir ecclesiastical autonomy was more completely suppressed" than that of the Greeks.[6] In other words, Brailsford saw national identity (as some still do) as a concept that simply could lay dormant for centuries, safely entombed within different church traditions, only to be woken up when the time was right. Religion, therefore, was important, but only insofar as it preserved the core identity of a nation, not in and of itself.

It is interesting to contrast this view of religion as an incubator (and religious difference as derivative of national difference), which follows logically from primordialist understandings of national identity, with that of Benedict Anderson, who sees religion as "the basis of very old, very stable imagined communities not in the least aligned with the secular [colonial] state's authoritarian grid-map." The stabilizing influence of religion on local communities could not easily be dismissed by colonial authorities, who in the end had to contend with it through regulation and subordination, rather

---

In contrast, Skopetea attributes a stronger role to religion in the creation of Greek nationhood in post-revolutionary Greece; Ellē Skopetea, *To "Protypo Vaseileio" kai ē Megalē Idea, Opseis tou ethnikou provlēmatos stēn Ellada, 1830–1880* (Athens, 1988), 119–34.

4. Gazi, "Revisiting Religion and Nationalism," 95–106.
5. Brailsford, *Macedonia, Its Races and Their Future*, 99.
6. According to Brailsford, even the Serbs were luckier in this respect for various reasons, but "[Bulgarians] were within easy striking distance of the capital." Ibid., 99–100.

than complete eradication. Sacred spaces such as temples, mosques, and schools fell outside the topographic order of the colonial state, an anomaly that facilitated the transformation of these spaces into "zones of freedom and—in time—fortresses from which religious, later nationalist, anticolonials could go forth to battle."[7] That religion was easily transformed into a basis for anticolonial liberation struggles because of the spatial and spiritual autonomy it provided to the colonized is a hypothesis that seems to stand in close conceptual proximity to primordialist accounts of the role of the Orthodox Church as the vault where the core of national identity was kept and, later, as a base from which the fight for national independence was launched. By contrasting the categories introduced and imposed by the colonial rulers with an already existing and "stable" marker of identity, namely, religion, Anderson accords religion a privileged position in the resistance against colonial regimes.

Sumit Guha has justifiably criticized Anderson's stance with regard to the role of religion as an innately suitable anchor for anticolonial struggles. Most significantly, Guha contends that "Anderson does not consider *how religious identities were socially reproduced and propagated*—as they must have been to survive"[8] Before throwing out the baby with the bathwater, however, we must take note of the conclusion to Anderson's argument, which is that the resilience of religious markers compelled "frequent endeavours to force a better alignment of census with religious communities by—so far as possible—politically and juridically *ethnicizing* the latter."[9] More than the myriad possible premodern, precolonial, and prenational identity markers generated by a complex web of social and political networks that, according to Guha, were neglected by Anderson in favor of religion, the key notion that is relevant here is the "ethnicizing" of religious identity—a process that is not derivative of preexisting categories of collective identity but, rather, imbues those preexisting categories with new meaning. This process also explains the dramatic changes with respect to the meaning of religious difference in Ottoman Macedonia at the turn of the twentieth century.

Singling out religion as the primary marker of collective identity is not to replace one form of primordialism with another. Nor do I privilege religious identity as the authentic collective identity of the Balkan peasant that existed from time immemorial as opposed to an alien social construct. It is clear that religion is a highly contested territory, no matter the context, and as Guha notes, religious identity itself is "socially reproduced and propagated." These specific social processes, however, were part of how and why religion and nationality came to define one another in Macedonia—in other words, how Orthodoxy became ethnicized. The ethnicization of Orthodoxy

---

7. Anderson, *Imagined Communities*, 169–70.
8. Guha, "Politics of Identity," 149.
9. Anderson, *Imagined Communities*, 170. (Emphasis added.)

was a process that involved the transformation of preexisting social value systems into a depository of national consciousness and, more important, a reference for immutable differences. For the purposes of the national elites, "who had to weld the isolated Macedonian villages ... into a conscious nation," church affiliation served as a readily available blueprint for their ambitious project.[10] The religiously observant peasant masses, who regarded religion as the center of their social as well as spiritual worlds, would be drafted into this same project of nation-building through the gate of church affiliation. The readily available and universally accepted principle of religious observance required yet another element to be ultimately enforceable, namely coercion, whose means became increasingly violent as the project grew more contested. Ultimately, it was not merely the introduction of an alternative church and its rivalry with the preexisting one that molded and fixed the national identities of Christian Macedonian peasants but the *violence* that accompanied it. Ideology did not induce a mass mobilization of the peasantry until it was activated through violence.

In this chapter, I question the presumed causal link between religious difference and conflict by tracing the experience of the Exarchist-Patriarchist schism "on the ground." Taking a closer look at how the Exarchists and Patriarchists came to be two separate and antagonistic communities shows that the link is more complicated than the clear formula of "one church, one language, one nation." First, religious differences did not necessarily correspond to linguistic ones, and second, they were not the result of the need to reconcile national consciousness with religion. Finally, these two communities had been entirely capable of working out their differences, if grudgingly, without resorting to violence, prior to the activities of insurgent bands in the region.

Religion was important in forging national identities because it superseded any ideological alternatives in terms of its potential for unifying or dividing the rural Christian population. Yet its role was not one of logically following a preceding national division. Religion as dogma was not nearly as important as the daily practice of religion in this context. The symbolic nature of many of the conflicts centering around sacred spaces and the clergy was not simply coincidence but a deliberate motion aimed at exploiting the rules, customs, and practices through which people made sense of this world and the next. Acts such as defrocking a priest, confiscation of liturgical books, denial of sacraments, and the theft of a ceremonial robe were important not in and of themselves but because they struck a chord by directly usurping the system of symbols that the peasants had been using as a bridge between spirituality and everyday existence. Targeting a church during mass was not a random act of violence but one designed for maximum impact, spiritually

---

10. Brailsford, *Macedonia, Its Races and Their Future,* 116.

A Leap of Faith: Disputes over Sacred Space → 173

and physically, and for replacing communal coexistence with communal boundaries, enforced by guns if necessary.

Religion and Religious Authority

In the eyes of western Europeans, Catholic or Protestant, clergy or lay, Christians of the Eastern rite, although deserving the support and sympathy of their co-religionists, practiced a strange, if not pagan, version of Christianity that bore little resemblance to the faith practiced in more civilized parts of the world, save for the cross that symbolized it. Members of the Orthodox clergy were viewed with suspicion and amusement, attached as they were to their bizarre rituals bordering on the occult, performed in languages they themselves were not able to understand, let alone convey the message to their flock.

Ruggiero Giuseppe Boscovich, a Jesuit priest accompanying the party of James Porter, the English ambassador to the Sublime Porte, on his return journey in 1762, was an early observer of Orthodox priests' woeful ignorance.[11] Thanks to his Slavic roots, he was able to communicate with a (presumably) Bulgarian priest whom the party met on their journey, in a village (most likely) in Thrace. The impressions he gathered from this exchange of the young, married priest were quite unflattering: "His ignorance, and that of all these poor people, is incredible. They do not know anything of their religion except for the fasts and holidays, the sign of the cross, the cult of some image, of which one encounters now and then among them some quite horrid and ugly ones, and the name of a Christian. To the extent that I could discover that evening, speaking my language, and also having inquiries made in Turkish, which is commonly understood among them, they know neither the Pater Noster, nor the Credo, nor the essential mysteries of the religion."[12]

More than a century later, H. N. Brailsford (a Methodist) was equally condescending, if slightly more sympathetic, to the village priests:

> To go for ethical guidance to the average village priest would indeed be too ridiculous. The married priests outside the larger towns are for the most part almost totally uneducated, and lead the life of peasants. ... They can read enough to mumble through the ritual, and write sufficiently well to keep the parish

---

11. Boscovich was born in Ragusa in 1711. In addition to being a Jesuit a priest, he was also "a Copernican astronomer and Newtonian physicist of international reputation, and furthermore an eminent scientific geographer." He had a Serbian father and Italian mother, but his education and early socialization were decidedly Italian; Wolff, *Inventing Eastern Europe*, 172.

12. Ruggiero Guiseppe Boscovich, *Giornale di un Viaggio da Constantinopoli in Polonia dell'abate Ruggiero Guiseppe Boscovich* (Milan, 1966), 35, quoted in ibid., 175.

registers; but there the superiority to the peasant ends. Preaching is practically unknown. Their function is not that of the pastor or the teacher. They are simply petty officials who perform the rites appropriate to the crossing of the frontier between this world and the next.[13]

Unlike Boscovich, Brailsford placed the blame for the deplorable state of the priests and higher clergy primarily on "Turkish rule" that "crushed every form of intellectual life" and partly on the church hierarchy itself. "There is no heresy in the Eastern Church," he wrote, "because there is no real interest in religion."[14] Even though a few Greek bishops had benefitted from education in Oxford and Leipzig, the "incorrigibly Byzantine habits of thought" rendered this exposure useless and their ignorance more offensive. Many members of the Bulgarian clergy had been trained in seminaries in Russia, where "modern and Western ideas [were] very jealously excluded."[15] Given the sad state of affairs with regard to the clergy, it was no wonder that their flock fared even worse in the recollections of Europeans with regard to their religiosity. Travelers noted, usually with surprise and often with condescension, how time was anchored to the procession of what seemed to be an infinite number of saints' days; how people seemed to fast for almost the entire year; and worse, how the observance of so many religious holidays bred "laziness."[16]

Needless to say, pious observance of religious rules among the peasantry was not unique to the Christian Orthodox of the Ottoman Empire. It was the norm in such communities all over Europe. Rather than a pure matter of conscience, religion was a set of guidelines and rituals according to which the rhythm of daily life was set. The rites and rituals not only fulfilled indispensable social functions but also evolved with them. Certain practices, such as fasting, were as much the result of exigency as of piety. If the descriptions in the travel literature reflect the actual situation with any degree of certitude, the diet of Ottoman peasants in Rumeli was comparable to that of other rural populations in eastern and most of western Europe, which meant that animal products were considered a luxury and reserved for festive occasions. Saints' days ensured temporal continuity, marked the changing of seasons, and normalized time—it was no coincidence, for instance, that the Ilinden Uprising took place on the day that it did—not simply August 2, but the day of Saint Elijah.

Brailsford predicted that the theocratic hold of the church over the peasantry would be lifted along with the disappearance of Turkish authority. He obviously viewed the insurgency in Macedonia as a western-leaning, if

---

13. Brailsford, *Macedonia, Its Races and Their Future*, 69.
14. Ibid., 66.
15. Ibid., 62–65.
16. See, for instance, Baker, *Turkey in Europe*, 102.

not entirely secular, movement. The armed revolutionaries were pioneers of democratic freedom in a land of religious tyranny of both the Muslim and the Christian sort. "Already the Bulgarian Committee [IMRO] represents a movement of democratic revolt against these princes of the Church," he noted, disregarding the fact that the Church was instrumental in propagating a distinct Bulgarian national consciousness among the youths who were educated at its schools—a point he himself made later in the same book.[17] More important, the "democratic" revolutionaries relied heavily on the Church for several of their logistical and other organizational needs, not to mention that the Church itself was directly involved in the revolutionary movement through its radicalized priests and schoolteachers. It is true that the relationship between the higher ranks of the Exarchate in Constantinople and the revolutionaries was often strained because of the former's preference for a more prudent policy for the national cause and disapproval of the insurgents' provocative methods. Yet the insurgents knew they could not carry out their agenda without the assistance of the Church—not least because that was the most direct way of reaching out to the peasants.

The insurgents' reliance on Church officials to provide cover for their operations could occasionally end up in completely unforeseen blunders, such as the case of the Exarchist assistant bishop of Tikveş/Kafadar [Kavadarci]. Assistant Bishop Methodii disappeared from his seat without anyone's knowledge on April 18, 1905, apparently leaving town on foot. The authorities later found out that he had managed to catch a train to Salonika and had sent a letter to a confidant (who evidently was not as trustworthy as he had assumed), asking for his personal belongings to be shipped to Salonika. Rumor had it that the assistant bishop had fled in haste because he was afraid that the "Committee" was about to find out that he had been embezzling funds the church had collected on its behalf. The prefect found it unlikely that Bishop Methodii had indeed been embezzling money. But, anticipating the uproar that was probably brewing among the people who had apparently been swindled, he decided to err on the side of caution and requested the dispatch of a 150-strong detachment in addition to the troops already in the provincial center, lest there be an uprising.[18] Although the assistant bishop's behavior lends some credence to Brailsford's opinions about the Orthodox clergy's rapaciousness, I must note that this example is more illustrative as an exception rather than as the rule. Although there certainly must have been several corrupt individuals among the clergy, as well as laypeople, collecting "taxes" on behalf of the Committee, it is not possible to conclude there was endemic corruption among Church members, of the Exarchate or the Patriarchate, based on occasional examples. Moreover,

---

17. Brailsford, *Macedonia, Its Races and Their Future*, 66; cf. *Macedonia, Documents and Material*, 116.
18. BOA, TFR.I.SL Tikveş. Prefecture to the Inspectorate, April 20, 1905.

failing to follow the rules of the committee resulted in serious punishments, including death, which acted as an effective deterrent against such slip ups; the bishop actually had good reason to be afraid.

Bishop Methodii's misadventure with the Committee money notwithstanding, clergy belonging both to the Exarchist and the Patriarchist sides carried immense moral authority over the peasants. In fact, that is what made his transgression all the more egregious. Brailsford, for all his condescension toward the clergy as "petty officials," was accurate in highlighting their role in performing "the rites appropriate to the crossing of the frontier between this world and the next." What he failed to fully comprehend was the importance of that role among people who truly believed that they needed the comfort of faith, and the priests who affirmed that faith, when "the frontier between this world and next" was so narrow.

Worship in Contested Churches

During the last decade of the nineteenth century, the "church contest" had become a palpable source of tension in Macedonia, one that involved not only disputes at the level of the clergy but also struggles centered on the physical church buildings and the worshippers within. The relations between the Ecumenical Patriarchate and the Sublime Porte had been quite tense since the establishment of the Exarchate, but it was not only the recognition of a separate church directly challenging the Patriarchate's authority among the faithful that caused the tension. A paradox of the post-*Tanzimat* organization of autonomous religious communities—or *millets,* in the true sense of the term, with internal constitutions and an official representative, the *milletbaşı*—also unleashed a process that gradually eroded the authority of the Patriarchate over the Greek Orthodox community.[19] The reforms accorded lay members of the community more control over the Holy Synod through the "mixed national council" (*karma milli meclis* or *mikto ethniko symvoulio*).[20] As Greek Orthodox members of the Ottoman administration joined the council, the control of the Ottoman bureaucracy over the Patriarchate increased, although indirectly. In 1883, the growing concerns of the Patriarchate about Ottoman government involvement in the communal affairs of the *millets,* considered to be a set of "privileges" accorded to the Ecumenical Patriarchate since earlier times, resulted in a crisis. The immediate reasons involved the increased secularization of the

---

19. On the establishment myths of the Ottoman *millet* system, see Benjamin Braude, "Foundation Myths of the Millet System," in *Christians and Jews in the Ottoman Empire: the Functioning of a Plural Society,* Vol. 1, *The Central Lands,* edited by Benjamin Braude and Bernard Lewis (New York, 1982), 69–88.

20. For more on this development, see Stamatopoulos, *Metarrythmisē kai Ekkosmikeusē.*

judiciary and government control over schools, which had been the purview of the Patriarchate.[21] These interventions curtailed the legal authority of the Patriarchate over its own members; it made clergy members subject to civil laws in criminal cases, and the curricula and teachers of Greek schools subject to bureaucratic scrutiny. Finally, Patriarch Ioachim III cited restrictions imposed on the construction and repairs of churches in his protest to the Sublime Porte, and resigned. Greek Orthodox churches remained closed over Christmas that year.[22] An imperial decree was issued in 1884 affirming the rights of the Patriarchate, but another crisis broke out in 1890, this time over the declared intention of the Sublime Porte to regulate the appointment of teachers and trustees of Greek schools. Adding insult to injury, the government had also issued *berats* for Exarchist bishoprics in Skopje and Ohrid. Patriarch Dionysios V resigned, declaring that he would not "renew his permission to his priests to perform divine service in their churches this year."[23] The Greek Orthodox churches in Constantinople followed suit by suspending their services, an action also followed by the Metropolitans in the Macedonian provinces. In Serres, for instance, all district churches remained closed in December 1890, until the community reached a compromise with the Metropolitan of Menlik (Melnik) that restored access to the churches also in Cuma-i Bâlâ (Blagoevgrad), Petriç (Petrich), and Demirhisar/Valovishta (Sidirokastro).[24] The decision, celebrated by congregations anxious to reclaim their venues of worship, owed much to the resourcefulness of the *kaymakam* (prefect) of Menlik, who apparently persuaded the Metropolitan by promising him that he would not let the Bulgarians invoke the name of the Exarch in liturgy.[25] The rest of the province was not as lucky, and their churches remained closed.

As communities remained without access to their churches, the fact that the clerical strike occurred during a time of heightened religious sentiment, when most people were fasting and Christmas celebrations were around the corner, exacerbated the overall restlessness. On December 18, the day of St. Nicholas (Julian calendar), the Greek Orthodox inhabitants of Serres pleaded with the Metropolitan and submitted a petition to the sultan to have their churches reopened. As we will see shortly, it was not a coincidence that such tensions happened to mount right around the major holidays of the Orthodox calendar. For the most part, it was the clear symbolic power of these dates and the increased sensitivity of the population that accounted

---

21. Kofos, "Patriarch Joachim," 114.
22. For a summary of these events see Vangelis Kechriotis, "The Modernization of the Empire and the Community 'Privileges': Greek Orthodox Responses to Young Turk Policies," in *The State and the Subaltern: Modernization, Society and the State in Turkey and Iran,* edited by Touraj Atabeki (London, 2007), 53–70.
23. PRO, FO 195/1692, Vice Consul Capety to Consul Blunt, November 5, 1890.
24. PRO, FO 195/1692, Vice Consul Capety to Consul Blunt, December 6, 1890.
25. PRO, FO 195/1962, Vice Consul Capety to Consul Blunt, Serres, December 20, 1890.

for this phenomenon, but there was also the simple fact that these were the times when access to churches was in highest demand.[26]

Archival records of sectarian conflict reveal that incidents of church access–related violence, especially in the countryside, started to escalate gradually, beginning with the first years of the twentieth century. After 1903, reports of such incidents appeared on an almost daily basis in consular as well as Ottoman state documents. When the contested churches and chapels became a nuisance for the Ottoman authorities, they started closing them down as a temporary measure, not allowing access to either community. Even Easter, the most important holiday of the year—normally a festive occasion for celebrating not only the resurrection of Christ but also the arrival of spring—fell victim to the poisoned atmosphere. Attending Easter service, one of the basic tenets of religious observance for all Orthodox faithful, turned into a risky undertaking for most, and was impossible for some, because of the number of contested and therefore closed churches. One such church, in Visoçen (Xiropotamos), had been closed for three years when the Metropolitan petitioned the Inspectorate requesting permission to open the church for Easter service in April 1903; the response was negative. The Inspector pointed out that the church had been closed in 1900 because the conflict among the Greeks and Bulgarians had escalated to the point where the two parties were inflicting physical harm (*"darb ve cerh"*) on each other. Until a general decree was issued about the matter, all similar local conflicts would be dealt with in the same manner (i.e., the Inspectorate would not issue exceptions for special circumstances).[27]

Meanwhile, the Greek Orthodox community, wanting to keep the issue current and maintain proprietorship of the contested churches until such time when they reopened, became more vocal in their protests. Unlike a decade earlier, however, when the government treated the Exarchate and the Patriarchate as equals (at least in the eyes of the Patriarchists), the Ottoman officials were now—after the incursions of Bulgarian bands into Macedonia became an immediate threat—more likely to bestow favors on the Patriarchate at the expense of the Exarchate. Even the smallest village chapel could become a rallying point against the rival community by the other community claiming ownership of or simply access to it. Take, for instance, the small village of Koula (Palaiokastro), a *çiftlik* (estate or farm) of not more than twenty-four households, probably entirely owned by one

---

26. When Capety, the vice consul himself, was attacked at the Serres Metropolitan church a year later, after writing the reports above (notes 23–25), he was there for the celebration of his name day, May 21, which corresponds to the day of saints Konstantinos and Eleni, two most common Greek Orthodox names; this suggests that the church must have been packed. PRO, FO 195/1768, Serres, June 3, 1891.

27. BOA, TFR.I.SL 9/804, Bishop of Drama [Drama Metropolidi] to the Inspectorate, April 16, 1903; Inspectorate to the Subgovernorate of Drama, April 17, 1903.

proprietor.²⁸ The village had a small convent that was traditionally visited by people from neighboring villages on September 14/27, for the observation of the "Exaltation of the Holy Cross [Ypsōsē tou Timiou Staurou]." In 1904, however, local authorities canceled the celebration to prevent any disturbance that might arise because the residents of Koula had just signed a petition to join the Exarchate. In the words of the British Vice Consul J. M. Theodorides, who was in fact a Greek Orthodox local, the villagers had expressed their desire to be considered "among the Schismatic Bulgarians" while the neighboring villages were all "Orthodox."²⁹

It appears that the Greek Orthodox community of Serres took the matter of this small village very seriously, and a large crowd estimated at 5,000 people gathered in town. They first went to the acting Greek Metropolitan and then, accompanied by him and the representative committees of the town, made for the *mutasarrıf*'s (subgovernor, or district governor's) office. The subgovernor, Theodorides reported, had to give in to the pressing demands of the crowd and permitted the people to go to the convent for celebrations, adding that he would take all measures, including sending a military escort, to make sure that order would be preserved. Content with the assurances of the subgovernor, everyone left in good order.³⁰ Even though Theodorides does not mention how the inhabitants of Koula celebrated the festival, it is questionable whether they dared to go to the little convent given the presence of a large Greek Orthodox crowd, which had contested the right to celebrate and won. It is also significant that a practice that, until recently, had been a routine observance turned into a political issue requiring the involvement of civilian and military authorities.

The demonstration of the Greek Orthodox community in Serres was not the first of its kind that year. Similar demonstrations asking for support from the Ottoman authorities sprang up across the region. The community in Salonika organized an impressive gathering on March 6, 1904. Reportedly, the community had informed the government officials a day earlier that it would meet at the Church of Aghios Nikolaos in the Eski Cuma neighborhood to observe the "Aya Nikola Palamas" [sic] holiday and then march to the governor's mansion *(hükümet)* to present a petition about the "atrocities and aggression" of the Bulgarians.³¹ Having been advised by the

---

28. *Cartes Ethnographiques.* G. F. Abbott, who passed through the village in 1900, did not provide any information on the language spoken by the peasants or their religious affiliation, but he noted that his party had to leave in haste because they were warned that an armed band was in the area; the band did, in fact, come to the *chiftlik* to pick up provisions shortly after Abbot's party had left; Abbott, *Tale of a Tour,* 112–13.

29. PRO, FO 195/2183, Vice Consul Theodorides to Gérant du Vallon Serres, September 26, 1904. Consular staff employed by the European Powers in the Ottoman Empire were often recruited from among the local Christians.

30. Ibid.

31. The clerk drafting the letter is wrong about the holiday in question; probably he confused the name of the church where the ceremony would be held with the saint's name.

governor that marching en masse from the church to the governor's mansion would be "inappropriate," the Metropolitan Alexander pledged to present the petition himself. Indeed, a large crowd that seemed to include "the entire Greek Orthodox community of Salonika" filled the church and listened to the service that went from noon until 5 p.m. The Metropolitan was politically savvy enough to pray for the sultan as the congregation cheered with cries of "Zito! [Long live!]." Instead of dispersing after the service, the crowd started to march on the Hamidiye Avenue (one of the main paved arteries of the city), passing by the consulates and ending up in front of the imperial barracks, where the marchers "showed their respect" with more cries of "Zito!" Their final destination was the Metropolitan Cathedral, where Archbishop Alexander repeated his speech at the church and further cries of "Zito" were heard before the crowd dispersed peacefully.[32] This was a carefully choreographed event that pushed all the right buttons to garner sympathy for the Greek side in the ecclesiastical struggle. Timing the gathering with an important local holiday, following official guidelines to the letter, vocal expressions of gratitude to the sultan and respect to the military, making the crowd visible by marching across the city, and passing monuments and the foreign consulates (which were carefully left out of the official petition) were all elements of a cleverly designed show of power that managed not to transgress any norms of propriety. The petition itself, which praised the sultan and reaffirmed the loyalty of his Greek Orthodox subjects, contrasting their exalted and long-established place in Ottoman society with the rebellious and uncouth "Bulgarian evil-doers," was another document of political sophistication.[33]

The Bulgarian Exarchist community was perhaps not as talented in soliciting protection from the Ottoman officials, but it did not necessarily lag behind its rivals in resourcefulness in the fight over the churches. On June 11, 1905, the Inspectorate sent an inquiry to the *kaymakamlık* (prefecture) of Yenice (Giannitsa) demanding information about the inhabitants of the villages of Pirolik (Pentaplatano), Kruşar/Krusari (Ampelies), Hisarbey (Drosero), Vardiçe/Vadrishta (Palios Milotopos), Vehdi Pazar (Palaio Giannitson), and Dalyan. According to information delivered by the Bulgarian commercial agent in Salonika to the Inspectorate, all churches in these villages had been closed down and, when the villagers put up fences to create some makeshift open-air churches, the gendarmes had demolished them. The villagers had also been forced to sign papers stating that they would

---

There is no Saint Nikolaos Palamas, but given the date, he is almost certainly referring to Agios Grigorios Palamas of Thessaloniki, and the church in question could be Agios Nikolas Orfanos.

32. BOA, TFR.I.SL 32/3190, Governorship of Salonika to the Inspectorate, March 6, 1904.

33. BOA, TFR.I.SL 33/3228, Greek Community of Salonika to the Inspectorate, March 6, 1904.

not try again to erect these enclosures made of tree branches and rugs, and would no longer assemble for prayer.

The prefect's response was that the villages of Pirolik, Kruşar, Hisarbey, Eskice (also part of Palaio Giannitson), and Sukutlu (Palatades) had petitioned to join the Exarchate following threats from the "brigands" even though they had been loyal to the Patriarchate until 1904. The standing order was that such petitions would not be accepted until the security threats in the region were driven away, and it was also applied in this case. However, the villagers had persisted in performing services in "Bulgarian" with "Bulgarian" priests. For this reason, the prefect explained, their churches had been closed down and their keys temporarily confiscated by the state. Following this, the villagers built fences of wood and tree branches around the churches, and Bulgarian priests continued to officiate in these enclosed areas. Not only was it "inappropriate for Bulgarian priests to perform divine liturgy," continued the prefect, given that the churches belonged to the Patriarchate, but the fences also posed a fire hazard. Therefore, the villagers were told not to build such fences, but it was not true, he averred, that they had been forced to sign papers.[34]

Considering the general attitude of the Ottoman gendarmerie toward Exarchist villagers, the prefect's assertion that nobody had forced them to sign papers is highly suspect. It is also highly unlikely that this "worship al fresco" was a spontaneous and improvised solution to the hardship posed by the locked churches because the same particular (and somewhat peculiar) pattern had sprung up simultaneously in five villages. The main motivation for the attempts by each community to defy the ban on using closed churches was the principle of squatters' rights. There was no guarantee that either of the communities could successfully claim proprietorship of the churches when the disputes were finally resolved, not only because there was no sign of an attempt to issue uniform and coherent guidelines on the part of the Ottoman government but also because it was not clear whether the Ottoman state would be the ultimate arbiter resolving the issue. Given the overall uncertainty, it was safe to assume that a community that had managed to somehow "occupy" the church when it was shut down would have a better shot at claiming it in the future.

Interruptions of religious rites were common occurrences, but sometimes they were carried out in the most unexpected manner, such as the strategically executed theft of a ceremonial robe. On January 17, 1905, for instance, his congregants noticed that Bishop "Yerasim Efendi" was missing from church during the observance of the rite of the New Year (probably Bulgarian Christmas, Boujik; the bishop in question was a representative

---

34. BOA, TFR.I.SL 75/7481, A. Schopoff, Bulgarian Commercial Agent to Hüseyin Hilmi Pasha, May 24, 1905; Inspectorate to the Prefecture of Yenice, June 11, 1905; Yenice Prefect to the Inspectorate, June 20, 1905.

of the Exarchate). His absence being rather conspicuous, the Inspectorate requested an inquiry from the prefecture of Usturumca/Strumnitza (Strumica) concerning the bishop's whereabouts. It was soon understood that the bishop had been unable to officiate because two individuals had broken into the church the night before and stolen his ceremonial robe from the caretaker. Further inquiry revealed that the perpetrators were from the band of the famous Chernopeyef (an IMRO affiliate) and that they had been sent there because the bishop had refused to pay the (quite hefty) sum of 200 liras demanded earlier.[35] Interestingly enough, the robe was returned the day after, leaving us to wonder whether the *komitajis,* certainly aware of the symbolic value of this article of clothing, also had enough faith in its spiritual value that they felt pressed to return it, risking capture by the authorities. The moral value of clerical ornaments, liturgical objects and books, and, most important, icons, which served as a direct link to the spiritual world, was so exalted in the eyes of the locals that even Ottoman authorities were occasionally forced to acknowledge the direness of an assault on these venerated objects. The commander of the troops searching for weapons in the church of an Exarchist village in the district of Avrethisar (Ginaikokastro) found this out the hard way when he was immediately arrested on the villagers' complaints that soldiers under his command "broke the icons and toppled the sacraments."[36]

The priest's robe, not only the elaborate pieces worn for special occasions such as Easter or Theofania but also the simple everyday article, was a symbol that distinguished him from his flock and made him instantly recognizable. The Greek Orthodox Church did not harbor much sympathy for members who defected to the Bulgarian Exarchate and obviously did not see them as worthy of the robes they wore, as the "defrocking" of Papa Iovan Iconoff of Karlikovo (Mikropoli) of the *kaza* of Zihna (Palia Zichni) testifies. Karlikovo was a mid-size, Slavic-speaking Patriarchist village, possibly with Greek- and Vlach-speaking minorities.[37] In other words, Karlikovo was one of those villages whose allegiance was up for grabs by either party, and at the beginning of 1905, its inhabitants had (partially) petitioned to join the Exarchate.[38] Ottoman officials alleged that the village had been attached to the Patriarchate "since old times" and that the desire to join the

---

35. BOA, TFR.I.SL 61/6121, Inspectorate to the Prefecture of Usturumca, January 17, 1905.

36. The incident took place in Tchigontzi (Tchougountzi) on January 20, 1905. MAE, Constantinople Serie E 147, Consul General's report to the Embassy in Constantinople, Salonika, January 28, 1905.

37. According to the pro-Bulgarian *Cartes Ethnographiques,* Karlikovo was a mixed village of 380 households. Mishev cites it as a village of 1,500 souls, 1,440 of whom were Patriarchist Bulgarians and 60 of whom were Vlachs.

38. PRO, FO 195/2232, Consul Graves to the Ambassador, February 6, 1906. Even though the British consul's and Ottoman officials' initial reports give the impression that the entire village had petitioned to join the Exarchate (see BOA, TFR.I.SL 100/9992, Inspectorate

Exarchate was motivated by the threats of the "Bulgarian brigands." In any case, because their petition was presented after August 1903 (the date that had been declared final by the Inspectorate for official recognition of conversions to and from the Bulgarian Exarchate) the village would officially continue to be counted as Patriarchist.[39]

This may have been the official status of Karlikovo, but because their priest, formerly a representative of the Greek Orthodox Patriarchate, had also converted with the villagers (or more likely, had persuaded them to convert), the higher Greek Orthodox clergy of Drama found the situation extremely disturbing and took measures accordingly.[40] In the words of Consul Graves:

> It appears that the [Greek Orthodox] Metropolitan requested the Mutasarrif to have the priest of Karlikovo brought to Drama to answer a charge of uncanonical conduct. This request was transmitted by the Mutasarrif to the *kaymakam* of Zihna, by whose orders, after reference to the Mutasarrif of Serres, two gendarmes took charge of the priest on the 20th of January and conveyed him to the frontier of the Drama Sandjak where he was handed over to the Drama patrol by whom he was conducted to the Government House at Drama. Thence he was taken by a policeman to the residence of the Greek Metropolitan, where he was kept a prisoner until nearly midnight. The Metropolitan's Cavass, accompanied by a deacon and two other men, then entered the room, and while the Cavass held a revolver pointed at the head of this old man of eighty-four years of age, his hair and beard were cut off with a clipping-machine, his priest's hat and robes were removed, and he was dressed in peasant's clothes, and a fes placed upon his head.[41]

The details of the literal "defrocking" of the priest, such as the acts of shaving his hair and beard, and replacing his robe with a peasant's outfit complete with a fez, signified more than a simple lesson taught through humiliation. The habits of the Exarchist clergy had long been a sore spot for the Patriarchate, which had made various unsuccessful attempts to deny them, from the very beginning, the right to wear the distinctive attire of the Orthodox Church.[42] The issue had become even more inflammatory after the Exarchate started acquiring bishoprics, such as Nevrekop (Gotse Delchev) and Veles/Köprülü (Veles) in 1894, in areas that were considered outside the accepted "Bulgarian" sphere of influence. The appointment of

---

to the Grand Vezirate, February 16, 1906), it is clear from subsequent correspondence that part of the village had remained attached to the Patriarchate (BOA, TFR.I.SL 129/128580).

39. BOA, TFR.I.SL 100/9992, Inspectorate to the Grand Vezirate, February 16, 1906.
40. Karlikovo was administratively under the jurisdiction of the *kaza* of Zihna but ecclesiastically under that of Drama.
41. PRO, FO 195/2232, Consul Graves to the Ambassador, February 6, 1906.
42. Kofos, "Attempts at Mending," 353.

an Exarchist bishop in Nevrekop, for instance, caused protests in Menlik, Demirhisar, Zihna, and Drama by the Muslim as well as the Greek Orthodox population.[43] One of the issues that the Greek Orthodox emphasized in their petition to the governor was the garb of the Exarchist clergy in these areas. In the words of the French consul in Salonika:

> In their petitions, the protesters assert that there is but one Orthodox church, and therefore, there should not be two distinct ecclesiastical authorities; in case that there would be schism, they demand, at least, that the exarchist priests should no longer be authorized to carry the costume of Greek priests; the form and the color of the cap present, in their eyes, a real importance. ... The orthodox fear, justifiably, that the same peasants will rally around the Exarchate the day the priests and bishops, speaking the same language as them and not having discernible differences with other priests either in their costumes or their rites are officially permitted to oversee the administration of civil and religious affairs.[44]

In the eyes of the Greek Orthodox, the Exarchist clergy was cheating by not giving up the garb and the distinctive cap (*kalymauchi*) of the Orthodox Church because this visual continuity failed to signal to the peasants that the Church they now attended was not the Church that they had belonged to for generations. And when they seized the opportunity, higher members of the Patriarchate did not refrain from removing these symbols of the "genuine" Orthodox Church from the person of Exarchist priests. In 1894, almost a decade before the defrocking of the priest of Karlikovo, when the outrage against the assignment of new bishoprics to the Exarchate was at its height, the priest of a small village named Klepousna (Agriani) suffered a similar humiliation. He was defrocked four years after 90 of the 140 households of the village signed a petition expressing their desire to attach themselves to the Exarchate. Before he was taken into the room where the district manager and the Metropolitan were waiting for him to hear his defense, the Metropolitan's deacon seized the priest's cap, saying, as it was reported by the British consul, "we made you a priest, and we depose you." The priest had to "enter the room bareheaded which was regarded as a great disgrace to him."[45]

The removal of the priest's cap and the "defrocking" of the priest of Karlikovo followed a formula meant to deliver a message not only to the priests who had thus been stripped of their ecclesiastical authority but also to the Exarchate. In the case of Karlikovo, further correspondence reveals that the Metropolitan, who was single-handedly responsible for the priest's public

---

43. PRO, FO 195/1849, Vice Consul Capety to Consul Blunt, Serres, May 14, 1894.
44. MAE, vol. 9, Consul to Casimir Perier, Selanik, May 9, 1894.
45. PRO, FO 195/1849, Report of the Consul [in Salonika], Samokov, December 11, 1894.

humiliation, defended his conduct on the grounds that he was "acting under the orders of the Patriarchate and strictly within his rights" in punishing a rebellious priest of the Church. After the matter was brought to the attention of Hüseyin Hilmi Pasha, however, the prefect of Zihna and his deputy were removed from their posts, a measure much appreciated by representatives of the European Powers in the region—with the exception of the British vice consul at Drama, Mr. Gregoriades, who, no doubt owing to his own affiliation with the Greek Orthodox Church, found the conduct of the Metropolitan "quite justifiable" and "accused the Turkish authorities of interfering in a purely ecclesiastical matter in which they were not concerned."[46] The conflict soon spread from the domain of the church officials to their parishioners. The Exarchists of Karlikovo, who obviously did not appreciate the way their priest had been treated by the Greek Metropolitan and the Ottoman authorities, turned their resentment against their Patriarchist neighbors and attacked them.[47]

Giving someone a haircut and shave may not strike modern sensibilities as an exceptionally offensive act, but in this specific context it was nothing less than a violation of the priest's ecclesiastical identity, a violent intervention to directly decommission the priest and nullify his social capital. The first sentence of a petition presented by Karlikovo's communal representatives to the Inspectorate substantiates the exact nature of the violation involved in the shaving of an Orthodox priest's hair and beard; the letter starts with an expression of gratitude for permission to continue observing divine liturgy officiated "by a newly appointed priest" who would serve them "until the beard of our priest Papa Yovan Ikonov grows back."[48] A priest was no longer a priest without his beard.

It appears that temporarily losing their priest was not the last indignity these villagers had suffered. On February 16, a man by the name of Atanas Girkof had passed away. The priests Tanasis, Yovan, and Dimitri, who were responsible for Papa Yovan Ikonov's suffering, were now determined to prevent the new priest from performing the last rites for the dead man and burying him in the village cemetery. The Exarchists needed a separate lot for a cemetery, the petitioners reasoned, so that "the occurrence and repetition of such inappropriate situations would not be allowed." "Inappropriate" is an understatement for the situation: it is difficult to say for how long the burial was delayed, but the Inspectorate's response, written on March 22, mentioning that the body had been "left in the open [açıkta kaldığı]," is disturbing enough. The recommendation of the Inspectorate was to establish whether it was possible to divide the existing cemetery between the two communities

---

46. PRO, FO 195/2232, Consul Graves to the Ambassador, February 6, 1906.
47. MAE, vol. 51, December 28, 1906. There were no injuries or death reported, but the attacks seem to have been repeated.
48. BOA, TFR.I.SL 100/9927, March 18, 1905.

and, if that seemed unworkable, to issue permission to the Bulgarian community for a separate cemetery in an appropriate location.[49] Note that the Greek Orthodox clergy chose to reassert their authority at a time and occasion when the Exarchist community was extremely vulnerable. It is even more noteworthy that the Exarchists chose to hold on to a rotting corpse rather than have a Greek Orthodox priest say the last rites for the deceased man.[50] No sacrament, it seems, was too sacred for these clergy members, who were in the fight until the bitter end. Perhaps less extreme than the denial of last rites, but still cruel, were the denial of the first rite (baptism) and the most important one in between (the bestowal of wedding wreaths). All these were rituals of life that not only marked the transition from one stage to the next but were also required of the faithful. These were the most precious instances in which Orthodox clergy could interfere between God and those who had strayed, and interfere they did.[51]

Priests were at the forefront of the struggle for the churches, sometimes as unwitting bystanders and often as active participants, but as this case suggests, their struggle was not seen as a religious matter by any of the concerned authorities, including that of the office of the Ottoman General Inspector, even though their congregations considered them the gatekeepers of eternal salvation. The peasants venerated the clergy not for their temporal but for their spiritual power, and they feared them for the same reason. It is not surprising that the clergy members were not shy about using this power to further their political agendas, as in the case of the Bulgarian bishop (*re'is-i ruhânî*)[52] of Nevrekop, who apparently banned his flock from engaging in any sort of commercial activity with the Greek (Orthodox) and from attending their churches.[53] One of the punishments that the noncompliant risked was monetary—a fine of 1 Ottoman lira (a very large sum for the peasants) presumably to be paid to the coffers of the Bulgarian church of Nevrekop.

---

49. BOA, TFR.I.SL 100/9927, The Inspectorate to the Salonika Province, March 22, 1905.

50. Refusal to bury the dead was a resistance method employed not only in protesting the Greek Orthodox clergy but also Ottoman officials when appropriate, as happened after the massacre in Mravintza *çiftlik* in January 1905. Ten men were killed by Greek *komitadjis* dressed like Ottoman soldiers. The wives of the dead refused to bury their husbands despite the prefect's offer to pay 2 *mecidiye* each as an incentive. The women wanted to take their protest to Salonika and presumably demand autopsies. MAE, Constantinople E 147, Verbal Deposition of Risto Costandi, Mitre Gochi and Risto Lazo recorded at the French Consulate, January 22, 1905.

51. The Metropolitan of Vodine, having secured the assistance of government authorities to expel Bulgarian-speaking priests and teachers from Patriarchist villages, would not allow residents of the same villages to travel to another village to be married or have their children baptized by an Exarchist priest. Even the Ottoman official writing about the issue did not hide his shock at the Metropolitan's conduct; BOA, TFR.I.SL 60/5920, Vodine Prefecture to the Inspectorate, December 24, 1904.

52. It seems that in the language of Ottoman bureaucracy, *reis-i ruhânî* (lit. "spiritual leader") was generally used for bishops of the Exarchate, whereas the term *metropolit* was reserved for their Greek Orthodox counterparts.

53. BOA, TFR.I.SL 9/838, Subgovernorate of Serres to the Inspectorate, April 17, 1903.

The fee was only part of the deterrence factor, however; the transgressors also faced excommunication for the dire offense of buying so much as a head of lettuce from a Greek Orthodox shopkeeper.[54] In addition to all the horrible consequences of excommunication we may imagine for the faithful, we must also note fears that would be considered "superstitious" in our times. In the Balkan folk tradition, excommunication was associated, among other things, with vampires. In his travelogue Tozer noted, "The principal causes which change persons into *vrykolakas* [vampires] after death are excommunication, heinous sins, the curse of parents, and tampering with magic arts. The first of these is the most common and most important and dates from very early times."[55]

It is remarkable that the bishop's announcement to his flock through the intermediary of priests coincided with the *Megali Evdomada,* the week before Easter Sunday, when the fast is most austere, religious sentiments run high, and, perhaps most important, the markets are busiest because of all the shopping going on in preparation for the holiday. Oddly enough, according to the report of the prefecture of Nevrekop, during the *Paskalya Pazarı,* or Easter Market, that was set up on Friday, no Bulgarians were seen shopping from Greek Orthodox vendors. When questioned about this peculiar phenomenon, the bishop's response was that it was possible they had found what they desired being sold by Bulgarian vendors and not the Greek Orthodox or perhaps that the latter were selling at more expensive rates. Anyway, he added, they would be buying from them again in a couple of weeks. When asked why they would start buying from them in a couple of weeks if they did not yesterday, the bishop was quiet.[56]

The bishop's ban was clearly aimed at reducing or completely eliminating whatever daily contact remained between the Exarchist and Patriarchist communities that protected the threadbare social fabric from disappearing entirely.[57] The marketplace in Nevrekop was one place where people interacted with one another despite their sectarian, linguistic or national differences very similar to the way these markets still function in Macedonia.[58] In other

---

54. BOA, TFR.I.SL 9/838, Prefecture of Nevrekop to the Subgovernorate of Serres, April 15, 1903; Governorship of Salonika to the Inspectorate, April 18, 1903.
55. Tozer, *Researches in the Highlands of Turkey,* Vol. 2: 86.
56. BOA, TFR.I.SL 9/838, Prefecture of Nevrekop to the of Serres; Subgovernorate of Serres to the Inspectorate, April 21, 1903.
57. Declarations by both parties banning all transactions would become commonplace within a few years. For instance, a Greek Orthodox who, despite threats from the "Greek party," negotiated the sale of a house that he owned to the Bulgarian commercial agent in Serres, was killed by a Turk allegedly working for the Greeks; MAE, vol. 147, Colonel Vérand to the Ambassador, Serres, January 31 and February 15, 1905. In the same town, a notable Greek lady, who had been renting a building to Bulgarian tenants, was threatened by the Greek committee; PRO, FO 195/2263, British Vice Consul Bosanquet to Consul Graves, Serres, May 30, 1907. The ban would later be transformed into an extensive boycott in most parts of the province in Salonika, FO 195/2263, Salonika, Consul Graves to O'Connor, June 18, 1907.
58. See Karakasidou, *Fields of Wheat, Hills of Blood,* esp. 74–76.

words, the bishop was using his ecclesiastical authority to intervene in an entirely secular space of interaction to divide it along sectarian lines. What is even more striking than the order to boycott the businesses of the other community was the ban on attending its church. It reveals, yet again, that church segregation was not as rigidly practiced as we might expect, even as late as 1903, three decades after the sectarian split.

Compromise and Coexistence—Church Rotation, a Viable Alternative?

In many villages with mixed populations of Greek Orthodox and Bulgarian Exarchists, "church rotation," a compromise whereby the two communities took turns holding services in a single church, seems to have prevented serious conflicts for many years. The practice was widespread enough in the early 1900s to be noted by astonished European visitors, such as H. N. Brailsford, who wrote: "the absurdity of this use of spiritual weapons in carnal warfare is so patent that 'Greeks' and 'Schismatics' frequently share the same church, and say Mass on alternate Sundays in Greek and Slavonic from the same altar."[59]

As the propaganda activities in Macedonia intensified, however, it became increasingly difficult to maintain this compromise. The only church of Spatovo (Kimisi), a medium-size village in the district of Demirhisar, was one such building that had been used in rotation by the villagers, who were all Slavic-speaking.[60] The village church was first brought to the attention of Ottoman authorities in March 1904 when the Bulgarian Exarchist community sent a petition to Hüseyin Hilmi Pasha demanding the restoration of the practice of church rotation.[61]

According to the petitioners, the entire village had converted to the Exarchate fifteen years earlier (in 1889), after which date they started to perform their rites in the village church in "Slavic [*Islavca*, i.e., Church Slavonic]" and the children of the village were also instructed in "Slavic."[62] The petitioners alleged that twenty-five households had reverted back to the Patriarchate in 1898 because of pressures from the Greeks. The villagers, to prevent a conflict, had consented to take turns using the church with the Patriarchists. According to the arrangement that they had worked out, the Patriarchists would have use of the church every third Sunday because they

---

59. Brailsford, *Macedonia, Its Races and Their Future*, 72.
60. According to the *Cartes Ethnographiques*, the village consisted of 201 Bulgarian households. Mishev cites a total population of 2,000, 1,280 of whom were Exarchist and the rest Patriarchist Bulgarians.
61. BOA, TFR.I.SL 67/6606, petition to Hüseyin Hilmi Pasha, March 31, 1904.
62. Note that the petitioners did not call the language of instruction "Bulgarian," which was often used in reference to both the local dialects and Church Slavonic.

were in the minority and did not contribute to the expenses of the church. Through a similar arrangement, one of the smaller rooms of the school building was also allocated for the children of the Patriarchists. The community had two *muhtars* (leaders, chiefs), one for each group, and two *mühürs* (official seals).

According to the letter, the remainder of the village had also attached itself back to the Patriarchate in summer 1903 because of the threats of "the ill-omened Greek Orthodox [*Rum meş'umları*]" and out of fear of persecution by the authorities, especially after the "disturbances" in May and June 1903. Even though the villagers had remained "loyal to the state" during these acts of "murder and brigandage," six of them had been arrested and placed in custody in Serres, and many of them had been detained several times in Demirhisar. The official seal of the Exarchist community had also been removed. After the arrival of the Greek Orthodox Metropolitan of Menlik in July 1903 in Spatovo to conduct services, the keys to the church had been handed over to the Greek Orthodox trustees and the icons of Cyrill and Methodios had been confiscated along with twenty-six volumes of religious books in Slavonic.

In February 1904, after the area had calmed down and become relatively secure, 133 households applied to the prefecture of Demirhisar with the intention of rejoining the Exarchate. The prefecture gave them verbal affirmation of the approval of their petition. Despite this, the *Kaymakam muavini* (deputy prefect), a Greek Orthodox man, prevented the restoration of their rights over the church and the school. Neither their icons nor their liturgical books were returned because of this man's interference. Actually, this was not the first recorded grievance against this particular deputy prefect, who, according to the allegations of the Bulgarian Exarch in November 1903, had publicly announced to the Bulgarians that those who "recognized the Patriarchate would indefinitely be safe from all persecution and repression, and even the Bulgarians who were incarcerated would be pardoned if they acquiesced to the same offer."[63] Spatovo was obviously one of the villages where the locals had not heeded his advice. The long petition by the villagers ended with a restatement of their wish to reinstitute the practice of using the church in rotation, to restore the school building to their community, and to have their confiscated icons, books, and the official seal of the community returned.

The Inspectorate ordered the prefecture of Demirhisar to carry out a preliminary investigation and ascertain whether the claims of the Exarchist villagers were correct.[64] According to the prefect's report, the village consisted of 190 households, which had been adherents of the Patriarchate

---

63. MAE, vol. 39, Petition of the Bulgarian Exarch to the Grand Vezir, November 21, 1903.
64. BOA, TFR.I.SL 67/6606, Inspectorate to the Prefecture, April 2, 1904.

"since old times," but 160 of them had attached themselves to the Exarchate in 1896–1897. For four years following this, the Exarchist majority had shared the church with the Patriarchist minority, and the two communities had attended church *together*. In 1900–1901, after a dispute among them, they had started the practice of rotation instead of sharing the church simultaneously. In August 1903, they had returned to the Patriarchate, and seven months later, in February 1904, they reverted back to the Exarchate. At this point, the prefect noted that the Bulgarians apparently could not stick to one sect (*"bir mezhebde sebât etmemeleri"*); they did not consent to the method of rotation; and that the church had originally been constructed under the name of the Greek Orthodox community. He had asked for counsel from his superior on how to proceed with the matter given these facts, but he had not received an answer. Regarding the liturgical objects, the prefect implied that they had not been seized by force; the villagers themselves had handed them over to the Metropolitan Ioachim Efendi.[65]

A few days later, another petition from a representative of the Exarchist community of Spatovo was on the desk of the Inspector General, explaining why the prefect's interpretation of the events was partial to the Greek side.[66] According to the petitioner, Avram Konstantin, the Greek Orthodox deputy prefect had convinced the prefect through "tricks and lies [*hiyel ve desâis*]" to summon the members of the Exarchist community of Spatovo to his office and tell them that they could have their liturgical books and other objects back, but that the practice of rotation would no longer be allowed. He also told them that they were not to go near the church when the Greek Orthodox were there, that they would have to give up their official seal, and that they would be officially represented by the Greek Orthodox *muhtar*. It was no doubt a safer bet for Avram Konstantin to place the blame entirely on the Greek Orthodox deputy and absolve the Muslim official of any wrongdoing than to complain about the conduct of both. Two days later, the Exarchist community sent yet another telegram, informing the authorities that they could not get into their church even though it was Easter Sunday and that the village consisted mostly of Exarchists.[67]

The Exarchist villagers of Spatovo apparently found a more sympathetic ear with the Inspectorate than the local authorities. A telegram sent on April 11, 1904, from the Inspectorate to the governorship of Salonika ordered that the requests of the Exarchist community be granted.[68] Each community would enjoy use of the church every other week according to

---

65. BOA, TFR.I.SL 67/6606, Prefect Ramiz to the Inspectorate, April 4, 1904.
66. BOA, TFR.I.SL 67/6606, Avram Konstantin of Spatovo to the Inspector General, April 6, 1904.
67. BOA, TFR.I.SL 67/6606, Vangel Atanas and his 39 companions of Spatovo to the Inspectorate, April 8, 1904.
68. BOA, TFR.I.SL 67/6606, Inspectorate to the Governorship of Salonika, April 11, 1904.

the new arrangement. Not two weeks had passed after this order was issued, however, than the Metropolitan of Menlik sent an angry protest telegram to the Inspector General. According to the Metropolitan, the Inspector had been deceived by a group of evil-doers consisting of five or six people (*"beş altı neferden ibâret fitne-engiz takımı'"*).[69]

According to the Metropolitan, the dispute in Spatovo was not an issue of religion, or one of "Orthodoxy and Schismatism," as he put it, but was all about the endowment of the church, which was estimated at 100 Ottoman liras. The "evil-doers" had duped the villagers into signing the petition by saying that it was for the appointment of a *kocabaşı* (Christian village elder). These evil-doers, he continued, incited the population to achieve their "atrocious and malevolent" ideas under the pretext and defense of "Bulgarianness" (*"vicdansız ve su'i-mekâsıd efkârlarına na'il ve muvaffak olabilmek içün Bulgarlığı siper ve vâsıta isti'mâl ile ahaliyi teşvîş ederler"*). He claimed that the village consisted of 230 households, about 15 or 20 of which had been misled to take sides with the evil-doers. The total number of "Schismatic" households, according to the Metropolitan, was not more than 30 (consistent with the prefect's report), an insignificant minority in comparison to the more than 200 Greek Orthodox households. He maintained that it could be easily verified that this was not a "national or a spiritual" matter if the "Schismatics" were granted permission to build another church or to convert a building into one. They would not accept such a solution, the Metropolitan contended, because their purpose was not to found a new church, but to seize the present one's endowment (*"bunların efkâr ve mekâsıdı kilise temellük etmek olmayub vâridâtını almakdır"*). He would even have allowed them to use Slavic in the church had he been convinced that the issue could be resolved in this manner, but their purposes were entirely at odds with religion and motivated purely by the desire to harm the Greek Orthodox. Therefore, he was asking that the order allowing the Exarchists to use the church every other week be reversed.

It is clear from the correspondence between the Inspectorate and the *mutasarrıflık* (subgovernorate or district governorate) of Serres that the Metropolitan's argument was not found to be convincing by Hüseyin Hilmi Pasha's staff, who sent persistent telegrams to the provincial authorities inquiring about the status of the liturgical books and the church in Spatovo.[70] The same correspondence also reveals that the local authorities dragged their feet in carrying out the urgent orders of the Inspectorate. As a response to the repeated demands, the prefecture of Demirhisar assured the subgovernorate that the Exarchist community would be allowed to have liturgy at

---

69. BOA, TFR.I.SL 67/6606, Greek Orthodox Metropolitan of Menlik to the Inspector General, April 21, 1904.

70. BOA, TFR.I.SL 67/6606, Inspectorate to the Subgovernorate, April 22, 1904; Subgovernor of Serres to the Inspector General, April 23, 1904.

the village church the following Sunday (April 24) and that one room of the school had been transferred to the Exarchists for instruction in Slavic. But the Exarchists would have to give up whatever hope they may have had of retrieving their books and icons for reasons bordering on the absurd: the subgovernor claimed that the Greek Metropolitan's predecessor had handed the liturgical objects over to the Demirhisar *Rum mütevellisi* (Greek Orthodox council member) for "safe keeping" in his shop, which, unfortunately, had burned down.[71] The Greek consul in Serres subsequently attempted a final effort terminate service rotation at the church in Spatovo by contacting the Inspectorate and claiming that the practice was causing conflict, but an investigation revealed that there was no such conflict between the two communities.[72]

We would hope that all this brokering, scheduling, and monitoring and the compromise that was finally accomplished ensured that these two communities managed to exist side by side as they had done "since old times." This indeed seems to have been the case at least for another eight months after the completion of the correspondence related here. Whatever disputes and tensions the peasants of Spatovo may have had during this time, they were not serious enough to leave an archival record, which is significant, given their previous propensity to drop a few lines to the Inspector General describing their grievances.[73] In December, however, the name of the village was back on Hüseyin Hilmi Pasha's agenda, and this time the issue centered on the church school. The children of the Exarchists had been thrown out of their classroom, along with their school materials, on December 2 by the usual suspects: the Metropolitan of Menlik, accompanied by two gendarmes assigned for his service by the prefect of Demirhisar.[74]

Communal Schools as Boundary Markers

At the local level, it is impossible to distinguish the school disputes from the broader sectarian rift. They were two sides of the same coin, and school disputes in small rural communities such as Spatovo usually paralleled the development and aggravation of disputes over use of a church building by the communities. They served as a wedge between the two communities,

---

71. BOA, TFR.I.SL 67/6606, Attachment to the telegram from the Subgovernor of Serres to the Inspector General, April 23, 1904.

72. BOA, TFR.I.SL 67/6606, Subgovernor of Serres to the Inspector General, April 29, 1904.

73. All the correspondence concerning Spatovo was placed in one file at the Rumeli Müfettişliği archives, which makes it quite unlikely that there were any missing petitions or telegrams between the two clusters of documents.

74. BOA, TFR.I.SL 67/6606, petition from the Exarchists of Spatovo to the Inspector General, December 16, 1904.

and another tangible marker of the boundaries dividing them, rendering coexistence more difficult, if not impossible. In this regard, it was not what the schools taught but what they stood for that made them an instrument of nation-making among the peasantry. As we have seen in chapter 2, education in the service of nationalization in Macedonia was a two-tiered process that involved the network of parish schools in the countryside and more sophisticated institutions such as gymnasia in larger centers that had different but complementary agendas. The leadership and influence of the national elites were considerably more pronounced in the top tier of this process, that is, the high schools.

Despite the rudimentary conditions in which they operated, the village schools, overall, were successful centers for recruitment to the national cause. It is remarkable that even small villages with fifty or seventy households had at least one primary school — and sometimes more.[75] Nevertheless, we can hardly argue that it was ultimately a successful educational campaign that created Greeks and Bulgarians out of the children of Christian peasants in Macedonia. It is true that the schools in urban centers played an immensely important role in the making of national leaders, some of whom, as we have seen, took their mission to villages across Macedonia as schoolteachers. As influential as they were, these teachers were still the minority among those educating the rural parishioners' children, many of whom could not attend school regularly due to their families' reliance on them as extra labor. The dearth of teachers and the unwillingness of some communities to accept teachers who did not speak their language meant that not all schools were open all the time. The committees also interfered with the functioning of schools if they could not fully collaborate with the overseeing eparchy. Most important, the educational projects of Greek and Bulgarian national elites lacked the means and the ideological unity that could be guaranteed only through the resources of a central state, even as the Greek and Bulgarian states coordinated their efforts with the local religious authorities. The contribution of rural schools to nationalization therefore should be attributed more to their role in further delineating and politicizing communal differences than to large-scale indoctrination.

The dispute over the church building in Spatovo, which eventually spilled over into a dispute about the school building, encapsulates the process through which communal boundaries were hardened. Even after the laborious efforts of several authorities to mediate the conflict in Spatovo, which seemed to have been successfully resolved, the question of fair access to the school reanimated the dispute between Exarchists and Patriarchists. As the negotiations for the church building were finalized, both parties had consented to an arrangement whereby the extra room of the village school

---

75. *Carte des Écoles Chrétiennes;* Brancoff [Mishev], *La Macédoine et sa Population Chrétienne.*

194 → Chapter 5

would be assigned to the children of the Exarchists because they outnumbered the Patriarchists by five to one. Unfortunately, this arrangement lasted only until the arrival of the Greek Metropolitan at the village months later. The Metropolitan demanded that the extra room assigned to the Exarchists now be divided into two sections, one of which would be allocated to the Patriarchists. When the Exarchists refused to give up half of the room, the Metropolitan had the Exarchists' children removed from the room and gave it to the Greeks (*"Rum"*). The incident was reported by the Bulgarian bishop and corroborated by the Greek Metropolitan. The local authorities then advised the leaders of the two communities and the Greek Metropolitan to manage the situation according to the old arrangement, which previously had worked without any complaints from either side. The Greek community, however, now refused to accept any arrangement other than the Metropolitan's, and the Exarchist community, further emboldened by the Metropolitan's interference, refused to give up half of the room, arguing that it was not big enough to accommodate their children, who constituted the majority.[76]

Determining the exact number of rooms in the village school, their dimensions, and the manner in which they were used by the two communities in the last years occupied the officials of the Inspectorate for several months, and the Austro-Hungarian consul in Salonika also got involved in the matter.[77] It appears that they were able to convince the Exarchists to share one of the smaller rooms with the Patriarchists, but the fragile status quo was disturbed yet again in March, this time by the Exarchists, who allegedly confiscated one of the rooms. According to the Greek Metropolitan, the Exarchists had called on the children, who normally would have been tending the cows in the fields, to convince the local authorities that they constituted the majority (*"ekseriyeti kazanmak içün sığırlarını güden çocukları mektebe idhal ve mahallî hükümet memurlarını bu suretle iknâ edebilerek."*). As a result, he continued, not only had the Exarchists almost managed to transform the Greek community school into a Bulgarian one but they had also forced the Greek teachers to instruct all children, boys and girls, in the same room, which surely was unacceptable to the sultan and the General Inspector.[78]

A report prepared by a police officer from Serres, and approved by the representatives of the two communities of Spatovo, finally clarified the confusing matter of the number, division, and use of the rooms of the school. The room that the Exarchists had started using in December 1904 had not been seized from the Greek community; it had been created by dividing in

---

76. BOA, TFR.I.SL 67/6606, report [copy] to the Prefecture of Demirhisar, December 20, 1904; Governorship of Salonika to the Inspectorate, December 25, 1904.
77. BOA, TFR.I.SL 67/6606, Inspectorate to Governorship of Salonika, December 31, 1904 and January 2, 1905; petition from the Exarchists of Spatovo to the Consul of Austria-Hungary, January 6, 1905.
78. BOA, TFR.I.SL 67/6606, petition from the Metropolitan of Menlik and Demirhisar to the Inspector, March 6, 1905.

two the large room on the first floor of the school building that they had already been using. The Greek Metropolitan had come in, removed the children from the small room on the second floor, and locked it up in January. A police officer and a gendarme had been sent to open up the room and return it to the Exarchists' use in February. According to the report, there was no conflict arising from the division of the school in this manner, and female and male teachers (*"daskal ve daskaliçeleri"*) also stated that they got along well.[79] The recommendation of the *vilâyet* to the Inspectorate based on this report was not to intervene in light of the fact that the previous arrangement had been restored and no conflict seemed to have arisen from it.[80]

Did the statements of the teachers to the Ottoman authorities that they were getting along reflect the actual situation? Perhaps, but it is hard to imagine the Slavic-speaking teachers reconciling with their Greek colleagues, whose religious leader had thrown the Exarchists' children out of the school building with the complicity of local officials. Nor would the Greek teachers accept with joy the dwindling number of their student body and their relegation to a minority status in what they considered to be a building and institution that belonged to their community. In other words, there is not much reason to expect that relations between these two communities were as amicable as they appeared in the police officer's report, even though the names of representatives of both sides were signed on it.

On the other hand, the correspondence over the church and school building of Spatovo over the course of a year also reveals that this village was a location where Exarchist and Patriarchist communities had worked out an arrangement between themselves that allowed a sustainable, if not harmonious, form of coexistence. Paradoxically, in Spatovo and countless other mixed villages, the church and the school, the two institutions around which the life of a community revolved and the early socialization of its members occurred, not only constituted the main source of conflict but were also the domain where the factions had to continue to be together. The trajectory of the conflict that followed the division of the Orthodox faith into two different camps in Macedonia was not a straight line tracing a fracture that would inevitably end in violence. It was violence and coercion that made dead-ends out of the various bypasses that existed and might have been taken.

Violence and Religion

Villages with Slavic-speaking populations that had remained loyal to the Patriarchate were the terrain on which the struggle for Macedonia—ecclesiastical,

---

79. BOA, TFR.I.SL 67/6606, Report of the police officer Mahmud bin Mustafa, March 20, 1905.
80. BOA, TFR.I.SL 67/6606, Governorship of Salonika to the Inspectorate, March 27, 1905.

scholastic, demographic, and military—was carried out. Valandova (Valandovo) of the prefecture of Doyran (Macedonian portion: Nov Dojran; Greek portion: Kilkis) was one such village, first brought to the attention of authorities by the Greek Metropolitan of Usturumca/Strumnitza on January 12, 1905, in a letter complaining about the occupation of the community church and school by Exarchists and requesting the restoration of both to the Greek Orthodox community.[81] The Inspectorate demanded an immediate investigation from the prefecture in response. The investigating committee dispatched to the village consisted of Kemal Efendi, a police chief; Atanas, a member of the town's administrative council (who, it seems, was a Slavophone Patriarchist); Hristo Nano of the municipal council, and Esmen Ağa.[82]

The Greek Orthodox villagers told the investigators that they had never abandoned their religion. According to their version of the events, a couple of months earlier their teachers had left the village and returned to their hometowns, scared away by the killings of a female teacher and a few locals in Garçişte (Grchiste) by a Bulgarian *komite*. Naturally, the school had closed down, but the villagers temporarily sent their children to the "Bulgarian school that remained open, instead of leaving them ignorant and without instruction, given that they spoke Bulgarian anyway [*bi't-tabi' mekteb ta'til olunduğu ve bu cihetle etfâlin bilâ-tedâris cahilâne bulunmaktan ise zâten öteden beri Bulgar lisânıyla tekellüm etmelerinden nâşi açık bulunan Bulgar mektebine suret-i muvakkatede berây-ı tedris gönderildiklerini*]." It was also true that a Bulgarian priest had come into their church, although their own priest was present, and that he had conducted services during a holiday, taking turns with the other priest and conducting the service in Bulgarian. It was not true, however, that any coercion was involved, and because this had happened only once, and all the villagers were familiar with Bulgarian (*"cümlesi Bulgar lisânına âşinâ olmalarından dolayı"*), they had not refused him. They asserted that they had never severed their ties with the Patriarchate, and they were not subject to any hidden or explicit threats.

The prefect of Doyran, who related the report of the investigating committee to the Inspectorate, noted that it was quite likely that the villagers were not revealing the complete story. The fact of the matter, he continued, was that there was only one church in Valandova, and it belonged to the Patriarchate and was reserved for the use of the Greek Orthodox community. Moreover, the people who lived in the vicinity of the church, like the majority of the village population, were Greek Orthodox, and the number of Exarchist households was only twenty. Yet the Greek Orthodox population had recently come under pressure to keep their school vacant

---

81. BOA, TFR.I.SL 62/6171, Greek Metropolitan of Usturumca to the Inspectorate, January 12, 1905.

82. BOA, TFR.I.SL 62/6171, Prefecture of Doyran to the Inspectorate, January 15, 1905.

and send their children to the Bulgarian school. Even though they had not been able to find any tangible proof suggesting that the Bulgarian brigands ("*Bulgar eşkiyası*") had passed through the village, a police report had observed that the Greek Orthodox community had lately altered their behavior, which the report attributed to the committee or other "harmful individuals." The prefect himself had received intelligence from an anonymous source that the inhabitants of Valandova had been severely threatened and pressured by a Bulgarian band forty days earlier. In his report, he emphatically recommended that the village be sheltered from the pressure of the *komites* and that the Greek Orthodox teachers and priests be brought back. Finally, the prefect inquired whether legal action would be required against the Bulgarian priest who conducted service in Bulgarian in a church that belonged to the Patriarchate without official permission or authorization. The Inspectorate's response sent to the prefecture on January 26 was that all necessary measures must be taken to prevent such unauthorized interventions in churches belonging to the Patriarchate.[83]

It is interesting to note that the same village was mentioned again in a correspondence of the prefecture of Doyran to the Inspectorate, five months later during the census.[84] It appears that the church had been restored to the Greek Orthodox community because the Exarchists were now asking for a license to build their own church. The local authorities had granted them a temporary building license until an imperial order could be issued. The prefect also recommended registering these twenty households as "Exarchist Bulgars" to prevent the complaints and hardships that were sure to follow if they were not granted this right, even though, having converted in 1900, they were not included in the older register of 1893 as "Bulgars."[85]

The level of tension in such a small village must have been palpable. They had apparently shared one church and one school until five years earlier, sometimes using the church simultaneously and speaking the same language, but they were now split over who possessed the right to use the same buildings. It is also noteworthy, however, that there is no indication in any of the correspondence regarding Valandova that the church split resulted in any prior acts of conflict during the five years that the twenty households had turned Exarchist. The statements of the villagers to the investigators that they sent their children to the Bulgarian school instead of "leaving them ignorant" and because they all "spoke Bulgarian anyway," and did not refuse the Bulgarian priest for the same reason, were probably inspired by

---

83. BOA, TFR.I.SL 62/6171, Inspectorate to Doyran Prefecture, January 26, 1905.
84. BOA, TFR.I.SL 74/7301, Doyran Prefecture; to the Inspectorate, June 3, 1905.
85. The population figures provided by Mishev for this village were 312 "Exarchist Bulgarians" and 560 "Hellenizing Patriarchist Bulgarians," which, although slightly inflated, also correspond to the description in the Ottoman prefect's report; Brancoff [Mishev], *La Macédoine et sa Population Chrétienne*, 100.

the Bulgarian *komite*s in the region, who no doubt protected the twenty-household Exarchist minority of the village.

We should not lose sight of the fact that the villagers were giving this statement to a committee of Ottoman officials, consisting of Muslims and Patriarchists, which suggests that there might have been a kernel of truth in their implied indifference to the presence of Bulgarian clergy and teachers in their midst. Between the *komite* and proselytizing Exarchist priests, on the one hand, and Ottoman officials and the overbearing Patriarchate, on the other, there is seemingly little hope that Valandova managed to maintain this delicate balance of coexistence for long, but, surprisingly, the name of the village does not appear at all in later reports of conflict between Patriarchists and Exarchists. This may, of course, be because of a hole in the archival record, but it also points to the likelihood that Valandova was spared the violence that afflicted similar villages.

Nevertheless, the feeling that violence was the imminent consequence of their communities' being pulled apart by external forces beyond their control was increasingly accepted among the population, as exemplified by the statement, in unison, of a Patriarchist priest and an Exarchist council member from the mixed village of Ravna (Isoma) that their church dispute would not be resolved without bloodshed.[86] The subgovernorate deemed the statement so explosive that they dispatched a significant gendarmerie force and infantry to this small village to prevent the gloomy forecast of the priest and the council member.[87] Four years later, however, the dreaded resolution happened. A Bulgarian band of six entered the village on January 12, 1908, and retreated, leaving behind four people dead and seven houses burned. The attack followed a typical church dispute: the Greek community had obtained a permit to build a new church that the Muslim half of the village was opposing. Because of their pressure, the subgovernor was hardly able to enforce the decision that guaranteed the right to build the church, but he finally managed, and construction started. This time, however, the Greeks did not want to abide by the arrangement that allocated the use of the existing church to the Exarchist and Patriarchist communities in rotation and insisted on their right to use both churches exclusively. Shortly after this, the Exarchist priest of the village was killed, and according to Major Foulon of the French gendarmerie stationed in the area, there was no doubt that the band that later attacked the village was avenging the killing of this priest.[88]

The village of Graçen/Gratsiani (Agiochori) is another example of a Slavic-speaking Patriarchist village being more vulnerable to agitation by armed

---

86. BOA, TFR.I.SL 52/5144, Subgovernor of Serres to the Inspectorate, September 11, 1904; Inspectorate to the Subgovernorate, September 17, 1904.
87. BOA, TFR.I.SL 52/5144, Inspectorate to the Subgovernorate September 16, 1904; Subgovernorate to the Inspectorate, September 17, 1904.
88. MAE, no. 150, Rapport du Major Foulon, Serres, January 21, 1908.

bands through their churches and schools. Graçen was a Patriarchist village of approximately 295. On August 18, 1906, the village Greek Orthodox priest (it is not clear from the report detailing the incident whether he was Slavic-speaking—which is very likely—or Greek-speaking Greek Orthodox) was killed by Bulgarian *komitajis*. The village presumably remained without a priest after this incident until October, when, according to the vice consul, a new priest from the nearby Alistrat (Alistrati) named Leonidas came and held services "with a rifle in his hand and a cartridge-belt over his shoulder." The villagers must not have appreciated the new priest's combative worship style, given that they immediately reported him to the military authorities. The vice consul reported that Father Leonidas was arrested, along with three Greeks (probably teachers from the Hellenic Kingdom), and that 3 Gras rifles and 109 cartridges were recovered from his possession. The villagers requested a priest and schoolmaster who understood their language to replace the ones who had just been apprehended, but to no avail.

At the end of January, a Bulgarian band of five took shelter in the village. A Greek band, apparently in pursuit, arrived after them and set some houses and the village bakery on fire. The *komitadjis* retaliated with bombs, and by the time a local detachment of soldiers and reinforcements arrived, three people were dead and three others injured. The next day, as the soldiers were searching the village for arms, they were met with fire from the *komitadjis*, who had been in hiding and who tried to flee as the soldiers closed in. Two of them were killed.[89]

It is certain that Graçen was a Patriarchist village—especially given that pro-Bulgarian sources of the period record it as such. It is quite remarkable that the village, at least according to the British vice consul, had remained Patriarchist until August or September 1906, quite late and well after the church disputes took a violent turn. In fact, it is not even clear that the villagers ever officially petitioned to join the Exarchate, but the vice consul, who related the incident, had reached that conclusion based on the villagers' demands for a "priest and schoolmaster who understood their language." As the case of the defrocked priest of Karlikovo reveals, the Greek Orthodox Church, thanks to its status as the older and more established ecclesiastical institution, included Slavic-speaking representatives even during the worst stages of the struggle for Macedonia. We have also seen that the Patriarchate could be accommodating in meeting demands for Slavic-speaking priests and schoolteachers as long as they did not preach for the Exarchate. Following the establishment of the Exarchate, conversions in the region did not occur en masse, and a good segment of the Slavic-speaking lower clergy remained within the ranks of the Patriarchate. Therefore, it is highly likely

---

89. PRO, FO 195/2263, Vice consul Bosanquet to Consul Graves, February 16, 1907; MAE, Constantinople, Serie E Macédoine, no. 144, f. 179 A, Colonel Vérand to the French Ambassador in Istanbul, Serres, February 6 and February 19, 1907.

that Graçen had remained among the followers of the Patriarchate, even though its priest and inhabitants were Slavic-speakers and, like many others, opted to preserve the older local religious practices instead of getting involved in a dispute originating in the imperial center. This choice is not extremely surprising, given most people's attachment to the spiritual tradition they were born into and the physical isolation of some of these villages, which made them more immune to (or detached from) calls to switch their Church affiliation. In either case, the communal decision to convert, or not, became a source of acute conflict only after these decisions became politicized thanks to the violent means of coercion employed by the insurgents fighting to establish dominance.

There were no rules of conduct exempting the sacred, even though preserving the sacred from encroachment was presumably what the insurgents were fighting for. The rifle and cartridges that Leonidas, the Greek priest, held close as he was overseeing the liturgy were a relatively minor effrontery and could even be seen as a necessity, considering that no church was safe from the physical assaults of the rival *komites*. Papa Dimitri of Baraklı Cuma/Dolna Djoumaya (Irakleia), who was shot dead on May 25, 1907, while he was conducting services in his church, and his wounded colleague, Papa Stoyan, might even testify that keeping a rifle next to the liturgical objects could have come in handy. According to the reports of the British vice consul, the band entered the church, which was enclosed in a yard, from its two entry points simultaneously. The *cavass* (guard) was caught unaware and killed. The band then proceeded inside and shot the two officiating priests and two women who happened to be attending services at the time. The vice consul's inference was that the attack was in revenge for the killings of two Patriarchists of the same area earlier in the day by a Bulgarian band.[90]

Priests were held personally responsible not only for their own actions and affiliations, but also for the actions of their parishioners, which made them viable targets for disgruntled locals and bands clamoring to impose their own rules on the population. In Usturumca/Strumnitza in April 1904, the French consul general reported that the church dispute had agitated people to such an extent that a "grécisant" (i.e., Patriarchist) named Zographos had been attacked by a Bulgarian, who had fled town after his failed murder attempt. Zographos, having survived the bullet wound, and certainly full of rage that his attacker was nowhere to be found, sought revenge by shooting the Exarchist priest Gerassimos, who, fortunately, was not harmed.[91]

As we have already seen, the general conduct of the priests did not contribute much in the way of dispelling the common notion that they were

---

90. PRO, FO 195/2263, Vice consul Bosanquet to Consul Graves, Serres, May 28 and June 7, 1907.
91. MAE, vol. 40, Consul General Steeg to the Ministry of Foreign Affairs, April 12, 1904.

the principal instigators of the conflict. Adherence to a national cause did have its detractors among the hundreds of priests serving in Macedonia, but those who did follow a nationalist agenda used everything in their power to make sure that their flocks followed suit, even if it meant going against the policies of the Patriarchate or the Exarchate. Consider a few more examples. The Bulgarian Exarch presented a letter to the Grand Vezir in November 1903 about a Greek Orthodox priest and a *muhtar* in Serres who had been circulating the district. They were knocking on the doors of Exarchists, accompanied by a police officer, and telling them that they would be banished from their homes unless they attached themselves to the Patriarchate. The same letter alleged that the Greek priest of Rondi-i Bâlâ (Ano Vrondou), under orders of the Greek Metropolitan, had entered the Bulgarian church by force and, after conducting mass, had removed all the liturgical objects and taken them to the seat of the Metropolitan.[92] Naturally, Exarchist clergy were the subject of similar complaints by their Patriarchist counterparts, especially concerning their collaboration with the *komites* in the region. Take, for instance, the Greek Orthodox Metropolitan of Usturumca/Strumnitza, who intercepted a letter in February 1905 and immediately presented it to the local authorities as proof that the Exarchate was in cahoots with the "brigands." The letter was written by Christo Gorki, the assistant of Chernopeyef, the famous band leader, and addressed to the heads of *komites* in Patriarchist Christian villages. While the Russians were there, the villagers were told, they should go to the Bulgarian Metropolitan and declare their allegiance to the Exarchate.[93] Although the Exarchist and Patriarchist clergy did not unanimously share the goals of the bands, much less condone their tactics, it is true that most of them harbored and protected the guerrillas when the situation called for it and that a smaller but more influential segment actually participated in masterminding the activities of both factions in the region.

It is also important to note that no matter what policy was dictated by Constantinople, the priests had to serve in areas where insurgent bands had either established control or were fighting to achieve that goal. Members of the clergy refusing to comply with the demands of the insurgent bands did not have much recourse other than asking for assistance from the Ottoman authorities or pleading with the representatives of the European Powers. Neither of these were effective measures against the immediate threat posed by the guerrillas, especially in the case of Exarchist priests, given the reluctance of the local Ottoman rank and file to protect anyone associated with the Exarchate, opposed as they might be to the revolutionaries' tactics. Even though the Inspector's office maintained at least the appearance of

---

92. MAE, vol. 39, Petition of the Bulgarian Exarch to the Grand Vezir, November 21, 1903.

93. BOA, TFR.I.SL 65/6434, Usturumca Prefect to the Inspectorate, March 8, 1905.

objectivity when dealing with Exarchist and Patriarchist clergy, the suspicious attitude toward the Exarchate went high up the chain of command to the level of the officers and district governors, who reasoned that the persistent presence of radicals among the priests and schoolteachers even after the wave of arrests and amnesties following the Ilinden Uprising compromised the entire Exarchist establishment. The French consul general in Salonika, M. Steeg, remarked in a report to the embassy in Constantinople, "Hilmi Pasha does not conceal the vivid repugnance he feels to let the functions of priests and teachers be filled with ex-agitators." The consul found Hilmi Paşa's reaction exaggerated because, as he put it, "the nominations of new priests and teachers done by the bishops of the Exarchate are dictated to them most often by the committees." As a matter of fact, the bishop whose ceremonial robe was stolen right before Christmas mass was one of those who did not comply with the orders of the committee. Not only was he humiliated in the eyes of his congregation because of the theft, but, he was also helpless in reopening the schools of his eparchy, which the revolutionaries kept shut down because of his infraction.[94]

Churches as Property, Disenfranchising the Exarchate

The Patriarchate certainly made good use of the suspicion of authorities toward the Exarchists—especially after the Ilinden Uprising—in presenting the cases of disputed churches from their point of view. It was convincing to argue that the communities in question were only recent converts and that, even if they were sincere in their claims of "Bulgarianness," they had no legal entitlement to property belonging to the Patriarchate through the Greek Orthodox community, such as churches. The ownership issue, articulated as a purely legal matter, did not simplify the resolution of the disputes. It did, however, considerably strengthen the hand of the Patriarchate because most of these churches had been constructed during a time when there were no Exarchists to speak of. Even in cases where the churches were built with donations from communities, most of which had subsequently converted to the Exarchate, the Patriarchate could produce titles and records and formulate a convincing legal argument that the churches in question were Patriarchists' property and thus could not be handed over to the Exarchist villages without their consent. This argument was presented as a legitimate reason to keep disputed churches under the control of the Patriarchate as late as 1910. When the Senate was holding discussions on the new *kiliseler kanunu* (Law of Churches), Deputy Alexander Mavrogenis concluded that the issue was simply one of "real estate" and that the Exarchists had no legitimate claim

---

94. MAE, Constantinople E 147, Consul General to the Embassy in Constantinople, Salonika, January 28, 1905.

to the churches built by the Greek Orthodox community for the "spiritual center." Interestingly, Besarya Efendi countered that it was not the church, but the government, that had ultimate authority over such decisions, and his point of view ultimately prevailed in the drafting of the resulting law.[95]

Another factor in favor of the Patriarchists was that, even though villagers were within their rights to present petitions stating that they wished to adhere to the Exarchate, in regions where the Exarchate did not officially have bishoprics, the local parishes that converted to the Exarchate were practically on their own and, at least in principle, still under the ecclesiastical jurisdiction of the Patriarchate. In the case of localities wishing to join the Exarchate where the Exarchate had a bishopric, the legal recourse for Patriarchists contesting church rights was more limited. But some overcame these hurdles through more creative methods that ensured the intervention of the Ottoman authorities against Exarchist communities. An example of this is a disputed lot in Usturumca, purchased by the Bulgarian community for the sum of 900 pounds to build a church. The lot remained vacant for a number of years because the Greek community successfully litigated to "prevent its being even enclosed."[96] The Exarchist community finally obtained the official construction license for the lot on March 22, 1904. Not a week had passed after the work started when shots were fired into a Greek café in town. A Greek Orthodox man by the name of Vassil Christomanos claimed that he had been attacked by Bulgarian *komitajis* in the café, but his story was discredited because he was with friends at the time and no one reported seeing any Bulgarians. It also appears that no injuries were reported. The alleged attack, however, served as a justification for Christomanos's actions the next day, when he shot—and fortunately missed—the Bulgarian Metropolitan who was inspecting the construction. The consul mentioned the agitation that this event stirred up in town, especially considering "the approaching Easter Feasts." This was yet another example of a religious holiday spoiled because of sectarian rivalry.

More complicated were cases involving small community churches in regions exclusively under Patriarchate authority. In such cases, the outcome usually favored the Patriarchist side, given the propensity of the Ottoman authorities for holding up the claims and demands of the Greek Orthodox as a counterweight to Exarchist influence. The Ottoman officials largely shared with the Greek Orthodox clergy the belief that the most effective way to end revolutionary activity in the region was to keep as large a segment of the population as possible within the grip of the Patriarchate. In a report written for the British Blue Book on May 5, 1903, British Vice Consul Theodorides

---

95. Kechriotis, "Modernization of the Empire," 68.
96. PRO, FO 195/2182, Consul Graves to O'Connor, Salonika, April 5, 1904. The consul's report does not make it clear exactly how long the lot had remained vacant. The Exarchate had obtained the bishopric in Strumnitza in 1889.

opined that the villagers should be "encouraged" to return to the Patriarchate because "Exarchist signifies *comitadji* and a real blow cannot be dealt the revolutionary organization except by making the Exarchists return to their original church."[97] In a subsequent report, the same vice consul pronounced the type of encouragement he had in mind more clearly. After a skirmish in Baniçe/Banitsa (Karies) between the troops and an insurgent band, more than 500 arrests had been made in various districts of Serres, followed by petitions from 1,700 households to return to the Patriarchate.[98] Therefore, Theodorides noted approvingly, "there remains no village in the caza [Serres] to the Schismatics."[99] The subgovernor of Serres concurred with Vice Consul Theodorides in his report to the Inspectorate about the incident and the petitions that followed:

> Owing to the military precautions implemented under the auspices of his majesty the sultan, the Bulgarian evil-doers have been exposed. Some villages now come to understand that they were deceived [*iğfal olunmuş*] by the evil propaganda of the Bulgarian priests and teachers installed in their midst, and those villages that have been inclined towards the evil-doers with the encouragement and threats of the Committees, even though they had been attached to the Patriarchate since old times, have applied to the government and stated that they are *Rum* as in the past, and petitioned for the appointment of *Rum* teachers and priests to the Metropolitan, and their registry of under the *Rum* community.[100]

The resemblance in the expression of opinions describing the Exarchists as "evil-doers" and "schismatics," and calling for their conversion back to the Patriarchate by all necessary means, is not merely a coincidence, given that the British Vice Consul Theodorides was a "respected consultant" of both the Greek Metropolitan and the Ottoman subgovernor.[101] Alliances of this sort between the local Ottoman officials and the representatives of Greek Orthodox interests in the area undoubtedly multiplied the resentment of the population against the two sources of authority, the state and the church. Moreover, the accomplishments of the policy of what may be termed "containment by conversion," so exalted by the vice consul and the *mutassarrıf*, did not last for very long.[102] After the reestablishment of relative calm in

---

97. MAE, vol. 40, Appendix to the correspondence of French Consul in Salonika to the Ministry of Foreign Affairs, March 10, 1904, excerpt from a report written by Theodorides on May 5, 1903.
98. Gotse Delchev was among those killed at this battle.
99. MAE, vol. 40, Appendix to the correspondence of French Consul in Salonika to the Ministry of Foreign Affairs, Theodorides's report dated May 26, 1903.
100. BOA, TFR.I.SL 14/1317, Subgovernor Rükneddin to the Inspectorate, June 1, 1903. The mentioned villages were Fraştan-i Bâlâ/Dolna Frachtani, Diranova/Drianovo, Dutlu/Doutlia, Baniçe/Banitsa, Hristos, Marhat/Marsena, and Lakos.
101. MAE, vol. 40, French Consul to the Ministry of Foreign Affairs, March 10, 1904.
102. Shortly after writing this report, the Subgovernor was replaced by Hıfzı Recep Pasha.

the Serres region and the sensible interventions of Hüseyin Hilmi Pasha in favor of the Exarchists, acknowledged by the French consul in Salonika, some of the villages started going back to the Exarchate.[103] Furthermore, the policy of "containment by conversion" would become impossible to sustain, despite the best efforts of the local officials and the Greek clergy, after the order of the Inspectorate to recognize the date of the Ilinden Uprising as a cut-off date for the official recognition of all conversions, including those asking to rejoin the Patriarchate. Finally and more important, this was a self-destructive policy in the sense that, by singling out the Greek Orthodox as the community to be preserved, it made the Slavophone Patriarchists a more attractive target for the wrath of the Bulgarian *komitajis*, who found a ready group of volunteers among the Exarchist peasants disgruntled enough to turn against their neighbors.

Despite the attempts of the office of Hüseyin Hilmi Pasha at reconciliation, the coercion of local Ottoman officials and the repression of the Patriarchate, from one side, and the guerrilla attacks, from the other, irrevocably polarized the Christian population. As the conflicts intensified to the point where going to church on Sunday might mean death, it became impossible for the two communities to use village churches alternately, let alone share them simultaneously, which had once been the accepted practice. After 1904, designating separate lots for each community to build its own church was advanced as another option in official correspondence.[104] Even that, however, would not resolve the problem because by this time the relative centrality of the location of the new church also became a source of conflict.[105] Reluctance to compromise was such a blinding force that the parties would—at least in one case that we know about—rather burn down a church than share it.[106]

A Leap of Faith: Religion and National Identity

Macedonia is a place with plural geographies, borders, and pasts, corresponding to the national vantage point one takes. These divergent and contesting notions of space and identity became calcified behind national borders, stamping the people on either side as belonging to one and only one group, only relatively recently; and even today, they cannot mask the heterogeneity that once characterized these regions entirely. A visitor to one of the border towns of Macedonia on a market day before Easter will

---

103. MAE, vol. 40, French Consul to the Ministry of Foreign Affairs, March 10, 1904.
104. BOA, TFR.I.SL 52/5144, Subgovernor of Serres to the Inspectorate, September 17, 1904.
105. MAE, vol. 40, French Consul to the Minister of Foreign Affairs, April 12, 1904.
106. MAE, Constantinople, Serie E Macédoine, no. 144, f. 191, Captain Sarrou to Colonel Vérand, May 23, 1907.

witness a scene not that far removed from those a century ago, as I did a few years back in Demirhisar/Sidhirokastro (synonyms in Greek and Turkish for "Iron Fortress"), a town mentioned several times throughout this book. True, there were some obvious differences: motor-driven cars had replaced the horse- and oxen-drawn predecessors, and instead of *bijouterie* from France, knick-knacks made in China dominated the stalls. The blaring music and cries of ambitious vendors hawking their wares with the help of audio amplifiers made me nostalgic for the days without such modern amenities, but the produce was alluring even on an unseasonably cold and drab day. A shopper could find anything a household might need before the holiday, from vegetables to cooking utensils to children's clothes. And the place was teeming with shoppers, exactly as it would have been a century ago, making it the best day of business for the nearby coffeehouses that served the exhausted shoppers and leisurely onlookers the same kind of coffee that people have been drinking in the Balkans, Asia Minor, and a large part of the Middle East since the sixteenth century—although it goes by a different name in these parts nowadays: *elliniko* rather than *tourkiko*. I was on the Greek side of the border, but I could discern Greek mixing with Slavic dialects. A woman, the descendant of Asia Minor refugees and married to a Vlach, chatted with me, eager to seize the opportunity to practice her rusty mother tongue, a quaint dialect of Turkish that she had not spoken since her mother had passed away. A live performance by Roma musicians provided a respite from the *skiladika* emanating from the speakers. I could clearly hear the "whispers of assorted pasts," to paraphrase Anastasia Karakasidou.[107]

It was hard to imagine, in such an environment, how people could decide where to buy the dill and parsley for their *mageiritsa* (Easter soup) based not on freshness and price but on the church the vendor would attend the next evening, as the bishop of Nevrekop had demanded of his flock during the *Megali Evdomada* (Holy Week) in 1903. As if to remind me of what I should not lose sight of, two women, who realized I must be a foreigner, stopped me on my way out of the market and insisted that I not leave town without visiting "*our* monastery." Making that monastery "ours," and not "theirs," was the same process that had created Greeks, Bulgarians, and Macedonians out of Orthodox Christians. The muted sounds I heard attested to the "assorted pasts," but it seemed they were destined to fade into oblivion.

The Balkan elites were quick to embrace nationalism as a way out of the defunct and anachronistic political formations that dominated all aspects of their lives—political, social, religious, and economic. Nationalism was a secular ideology closely associated with the notions of mass political participation and representative government, which made it attractive to the nascent bourgeoisie, and to the men and women of letters, who were not

---

107. Karakasidou, *Fields of Wheat, Hills of Blood*, 5.

content within the confines of the old imperial order, including the church. The ideas of the Enlightenment and the French Revolution made a great impression on the pioneering nationalists of the Balkans as they adopted the concepts of scientific rationality, linear time, and teleological history to their circumstances. Religion did not occupy center stage in such bourgeois understandings of the world and their place in it. It may seem paradoxical, then, that the development of secular—or perhaps "vernacular"—cultural movements in the Balkans in the nineteenth century subsequently spearheaded national movements that consolidated religious identities into national ones, rather than entirely supplanting them. Considering the social realities of the human material that the elites needed to recruit for the ultimate success of their national projects, however, the leap from a secular literary culture into a nationalist ideology, formulated and presented through the medium of a "national" church, does not seem that great. The imagined community provided by, and experienced through, the church was the only one that the peasants could make sense of as a union that extended far beyond their otherwise insular worlds. Therefore, for the Balkan nationalist elites, the course of action that had the best shot at success was to create national markers out of religious ones. Victor Roudometof, a historian of the Balkans, has called this plan of action "the redeployment of Orthodoxy," which, he argues, was a direct response of the Balkan intelligentsias to the "articulation of the Greek *ethnie* as a secular nation."[108] But the centrality of religion to the project of nation-making in the Balkans leads me to conclude differently. Although the Greek model indeed pioneered the movement for bourgeois-secular national cultures, the impact of a secular Greek *ethnos* on the rest of the Balkan bourgeoisies and intelligentsias did not emanate in one direction, from the Greek elites to their peripheral Balkan counterparts. Especially after the second half of the nineteenth century, when the church struggle entered a course that would ultimately end with the schism and the formation of national churches in newly emergent Balkan states, religion became an issue of utmost importance also for the supposedly secular Greek elites.[109] Despite its impressive accomplishments, the Greek national project was far from complete at this time, at least as far as the new generation of nationalist intellectuals and statesmen in Athens were concerned. The secular/classical model was insufficient as an ideological support capable of sustaining irredentism in Macedonia (and eventually Asia Minor) when it was confronted with a Slavic-speaking population asserting its collectivity through an alternative ecclesiastical organization. In a sense, rather than the Greek intelligentsia dictating the terms of secular nationhood to the

---

108. Roudometof, *Nationalism, Globalization and Orthodoxy*, 235.
109. According to Kitromilides the "antinomy between Orthodoxy and nationalism" was overcome only after "nation-states had nationalized their churches." Kitromilides, "'Imagined Communities,'" 59.

Bulgarians and religious *Rum,* they would redefine nationhood according to religious criteria. In the end, the threat of Bulgarian nationalism, propagated in Macedonia through the Exarchate, was an important factor embedding Orthodoxy at center stage in the newly cast definition of the Greek ethnos.

Although religion turned out to be the most potent device of nation-making available to the elites, there was more to this process than just the radicalization of sectarian differences. The evidence presented here demonstrates that the mere provision of a new theological alternative that appeased their social and cultural sensibilities did not guarantee mass participation by the peasants, Exarchist and Patriarchist alike, and that the religion question in Macedonia was not solely a matter that followed the formation of an alternative Church. The Exarchate was originally a Church based in Constantinople, the imperial capital, rather than in a place more appropriate to Bulgarian national narratives, such as Tirnovo. It was not a logical consequence and embodiment of Bulgarian national awakening. On the other hand, Bulgarian nationalists would probably have created it by 1900 if it had not already been instituted with an imperial *ferman.* For the elite and the nationalist visionaries on both sides, the Church was the next frontier in the battle for national sovereignty, and the schism was inevitable because of the political imperative of the nation. But the dispute had to be worked out also at a second level, the level of the people, and there expectations of a lasting solution became inextricably entangled with violence. As an Exarchist and a Patriarchist from the village of Ravna put it, there was no redemption until "blood was spilled."

CHAPTER SIX

Logic and Legitimacy in Violence

Even in turbulent Macedonia peace and quiet are a normal condition and violence the exception, though the exception is frequent enough there to render the nerves susceptible to an atmosphere overcharged with the electricity of human emotions.
—Albert Sonnichsen, *Confessions of a Macedonian Bandit*, 1909

The photographs of Leonidas Papazoglou, saved from oblivion thanks to a selection published in 2004 by the Thessaloniki Museum of Photography, provide a rare panorama of life in Ottoman Macedonia, more specifically in the province of Monastir, during the time of the struggle for Macedonia.[1] Through Papazoglou's lens, we catch glimpses of newlyweds, street vendors, actors, and entertainers, the well-heeled and the modest, urban dandies and pastoral tradition, all, of course, mediated through Leonidas Papazoglou's own sense of mise en scène. The album also is a sobering reminder of the extent to which violence was a part of the daily experience of the same people who were posing for the camera—the playful images of young lovers and dapper-looking youths are interspersed with those of guerrillas, real or aspiring, victims of the former, and more macabre compositions involving naked bodies in rigor mortis.

That violence was tenaciously present in the lives of ordinary people of Ottoman Macedonia at the turn of the twentieth century is not a surprising statement at all. The images captured by Papazoglou are starkly indicative of what we have already seen in the preceding chapters and relay through the camera lens what the Albert Sonnichsen, journalist, relayed through the words that open this chapter, taken from in his account of travels with the "Macedonian Bandits." Life as usual went on through the violence; people married, had children, and found ways to make a living and even have a little fun as the struggle for the territory that encompassed their homes was closing in and claiming lives by the hundreds, because that is what human beings are hardwired to do.

---

1. Leōnidas Papazoglou, *Phōtographika Portraita apo tēn Kastoria kai tēn periochē tēs tēn periodo tou Makedonikou Agōna* (Thessaloniki, 2004).

210 → *Chapter 6*

6. Father and son with oxen.

In this chapter, I sharpen the focus on instances of violence for two reasons: first, to separate violence from the struggle taking place and analyze it in its own right rather than write it off as a self-explanatory occurrence under the circumstances, and, second, to look beyond the seemingly ubiquitous incidents of violence to understand what, if any, alternative modes of interaction were available to the warring factions. The relation between conflict and violence should not be considered a robust and self-evident mechanism but a context-specific process, the logic of which remains to be explored.

In an article that sets forth the desiderata for a new approach to ethnic and nationalist violence, Rogers Brubaker and David Laitin urge caution in making precisely this type of association between preexisting conflict and violence, arguing that violence "should not be treated as a self-explanatory outgrowth of such conflict, something that occurs automatically when the conflict reaches a certain intensity, a certain 'temperature.'" The important distinction, according to Brubaker and Laitin is that "[v]iolence is not a quantitative degree of conflict but a qualitative form of conflict, with its own dynamics."[2]

---

2. Rogers Brubaker and David D. Laitin, "Ethnic and Nationalist Violence," *Annual Review of Sociology* 24 (1998), 426.

7. Couple from Kastoria.

8. Peasant couple.

9. Imam and daughter.

10. Dancers.

11. Wedding.

12. Funeral.

13. Smokers.

Following this approach, I show that violence was a necessary condition for, and not a natural by-product of, a strong ethnonational consciousness among the rural population. In other words, violence played a role in engendering that very same feeling of difference and boundaries that purportedly were its cause. The systemic, targeted, and (tragically) efficient violence, examples of which I describe in this chapter, was not simply an epiphenomenon but a prerequisite to the politicization of communal difference. Just the simple fact that both the perpetrators and the victims were Slavic-speaking in a majority of the cases discussed in this chapter should throw notions of ethnic warfare fought among clearly defined groups in doubt. The violence inflicted by the Ottoman military and paramilitary groups, on the one hand, and several factions of militias, on the other, worked in tandem to create the conditions under which the notion of national belonging penetrated the consciousness of a large segment of the peasant population. This process functioned through two principal channels of boundary-creation and -activation mechanisms: first, it rendered impossible the option for individuals to remain bystanders by creating an atmosphere of inescapable terror, and second, it made people aware of their ties to a larger community outside their immediate vicinity—they were now tied by blood to an imagined community.

This should not, however, lead us to conclude that violence was an indisputably effective tool in disseminating an ideology and creating committed converts to one movement or the other. Although the utility of violence as both a tactical and strategic instrument was clear to those who wielded it, the results achieved were mixed at best in terms of winning the hearts and minds of the people on whose behalf the insurgents were fighting. Without discounting the dedication or the faith of the insurgents, we should not lose sight of the fact that as many people picked up arms out of an instinct to survive as did out of ideological commitment. This is not to suggest that most of the guerrillas were hapless tools without any agency of their own; nor should we attribute an idealized innocence to those who denounced their comrades, turned in their neighbors, or hid weapons in their barns. We need to exercise caution, however, in attributing purely ideological motives to individuals' participation in episodes of violence carried out against the putative enemies of the nation.

The question of agency is implicitly linked to a problem with narration; more specifically, the problem of naming the members of different armed groups without setting off ideological alarm bells. Although I am not entirely persuaded by the analytical utility (or even the possibility) of devising a normative terminology, I think it is necessary to clarify, or at least underline, a few keywords that appear repeatedly in the primary sources as well as secondary accounts, scholarly and popular, of some of the events in question. The arbitrariness of ascribing meaning to the difference between a brigand and a guerrilla is well encapsulated in the clichéd expression "one man's terrorist is another's freedom fighter." We have already seen the refusal of the Ottoman bureaucracy to assign any name other than "*brigand* to those who joined insurgent bands; doing so would have been an acknowledgement of a substantive difference between highway robbers and members of the revolutionary organizations. Nevertheless, the Ottoman government did apply a similar distinction by trying the captured insurgents in different courts; according to official reasoning, which court tried the case depended on whether the crimes committed fell under the purview of criminal law or extraordinary regulations regarding state security. In practice, this usually translated into Greek insurgents being transferred to the criminal courts for trial and sentencing but their Bulgarian counterparts being tried in the "extraordinary courts."[3] It is worth noting that the term *brigand* was also used by foreign representatives of the international reform initiative in Macedonia in reference to the members of revolutionary organizations, despite the fact that they were often tacitly sympathetic to one side rather than the other.

Although I could avoid, if not entirely resolve, this issue by resorting to the relatively neutral term *militia,* this semantic strategy would not address the more problematic distinction from the point of view of a historian, the one between the categories "peasant" and "militia." The struggle for Macedonia was fought not between sovereign states but as an insurgency.[4] As in any other conflict of this nature, and as the Ottoman administrators readily acknowledged, the majority of the fighters were not foreign agitators but locals, ordinary people, who had a frustrating ability to resume their daily work and blend into the peasantry as soon as there was news that the Ottoman military was getting ready to make a move. As in Mao Zedong's famous metaphor, they moved among the peasantry as "a fish swims in the sea." An Ottoman official put it more bluntly, they were simply "indistinguishable" from the general population.[5]

The source of frustration for the Ottoman administrator is the same thing that makes the task of the historian much more complex, namely, that the peasants were indistinguishable from the militia members simply because they sometimes were one and the same. This statement does not imply that every single peasant led a parallel life as an active combatant. Rather, it underscores the ambiguity of agency when it comes to the involvement of the peasants themselves in the fight to capture their bodies and minds. We should not forget that participation in the insurgency did not necessarily require an individual to pick up a rifle and join the roaming bands of men

---

3. MAE Constantinople, Serie E 147, Macédoine, February 28, 1905.
4. The definition of *insurgency* adopted here is from James D. Fearon and David D. Laitin: "a technology of military conflict characterized by small, lightly armed bands practicing guerrilla warfare from rural base areas." "Ethnicity, Insurgency, and Civil War," *American Political Science Review* 97, no. 1 (2003), 79.
5. BOA, TFR.I.AS 62/6160, June 24, 1908.

in the mountains. The bulk of the planning, coordinating, and enabling was carried out by noncombatant locals, who were more vulnerable to violent retaliation by the state or rival groups than their protectors at large. Even though the perils of an ex post facto attribution of political motives to the actions of the peasants are obvious, we cannot discount their involvement as a reflex response to propaganda or simply chalk it up to coercion. In other words, although the categories "peasant" and "militia" should not be conflated, the overlap between the two makes it imperative that we discount approaches that assume clear boundaries dividing them.

We need not distinguish between guerrillas and security forces based on the respective sources of legitimacy for their actions; this is immaterial in accounting for the mechanisms through which violence created, activated, and reinforced social boundaries. How, then, do we start to make sense of such a complex sociological picture where we cannot assign the actors into neat and self-contained drawers with labels such as "peasant," "soldier," "guerrilla"? I propose, as a starting point, to borrow a few conceptual tools from Charles Tilly's work. Tilly argues that "no simple distinction between 'insurgents' and 'forces of order' can possibly capture the complex social interactions that generate collective violence." His emphasis is, instead, on intermediate political actors with a significant amount of overlap and collaboration (as well as contention) between them. Two such groups, whose interactions are especially significant in shaping collective violence, are the "political entrepreneurs" and "specialists in violence."[6]

In the first group are those who "specialize in activation, connection, coordination, and representation."[7] In our case, the prime example for political actors in this group were the teachers employed at the village schools and gymnasiums across the region, who not only molded young minds and instilled "national pride" in their hearts but agitated the locals for the political committees or the nation-states they served. Politically active priests were also in this category. They were in a unique position to wield religious authority, a particularly mighty force in this context, to activate and reinforce communal boundaries. They also acted as power brokers and negotiators between the people, the guerrillas, and state actors such as Ottoman officials and the representatives of foreign powers. In addition to these "usual suspects," the category "political entrepreneur" is flexible enough to include, for instance, the shepherds who transmitted information on behalf of the guerrillas, the village grocer who coordinated the "contributions" for provisioning of the same, and the sharecropper who got rid of an adversary by ratting him out as a government informer. Representation is another purpose that political entrepreneurs serve, as in the example of the village headmen who supposedly spoke for the interests and wishes of all individuals

---

6. Charles Tilly, *The Politics of Collective Violence* (Cambridge, 2003), 40.
7. Ibid., 34.

in their community and who interfaced between them and agents of the government.

In the category "violent specialist" we have not only the coercive agents of the state, such as the troops, gendarmes, police, security guards of the *Régie*, and village guards, but also the guerrillas, thugs, and sundry bandits. It would be counterproductive to try to classify these agents according to their proclaimed source of legitimacy, political agenda, or lack thereof. It is, however, important to note that these two categories—"political entrepreneur" and "violent specialist"—sometimes overlap, creating great potential for the emergence of particularly effective warlords such as Sandansky and Enver Bey (later, Enver Pasha).

What follows is an account of the work of these actors, the political entrepreneurs and violence specialists, and my analysis. In the first part of the chapter, I take stock of their actions and formulate a taxonomy of violence as witnessed, experienced, and exercised by the people of Macedonia. This allows us to gauge the level of penetration of violence into daily life, its performative aspect, its intimacy, its politicization, and the channels through which it rendered nonparticipation a defunct option. In the second part, I shift the emphasis to the logic of this violence: what distinguished it qualitatively from what preceded and what followed, what its escalation patterns and tipping points were, and how selective violence was gradually overtaken by violence of a more indiscriminate nature. My reading of these events has been strongly influenced by Stathis Kalyvas's theory of violence in civil war, although my analysis is not strictly an application of his model. I have taken heed of his warning against seeing violence as an outcome rather than a process. Although there are many instances of violence presented here, and I do argue that violence should be treated as a category in its own right, my purpose is not to hone in on instances of violence in isolation and present a picture of a world "populated only by victims and perpetrators, combined with the flawed perception that victimhood and guilt are mutually exclusive categories."[8] Victims can indeed also be guilty, and denying that would be denying the individuals who participated in this conflict their historical agency. Nevertheless, this is not a cynical take on the experience of violence; conceding that the line separating victims from perpetrators may be more porous than we tend to assume is not, of course, tantamount to suggesting that the priest had it coming or the informer deserved to be executed. It does require, however, that we engage with the inherent ambivalence of ascriptive categories and accept the uncomfortable truth that it was impossible to sustain the kind of communal warfare we see in this region without significant participation on the part of the "civilians" in acts of aggression against their "friends and neighbors."

---

8. Stathis Kalyvas, *The Logic of Violence in Civil War* (Cambridge, 2006), 21.

Violence: A Post-Mortem Analysis

A man from the village of Eğridere (Kallithea) alerted the authorities about a multiple homicide outside his village in January 1906. The investigators sent to the scene of the crime described it as "savage." The victims were three Greek Orthodox men from Eğridere: Taşo and Koço, the sons of Mihal, the village headman; and Nikola Todor, another Greek Orthodox man from the same village. A fourteen-year-old who ran errands for an Exarchist man had been sent off to deliver animals to the three men for their return journey from the district center. The boy had disappeared without a trace, and the corpses of the party he was supposed to meet were found in a riverbed along the road between Graçen/Gratsiani (Agiochori) and Eğridere.

According to the investigators' report, the shape and size of the entry and exit wounds on the twenty-four-year-old Taşo Mihal's body suggested that the bullets had been fired from a Mannlicher rifle and from some distance above the victims—probably from an ambush position facing the direction of Skirçova/Skrijovo (Skopia).[9] These wounds were not the cause of death, however. All three victims also had wounds consistent with a distinctly large knife commonly used by the "brigands," and they had been "slaughtered" after they were blindfolded with their hands tied in their backs. Nikola Todor's detached head had been placed next to the feet of his corpse. The personal effects of the victims were found nearby, abandoned to give the impression that the attackers had taken off in the direction of Iskirçova, but the report noted that the "tidiness of the pile" and the "discovery of the three men's animals tethered in Eğridere" suggested this was a diversionary trick. Heavy rains following the incident had cleared whatever tracks might have been left behind. Subsequent interviews with two shepherds who had been in the vicinity a few days earlier and the questioning of the village guard as well as the victims' parents yielded no results. Ultimately, the report revealed a motive that might link the murders to the Bulgarian committees more strongly than the (rather impressive) forensic evidence collected from the crime scene: the men had been returning from Serres after having testified at the criminal court against a Bulgarian man from their village.[10]

The extraordinarily detailed crime scene investigation report distinguishes it from more common incident sheets, but the incident itself carries features shared by similar violent crimes registered by the authorities. The first is its performative aspect: the spectacular, almost ritualistic grisliness of the act, or its gratuitous "savagery," to cite the inquiry report, that put a memorable mark on the murders. The second is the possible involvement of

---

9. Mannlicher rifles, state-of-the-art weaponry of the time, were used almost exclusively by Bulgarian bands.
10. BOA, TFR.I.SL 95/9494, January 31, 1906.

neighbors, people who had been living within close proximity to each other regardless of their differences and who would continue to do so after the investigators left, in the planning of the attack and thus the blurring of personal and political motives. The third is the difficulty of gathering information about the incident, the refusal of the victims' relatives to collaborate and provide information, which was a problem faced not only by the state actors but by the guerrillas as well. And finally, there was the location of the incident as well as the origin of the victims: as it will become clear from the examples below, certain areas were more prone to violence than others. Eğridere was among the cluster of villages that also included Graçen/Gratsiani, Alistrat (Alistrati), and Iskirçova/Skrijovo, which were all within an approximately 15-mile radius and which witnessed a disproportionately large number of violent incidents.

Violence as Spectacle

The human body provides a perfect medium for the display of power through humiliation. While alive, its integrity can be offended by relatively inane tactile methods such as the removal of garments covering it, or by more invasive ones such as shaving off facial hair, or through the infliction of physical pain and permanent damage such as the severing of a digit or an ear. The very act of draining life out of a body can be placed on public display for effect, as in public executions (killings carried out in view of bystanders). Even after it no longer has a pulse, the body can be dismembered or desecrated in myriad ways to deliver a message. The message of the examples presented in this section is one of territorial hegemony delivered through the human body. We have seen how the fight over territory in Macedonia was carried out on paper through cartography, in census figures through a body count, and in the spiritual realm through attempts to capture souls by rival sects. The ultimate terrain through which this struggle was dragged, it seems, was made up of mangled bodies.

The articulation of power through the medium of the (tortured) human body was practiced by "specialists in inflicting physical damage." This group included state agents such as soldiers, gendarmes, and the police as well as executers of a certain ideology and the motley crew of brigands and simple thugs.[11] Among the tools used by this group, public executions, which were essentially murders committed in plain sight and in defiance of accepted moral norms, carried a significance that was far weightier than their immediate function as demonstrations of deterrence. They were shows of control and power meant to inspire fear among enemies and awe among supporters, deriving legitimacy through the sheer audacity of their commission.

---

11. Tilly, *Politics of Collective Violence*, 4.

14. Apostol Petkov. Courtesy Princeton University Library.

In September 1904, Apostol, the notorious band leader, personally carried out such an execution. His victim was a man from Baravitçe/Barovitsa (Kastaneri) who had allegedly been hired by the government to spy on Apostol. His punishment was to have his head cut off in his house, in front of his wife and children. Lest the rumor mill mistake the author and motives of this grisly act, Apostol dispatched a letter to the governor of the province claiming full responsibility and daring the officials to enlist more informers to catch him: "Those who denounce will not be spared our knives and guns. Whether they are Muslim or Christian, we do not touch those who do not denounce, we give no harm to nice people, we kill the bad. [He] would supposedly deliver my head to you in return for the gold he received. Instead of him handing over my head, here I am cutting his head off in front of his family, those who see this, if it pleases them they can also continue to snitch." The conclusion of the letter was even more defiant, warning the authorities not to crowd the village with soldiers to gather information because there was nothing to inquire about; he was confirming that the murder was his doing. "If the soldiers swarm in and abuse the villagers, it won't be good, if you want to see us, we are always here, if you want to meet us, we are always in the vicinity," were the last words of Apostol's letter.[12]

A flurry of correspondence between military and civilian authorities followed the receipt of Apostol's message. The region of Mayadağ had been under this guerrilla leader's sway for a while, and he had not only committed a crime and seemingly gotten away with it but was also challenging the government to seize him on what he was clearly claiming as his own turf, with the intended consequence of frustrating the local administrators to no end. Here was a man who had made numerous enemies while building his reputation as a ruthless warlord and yet seemed to evade arrest thanks to that very same reputation. The apparent shortcomings of the troops on the ground did not help the situation either. Interestingly enough, the victim, at least according to the authorities, was not even an informer.[13]

It is impossible to ascertain whether the man really was a government spy or not. When informants were killed, they were usually acknowledged in official records as such, and authorities demanded extra care in the pursuit and capture of those who had assaulted people working for the government.[14] In other words, there was no reason for the authorities to deny that this person indeed had been serving as an informer. It is more likely, however, that he was suspected of helping rival Greek bands because he had violated the ban against interacting with members of the Greek Orthodox

---

12. BOA, TFR.I.SL 52/5169, September 1904.
13. Ibid., esp. Yenice prefect's telegram to the General Inspectorate, September 19, 1904.
14. See, for instance, BOA, TFR.I.SL 13/1268, June 23, 1903.

community.¹⁵ Whether or not the man was indeed an informer, his execution clearly had the desired effect by demoralizing the local authorities, communicating to the locals who wielded real power in the region, and ultimately warning them to stay within the limits set by Apostol. Even the Ottoman officials who, we assume, would have been jaded by the damage and pain they witnessed (and inflicted) daily, repeatedly emphasized the heinousness of the crime, revealing the potency of the medium in which Apostol had chosen to deliver his message to bolster and assert his authority.

Having presented this sequence of revolting scenes, I add here a few words of caution about their interpretation: it is indeed possible to read too much into these deliberately staged acts of ghoulish murder, which can easily be viewed as instances of "expressive" or "ritualistic" violence. The first problem with this conclusion is that "ritualization of violence often serves instrumental purposes."¹⁶ In other words, there is a larger purpose that the seemingly gratuitous cruelty serves—in this case, a claim to territory—which implies that the very "gratuity" of the act is suspect. And although it is tempting to question whether any of this ritualistic violence could be the work of individuals with extreme personality disorders—especially after viewing Apostol's studio photograph in which he is posing gloriously with a pal, rifle in hand and a human skull between his feet¹⁷—that turns out to be an unlikely scenario. The literature on comparative cases suggests that people such as Apostol do carry certain traits that enable them to rise to positions of prominence under extraordinary societal conditions but that they are hardly "abnormal in a clinical sense."¹⁸

We also need to keep in mind that decapitations were part and parcel of the collective memory of punishment in this region, the apparent shock and horror of the Ottoman bureaucrats recording these incidents notwithstanding. We can see this as an extension of Charles Tilly's notion that societies have a "limited repertoire of social action," and "people tend to act within known limits, to innovate at the margins of existing forms."¹⁹ Execution by decapitation and the exhibition of the severed heads of the "enemies of the state" had a long tradition in the Ottoman Empire, providing emphatic material for the histories of a cruel and arbitrary Ottoman yoke in the Balkans; however, we should note that the practice was not exclusively an Ottoman form of punishment and that its use did not necessarily distinguish among

---

15. BOA, TFR.I.SL 52/5169, Prefect of Yenice to the General Inspectorate, September 20, 1904. The Prefect reconfirmed that the victim had not been in the employ of the government, but there were rumors that he had been "in contact with the *Rums.*"

16. Kalyvas, *Logic of Violence in Civil War*, 25.

17. This image can be viewed at "Apostol Petkov," Wikimedia commons, http://en.wikipedia.org/wiki/File:Tane_Nikolov_Apostol_Petkov_jpg.jpg (accessed October 29, 2012).

18. See, for instance, Kakar's work on the "wrestlers" in Hyderabad; Sudhir Kakar, *The Colors of Violence: Cultural Identities, Religion and Conflict* (Chicago, 1996), 81.

19. Charles Tilly, *The Contentious French: Four Centuries of Popular Struggle* (Cambridge, 1986), 390.

regions or the ethnicity of the victims. What is important to note is that the act of decapitation itself, as offensive as it was even then, did not transgress an established norm. The transgression was, rather, in the appropriation of the authority to perform that act, by the "bandit" in this instance.

During the sixteenth-century French religious riots, Natalie Davis observes, "*official* acts torture and *official* acts of desecration of the corpses of certain criminals anticipate some of the acts performed by riotous crowds."[20] We can argue that the examples presented here follow a similar pattern, but that should not give us an excuse to overlook the subtle (and sometimes not so subtle) shifts in the deployment of this macabre display of force. These shifts reflect a change in not only the medium but also the substance of the message it aimed to impart. To start with, we need to draw a distinction between public executions by decapitation (or other methods) and the display of post-mortem severed heads, a morbidly fascinating practice with apparently more uses than we might expect.

In the post-*Tanzimat* Ottoman Empire, public executions, including decapitations, were an all but extinct practice. What was more common, even as late as the turn of the twentieth century, was the display of the corpses or the severed heads of "bandits" killed in clashes with security forces (who were sometimes ex-bandits themselves), especially those of some renown, in a public place, ideally to those who were familiar with the deeds of the deceased. An obvious interpretation of this grim pageantry of post-mortem humiliation is that it was meant to strip the "bandits" completely of the power—moral as well as physical—they once wielded in challenging the authority of the state, ensuring that they were not only dead but were also denied the right to preserve somatic integrity as a minimal degree of dignity for the dead. It also confirmed the identity of the deceased to a large audience, who witnessed his inglorious end with their own eyes, lest the legend of the dead "bandit" outlast his biological life.

This state-centric interpretation is complicated by photographic evidence showing guerrillas posing with the cut-off head of one of their comrades, resting on a podium covered with a cloth and framed by a funerary laurel wreath. Here, the intended humiliation was completely displaced and the deceased was honored as a hero through the photograph of his desecrated remains.[21] In either case, the image of a head without a body was an extremely potent one, capable of creating what seem to be contradictory paths of commemoration.

The Ottoman government was adamant in refusing any formal acknowledgement of a distinction between militias fighting for political independence

---

20. Natalie Z. Davis, "The Rites of Violence: Religious Riot in Sixteenth-Century France," *Past and Present* 59 (May 1973), 59.

21. It is tempting to read this image as a neo-icon channeling the image of St. John the Baptist, with the guerrilla replacing the saint as a martyr to the just cause.

15. *L'Illustration* cover, February 28, 1903. Ottoman gendarmes and police with severed heads. Private collection of Edhem Eldem. Used with permission.

16. Guerrillas with severed head. From Leonidas Papazoglou, "Photographic Portraits from Kastoria and Its Vicinity at the Time of the Macedonian Struggle," George Golobias Collection, Museum of Photography, Thessaloniki. Used with permission.

and highway robbers or simple "brigands." Despite the occasional overlap between these two categories and the Ottoman authorities' hypocrisy in trying Bulgarian and Greek guerrillas in separate courts, however, they were indisputably distinct from one another by the turn of the twentieth century. The highway robbers might be harking back to the romantic tradition of "noble thieves" living in the mountains unencumbered by the norms of settled society and peasant submissiveness, but they did not carry the same moral clout accorded to independence fighters in liberal European public opinion. Moreover, the guerrillas themselves were committed, at least in principle, to maintaining that distinction.

It is not surprising, then, that the Ottomans found themselves in a publicity nightmare that could not be undone, despite the deployment of the Hamidian "image management" machinery, following the publication on February 28, 1903, on the front page of *L'Illustration* of Paris, of an image of Ottoman gendarmes posing around what was captioned as the decapitated heads of "Macedonian rebels." Even though the officials in Monastir eventually identified the heads in the image as those of "Greek brigands" killed in Gorice (Goritsa) in 1891, and assured the palace that no such acts were carried out anymore, there were enough similar compositions in circulation to suggest that it was fairly common to have such photographs taken as "trophies."[22]

That is, although the state was certainly willing to receive full credit for the capture and annihilation of its enemies, and was complicit in the desecration of their bodies, the resulting photographic compositions were not intended as a tool in its display of hegemony through human bodies. The moment the corpses or severed heads of guerrillas killed elsewhere were placed on public display in a town center the state mission was complete. When these images were captured by a photographic lens, however, they acquired an independent meaning. As fascinating as it is, the pursuit of this meaning would be a digression from the main thread we have been following so far—the use of state-induced or state-endorsed violence to communicate territoriality. Suffice it to say that the state was concerned with these images only to prevent their dissemination from infringing on its already shaky legitimacy.

The Ottoman government under Abdülhamid II went after those who opposed its authority with a vengeance, but for all its show of absolutism, its punishments were always juxtaposed with the paternalistic leniency of a regime that jailed entire villages following an uprising and yet pardoned "ex-bandits" who expressed their regrets, often honoring their requests to be enlisted in the gendarmerie.[23] "His august majesty's clemency" was extended not only to remorseful "brigands" who surrendered but to those already arrested and sentenced to death for involvement in the revolutionary committees. Consider the case of Konstantin Goroyif, for instance. Previously arrested and sentenced to death for leading a group of "bandits," he was not only pardoned but also appointed as a teacher in the district of Yenice Vardar (Giannitsa), despite the general policy banning individuals associated with revolutionary committees (let alone leading one) from employment at schools, which were (fairly) viewed as staging centers for propaganda activities.[24]

A perusal of records on the death penalty suggests that it was mostly reserved for nonpolitical crimes and often commuted to life or long-term imprisonment. One convicted criminal, a certain Hüseyin Ali, apparently took notice of this asymmetry in the application of criminal law when he sent a petition asking to be pardoned, just like "Bulgarian and Rum evil-doers

---

22. BOA, TFR.I.A 4/380, March 1903. The same folder of correspondence reveals that 350 copies of a similar photograph was found in Salonika in the photography studio of a German national by the name of Bader. The photographs were clearly intended as "souvenirs" from the region. I borrow the term Ottoman "image management" from Deringil, *The Well-Protected Domains*.

23. See, for instance, BOA, Y.A.RES 151/55, December 10, 1907; TFR.I. SL 13/1300, June 28, 1903.

24. BOA, TFR.I.MN 52/5103, May 5, 1904.

230 → *Chapter 6*

who have been set free despite being sentenced to death."[25] There was no indication, however, that this "me too" wish of the detainee was granted.

Two public executions that took place in the market square of Serres in 1907 indicate a clean break from this established practice. The first of these must have been a shocking sight. Dimitri Trandafil and Yovan Gilo Mihal were brought before the gallows at 6:30 a.m. on October 31, 1907. Their incarceration had taken place only months before, thanks to the confessions of Giorgi Kiatibof, a "notorious comitadji" on the loose for many years, who had turned himself in to the authorities in Rondi/Vrondi (Vrondou) in June. Kiatibof's confessions had inculpated a large number of Vrondi locals, among them Dimitri Trandafil, the village teacher, and Yovan Gilo Mihal, grocer and former *muhtar* (headman). Kiatibof had identified the two as the section chiefs of the revolutionary committee (presumably IMRO) in Vrondi, which was confirmed by another guerrilla who had surrendered to the authorities, as well as by witnesses from the village. They had coordinated the storage of arms and munitions, coordinated the provision of shelter to the guerrillas, and, more important, delivered judgments on executions to be carried out by the bands. That their comrades attempted to assassinate Giorgi Kiatibof and his associate after these arrests must have been a contributing factor in the harshness of their punishment. Whereas Kiatibof survived the plot and went up the social ladder, having been appointed a police officer, his friend was killed.[26] After a trial at the extraordinary court of Salonika, Trandafil and Mihal were sentenced to death, and their execution took place soon after the sentencing.[27] The following excerpt from the report of Major Foulon conveys in detail the theatrics involved:

> Two gallows had been erected by gypsies who would proceed with the execution themselves. The two Bulgarians were made to climb on a stool on a table and after passing around their neck a rope coated with soap and oil they toppled the table and the stool, as a result of this fall from about a meter, death should be almost instantaneous, in any case, no convulsions were observed on either of the corpses. After a display of three hours, during which a large group of people—where the Christian element was scarcely represented—went around the gallows, the corpses were placed in caskets. The mutasarrif himself came to the place and lectured the crowd, essentially telling them that from that moment on, the imperial government which until then had shown much leniency toward the trouble makers was firmly resolved to let the people who had been convicted of crimes such as [these] be executed, and consequently in the future

---

25. BOA, TFR.I.ŞKT 97/9654, March 31, 1906.
26. This assassination attempt is described in detail later in the chapter. Katibof initially requested a position at the tax office in Vrundi, but the position of police officer was deemed more suitable by the authorities. Kaitibof reportedly accepted the position with enthusiasm; BOA, TFR.I.AS 48/4798, July 13–15, 1907.
27. BOA, TFR.I.SL 161/16035, October 14, 1907.

people would take care to refrain from such acts. Before the execution, the death sentence was read publicly, an excerpt from this sentencing, written in large letters was attached to the chests of the condemned. After the public display, the corpses were transported to the Bulgarian church where a service was held.[28]

Shocking as it was, this public execution was not the real clincher; that took place less than two months later, again in a public square in Serres. This time, it was two Greek *andartes* who stood before the gallows. Nico Dimitri Panayiot, a Greek national, and Vano Orde Athanas, from the village of Homondos/Houmandos (Mitrousi), were hanged at 6 a.m. on December 16, 1907, amid the shocked horror of the *Rum* community of the town, the Metropolitan, and staff of the Greek consulate. This was not only a break with the custom of pardoning political prisoners but also an open reversal of the policy of tacit collaboration with the Greek bands and turning a blind eye on their increasingly audacious activities. Despite the repeated pleas of the Greek consul in Serres to the subgovernor and, subsequently, the governor of the province, the executions were carried out as planned.[29] The two men had been arrested during the course of an attack after they had killed the main commissioner of the locality, a police agent, and two soldiers, which may explain why the local authorities were less inclined to take the necessary steps to arrange a clemency hearing for the two. Nevertheless, this public execution, coupled with the growing tension between the subgovernor and the consul, denotes a significant shift in the attitudes of the Ottoman authorities toward Greek militia activities in the region.

Following these two incidents, there were other executions of death sentences elsewhere in Macedonia during the first half of 1908.[30] Although they were still quite few in number, this apparent shift in policy toward political prisoners, and especially the manner in which the executions were carried out—in full view of the public and with the bodies deliberately left on display for hours—raises the question "why?" The answer lies in the broader international context and the direction the Macedonian reforms were taking at that particular time. The speech of the subgovernor to the crowd (most of whom were Muslims, reportedly) watching the hangings, warning them that the imperial government would no longer tolerate the misdeeds of the committees, is a clear indication that these executions were staged more for political effect than for carrying out the rulings of the extraordinary court. The intended audience was not only the present crowd but the representatives of

---

28. MAE, Constantinople, Série E 144, October 31, 1907.
29. BOA, TFR.I.A 36/3581, December 17, 1907; MAE, Constantinople, Série E 144, December 16, 1907.
30. I was able to track a total of five, all but one of them carried out in Monastir: BOA, TFR.I.MN 152/15168, January 8, 1908; TFR.I.KV 187/18606, January 1, 1908; TFR.I.MN 162/16153, April 4, 1908; TFR.I.MN 169/16855, June 6, 1908; TFR.I.MN 173/17248, June 6, 1908.

the European Powers responsible for supervising the reforms. The mandate allowing their presence was up for renewal at the end of 1907, but reciprocal foot dragging by Britain, the other powers, and the Ottomans had created a crisis. Britain was seemingly determined to take over leadership of the reforms from Russia and Austria-Hungary, and to impose more stringent measures on the Ottomans. Among the British demands from the Sublime Porte was an end to the complicity between the Ottomans and the Greek bands. The civil agents lent support to this demand, and by the end of the year, the Ottoman military had started a more energetic pursuit of the Greek bands.[31] The executions of Bulgarian and Greek fighters within a two-month period should therefore be seen as proof by the Ottoman administration of its commitment to stamping out guerrilla activity, regardless of the side a particular band was fighting for.

Intimacy of Violence and the "Dark Face of Social Capital"

May 29, 1908. Early in the evening, a Greek Orthodox youth, approximately twelve years of age, walked into Nikola Trayko's shop to buy some yogurt. Having made his purchase, he started toward his house. He was about 30 feet from the store when pandemonium erupted over the bowl of yogurt. Nikola Petre, identified by the report as fifteen years old, a sawyer by occupation, and a resident of the Hamidiye quarter in the vicinity of the Armenian church, had apparently been observing the transaction from his store. He walked out and stopped the child: "Why do you buy yogurt from a Bulgarian when there are Greek shops here?" he demanded. As Nikola Petre was attempting to spill the contents of the hapless child's yogurt bowl, *kalayci* (tinner) Hasan ran up to them: "Why are you doing this?" he asked of Nikola. In response, Nikola claimed he had been declared the "despot"[32] and that he would prevent the Greek Orthodox from buying yogurt or other things from Bulgarians. He was wielding a knife and about to charge at Hasan when Çerkes (Circassian) Said Efendi, a market inspector, interfered and seized him and had him removed to the police station for questioning.[33]

This episode took place in Salonika, Macedonia's largest port city and the "window into the world." The narrative of this document partially reflects the ethnic and religious mixture that was the defining characteristic of the city—with the exception of the Jewish element, which was the dominant ethnic group in the city, we hear about all the major groups in the city and their intermingling. It also reveals that the practice of boycotting the

---

31. At the same time, the European Powers started exerting more pressure on the Greek government to prevent Greek officers from crossing the border to organize and engage in the activities of armed Greek bands; Dakin, *Greek Struggle in Macedonia*, 314–20.

32. The term *despot* in this context means "person in charge."

33. BOA, TFR.I.SL 184/18394, Salonika Police Bureau to the Inspector General, May 30, 1908.

businesses of rival ethnic groups, long in effect in some provincial centers, had also spread to Salonika, whose cosmopolitanism was apparently eroding under the new rules aimed at keeping different ethnic groups separate from each other.

Small-business boycotts relied on voluntary enforcers such as Nikola Petre, and their zealous participation should itself serve as a reminder that these boycotts were not always very effective—especially in a large port city such as Salonika where social pressures were considerably lighter. Their impact, however, should not be measured by the economic damage they were meant to impose on the other community but seen as part of a larger strategy that aimed to minimize intercommunal contact. This strategy involved several methods to keep communities separate, such as orders against house visits, attending baptisms and marriages, and sharing sacred space, examples that we have seen in the previous chapters. Limiting the exchange of greetings and small talk in what should have been the "safe zone" around the marketplace was a far more destructive result of these boycotts than any material damage they might have caused because it served to make strangers out of one's neighbors and to make a threat out of the mundane and the familiar. This alienation was a significant (and necessary) element in the normalization of acts of violence against the separated "other" because it served the very human need to put a distance between an individual and his or her deeds that might result in harm to another person, by making that distance much greater than it used to be.[34]

The alienation or "dehumanization of the other" has been identified as a necessary step on the road to mass killings in a wide range of history, from sixteenth-century religious riots in France to the Holocaust.[35] In his work on Hindu-Muslim riots in India, Sudhir Kakar follows this well-established notion that dehumanization of the victim is integral to the (social, ethical, and psychological) legitimation of violence.[36] Even though Kakar's focus is on a particular kind of violence, namely urban riots, which does not readily present a parallel to the rural violence in Macedonia at the turn of the twentieth century, his ethnographic conclusions have broader applicability. Sarkar's case studies reveal a process that runs parallel to the construction

---

34. For a detailed analysis of the psychological processes that shape people's behavior during ethnic conflicts, see Vamik Volkan, "Psychoanalytic Aspects of Ethnic Conflicts," in *Conflict and Peacemaking in Multiethnic Societies*, edited by Joseph V. Montville (Lexington, 1991), 81–92.

35. Natalie Z. Davis, in articulating this notion, argues that the ceremonial accompanying acts of violence performs the function of hiding from sixteenth-century religious rioters "a full knowledge of what they are doing." "Rites of Violence," 85. Several studies following the culturalist approaches to ethnic and nationalist violence place the process of dehumanization at the center of their analyses, and they consider the "cultural construction of fear" to be a necessary part of it. For a discussion and an introductory bibliography, see Brubaker and Laitin, "Ethnic and Nationalist Violence."

36. Kakar, *Colors of Violence*.

of a dehumanized "other" from one's neighbors, namely, the strategies devised to deal with the guilt that accompanies participation in riots despite the early socialization vilifying members of the other community that each person goes through: "It is easier to kill men who are strangers, to obliterate faces which have not smiled on one in recognition. It is easier to burn down houses which have never welcomed one as a guest," Kakar remarks, capturing the essence of the dilemma any human being must face before causing harm and pain to another.[37] This is why, he explains, it was more common for mobs to go foraging in distant corners of their town rather than attacking their immediate neighbors: that task was left for a mob from another corner of the city.

It is not far-fetched to suggest, then, that for many who wound up "denouncing" their neighbors by guiding a band to their house there must have been a great psychic distance between what they were doing and, say, participating in a massacre; the guerrillas can be seen as the counterpart to the "mob from another part of town" in this version, assigned the task of "cleaning up" without compromising the larger public's sense of decency. As Stathis Kalyvas puts it, "[C]ivil wars are bloody not so much because people are inherently violent, but because they are not: most are repelled by the prospect of acting violently, and so they will not, unless someone else handles the gory details while shielding them." The ease with which violence can be outsourced, or the abundance of "opportunities for indirect violence," is precisely what makes civil wars so unusually violent.[38] On the other hand, we should also note that the guerrillas, whose job it was to "handle the gory details," occupied a moral space separate from the rest of the members of society, just like the soldiers whose use of coercion was sanctioned and legitimized by the higher interests of the state. They knew their moral purity was compromised, but they had volunteered for this position out of their commitment to a legitimate political cause (and no doubt, at least for some, out of less "noble" motives such as the lure of pursuing a romantic ideal of manhood).

Apostol, one of these self-declared "avengers" of the people, and his band were in action again in November 1904.[39] They stopped by Garçişte (Grchiste) to look for a Greek band that had reportedly taken shelter there. Their search did not yield any results, but they did not leave without telling the villagers to convert to the Exarchate and expel their schoolmistress, Catherina Hadgi-Yorgi. Miss Hadgi-Yorgi, in her twenties and originally from Gevgeli (Gevgelija), had resided there for the past five years. Shaken

---

37. Ibid., 29. The exceptions being, I assume, sociopaths or those suffering from similar psychosocial anomalies—admittedly, unlike Kakar, I am entirely out of my area of expertise here.
38. Kalyvas, *Logic of Violence in Civil War*, 14.
39. MAE, Constantinople, Série E 143, Macédoine, Vice Consul in Salonika to the Chargé d'Affairs in Istanbul, November 2, 1904.

up by this event, she packed and left the village for her hometown. She came back several days later, however, apparently after being encouraged by the Greek notables in Gevgeli and given assurances by the elders of the village. Only two days after her return, on a Saturday evening, a band of fifty men appeared in the village and went directly to Angos Kiros's residence, where Catherina had been renting a room, and demanded to see the teacher. Clearly, their intention was not to have a casual conversation with her, so the landlord refused to open the door. The guerrillas then poured kerosene on the periphery of the house and on three adjacent ones and started a fire. The charred remains of Catherina were later found in the rubble of the house. Six others had also been killed in the conflagration, including two children.

The French consul who reported this incident noted that the village consisted of some eighty households, which had been members of the Bulgarian Catholic Church until a few years earlier, when the Patriarchate managed to enlist them among its followers even though the village was entirely Slavic-speaking. The Exarchists in neighboring villages were disturbed by this turn of events and did not approve of the presence of a Greek schoolteacher. The consul added that sources more sympathetic to the Bulgarian side claimed that there was a Greek band taking shelter in the house and differed in their accounts in insisting that the band had given the residents a chance to evacuate the premises before starting the fire. This version of events did not really hold up against the evidence because there had been no retaliatory shots from the house, and all the victims were unarmed residents. This type of justification was a common enough excuse presented to attenuate and possibly depersonalize the crime committed, but the truth remains that the guerrillas were rarely concerned about minimizing the collateral damage from their actions, often planned on the basis of information they gathered from the friends and neighbors of the targets.[40] This brings us to one of the thorniest issues related to intercommunal violence, namely the involvement of neighbors and acquaintances in acts of aggression. Countless examples from archival sources suggest that this was a chillingly common occurrence.

Such was the fate, for instance, of Mr. Stephanos, the *muhtar* of Leşka (Leshko) in the district of Cuma-i Bâlâ (Blagoevgrad) near the Bulgarian frontier. The investigation after the man's disappearance from his village in summer 1903 revealed that he had been kidnapped and killed by a band of eighty men acting on the orders of Donchev, a well-known guerrilla leader. Fifteen fellow villagers of Stephanos had guided the band to his home, from which he was taken to Lakadaş (Logodazh) and executed on a hill above the village church. The band reportedly stayed in Leşka for another two days after carrying out the order and then returned to Bulgaria. According to the *mutasarrıf* (subgovernor) of Serres, it was understood that Stephanos

---

40. See, for instance, Captain Campocasso's report: MAE, Constantinople, Serie E 144, Macédoine, Captain Campocasso to Colonel Vérand December 31, 1906.

236 → Chapter 6

was killed because he had assisted the Ottoman troops as a "guide" for an ambush that had resulted in the "annihilation of 51 brigands."[41]

The neighbors of Mr. Stephanos, as far as we can tell, retired to their houses after pointing out his residence to the band members, who carried out the execution of the "denouncer" at a distance from the village. There were also cases, albeit not as common, in which neighbors actively participated in the punishment of the offending party. We read about one such incident thanks to the dutiful record-keeping of Captain Campocasso, one of the French gendarmerie officers assigned to the reform mission in the Serres district. The captain's report vividly relates what transpired on the evening of December 25, 1906, in Klepousna/Klepouchna (Agriani), in the district of Zihna, but none of the details he includes addresses the problem of identifying the motive, other than self-evident animosity, of the behavior of the parties involved.[42]

Klepousna was a mixed village, consisting of approximately fifty Exarchist and one hundred Patriarchist households, both sides Bulgarian-speaking.[43] The Patriarchist community had been under pressure to switch its allegiance for some time. Bougdan Vanguel and Jovan Nicolas, two Exarchist men from the same village, took it upon themselves to warn Vanguel Papa Philippe, the Greek Orthodox priest, that he might soon meet the fate of his colleague in Kornitza, who had been killed in July, unless his congregation joined the Exarchate.

The two men's warnings materialized on December 25, 1906. A large band of Bulgarians entered the village as darkness fell, took their positions, and then doused the Papa Philippe family home with kerosene and set it on fire. In addition to the residence of the priest and his three brothers, eight other houses were completely burned down. The death toll was seven people: Anton Angel's parents, son, and wife; the priest's wife; and the parents of Caranfil Boujic. Caranfil Boujic was a teacher married to one of the brothers of the priest. The guerrillas had opened fire on the burning houses, and Caranfil caught a bullet in the knee as she was trying to flee the flames, yet she was luckier than the others in that she lived.

Vanguel Papa Philippe, who had miraculously survived the attack with slight injuries, was familiar enough with his attackers to identify five of them by name; two of these were Constantin Sotir, the Exarchist village teacher, and Dimitri Tchirka, the priest of İskirçova/Skrijovo, another village in the vicinity. Another man claimed that there were other people from Skrijovo

---

41. *Kılavuz* ("scout" of "guide") was the term the Ottoman administrators used for "informers"; BOA, TFR.I.SL 13/1268, Telegram from the Sub-governor of Serres, June 23, 1903. This incident bears resemblances to another execution of an alleged Ottoman-troop scout in the same district; BOA, TFR.I.AS 8/751, June 25, 1903.

42. MAE, Constantinople, Serie E 144, Macédoine, Captain Campocasso to Colonel Vérand, December 31, 1906.

43. Brancoff [Mishev], *Macédoine et sa Population Chrétienne*, 203.

in the band because he had heard their peculiar way of speaking. The captain also remarked that "surely some Bulgarian inhabitants of Klepouchina [sic] were accomplices and must have guided the band."[44] Indeed Athanas, one of the Papa Philippe brothers, had recognized four villagers among the attackers, one of whom was the Bulgarian *kocabaşi* [leader]. Dimitri Papa Philippe named five others: the Bulgarian schoolteacher; a tailor from Razlog; Bougdan Vanguel, who had conveyed the threat to the priest; a certain Guiorgui Cotcho; and a painter by the name of Jovan Todor.

The testimony of the survivors, abbreviated, translated, and recorded by the French gendarmerie officers, leaves the reader grasping for the dénouement that will mark the end of the story. Instead, we are left in suspense; we can only guess what it must have been like to see a familiar face hurling a torch into one's house and speculate that the tailor from Razlog was easily recognized because the village folk sought his services when they needed a new pair of trousers for a wedding or had the old ones repaired before going to church on Easter. There is no moral to this story other than the ease with which former neighbors can turn into enemies and inflict pain on each other.

How then, do we make sense of the arson in Klepousna and countless similar others? Is it even worth dwelling on the details of incident reports trying to reconstruct what really happened from the imperfect information rendered even more problematic because it was conveyed through the idiosyncratic verbiage of various military and civilian bureaucracies? My answer is yes, even knowing full well that perfect reconstructions may elude us, because those very details are germane to the questions of how and why violence becomes salient in the first place. Imperfect as they may be, these reconstructions are worth the effort because they occupy center stage in any endeavor to qualify the link between preconflict cleavages and post-conflict identities. Recent scholarship on ethnic and civil war violence has brought this presumed clear, linear connection under question.[45] Studies covering a wide geographical and methodological range point to a major fallacy in the assumption that ethnic plurality, even in the presence of "ethnic rivalry," is an indicator or a predictor of violent conflict.[46] Moreover, understanding violence at the grassroots level, with all its disturbing intimate details, rather than treating it in the stylized and sterilized form that commonly

---

44. MAE, Constantinople, Serie E 144, Macédoine, Captain Campocasso to Colonel Vérand, December 31, 1906.

45. See, for instance, Brubaker and Laitin, "Ethnic and Nationalist Violence"; Stathis Kalyvas, "The Ontology of 'Political Violence': Action and Identity in Civil Wars," *Perspectives on Politics* 1, no. 3 (2003): 475-94.

46. For a comparative analysis, see Fearon and Laitin, "Ethnicity, Insurgency, and Civil War." See also Gagnon, *Myth of Ethnic War;* Georgi Derlugian, *Bourdieau's Secret Admirer in the Caucasus* (Chicago, 2005). Present-day Macedonia, which, contrary to widespread expectations that it would "explode," remained relatively calm and peaceful, constitutes another telling example refuting the notion that there is only a brief stage of separation between ethnic tension and violent conflict.

accompanies national "awakening" or "liberation" narratives, moves us one step closer to understanding its *dynamics*, which also means accepting the notion that much of this violence may be "endogenous" to war. That violence is endogenous to war is not a tautology, as it may initially sound, but, "a strong qualification of the view that violence arises exclusively from prewar cleavages," to paraphrase Stathis Kalyvas.[47]

Another element that makes the task of revisiting the details of these incidents extremely difficult is the fact that participation in acts of violence is, by definition, a subjective process. No amount of archival documentation and triangulation of that evidence can change this fact; this means that we can grapple with the questions surrounding people's motives for killing and harming only to the extent that we are willing to tap into that subjectivity.

Consider, for instance, the fate of Anton Panteli, who was killed by his erstwhile friends and neighbors at the dinner table, and in front of his wife and five-year-old daughter, who was injured by a stray bullet. The story perfectly showcases the intimacy of communal violence and the indelible mark it imparts as it ravages established networks of kin, friendship, and neighborliness. The murder investigation report from July 1907 provides a rare, if incomplete, picture of that intimacy in relaying the preparation, the calculated gestures, and what looks like the final trepidations of an assassin before he participates in the execution of a former friend.

Anton Panteli, the victim, was a "Bulgarian" from the town of Rondi/ Vrundi in the district of Serres. He and a former associate named Georgi Katiboff had surrendered to the authorities after participating in the activities of the local revolutionary committee for some time.[48] We do not know what prompted their surrender, but we can be certain that they must have provided useful information to the authorities because reportedly Katiboff's testimony ultimately led to the arrest of Dimitri Trandafil and Yovan Gilo Mihal, revolutionary committee members, who, as we have seen, were executed in the Serres town square later that year. After giving their depositions in Serres at the provincial center, Panteli and Katiboff were released, and they asked to return to their hometown.

They were accompanied by a sizable detachment of soldiers for protection on the way home and reached their destination after an uneventful journey. A day later, on the evening of July 5, Anton Panteli was having dinner with his family when several men, initially unidentified, entered his house and opened fire, killing him. During the attack, a bullet scraped his daughter Katerina's cheek, who, luckily, survived her wound. A neighbor,

---

47. Kalyvas, *Logic of Violence in Civil War*, 83.
48. BOA, TFR.I.AS 48/4798, correspondence, June–July 1907. The incident was also reported in MAE, Constantinople, E 144, Crime report for the month of July, August 1, 1907.

hallac (cotton-dresser) Dimitri, who was there for dinner, was also injured in his left arm.[49]

The investigation proceeded promptly after the incident, and the perpetrators were seized within a matter of days. On July 7, Taşko, the miller, who was identified as the person who had pulled the trigger, was arrested, and three days later his accomplices Yovan Savati and Vasil, a shopkeeper and shepherd from the same village, were also captured, and all three were en route to the Serres prison. The speedy arrests were largely the result of prodding by the Inspector General, who had recently come under attack from General Degiorgis for the authorities' repeated failures to protect former guerrillas from revenge killings after they gave up their arms.[50]

The investigation report, dispatched by the district director of Rondi (Vrundi) on July 8 deflected some of the blame onto the victim, claiming that Anton had acted in a cavalier manner and not secured the door to his house properly—although further details clearly reveal that he would have opened up the door for his assailants, regardless, because they were acquaintances. The inquiry commission determined that Yovan Savati, the leader of the local revolutionary committee, had given the assassination orders. Yovan Savati was the recently elected successor to another Yovan, who had been arrested; the murder was retaliation for this Yovan's arrest. The new leader had commissioned two men named Taşko and Vasil to execute the committee sentence.

According to several witnesses, Taşko was seen acting suspiciously on the day that Anton and Georgi arrived in the village. Even though he should have been at work, either at the mill or in his field, he idled around the village all day, briefly went into Anton's house, and came out. He then searched for Georgi and ran into him walking back home from the marketplace. He said, "I am coming too," and joined Georgi on his walk. When they reached his home, Georgi said goodbye, but instead of leaving, Taşko stood by and waited in a bizarre manner, "twisting his moustache," until Georgi finally went inside and closed the door. As he was going in, Taşko said "oh well, we'll see each other tomorrow, right?"

Taşko reportedly went over to Yovan Savati's store right after this incident. Savati then closed down his shop early and disappeared. Taşko was later spotted in the village walking about aimlessly. After sunset, he walked to Anton's house, pushed open the unlocked door, and went up and joined the family at the table and had some *raki*. As they were still eating, he got up and "against established customs," noted the report, left the family at the table. As he was departing he said something incomprehensible in Turkish to Anton. He went downstairs, but nobody heard the door open and close. The

---

49. BOA, TFR.I.AS 48/4798, Subgovernor Reşid's telegram to the Inspectorate, July 5 1907.
50. BOA, TFR.I.AS 48/4798, Degiorgis to Hilmi Pasha, and Inspectorate to the Subgovernorate of Serres, July 5, 1907.

attack took place while the family was still at the dinner table. The sequence of events suggests that Taşko had either let the other assailants in or left the door open for them to sneak, and that, while he was having *raki* with Anton and his family, the others were hiding, waiting for his signal to attack.

There is something cruel and unusual about this kind of violence that cannot be mitigated by widely acknowledged processes of distancing, dehumanization, and finally rationalization. There is an inherent intimacy in these acts, an intimacy that clings to the victim and perpetrator no matter how salient their hatred of each other and that makes the shedding of blood all the more incomprehensible, distinguishing this sort of conflict from any other kind. "Intimacy is essential rather than incidental to civil war," affirms Stathis Kalyvas, but this intimacy is "puzzling only because we tend to assume the inherent goodness of intimate relations."[51] Tension is as likely to arise out of closeness as affection, however. As Kakar points out, "there is a special quality to the enmity I feel for a person who resembles me most but is not me. Next to my brother, it is my neighbor the Ten Commandments enjoin me to love as I do myself, precisely because my neighbor is the one I am most likely to consider as a rival."[52] It is this uncanny resemblance between neighbor and enemy that makes communal violence so disturbing. Stathis Kalyvas convincingly argues that violence is a "reflection rather than a transgression of neighborliness—though a perverse one." The ultimate betrayal of trust, namely denunciation, in his words, amounts to "the dark face of social capital."[53] The examples from the close-knit rural communities we have seen so far constitute further empirical proof of this statement.

Polarization and the "Privatization of Politics"

Even some homicides that were demonstrably of a political nature, such as the quadruple murder and subsequent beheading cited earlier, might have been precipitated by personal vendettas. Remember that the victims had just given a deposition in court against their fellow villager, Pasko; although the report did mention that there long had been a mutual enmity between the defendants and the victims, the nature of this enmity was nowhere made clear, raising the possibility that either the victims' testimony or the calling in of the guerrillas to punish their behavior was motivated by nothing other than sheer spite. This opinion was also voiced by Consul Steeg, the representative of the French Republic in Salonika, when he wrote to the *chargé d'affairs* after a tour of the *sancak* of Serres that "personal vengeance" must have been the motive of at least some of the crimes committed by the bands.[54]

---

51. Kalyvas, *Logic of Violence in Civil War*, 330-31.
52. Kakar, *The Colors of Violence*, 43.
53. Kalyvas, *Logic of Violence in Civil War*, 332.
54. MAE, Constantinople, 143 E, Macédoine, Consul Steeg to the Chargé d'Affairs, October 5, 1904.

Disputes that otherwise would have dragged on in court, perpetuate mutual irritation, or perhaps cause a scuffle were now more likely to escalate into violent confrontation; old grudges harmlessly festering under the seal of social norms could now break free in cathartic bloodshed. It is very important to recognize the distinction between personal and political motives because this distinction ultimately calls into question common assumptions about the nature of preconflict differences in determining the course and intensity of communal violence. The fact that most of the attacks on life and property occurred within a particular physical and human geography of extremely close-knit yet distinct communities, often accompanied by the indifference (if not active involvement) of fellow villagers, requires a better analysis than one of mere condemnation on our part. The relationship between the personal and the political was all the more relevant in such communities, where kinship networks and social interaction between neighbors played an important role in shaping all aspects of life.

We have already introduced the idea that the peasants, far from being passive pawns, could act in ways that accommodated multiple agendas, maximized their chances of survival, and, moreover, made them into political entrepreneurs. In their capacity as political entrepreneurs, they were commonly involved in the planning and execution of mechanisms that served to create and activate social boundaries and contribute to the increasing polarization of society. *Polarization,* in Tilly's definition, is the "widening of political and social space between claimants in a contentious episode and the gravitation of previously uncommitted or moderate actors toward one or both extremes."[55] For our present purposes, the words *previously uncommitted* should be emphasized. In other words, polarization should be understood as being conflict-dependent rather than as the cause and definition of the conflict itself.[56] That polarization occurred not only through the work of guerrillas, or specialists in violence, but through the actions of otherwise peaceful people who continued to participate in the functioning of the society that they were tearing apart is something that should give us pause; however, it becomes easier to understand when we consider the mix of motives that determined their actions.

Here, rather than concentrating exclusively on the politicization of private life through polarization, it may be more useful to consider another, parallel process precipitated by intimate violence—namely the "privatization of politics," to borrow another explanatory concept from Kalyvas.[57] This process entails the transformation of otherwise isolated, interpersonal,

---

55. Tilly, *Politics of Collective Violence,* 76.
56. This is one of the common explanations for the brutality of civil-war violence, especially found in macro-level accounts of conflict. Kalyvas points out that this approach, in effect, "reasons back from violence to the factors that are believed to have produced it" and that "polarization explains simultaneously the onset of a conflict, its content, and its violence." *Logic of Violence in Civil War,* 65.
57. Ibid., 332.

and even inane disputes and tensions into a basis of political mobilization that can subsequently serve as the basis of new collective identities. And it is quite common, as Kalyvas rightly points out, "for the trivial origins of these new identities to be lost in the fog of memory,"[58] as the following example illustrates.

A massacre took place in Eğridere in summer 1905, a day before one of the most important holidays on the Orthodox Calendar, the Dormition of the Mother of God. The set of events that culminated in the massacre were initially set off by a dispute concerning the small chapel of Aghia Paraskevi.[59] The name Eğridere was a familiar one in the government records; this small "mixed" village had an unusual intensity of conflict. The Exarchist and Patriarchist communities both claimed stewardship of the chapel and demanded intervention by the authorities.[60] The Inspectorate followed common procedure in response to the petitions of the two communities and demanded an inquiry to establish whether any "official" conversions had occurred in the village (i.e., a record of adherence to the Exarchate by all or part of the community, presented before summer 1903, that would entitle the Exarchists to a separate church and school). The initial response of the local authorities, which stated that the two communities shared the church and the school and that it was not clear whether any attempt at conversion had taken place, was not particularly helpful in resolving the dispute.[61] Sent back for another round of inquiries, the local officials finally determined that the entire village had adhered to the Patriarchate before 1903. There was, however, a petition requesting official approval to join the Exarchate on June 5, 1904.[62] The final decision was in favor of the Patriarchists, who were granted the right to appoint the headman for the village because the petition had been sent after the official cut-off date of August 1903.[63]

Nevertheless, the fiduciary rights over the chapel were still a contested issue not directly addressed by this decision. The construction of the chapel had started eighteen years earlier under the supervision of Marko Yorgi, who had incurred an expense of 4 liras, partially collected as donations

---

58. Ibid., 351.
59. BOA, TFR.I.SL 73/7284, Metropolitan of Drama to the Inspectorate, May 18, 1905. See also TFR.I.SL 75/7409, Metropolitan of Drama to the Inspectorate, May 29, 1905.
60. BOA, TFR.I.SL 75/7409, Petition from the Exarchists of Eğridere to the Inspectorate, March 21, 1905; Inspectorate to the Subgovernorate of Serres, March 23, 1905; Subgovernorate of Serres to the Inspectorate, April 17, 1905; Metropolitan of Drama to M. Muller, April 14, 1905.
61. BOA, TFR.I.SL 75/7409, Inspectorate to the Subgovernorate of Serres, April 20, 1905; Subgovernorate of Serres to the Inspectorate, April 25, 1905.
62. BOA, TFR.I.SL 75/7409, Subgovernorate of Serres to the Inspectorate, May 2, 1905; Subgovernorate of Serres to the Inspectorate, May 8, 1905.
63. BOA, TFR.I.SL 75/7409, Inspectorate to the Subgovernorate of Serres, May 10, 1905; Subgovernorate of Serres to the Inspectorate, May 18, 1905; Petition of the Metropolitan of Drama to the Inspectorate, May 29, 1905; Inspectorate to the Subgovernorate of Serres, May 30, 1905.

from neighboring villages but not obtained a permit for the construction.[64] The Patriarchists claimed that the chapel was a much older *vakıf*, (or pious endowment) and that the current edifice had been built by repairing (*tâmiren*) an extant one in 1888. They asserted that there were "no Bulgarians" in their village back then ("*Bulgar namıyla kimse olmayub*"). Moreover, the supervisor had been a man who had passed away six years earlier and not Yorgi, as he claimed. They also pointed out that there was an official record showing that the chapel belonged to the Greek Orthodox community. They did, however, concede that Yorgi had been a trustee of the chapel. He had, however, joined the group that had decided to adhere to the Exarchate and to make the chapel available to them for Easter service the previous year. The Greek Orthodox Metropolitan had dispatched a priest to dismiss Marko Yorgi from his trusteeship following this incident.

Even though Yorgi had indeed continued to pay taxes as the trustee of the chapel, the authorities restored the chapel to the Orthodox community—not an unusual outcome, as we have seen, given the blatant partiality of Ottoman officials for the Greek Orthodox side in intercommunal disputes.[65] The disgruntled Exarchists, it seems, sought revenge. On the evening of August 13, a Bulgarian band attacked the village and targeted the homes of Greek Orthodox notables. The attack followed the familiar script of gunfire and arson. Vasil Konboti, one of the notables, perished in the fire along with his wife and daughter. Their neighbor's son, a fifteen-year-old boy who happened to be looking out the window as the guerrillas started the fire, was also killed.[66] By the time the troops arrived on the scene, the band had had ample warning to escape. The report mentioned that the guerrillas had stood by watching the fire while the cries of the two women trying to climb out of the windows could be heard.[67]

The same band continued its mission in Melnikitch (Melenikitsi) a day later, where they killed two *çiftlik* guards, both Greek Orthodox and one of them a Vlach. Their mutilated corpses were found later by farm laborers.[68] While the band itself apparently did not consist of locals, according to some residents and relatives who were interviewed afterward, it was aided by a

---

64. BOA, TFR.I.SL 73/7284, Report of the Deputy prefect and Mal Müdîri, May 23, 1905.

65. Ibid. The Subgovernor recommended, in an addendum to the report, that the petitions for changing sects should not be taken seriously.

66. BOA, TFR.I.SL 83/8221, To the Prefecture of Zihne, August 13, 1905; PRO, FO 195/2207, Theodorides, the vice consul at Serres to the British Consul in Salonika, August 14, 1905; MAE, vol. 46, Note by the Légation de Grèce en France, August 17, 1905.

67. BOA, TFR.I.SL 83/82221, Subgovernor of Serres to the Inspectorate, August 14, 1905; PRO, FO 195/2207, Vice Consul Theodorides to the British Consul in Salonika, August 16, 1905.

68. PRO, FO 195/2207, Vice Consul Theodorides to the British Consul in Salonika, August 16, 1905.

group of forty to fifty men from Eğridere. One of the village guards was subsequently found to be responsible for bringing in the guerrillas.[69]

Often attacks that clearly had political overtones in planning and execution started out as much smaller disputes over property, access to resources, or the payment of dues or taxes. Even disputes over churches, chapels, and parish schools sometimes fell under this category, despite their apparent association with the much larger political conflict. Episodes of violence originating as such disputes over ecclesiastical property should be distinguished from other episodes on at least three distinct levels: (1) regardless of the final act of aggression, they usually originated in local disputes and not in two opposing camps clustered around universal and abstract political principles, (2) belonging in one particular sect or the other was not necessarily a condition of having access to spaces of worship, and (3) the fiduciary responsibility was as significant a concern for the parishioners as the ecclesiastical authority presiding over their church.

What happened in Eğridere is representative of other small communities caught up in the spiral of violence. At the initial stage, when sectarian difference was an identifiable yet new and narrowly defined notion, the probability of a violent outbreak was slim. Despite the presence of two competing paths to spiritual salvation, potential disputes were contained through strategies such as the rotation of the churches for religious services between the two communities or the simultaneous use of the ecclesiastical space. When other considerations such as regulating the use of tangible resources or sharing financial responsibility became pressing concerns, however, the dispute took another turn.

Yet, even in the presence of these preconditions of sectarian difference and communal tension we cannot argue that violent conflict is the necessary outcome. We have already seen that mixed communities continued to function without major outbreaks of violence when left to their own devices. Even in cases where disputes did break out, such as fights over who would have the church building on which Sunday, the details suggest that these were as much an indication of the possibility of accommodation as of irreversible conflict.

An example from 1907, a year quite advanced in the "polarization" of the communities, illustrates this point further. The village of Karlikovo (Mikropoli) (another familiar name from the archival records of conflict) was in the course of holiday celebrations on December 6, and the Greek Orthodox and Bulgarian Exarchist communities, apparently having buried their hatchets in honor of St. Nicholas, or under the appeasing influence of *tsipouro*, were dancing the *horo* together in the village square. Unfortunately, the festive occasion did not end well; the document that relates the incident

---

69. BOA, TFR.I.SL 82/8221, Subgovernor of Serres to the Inspectorate, August 17, 1905.

Logic and Legitimacy in Violence → 245

is unclear as to the nature of the argument that set off the chain of events, but there was a scuffle and Dimitri, the son of the Greek Orthodox village headman, assaulted Gorgi Hristo, an Exarchist, with a knife and injured him in the shoulder.[70] In the melee that followed, Dimitri escaped. Bojik Hristo, Gorgi Bojik, and two small children named Hristo and Angel from the Exarchist side, and Angel Petre and Yovan Angel from the Greek Orthodox side, were slightly injured. It is interesting to note that the names of those who were involved suggest the possibility that this intercommunal fight had a tint of family feud, which is not surprising in that kin networks usually supplement, and even act like, ideological bonds in many cases.[71]

The lesson here is that violent communal conflict should not be seen as a foregone conclusion in the presence of sectarian differences. There were, however, several other factors, the combination of which made violence very likely. To start with, the institutional arbiters that might have helped to dissipate the tension across the region that was home to numerous such villages, namely the Ottoman government and the representatives of European Powers, were quite far from being up to this task. The legal/institutional framework was compromised not only by the divergent interests and agendas of the Ottomans and the Europeans but also by the lack of a robust security force that could have been deployed to enforce the law rather than ignore, violate, or flout it. Second, the proliferation of guerrilla strongholds in certain areas made their peripheries more violence prone, not only by simple logic of proximity but because it provided easy access to violence specialists who enforced an alternative order and could be brought in by political entrepreneurs to settle local disputes with lethal effectiveness (or ineffectiveness) considering the pretext for revenge that such attacks prompted.

Brutalization and the Impossibility of Fence-Sitting

In August 1905, Komaina, a fifty-year-old widow of a certain Costadine, disappeared in Marikostina (Marikostonovo). A few weeks later, on September 8, "the Bulgarian Guerman Nicolas" of Livonovo (Levunovo) left for the market of Melnik and never returned.[72] In Serres, Helen Giorgieva contacted the authorities in December 1905 and reported her husband had been missing for some time. Georghi Ferzi, the husband, was later found

---

70. BOA, TFR.I.SL 129/12858, Zihne Prefect Halil Rifat to the Inspectorate, December 20, 1906.
71. There is a significant body of literature supporting this point; see Kalyvas, *Logic of Violence in Civil War*, 95n. 11.
72. MAE, Constantinople, Série E 147, Captain Bouvet to Colonel Vérand, September 23, 1905. It is interesting to note that, according to Mishev, both Livonovo and Marikostina were inhabited exclusively by Exarchists, and Zlatko, where another person had disappeared (he cites "Zlatkof-Tchiflik," which is very likely the same place) had a population of 224 Slavic-speaking Patriarchists. Brancoff [Mishev], *La Macédoine et sa Population Chrétienne*, 192.

by fishermen, his corpse had been stuffed into a bag found floating in the Karasu River. An investigation into the murder did not produce any immediate results.[73] Pavlo Velo, a milkman originally from Kosovo, left his house in Serres at dawn on May 28, 1907, to go to the creamery where he purchased the milk he distributed daily to his clients. His daily routine was interrupted before he reached his destination, and he died after suffering multiple knife wounds at the hands of an unknown assailant(s). Even though the French gendarmerie officer hastened to remark that the attackers were probably "of Greek nationality," they had left no clue as to the motive for their crime.[74]

As a matter of fact, countless telegrams and incident sheets in the archives attest to a large number of violent crimes that were presumed to be of a political nature simply because there was no other apparent reason for them. It is interesting to note that many of these victims were stabbed, rather than shot, suggesting a more personal motive for the crimes committed. Comparative evidence suggests it is more than likely that at least some of these were not of a political nature at all but were, rather, crimes of opportunity, committed with the knowledge that the mechanisms that would have attached and exacted a high price for taking another person's life no longer functioned normally, thus discounting the "opportunity cost" of murder.[75]

Consider another quadruple murder, for instance, that reportedly took place in sight of at least a dozen people early on the morning of October 31, 1907. Four Catholic Bulgarians from the village of Todorak (Theodoritsi) were on their way to the village of Boursouk (Limnochori) in the district of Barakli Cuma (Irakleia).[76] They were intercepted by a group of three "Turkish brigands," who robbed the four men, tied them up, and then shot them. While this robbery-homicide was progressing, three Muslim couples were working in a field approximately 50 meters from the scene. Moreover, several people had seen the bandits shortly before the incident, including a group of armed Albanian men and another party of gypsies. None of them, however, was willing to offer official testimony, according to Major Foulon, who drafted a report to his superior, Colonel Vérand, about the incident in a style evoking a clumsy and bureaucratic harbinger to the "Chronicle of a Death Foretold." Finally, a young shepherd stepped forward and stated that he had seen the bandits flee toward Lovichta (Kallikarpo) on the victims' horses. He also identified one of them as a young Turkish man from Külahlı

---

73. MAE, Constantinople, Série E 147, Excerpts of minutes drafted by Subgovernor Reşid Bey and Colonel Ali Rıza Bey, January 1905.

74. MAE. Constantinople, Série E 144, Macédoine, May 29, 1907. I was not able to locate any other record of this crime that might have allowed me to cross-check this information.

75. A superb fictional example for the possible consequences of a discounted price for murder and predation are the characters Snoop and Chris (played by Felicia Pearson and Gbenga Akinnagbe, respectively) in the HBO television series *The Wire*. See Lorrie Moore's review, "In the Life of 'The Wire,'" *New York Review of Books* 57, no. 15 (October 14, 2010): 23–31.

76. MAE, Constantinople, Série E 144, Macédoine, Major Foulon to Colonel Vérand, November 5, 1907.

(Korifoudi). The shepherd was apparently a brave citizen not cowed by the grim statistics of abducted, killed, and maimed fellow shepherds, or perhaps he had a personal axe to grind against this violent man—this is not to say that these were two mutually exclusive possibilities.

Thanks to the testimony of the shepherd, the gendarmes had no trouble locating the man that day at home with his wife and mother. When questioned, he denied having left the house all day, but his wife failed to back up his alibi. Even though it is tempting to speculate about a fed-up wife finally seizing her moment to get rid of this wretched man, the holes in his alibi were not the only things that gave away the part-time bandit. The gendarmes also found cases of Gras bullets, identical to the ones used in the homicide, in the house, and further investigation revealed that his accomplices were two Albanian men who had already taken off toward Poroy (Ano Poroia).

Major Foulon was appalled by the witnesses' callous disregard of a multiple homicide taking place within their sight. Their negligence was compounded by their lack of civic responsibility in refusing to testify. The moral outrage of the French officer, although quite justified, did not take into account what, in my opinion, was the more striking moral conundrum posed by the incident: How did a local "family man" with a known address become a part-time bandit who could kill and rob several people in the morning and then come back home to take a nap?

We could make an argument here that there had been a possible desensitization of the public to violence through repeated exposure, although I would caution against taking this reading to its logical conclusion of a complete societal breakdown. Anecdotal evidence suggests that the failures of law enforcement coupled with the presence of competing groups with access to the means of coercion engendered the conditions under which criminal activity became more common, but this is not to say that such activity became normalized or ubiquitous. In other words, the desensitization should be seen as a context-specific deterioration of social norms rather than their general dissolution into a Hobbesian catastrophe.

Especially after the Ilinden Uprising, the inhabitants of the countryside were subject to a low level of daily violence, which was a constant reminder that their lives could change or end abruptly in a moment, that all-out war was just around the corner. These daily hardships were of a different order than the murder and mayhem we have discussed so far in that they did not always end in grave bodily harm; nevertheless, the cumulative effects of navigating this dangerous obstacle course to keep body and soul together, day after day, amounted to a trauma that was comparable to witnessing or being subjected to physical violence.

Much of this daily trauma could be attributed to the presence of a large number of troops, regular and reserve, mobilized in the region to counter the insurgency. The problem was not their numbers, which were clearly insufficient to patrol the countryside effectively, but the dearth of resources to keep them fed and equipped. Further complicating the matter was the mutual hostility that characterized the interactions between the military and the Slav inhabitants of the region. A majority of the latter understandably viewed the troops as a threat to, rather than a protector of, their security. The soldiers, for their part, viewed the Slavs with suspicion as actual or potential collaborators with the guerrillas.

Thefts of food and livestock were common complaints made against the troops, and these were a direct result of the Ottoman Third Army command's ongoing failure to make timely payments to the contractors and purveyors who supplied the military with foodstuffs. Frustrated with the arrears in payments, the contractors occasionally stopped delivering the food for the soldiers' mess, which usually consisted of bread and beans with the occasional mutton.[77] That the soldiers preyed on the local population, stole food and other goods, and got involved in the contraband tobacco trade should not come as a surprise given the conditions under which these men were deployed, often for years with no certain date of discharge, among a population they overwhelmingly despised. What is more surprising is that there were not even more incidents of abuse, looting, and general breaches of discipline—which we can attribute to the harsh punishments such breaches could result in, such as being dispatched to Yemen, which was seen as tantamount to a death sentence.[78]

Searches for weapons and guerrillas hiding in villages constituted the most frequent pretexts for the abuse of villagers by the troops. To address this problem, the authorities required searches to be carried out only in the presence of the village headmen and the members of the village council—a rule that must have been violated as many times as it was observed, considering the frequency of the registered complaints and the assurances from local officials that it was indeed being followed. The nature and intensity of these abuses ran a wide spectrum from inconvenience and verbal and physical harassment to plundering, beatings, and unjustified arrests. Looting, rape, and torture were also not unheard of; they usually accompanied reprisals after uprisings or armed confrontations.

The investigations of allegations of abuse by the military seldom produced any substantive results that might assuage the fears of the locals or restore a degree of trust in official due process. In cases where there was an easily identifiable culprit acting without open endorsement from his superiors, the man, usually a low-ranking soldier, was court-martialed and punished

---

77. The situation was indeed dire, and the threat of malnutrition-related diseases such as scurvy was constant. The soldiers not only lacked adequate food but also basic equipment and clothing such as socks and shoes. For more details on the effects of this problem on morale and relations within the security forces, see I.K. Yosmaoğlu, "Marching on an Empty Stomach: Practical Aspects of Gendarmerie Reform in Ottoman Macedonia," in *Economy and Society on Both Shores of the Aegean,* edited by Lorans Tanatar Baruh and Vangelis Kechriotis (Athens, 2010), 277–96.

78. Many thanks to Şükrü Hanioğlu for alerting me to weight of the "Yemen threat" (personal communication, March 2008).

swiftly.[79] When an entire detachment was implicated, and there were hints of acquiescence or participation at the officer level, however, abuses were more difficult to investigate and prosecute. It seems that the burden of proof was placed on the abused rather than the accused soldiers or officers. This applied even in cases where the allegations were made not by civilian locals but by the gendarmes, who also occasionally drew the ire of the troops.[80] This often resulted in the cases being dropped or in punitive measures that barely amounted to a slap on the wrist.

A number of events that took place in Cuma-i Bâlâ in late 1904 are illustrative of the common type of brutalization of the locals by the troops. Cuma-i Bâlâ was in the northern part of the *sancak* of Serres, along the Bulgarian border, and a significant number of its Bulgarian population had fled to the principality during the reprisals carried out by the Ottoman regular army units and militias in the aftermath of the Ilinden Uprising. A year after the uprising, many of the refugees had come back, but the situation was still very tense.[81] The district had been a thoroughfare for insurgents going to and from the Bulgarian principality, and the Ottomans attempted to, and for a while managed to, control this traffic by intensifying the number of troops. Detachments from the Third Army were stationed in *karakols* across the district, some of them commandeered from the locals, such as the Bulgarian community school building in Selichte (Selishte) and the Bulgarian priest's residence in Pokrovnik. The army could not, however, prevent the infiltration of two large bands of about 140 men from the Bulgarian principality in December.[82]

The committees had forbidden the *keradjis* (muleteers) carrying goods on caravans between Cuma-i Bâlâ and Demirhisar (Sidirokastro) to serve "Turks or Greeks of the region."[83] This ban was then expanded to include doing any kind of business with Muslims. The Muslim community retaliated by blacklisting the Christian merchants: the *mufti* proclaimed the order, police surveillance in the marketplace ensured its observation, and the troops apparently lent assistance to its enforcement through punitive measures.[84] Muslims who purchased anything from Christian vendors were forced to

---

79. Civilian authorities, more sensitive to the locals' grievances, tried to make sure that offenses did not go unpunished. For instance, during a search in a village of Avrethisar on January 20, 1905, the soldiers broke icons in the Bulgarian church. When the villagers complained about what had happened, their officer was arrested; MAE, Constantinople E 147, Consul General to the Ambassador, January 28, 1905. Offenders at the bottom of the pecking order, such as the *Régie* guards were also quickly transferred to a criminal court; BOA, TFR.I.SL 50/4970, August 8, 1904.

80. BOA, TFR.I.AS 54/5387, July 1907.

81. BOA, TFR.I.SL 48/4762, Inspectorate to the Prefecture of Cuma, August 6, 1904.

82. Dakin, *Greek Struggle in Macedonia*, 167.

83. MAE, Constantinople, Série E 143, Colonel Vérand to the Chargé d'affairs, November 1904.

84. MAE, Constantinople, Série E 143, Consul General to the Ambassador, December 9, 1904.

return it. The ban was revised soon afterward when the Muslim notables decided to exempt the Greek Orthodox vendors from the boycott, limiting it to the Exarchists. There were reports of Muslims walking around at night, talking loudly about "killing the *giaours* [infidels]."[85] The tension was sustained as a result of local agitation, and the state of the relations between Bulgaria and the Ottoman Empire did not help either. The anticipation of a war breaking out stirred up already heightened emotions.[86] The *kaymakam* (prefect), who seems to have had an appeasing presence and who was regarded as a "perfectly fair man" by the Christian population, asked for leave in October, reportedly exasperated with the influence of Mirliva Salih Pasha, the commander of the forces in Cuma and his cronies.[87] The prefect's departure was unfortunate under the circumstances because he was the only government official who could be relied on to diffuse the tension and to monitor and report on the conduct of the troops to the Inspectorate.

The abuses took place at the end of November and beginning of December during searches for weapons and guerrillas in certain villages after the shootings and deaths of three soldiers in the vicinity.[88] The complaints that followed were grave enough to prompt the authorities to reluctantly carry out an investigation—a task the officials sloppily completed in great haste, according to Colonel Vérand, the French gendarmerie commander.[89] The following excerpt from the subsequent report lends credence to Colonel Vérand's claim that it was botched by design:

> A majority of the inhabitants indicated that they were very happy with the conduct of the soldiers in Pokrovnik. It is just that there were quite a few complaints about officers in the *karakols*. As already mentioned, measures will be taken about these. We also asked the notables of the village of Pokrovnik if they had any other complaints. They responded that they did not, they only requested that the searches, while legitimate, do not take place during the night, in an arbitrary manner, and that officers and soldiers be always accompanied by the *muhtar* or an *aza*. This was all related to the commander and the *kaymakam*.

It would not be going on a limb to suggest that the villagers probably viewed the inquiry as an interrogation rather than an investigation. They wanted to give the "right answers" to the officials' questions rather than talk about what actually had transpired, and they accomplished this with gusto,

---

85. MAE, Constantinople, Série E 143, Colonel Vérand to the Ambassador, December 11, 1904.
86. MAE, Constantinople, Série E 143, Colonel Vérand to the Ambassador, December 20, 1904.
87. MAE, Constantinople, Série E 143, Consul Steeg to the Chargé d'affaires, October 5, 1904.
88. BOA, TFR.I.SL 61/6046, January 8, 1905.
89. MAE, Constantinople, Série E 147, Colonel Vérand to the Ambassador, March 4, 1905.

providing a perfect quotation for the reporting official about the terms under which "legitimate" searches would be carried out, as if they had memorized the latest government memo on the subject.

The final remarks in the minutes acknowledged that the soldiers had gone into the village on their own, following tips that there were "among the inhabitants brigands and guns" and had carried out searches without the *muhtar* and the *azas,* and also "engaged in some excesses." This was as far as the investigation could proceed, however. According to the official's deposition, the obstacle blocking the inquiry was clearly insurmountable: "since the villagers do not know their [the abusive officers'] names, and many detachments passed through the village during that period, and these villagers cannot specify which detachment these officers belong to ... it is impossible to inquire further."[90] This feeble excuse justified the decision to end the inquiry. Colonel Vérand's remark that "the commission was not so much interested in finding out the truth as proving the allegations wrong..." was probably not far off the mark, but it neglected an even more pressing concern for the Ottoman officials handling the investigation, which was to keep the involvement of the European officers to a minimum.[91]

It is also worth noting that the same investigation commission dismissed as "completely unfounded" the allegations of rape, which they referred to as "attacks on women," because, as their reasoning went, the women had not mentioned anything to their parents or anyone else from the village and their "husbands and elders of the village denied any knowledge of such assaults."[92] Therefore, the commission found the allegations unworthy of their time and consideration.

Note that rape, although certainly represented in the "repertoire of contention" of the "violence specialists" in the region at the time, was not used as a systematic tool of suppression in the form of mass rapes.[93] This was probably due to the fact that none of the groups—including the Ottoman government—competing for territorial supremacy included in their short-term plans a vision for the forcible removal or annihilation of a certain segment of the population.[94] In other words, the stake they had in a stable government in the long term made mass rape a counterproductive

---

90. MAE, Constantinople, Série E 147, minutes of verbal report by Subgovernor Rechid Bey and Major Ali Riza, ca. January 15, 1905.
91. MAE, Constantinople, Série E 147, Colonel Vérand's report, March 4, 1905. Captain Enchéry, who filed the complaints, was the frequent target of allegations that he was not only partial to the Bulgarian side but also actively involved in subversive activities such as presiding over alternative "revolutionary" tribunals; see, for instance, BOA, TFR.I.SL 60/598, December 30, 1904. The French consul dismissed these allegations as "absurd" in his report to the ambassador; MAE, Constantinople, Série E 147, February 28, 1905.
92. MAE, Constantinople, Série E 147, ca. January 15, 1905.
93. Both terms are borrowed from Tilly, *Politics of Collective Violence.*
94. It was, however, clearly on the agenda during and in the immediate aftermath of the Balkan Wars.

tool.⁹⁵ Anecdotal evidence suggests that this was an explicitly defined rule for members of IMRO, who did not dare stray from this injunction, and "[e]ven the old time brigands, who knew no laws but their own, were not only careful observers of women's chastity themselves, but were ever ready to avenge such wrongs."⁹⁶ This observation was recorded by a journalist whose impartial observer status was compromised by his willing participation in several IMRO activities while "embedded" with the revolutionaries in 1906; nevertheless, the lack of substantial evidence from Ottoman and other archival sources attesting to the rape of local women by revolutionaries corroborates his statement. The assignment of Catherine Tsilka as "chaperon" to Ellen Stone during the latter's kidnapping by Sandansky's band is another indicator of the lengths some IMRO men would go to prove their commitment to the protection of a woman's honor. Mrs. Tsilka, a Bulgarian Protestant missionary and a minister's wife, was kidnapped along with Miss Stone, the real target, apparently because it would have been inappropriate for an unmarried woman to be alone in the mountains with a bunch of young men.⁹⁷ Given the aspiration of IMRO to become a legitimate protector of the people, this principle and its strict observance made perfect sense.

Rape was more often used as a sporadic tool of oppression against the local population by Ottoman troops and irregulars, especially in the immediate aftermath of uprisings or armed encounters, when male inhabitants tended to flee into the mountains, or during overzealous searches for weapons in rural dwellings, when opportunities for abuse were abundant and were only perfunctorily curbed by the intervention of disciplined officers.⁹⁸ Incidents of rape were also reported after attacks by Greek bands whose

---

95. This was unlike, for instance, the case of Ottoman Armenian women during World War I. Mass rape tends to accompany ethnic-cleansing operations, such as in Bosnia in the 1990s, rather than the selective violence of civil war, which more closely characterizes what was happening in Ottoman Macedonia at this time. This is not to say that all ethnic-cleansing operations are accompanied by mass rape or sexual violence (a much broader category). On the rarity or complete absence of sexual violence in conflicts, see Elisabeth Jean Wood, "Armed Groups and Sexual Violence: When Is Wartime Rape Rare?" *Politics & Society* 37 (March 2009): 131–62.

96. Albert Sonnichsen, *Confessions of a Macedonian Bandit* (New York, 1909), 152.

97. Tsilka was not the intended person for this role, but the more matronly and hence suitable candidate had fainted during the actual kidnapping, forcing the guerrillas to make a spontaneous decision to take another married woman from the group. Unbeknownst to them, Tsilka was pregnant and would become a great liability during the hard marches across the mountains in the dead of winter as negotiations for the release of the hostages dragged on interminably. She delivered her baby girl while still in captivity, and the two women were not released until the baby was a month old; Sherman, *Fires on the Mountain*.

98. This is not to suggest that rape was a natural course of action whenever the opportunity presented itself. I strongly disagree with the "substitution" arguments, which hold that there is a link between armed groups' access to prostitutes or other forms of sexual gratification (or lack thereof) and their propensity to rape. For a discussion of such approaches, see Elisabeth J. Wood, "Variation in Sexual Violence during War," *Politics & Society* 34 (September 2006): 307–41.

members came from outside the region.[99] In any case, it is reasonable to assume that the reports of rape that did find their way to various authorities (and hence to us, through the archival records) represent only a portion of the actual cases that occurred given the reluctance of victims to speak out for various reasons, including social stigma and the difficulty (if not futility) of seeking justice, as this case adequately illustrates.[100]

The troubles in Cuma-i Bâlâ and the brutalization of the inhabitants of Pokrovnik, Selichte, Leshko, and Karasu Çiftlik present another important element in the polarization of the population as a result of violence that was determined from the top down, embodied in this instance by the District Commander Salih Pasha, who was a perfect example of the violent specialist with a significant resume in political entrepreneurship. Fluent in French, personable and approachable, Salih Pasha was known as a "military man of energy and action." Obviously, this military man knew how to channel his reputed "energies" to more lucrative pursuits than commanding the Third Army regiments stationed in Cuma-i-Bâlâ, having amassed considerable wealth through the lavish use of his influence and not a small degree of opportunistic and predatory behavior. His first initiative was reportedly the purchase of a large *çiftlik* that was languishing by the barracks. Soon, he had set up a smooth-running operation, where "the manure from the cavalry fertilized the soil, the soldiers harvested the tobacco, maintained the roads, dug irrigation canals and lower level officers supervised the laborers and the harvesters."[101] When the proprietor of the land adjoining his property fled to Bulgaria during the Ilinden Uprising, Salih Pasha acquired his land as well as the mill on the property through a tenuous legal transaction. The sale of the property required an auction, but given Salih Pasha's reputation no one else dared to bid on it. After this acquisition, he blocked access to the fields between the two farms, which was lifted only after the intervention of the Inspector General. It was through the same channel that the land and the mill were subsequently restored to its original owner—for the price of the sale.[102] The hardships that the proprietor experienced to have restored what had essentially been illegally confiscated from him underscore

---

99. See, for instance, MAE, Constantinople, E 147, Salonika, French Consul General to the Embassy, January 28, 1905.

100. As discussed later in regards to the Kuklish affair, there is a simple explanation for why many women would refrain from adding to their agony by filing an official complaint—they were simply convinced that their allegations would not be investigated thoroughly and objectively.

101. MAE, Constantinople, Série E 143, Consul General Steeg to the Chargé d'affaires, October 5, 1904.

102. The activities of Salih Pasha left a long paper trail; for details in addition to Consuls Steeg's report, see BOA, TFR.I.SL 43/4266, May 23, 1904; TFR.I.SL 47/4662, July 30, 1907; TFR.I.SL 48/4744, August 6, 1904; TFR.I. SL 48/4762-4763, August 8, 1904. A resident composed an anonymous letter, which seems to have made an impression on the authorities; TFR. I.ŞKT 50/4920, August 28, 1904. The order restoring the mill to its previous owner was issued in January 1905; TFR.I.A 22/2112. And Salih Pasha was finally replaced by Osman

a different kind of violence that the survivors of the uprising endured even when they were not being beaten up by troops or assassinated by guerrillas. It was a violence of the mundane, such as a Sisyphean battle with the Ottoman bureaucracy. Fortunately for the proprietor, who probably had more access to authority than the typical dispossessed peasant (although this is not to suggest that the typical peasant did not know to speak the language of the bureaucracy), the matter was resolved, but only after intervention at the level of the Inspectorate.

To be fair to Salih Pasha, I must note that he was obviously an equal-opportunity oppressor in the sense that the victims of his chicanery and strong-arming included several Muslims as well as Christians. This we find out from a report by an Ottoman officer and from an anonymous letter sent to the Inspectorate.[103] In many cases, people whose property had been usurped or confiscated were forced to pay for the privilege of accessing their own land or its yield, adding insult to injury. Naim Ağa, for instance, had to buy the produce grown on the land seized from him. Salih Pasha's animals were pastured on land belonging to a certain Ahmed Ağa, the other half of which was leased to the army at an exorbitant rate for pasturing its animals. The proceeds from this operation, needless to say, went not to Ahmed Ağa but to Salih Pasha. Again at the expense of the army, using the soldiers as free labor, the resourceful Pasha had had irrigation canals dug to water his property. These canals diverted water to the detriment of Karaca Mahalle, whose inhabitants now had to pay 1 *mecidiye* to Salih Pasha per *dönüm* they watered, essentially paying for the water he was stealing from them. The laborers of the neighboring fields, who were not able to pay this amount had lost their tobacco crop. In the Varouch Mahalle, he installed sentries to block the villagers' access to free water. Even the *mufti* had his share of the Pasha's exactions when his stock of 1,500 *okkas* of hay was pilfered one night by the soldiers.[104] The muscle Salih Pasha employed in these operations included a sergeant named Boşnak Süleyman and a cavalry gendarme Boşnak Mustafa, hinting at some form of ethnic solidarity network in Salih Pasha's dealings as a violent specialist turned political entrepreneur.[105]

Pasha, the commander of the reserves in Serres later in the same month; TFR.I.A 22/2153, January 30, 1905.

103. BOA, TFR.I.ŞKT 50/4920, August 28, 1904; MAE, Constantinople, E 147, appendix to Colonel Vérand's report: "Faits reprochés au Général Salih Pasha," March 4, 1905.

104. These examples are among the more odious drawn from a long list that also includes items such as the removal of furniture from the office of the commander to be placed in Salih Pasha's *çiftlik*. MAE, Constantinople, E 147, appendix to Colonel Vérand's report: "Faits reprochés au Général Salih Pasha," March 4, 1905.

105. Ethnic-regional solidarity in professional networks, including networks of crime and coercion, was common in the Ottoman Empire from the early modern era into the twentieth century. Ryan Gingeras's work on the role of these networks in the South Marmara region in the aftermath of World War I argues that shared ethnicity, although important, was only one among many elements that shaped them; Ryan Gingeras, *Sorrowful Shores: Violence, Ethnicity, and the End of the Ottoman Empire, 1912–1923* (New York, 2009), 56–65.

Logic and Legitimacy in Violence → 255

The abuse of villagers in Cuma-i Bâlâ was clearly part of Salih Pasha's local reign of terror in the territory he had carved out as a personal fiefdom. Under the pretext of a search for weapons and "bandits," the inhabitants were beaten, tortured, arrested and raped. The extensive search apparently produced only three guns, one of them belonging to a village headman, who in all likelihood was authorized to carry it, suggesting that cowing the peasantry was the motivation, not uncovering a cache of weapons.[106] The institutional and political climate provided Salih Pasha an opportune situation for expanding his own sphere of influence by terrorizing people with impunity.

"When it comes to government-led deployment of coercion against challengers," Charles Tilly notes, "collective violence increases further to the extent that violent specialists' organization offers opportunities for private vengeance and incentives to predation. Where participation in organized violence opens paths to political and economic power, collective violence multiplies."[107] Indeed, one of the immediate consequences of Salih Pasha's exactions was a large number of people leaving their homes and families to join the bands.[108] The mechanism at work here was one with a built-in momentum, gaining traction from the multiple incentives present for opting into the armed struggle and the barriers making it increasingly difficult, if not impossible, to remain a fence-sitter.

Even so, we should still keep in mind that picking up arms and joining a band was not an irreversible decision. As the story of Hristo, a young man from the village of Karacaköy (Monokklisia) in Serres shows us, life as a guerrilla, although not without its rewards, was tough and not always as adventuresome as the aspiring warriors may have hoped.[109] Furthermore, there was no guarantee that the chance for vengeance would ever materialize. Hristo, along with eleven other men from his village and thirteen others from the neighboring Kalendra (Kala Dentra) had joined a revolutionary band in winter 1903–1904. After five months of wandering in the mountains, crossing the border into Bulgaria, meetings in Sofia and the Monastery of Rila, and even a brief stint as a farmhand under the supervision of a band leader named Koço in Tatarpazarcık (Pazardzhik), Hristo, apparently stricken with buyer's remorse, decided to end his tenure as a guerrilla. After the band had crossed the border back into Ottoman territory, he managed to ditch his handlers and turned himself in to the authorities in Barakova (Barakovo). In his testimony to the pardon commission, Hristo was talkative

---

106. MAE, Constantinople, Série E 147, Colonel Vérand to the Ambassador, March 4, 1905.
107. Tilly, *Politics of Collective Violence*, 41.
108. MAE, Constantinople, Série E 143, Consul General Steeg to the Embassy, December 21, 1904.
109. BOA, TFR.I.SL 34/3316, *Fezleke sureti*, Serres Subgovernorate, March 17, 1904.

when revealing the names and describing the movements of the leadership cadres he had traveled with, but he was careful to add that he had never engaged in armed confrontations with Ottoman forces. Hristo was also smart enough to claim that it was the senior guerrillas' responsibility to arrange for provisions, dodging questions about specific villages, which might then be held responsible for aiding and abetting the guerrillas. As for why he and his friends had decided to join the guerrillas in the first place, Hristo was clear: "out of fear that the soldiers who had arrived in the village would beat [us] up," invoking one of the main pitfalls of counterinsurgency, on the one hand, and reminding us about the inherent problems in assuming motives based on observed action, on the other.[110]

The Logic of Violence

If the residents of Ottoman Macedonia started to question the benevolence or the existence of the god they worshipped in their (now segregated) churches, mosques, and synagogues and to invoke his name with despair (if not irony) in the winter that connected 1904 to 1905, no one could have blamed them. The worst was yet to come in terms of political turmoil, but that year human-made disasters were compounded by what looked like the ire of higher forces. Not only was the winter exceptionally harsh, with snow blanketing the villages into isolation and frost hanging over the fields, orchards, and vineyards with extraordinary persistence, but a flu epidemic was also running rampant.[111] The one-two punch of winter and the flu was followed by a spring when the activities of the Greek committees started to intensify, with the apparent complicity and even support of Ottoman authorities, adding momentum to the spiral of attacks and reprisals. After the Ottoman security forces dealt a large blow to Apostol's band in the spring, rumors spread that the leader himself had been killed. The jubilations of the authorities on the occasion turned out to be premature—Apostol was alive and well and getting ready for revenge. Despite the unrelenting pressure of

---

110. Kalyvas points out the need to "distinguish between reasons for joining an organization and reasons for remaining in it" and proposes that we "bracket the question of individual motivations and ... adopt minimal, yet sensible, assumptions about support." *Logic of Violence in Civil War*, 100–101. The minimal and (I think) sensible assumption I make throughout this chapter about individual reasons for peasant participation in insurgency is that, although these reasons ran the whole gamut from complete ideological commitment to coercion, minimizing damage to oneself and one's loved ones was the principle factor in shaping this behavior. Cf. James C. Scott, *Weapons of the Weak: Everyday Forms of Peasant Resistance* (New Haven, 1985).

111. We could add to the list of natural catastrophes the earthquake in April 1904, which did not claim a significant number of lives but caused enough damage to leave many homeless. Luckily, the snow had just melted, but the weather was still not very clement in the high altitudes; BOA, TFR.I.SL 35/3452, April 4, 1904; TFR.I.AS 13/1289, April 6, 1904.

the guerrillas, constant abuse of Ottoman security forces and other militias, and endless vagaries of life caused by a seemingly angry god, the people of Macedonia moved on with the business of living and even having some fun. Archival records, by their very nature, rarely hold clues to the diversions that people enjoyed, and when they do, they more often than not describe a festive occasion gone sour, such as a wedding or dance ending in bloodshed, or a less tragic run in with the law, such as complaints about a tax collector trying to get a cut of the proceeds from a traveling magician's show, or the raunchy content of a popular play by a theater troupe that continues to be performed despite "repeated warnings" by the authorities.[112] However incomplete, these snippets of information hint at the way life was experienced under "normal" conditions and should remind us that not all was murder and mayhem, even during these depressing times, and make us reconsider the conditions under which people inflicted harm on each other. In Captain Sarrou's words, "These murders or score settling did not prevent the local population from living, working, and having fun. They did not do without holidays celebrated with enthusiasm. My childish eyes keeps the sight of costumes for carnival, the continuous farandole [dance?] of the red devils, of the *evzones*, of *Karagöz* (Punch), of clowns, of porters, of harlequins, of colombines, and the shower of confetti and streamers falling from balconies or windows of houses with one floor. The cries of joy did not bother the people eating grilled corn from the cob."[113] So far, we have looked at several cases that exposed the dynamics of communal conflict at the micro level and demonstrated that we cannot speak of an unqualified, straight path that links sectarian difference and tension with outbreaks of violence. In this section, I ask broader questions of similar case studies, this time turning our attention to the logic of communal violence and its limits.

Violence as a Universal Tool of Communication

In June 1904, Chief Jane Sandansky, the legendary leader of the left wing of the IMRO dispatched an "open letter" to the population of the subprovince of Serres and the representatives of the European Powers stationed there. The letter was about several murders in the district of Melnik, approximately halfway between the center of Serres subprovince and the Bulgarian border. The region was claimed by Sandansky and his men as the base for their operations. The issue in the letter was not that Sandansky's band was accused of murders they had not committed—they were indeed responsible, and the letter proudly owned up to this fact. The targets of Sandansky's

---

112. See, for instance, MAE, Constantinople, E 143, October 5, 1904; BOA, TFR.I.SL 5/429, Subgovernor Rükneddin to the Inspectorate, Serres, February 19, 1903.
113. Auguste Sarrou (ed.), *Le Capitaine Sarrou, un Officier Français au Service de l'Empire Ottoman* (Istanbul, 2002), 50.

vituperation were those who had the audacity to call these killings "murders" because they were the ones, in Sandansky's words, who "use force, and who, in order to augment that force and keep it in their hands, commit the greatest illegalities, the most arbitrary acts ... and those who, hand in hand with the creators of this tyranny, protected and covered by it, commit the greatest pillages, suck off the last drop of blood out of the people...." [114]

It may seem specious, or even ironic, that an outlaw living in the mountains off the spoils of robbery and exactions would protest "illegalities" and "arbitrary acts," but there was nothing ironic here as far as Sandansky and his comrades were concerned because their authority stemmed from the will of the "people." The money and resources they "collected" from the people were not exactions but "taxes." Likewise, there was nothing arbitrary about the summary executions they performed because they were the result of due deliberations and the just punishment for crimes committed by the perpetrators—not victims. In this regard, their moral logic was irreproachable. What prompted Sandansky to write the letter, however, suggests a problem in the dissemination of the guerrilla leader's broader message; the target audience—the representatives of European Powers and the inhabitants of the region they aimed to liberate—were obviously not entirely convinced that Sandansky and his mates were carrying out the requirements of the law, or that the revolutionary "penal code" that Sandansky insisted he was enforcing had any more legitimacy than the laws of the state they were rising against, for that matter.

Sandansky's apparent concern with the perceived legitimacy of the punishments meted out by his organization should not, however, be read as the leader's ambivalence about the destructive consequences of the methods pursued by the guerrillas as the only road to success; like any movement that embraces the principle of "freedom or death," the Macedonian revolutionaries rationalized the killing of civilians as a necessary sacrifice and could not see beyond the false dichotomy of dying as a victim versus dying as a hero. The misgivings Sandansky had about the publicity that their actions generated did not stem from remorse over the glib cruelty with which they were executed but from a determination to ensure that the message was delivered to the right address. This kind of publicity was precisely what they were after, and Sandansky was sanguine about the lengths they would reach for to achieve it: "Finally they accuse us of being cruel, of being ferocious, without pity. Yes! We are cruel and ferocious; without pity against informants and our enemies. Often we punish not only the latter, but also their wives, their children and their sons to give an example to others, in case they want to follow the way of the condemned. Mercy! Forgiveness! These words are strange and unknown to us. We are without mercy. We

---

114. MAE, Constantinople, Série E 143, Macédoine, July 16, and August 22, 1904.

have but one punishment, only one suffering for the guilty. Death! Death to the snitch! Death to the traitor! Death to all who give us trouble!"[115] Before writing off Sandansky's public relations strategy as one of a mad man's misguided attempt, we should remember that this self-declared cruelty was quite calculated and instrumental in that it aimed to exert coercive power for a specific goal: to prevent denunciations and collaboration to establish complete control over the targeted region. The same rhetoric formula was repeated endlessly in letters to communities, emphasizing that noncompliance with directives would spell destruction not only for the "men" the letters were addressed to but also for women and children.

One such letter, drafted by Captain Zakas, who considered it his "duty" to tell the residents of Bomboki (Stavropotamos) to forget "the stupid idea that Greek Macedonia can possibly become a Bulgarian country" and to warn the entire village (including its canine population) of what might happen if they did not reconsider their decision to attach themselves to the Exarchate, put it this way: "Come to your senses, and convert and become Greek Christians like before, because if you do not revert back until April 20, I will come into your village outraged, and I will not spare anything, not women, not children, not dogs. There is still time to think and act."[116]

Such threats were not merely empty rhetoric. The same message was delivered loud and clear, most commonly through mutilated corpses, sometimes accompanied, in a gesture of overkill, by a note identifying the purpose the victim's death was supposed to serve. Village raids targeting total destruction were relatively rare occurrences, but the annihilation of an entire family for a "crime" committed by one of its members was not uncommon, as the French Consul General Steeg observed in a report to his superior in Istanbul: "Very often the band's revenge [is not limited] to the person accused of having laid an obstacle to their plans. They also aim the extermination of his family. ... A few days before my transit through Nevrekop ... three brothers had been attacked the same day. One was killed, the other gravely injured. ... The third one having managed to escape, his wife had been killed. A few months earlier the father of the three brothers had been killed. A letter sent in the name of the committee had previously informed his [the father's] and all his relatives' condemnation."[117]

---

115. There are two translations of this letter, originally drafted in Bulgarian, and they differ slightly.

116. From the letter of Captain Zakas to the Bomboki community: "Valete mialo eis to kefali sas kai gyrisate palin eōs kai prin Ellēnes Christianē[oi], dioti ean mechri esis tas 20 Apriliou den gyrisēte tha emvō orismenos [sic] mea eis sto chorgio [sic] sas kai den tha aphēsō tipote, oute gynaika, oute paidia kai oute skylia. Einai kairos akomē skephtēte kai kamēte." The peculiar spelling and barely legible handwriting suggest that Zakas was not among the better-educated fighters; MAE, Constantinople, E 144, enclosure, ca. March 1907.

117. MAE, Constantinople, E 143, Consul Steeg to the Chargé d'Affairs, Salonika, October 5, 1904.

This and other examples we have seen in the previous section follow an easily distinguishable pattern of attacks and assassinations carried out to punish a deed, such as defection or collaboration with the enemy, denouncing, or simple failure to comply with orders. Although the collateral damage might include completely innocent children or the adult relatives of the condemned, these acts were largely "selective"; that is, they targeted a specific person or anyone associated with him for a reason. They served both as punishment for something that had already occurred and also as a deterrent to prevent further lapses.[118]

We also need to consider a separate set of cases here that seemed to be less "selective" and more "indiscriminate" to have a better appreciation of the full range of violent acts experienced during the struggle and of the tipping points in the escalation of communal violence. A striking set of cases illustrating such indiscriminate violence were attacks targeting migrant workers, who did not have any ethnic or kinship ties to their places of work, where they were killed; they were apparently murdered simply because of who they were.

A large number of migrant workers were employed in Ottoman Macedonia, mostly in public projects such as road and railroad building and maintenance but also as seasonal agricultural workers. Bulgarian-speaking communities scattered throughout the region supplied a significant portion of this workforce, but employing members of a community that was increasingly associated with disobedience if not outright insurgency against the government caused concern for some officials, who argued that projects of strategic importance, such as railroad maintenance, should replace Bulgarian workers with Muslims and Greeks. This point of view did have its opponents among the Ottoman administrators such as the governor of Salonika, Hasan Fehmi Pasha, who was dubious about its feasibility and advised against its adoption.[119] After the Ilinden Uprising, however, the commissioner for the Salonika-Monastir railroad recommended that the workers employed by the railroad company should consist of at least 70 percent Greeks and Muslims and that the current force of Bulgarian workers should be culled to reach the desired ratio.[120] This recommendation was evidently adopted in principle by the railroad company.[121] Implementation, however, turned out to be problematic simply because of the difficulty of recruiting workers from among the Muslim population, the majority of whom had

---

118. Stathis Kalyvas notes that the former is the tactical use of coercive violence, whereas the latter has a strategic goal; *Logic of Violence in Civil War,* 27.
119. BOA, TFR.I.SL 9/858, April 25, 1903.
120. BOA, TFR.I.SL 17/1682-2, August 29, 1903.
121. BOA, TFR.I.M 2/163, January 1, 1904.

been drafted into the army.¹²² As a result, projects requiring large amounts of migrant labor continued to rely on the Bulgarian population.¹²³

These groups made an easy target for the Greek bands, especially in the southern part of the province of Salonika.¹²⁴ In one instance, three workers (two Bulgarians and a Vlach) were kidnapped by a Greek band from the road construction site about 10 kilometers outside Salonika. The two Bulgarian workers were later found dead, but the Vlach worker remained missing, presumably having been spared thanks to his less offensive ethnic affiliation.¹²⁵ In 1907, there were at least three such incidents, and this time the death toll was much higher; again, all three of these took place in the vicinity of Salonika.¹²⁶

One of these attacks occurred in December 1907, when a group of 125 workers, originally from Razlog and Nevrekop (Gotse Delchev) in the northeast part of the province, were on their way back home from Salonika.¹²⁷ The group, accompanied by two gendarmes, was ambushed by a Greek band outside the village of Limpsasa (Olimpiada) in the district of Cassandra. The band was led by two men known by the *noms de guerre* of Yorghaki and Korici and was reinforced by Greek youths from villages in the vicinity, specifically Stano. The two gendarmes were overwhelmed by the attackers, and even though they started to retaliate, after someone shouted "*sauve qui peut*," they dispersed. Twenty-five of the workers were killed, three were gravely injured, and three others were unaccounted for after the attack.

---

122. BOA, TFR.I.AS 45/4409, April 4, 1907.

123. These projects required a considerable workforce, which was difficult to source locally. Sometimes entire populations of certain villages were employed in the construction of roads in their districts; BOA, TFR.I. SL 192/19112, July 17, 1907. Nevertheless, their numbers were not enough to meet the demand. The construction of the road between Drama and Nevrekop, for instance, required the employment of eight hundred workers in June 1906; TFR.I.SL 211/21007. Some of the migrant workers came from Istanbul or as far as the eastern provinces of the empire; TFR.I.SL 28/2766, March 13, 1909; TFR.I.SL 214/21380, July 29, 1909. They were not entirely content with their working conditions, however, and it seems that authorities had a difficult time "persuading" them to remain at their site of employment; TFR.I.SL 208/20792, May 10, 1909.

124. According to the records of the General Inspectorate of Rumeli, there were two such incidents, in 1905 and in 1906, and both took place in the district of Langaza; BOA, TFR.I.SL 91/9003, December 13, 1905; TFR.I.SL 112/11180, July 11, 1906. Salonika was the province where Greek activity was most intense. For 1905, French records indicate another attack that occurred on January 13, 1905; MAE, Constantinople, Sèrie E 147, Salonika, Report of the Consul General to the Embassy, January 28, 1905.

125. MAE, Constantinople, Sèrie E 147, Salonika, January 28,1905.

126. BOA, TFR.I.SL 135/13499, March 4, 1907; TFR.I.SL 36/ 3520, October 10, 1907; TFR.I.SL 54/5389, December 12, 1907. The other year for which such incidents are mentioned is 1908, when one man was killed en route from Poroiy to Todoric, two neighboring villages in the district of Demirhisar (TFR.I.SL 175/17483, March 8, 1908) and eight others were killed in a field in Gaskar, one and a half hours from Salonika (TFR.I.SL 62/6101, June 13, 1908). Both of these incidents involved agricultural workers, however.

127. MAE, Constantinople, Sèrie E 144, Macédoine, December 3, 1904.

What distinguishes this and other attacks against migrant laborers, is that they were carried out in areas where the Greek Orthodox were the uncontested majority among the Christian population against nonlocals who were targeted for no reason, it seems, other than their ethnoreligious affiliation. Nevrekop, where most of the workers came from, and Cassandra, where they were killed, were located at two opposite sides of the province, and under normal circumstances, people from these two regions would not even come in contact or give much thought to one another's existence. But they were now connected through an act of violence. When the residents of Nevrekop and Razlog found out where, how, and why their kin were killed, it would not take a complicated thought process, but only instinct, to form a mental map that located Cassandra on the other side of the fence, a place one ventured to at the risk of death, rather than an extension of the home base where a person could temporarily locate to make a living. This was an effective method of boundary building, and exactly what the Greek *andartes* aimed to achieve. They were not interested in expanding their base of operations to the northernmost part of the province, to regions where the Slavic-speaking population was the majority among the Christians (and we should not lose sight of the fact that these areas were also heavily populated by Muslims); the fight was carried out in areas where the allegiance of the population could still be contested.[128] As for places where Greek speakers were the majority among the Christians, such as Langaza (Langadas), they were now out of bounds for members of the rival ethnoreligious group.

Both categories of attacks introduced in this section—those selectively targeting a person and his loved ones, and the seemingly more random acts simply based on ethnoreligious affiliation—raise the question of why the insurgents would follow such ruthless tactics if they aimed to replace Ottoman authority with a more legitimate one based on the loyalty and the consent of the ruled. In other words, was it not counterproductive to exert violent force on a population when the ultimate purpose was to win their "hearts and minds"? The short and cynical answer is that this was not a fight for "hearts and minds" but for territory, above and before all. Although not necessarily untrue, this is an incomplete answer that discounts one of the most complicated puzzles in civil war violence—the issue of popular support. Furthermore, it overlooks the conditions under which the insurgency broke out in the first place and the overriding need of all parties involved in the fight to ensure control over the population through whatever means necessary.

We have seen in the first part of this chapter the extremely complex matrix of motivations that determined how the locals acted in response to the

---

128. The boundary was the Monastir-Gevgeli-Demirhisar line.

demands of the guerrillas and the Ottoman authorities, and the unpredictability of their behavior from any given attribute. Likewise, it would be naïve to assume that the support they did or did not lend to the guerrillas was dependent on a particular ideological agenda they subscribed to, either because one group made a better case for it through appeasement or because they did not agree with the unfair and brutish methods used by the other. More important, however, coercive violence *was* the most effective tool at the disposal of warring factions given the institutional parameters within which they were operating. This is not to condone their methods, of course, or even make a case for their effectiveness; this merely emphasizes my point that the participants in the insurgency had taken up weapons not only to fight against the Ottoman forces for abstract principles but also to establish their own territorial hegemony, which implied controlling the population that inhabited that territory, through force when necessary.[129] Targeting a group of workers based on their ethnic affiliation was certainly a different (and arguably more odious) kind of violence than targeting an alleged informer, but both were instrumental in much the same way—they aimed to establish boundaries, declare turf, and deter opposition.

Retaliations and Escalation of Violence

A sizable Greek band appeared in Garçişte on January 13, 1905. After the Greeks destroyed the Slavonic prayer books of the community and demanded that the village adhere to the Patriarchate, they left. This was the same village where the Greek schoolteacher, Catherina Hadgi-Yorgi, and six others had been killed by Apostol's band in November 1904. The same band had moved on to Mravintza (Moravintzi) on January 17, and this time they did not leave simply after making threats: they rounded up the men of the village, twenty-six in total, marched them out of the village, and shot them all. Ten died instantly, one died of his wounds later, and five were gravely injured. The remaining ten managed to escape.[130] One of the survivors, Risto Constandi, said in his testimony that the band consisted of about thirty men, some of them "dressed like Turkish soldiers." When they told the *kocabaşı* to round up the villagers in front of the church, the people were first resistant, but they ultimately complied, assuming that these individuals were "with the government." The men asked for the key to the church, which the villagers could not (or would not) locate. They then said Mehmed Bey, the owner of the *çiftlik*, wanted to have a word with

---

129. Or, as Charles Colson, Nixon's adviser, put it, "When you have them by the balls, their hearts and minds will follow." Jung Chang, *Wild Swans: Three Daughters of China* (New York, 1992), quoted in Kalyvas, *Logic of Violence in Civil War*, 115.

130. MAE, Constantinople, Série E 147, Macédoine, Consul General to Ambassador, Salonika, January 28, 1905.

them, which was apparently a pretext for marching the men out of the village. After the shooting, the band went in the direction of Kazim Daouli, a Turkish village. Risto did not recognize any of the assailants except for "Anton Dintze who was among the seven Greeks arrested in Bogdantzi [Bogdanci] and later released." Constandi added that his wife had been raped by the "Greek comitas" while the villagers "were gathering in front of the church."[131]

The timing and the proximity of the village to Garçişte immediately brings to mind the possibility that the attack was retaliation for Apostol's earlier assault. In fact, according to the Greek consul's version of events, this was precisely the motive because there were suspicions that the Mravintzans had not only provided shelter to Apostol and his men before the attack but that some of them had actually participated in it. Although Greek Consul Coromilas was probably being fanciful in adding that the guerrillas intended to "arrest" the men so that witnesses in Garçişte could confront and identify them, there is no doubt that this was a retaliatory assault.[132]

This act of retaliation stands out from other acts of selective violence we have seen because of two peculiar details: the involvement of men "dressed like Turkish soldiers" and the time of the day that the attack occurred. Although it is not entirely inconceivable that these men were Greek guerrillas in Ottoman military disguise, the more likely explanation is that they were Ottoman deserters who had joined the roaming bands in Macedonia, some of which were organizing for a rebellion against the Hamidian regime.[133] Even though the Ottoman authorities repeatedly denied the existence of Muslim bands operating in the region and averred that the government pursued Greek "brigands" with the same vehemence applied to Bulgarian "evil doers," there was a mounting body of evidence contradicting both of these assurances.[134] The audacity of such a large-scale attack in broad daylight reveals that the complacency of Ottoman officials was coupled with the

---

131. MAE, Constantinople Série E 147, Macédoine, "Verbal Deposition," January 28, 1905.

132. The consul also alleged that the deaths were the result of an ambush by a Bulgarian band as the "detainees" were being led to the neighboring village, but the Ottoman authorities had no record of this incident; MAE, Constantinople, Série E 147, Consul's report, January 28, 1905.

133. The Committee of Union and Progress tapped into this potential by organizing the already existing Muslim bands into their network and modeling their activities after tactics used by IMRO; Hanioğlu, *Preparation for a Revolution*, 222–27. This particular incident is also cited by Douglas Dakin in his encyclopedic account of armed Greek activity in Macedonia. Dakin mentions that the band consisted of some forty men and included Albanian village guards from Vodena; *Greek Struggle in Macedonia*, 232.

134. See, for instance, BOA, TFR.I.AS 49/4846, Third Army Command to the Inspectorate, July 27, 1907. The earliest reports of Turkish bands in the Struma Valley date to autumn 1904; MAE, Constantinople, Série E 143, Colonel Vérand's report, October 27, 1904. In November 1906, a band attacked Karadjovo (Kirdjovo), a small Exarchist village in the Cuma-i Bâlâ district, and killed twenty-five people. During the investigation, the survivors reported that the çetecis were speaking Turkish and Greek; BOA, TFR.I.AS 40/3954, November 8, 1906.

complicity of local Muslims in attacks against Exarchist Christians.[135] The testimony of Bulgarian Uniate villagers from the neighboring Pirava underscore this point:

> In our kaza there are only Bulgarian and Turkish villages, Greek bands can wander in broad daylight with impunity into Bulgarian villages where Bulgarian bands cannot attack them without being chased by the troops. They pass the nights in Turkish villages, the one that killed the peasants of Mravintza came from the Turkish village of Kazim-Daouli, they departed from there at dawn and returned after finishing their job. We were told that there were Turks with them, but we're not sure, not having seen them ourselves. What is obvious to us is that the Turks are in agreement with the Greek bands and watch them with pleasure fight the Bulgarians.[136]

What becomes clear from this and other examples is that, starting in winter 1905, the violence was not limited to targeted attacks against informers and their associates but had spilled into a more indiscriminate form simply based on ethnoreligious distinctions. In June 1905, two shepherds were killed outside Petriç (Petrich); a note left by the bodies said that all Bulgarians working for Turks would meet the same fate.[137] Another incident, which took place in the fall of the same year, illustrates the double bind faced by locals caught between the conflicting agendas of the multiple groups of violent specialists, which tested the limits of their considerable skills in fence-sitting or hedging their bets for survival. On September 11, 1905, two shepherds were minding the Belevis community flock. Accompanying the shepherds was Nicolas Zlatkov, a twelve-year-old boy who was the only survivor of the attack. They were attacked and killed by four Muslims, at least one of whom was from the nearby village of Slave. Nicolas told the investigators that the assailants had "accused them [the shepherds] of refusing to guard herds belonging to Turks." When the shepherds heard this, they responded they had been banned from tending the Turks' animals by the Bulgarian *komitadjis* under pain of death and that "they would surely be killed if they did not obey this order." The assailants, obviously not satisfied with this explanation, dragged the hapless men to a riverbed and shot them.[138]

---

135. This should not be taken to imply that the mistrust between Muslims and Slavic-speaking Christians characterized their relations exclusively and throughout the region. The French consul noted in October 1904 that in the extreme northern parts of the subprovince of Serres the Muslim and Christian population lived on good terms; MAE, Constantinople, Série E 143, Consul Steeg to the Chargé d'affairs, October 5, 1904.
136. MAE, Constantinople, Série E 147, Macédoine, Consul's report, January 28, 1905.
137. MAE, Constantinople, Série E 147, Macédoine, Colonel Vérand's report, Serres, June 26, 1905.
138. MAE, Constantinople, Série E 147, Macédoine, Captain Bouvet to Colonel Vérand, September 23, 1905.

As the snow melted in the Struma valley, it also removed the natural barrier against armed activity, giving way to a particularly violent spring and summer in 1905. The escalation was directly related with the increased involvement of Greek bands in the region, which were now on the offensive and collaborating with local Turks and Albanians.[139] The presence of mixed Turkish-Greek bands in the region had firmly been established by spring 1905.[140] More surprising than the participation of local Muslims in these guerrilla groups was the degree of their proximity to the Ottoman military authorities, who apparently lent assistance to the Greeks routinely as a measure of counterinsurgency. A "reliable local source" alleged that an emissary of the Greek consulate had given the bands in the Yenice area a "password" to be shared with the Ottoman troops in pursuit of Bulgarian bands.[141]

The increasing involvement of armed groups supported and organized by Greek officers and consular staff served to accelerate the violence, not only through the common route of retaliations but also because the activities of these groups consolidated the notion that one could become a target simply for crossing into the wrong side of the (until then) invisible boundary of ethnic turf. Moreover, as the French consul pointed out, the unabashed tolerance of these bands by Ottoman authorities provoked the ire of the Bulgarians, who in turn redoubled their efforts against the Greek Orthodox civilians.[142] The increased involvement of state actors at the local level and the diminished hopes for a diplomatic way out of the impasse were two principal factors that caused the violence to escalate into unprecedented forms and levels after winter 1904–1905. In 1906, the violence spread into Bulgaria, where Greek communities were targeted in retaliation for the actions of the Greek committees in Macedonia. The first reactions in Bulgaria had come in the form of protest demonstrations after a particularly brutal attack that killed seventy-eight Bulgarians in Macedonia, but in summer 1906 there was a full-blown, violent, "anti-Greek movement" in Bulgaria, largely instigated by a group called Bâlgarski Rodoliubets (Bulgarian Patriot).[143]

---

139. The Greek guerrilla organizations were following the plan of Konstantinos Mazarakis (aka Kapetan Akritas), which limited the areas where armed activity would be pursued to preserve the limited military sources that the Greek side could devote to the cause. This meant that centers with significant Greek Orthodox populations in the north, such as Krusevo, would initially be left to their own devices while mobilization concentrated in the south. For further details see Dakin, *Greek Struggle in Macedonia*, 214–15.

140. When one such band, consisting of eight Greeks and two Turks, was captured—by mistake, according to the Russian gendarmerie major in the area—in March 1905 in Doyran, the local Ottoman administrator was so embarrassed by the situation that he would have released them all had it not been for the intervention of the same Russian officer; MAE, Constantinople, Série E 147, Consul's Report, Salonika, April 3, 1905.

141. Ibid.

142. Ibid.

143. The anti-Greek movement of 1906 caused a quarter of the Greek population of Bulgaria to flee the country; Dragostinova, *Between Two Motherlands,* esp. 35–75.

Logic and Legitimacy in Violence → 267

The reforms had already proven to be only a temporary fix, and the chance of an all-out war between Bulgaria and the Ottoman Empire constantly occupied the rumor mills while the Ottoman security forces were adopting a new counterinsurgency plan based on deployments in smaller zones and units.[144] Bands organized, equipped, and often led by Greek officers were on the offensive in a campaign to save Macedonia and its Greek Orthodox population from absorption into a large Bulgarian state.[145] The left-wing of IMRO, led by Sandansky, meanwhile, was fending off the attacks of Vrhovists, who were more in line with the agenda of the Bulgarian state than local revolutionary committees. The convergence of these trends spelled catastrophe for the region. The lull in armed activity following the Ottoman constitutional revolution of 1908 proved to be only a brief respite from the violence that would finally be expressed in totally destructive force during the Balkan Wars.

Clusters of Violence: Cyclical and Geographical Patterns of Attacks

On May 10, 1908, the village head of Taşirince/Tristenitza (Kriopigi) sent a petition directly to Hüseyin Hilmi Pasha, complaining that the villagers were living in fear, not even able to go to the fields around their village because of the crimes and murders committed by the *komitadjis* harbored by their Bulgarian neighbors in Skrijova.[146] This was not the first time the name Skrijova was mentioned in relation to band-related activity and violence. In fact, one of the most striking features of the body of evidence from 1904–1908 documenting disputes and violence in the Struma Valley is the constant repetition of certain village names. In addition to İskirçova/Skrijova, the names Klepousna, Graçen, Alistrat, Eğridere, and Karlikovo surface so many times (and in a dizzying array of alternative spellings) in these documents that those who are not familiar with the region may assume they form nodes along "a corridor of violence" or represent centers of intense armed activity in the region. Both guesses are only partially true, however; these villages actually form a tiny cluster in the northeast of the district of Zihna and cover an area no larger than a large suburb of a North American city.

These specific villages did not, of course, constitute the only locations for violent attacks in the region, but this peculiar clustering pattern alone should make us reconsider any assumption that violence was endemic *across*

---

144. MAE, Constantinople, Série E 147, Consul's Report to the Ambassador, Salonika, January 28, 1905.
145. Volunteers from Crete made up a significant portion of the fighting force, and because they were Ottoman subjects, they could deny charges that they had been sent by Greece. There were also numerous local bands, some composed of *klephts* (bandits).
146. The original petition was drafted in Greek, apparently by an educated person; BOA, TFR.I.ŞKT 153/15236, May 22, 1908. Mishev lists Tristenitza as a village of 240 Greek Orthodox "Bulgarians." Brancoff [Mishev], *Macédoine et sa Population Chrétienne*, 203.

Macedonia during the decades before the Balkan Wars. This general observation is based on anecdotal evidence derived from a wide array of sources over a five-year period; nevertheless, a more targeted approach based on a complete data set covering violent crimes committed in the province of Serres during 1907 reveals a similar conclusion.[147] Consider these examples from just the first six months of the year:

- On January 25, five Patriarchists were killed by a Bulgarian band in Graçen.
- About a month later, on February 23, two Exarchists from Skrijovo were killed outside Graçen by unknown assailants.
- On March 8, an Exarchist from Karlikovo was killed in Alistrat by the *cavas* of the Greek Metropolit.
- On April 28, an Exarchist from Skrijova was assassinated outside Graçen.
- On May 9, four Greek Orthodox shepherds from Karlikovo were killed by "Bulgarian comitadjis."
- On June 2, a Greek Orthodox from Alistrat was killed in his village by a Bulgarian band.

The cycle of attacks follows a predictable pattern. When marked on a map, the locations of violent crimes, in the entire Serres district, also tend to cluster around specific areas rather than being scattered around in an ad hoc manner. Nor do they encompass the entire map. The resulting picture is even more striking than the repetition of certain village names because it is a visual representation of the absence, rather than the presence, of violence in large areas where we might expect to see it. It goes without saying that what is missing from the picture is at least as important as what is represented by the dots indicating locations of violent crime.

What the villages İskirçova/Skrijovo, Alistrat, Graçen, Klepousna, Eğridere, and Karlikovo had in common was, first, their proximity to mountainous terrain and marshlands, facilitating access and mobility by roaming bands. Such topographic features are closely related to how prone a location is to civil war violence.[148] Second, the inhabitants of these villages were Bulgarian speakers whose allegiance was contested by the Patriarchate and the Exarchate. Even according to the pro-Bulgarian work of D. M. Brancoff (Dimitar Mishev), these villages were divided in terms of their affiliation.[149]

---

147. I used the French gendarmerie command monthly incident reports from December 1906 to January 1908, the period for which all monthly reports were extant, to form the data set.

148. Fearon and Laitin find that rough terrain is one of the conditions strongly related to the onset of civil war violence, whereas ethnic and religious composition (and even prewar grievances) was not; "Ethnicity, Insurgency, and Civil War."

149. Mishev's figures do not mention groups of households in these villages, such as in Eğridere, whose attachment to the Exarchate was far from final. Even so, he did not manipulate figures where the entire village was still loyal to the Patriarchate, although his assertions

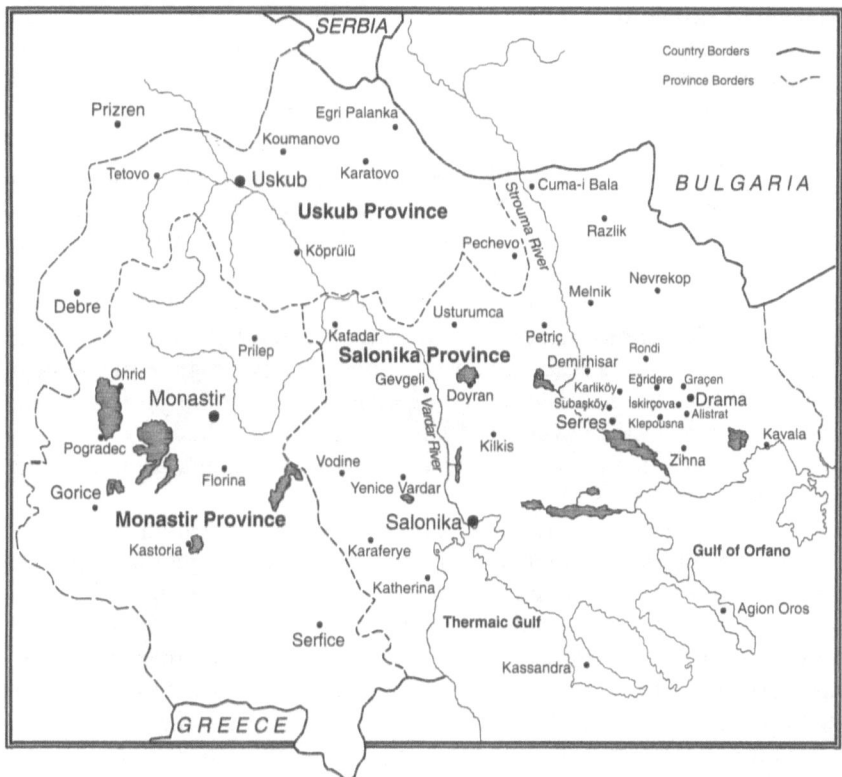

Map 1. Map of Ottoman Macedonia. The Provinces of Salonika, Uskub, and Monastir, ca. 1904.

Such locations were open to propaganda from both sides in the conflict and were more prone to violence, especially in regions within reach of the Greek *andartes*, such as the district of Zihna; easily accessible from the Gulf of Orfano; and considered to be part of Greek Macedonia by the Greek side.

Areas under the control of certain warlords such as Apostol or Sandansky were also more prone to attacks, not because these leaders had complete sway over their territories but because they had to contend with other, alternative sources of political power and legitimacy in the same areas. For Sandansky, this challenge came as much, and sometimes more, from the Bulgarian side as from the Ottoman. In 1907, most of the violence in the

---

about linguistic uniformity should be viewed with caution. The number of households he cited are 480 "Patriarchist Bulgarian" in Gratchen; 2,488 "Exarchist Bulgarian" in Skrijova; 880 "Exarchist Bulgarian" and 320 "Patriarchist Bulgarian" in Klepouchna; 5,200 "Patriarchist Bulgarian" in Alistrat; 1264 "Exarchist Bulgarian" in Egridere; and 1,440 "Patriarchist Bulgarian" in Kirlikovo. Brancoff [Mishev], *Macédoine et sa Population Chrétienne*, 203.

Melnik area could be attributed to the rivalry between IMRO left wing and the Vrhovists (or centralists), who tried to eliminate Sandansky's influence.

Similarly, violence was rampant in places where the Ottoman officers felt they were losing their grip and where the locals did not recognize state authority. Sightings of large armed bands on the move and reports of villagers sheltering bands were followed by searches by the military, which used a disproportionate force against the civilians, especially if the troops suspected that they had information about the killings of soldiers. Even when the searches did not turn up any incriminating evidence, the Slavic-speaking peasants were treated as if they were guilty until proven otherwise. The logic behind these exactions, which made the peasants resent Ottoman authority even more than they already did, was summarized by a high-level Ottoman officer, Mareşal İbrahim Pasha, the commander of the troops in Serres, who reportedly told Colonel Vérand, "There is but one method to control the population, and that is to inspire even greater terror among them than that exercised by the bands."[150]

"Inspiring terror" would be an understatement when used to describe the conduct of the Ottoman soldiers and gendarmes in February 1905, a few months after the commander uttered these words, during a nightmarish series of events in the village of Kukliş/Kuklish after the local military authorities received word that a band associated with Chernopeyef had been taking shelter in the village. This event was arguably one of the worst atrocities committed against Slavic-speaking peasants in Ottoman Macedonia since the suppression of the Ilinden Uprising and is worth relating in some detail here. The accounts found in French and Ottoman sources converge regarding the onset of the events. The accounts of what followed later, however, and the attribution of responsibility and blame after the village was left a smoldering ruin, has widely divergent versions, as we might expect, in the various sources.[151]

During their interrogation by the General Inspectorate officials, army Second Lieutenant Mahmud Efendi and gendarmerie First Lieutenant Hasan Efendi concurred that the district commander's office in Usturumca/Strumnitza ([Strumica) had dispatched them to Kuklish on the morning of February

---

150. MAE, Constantinople, Série E, Macédoine, Colonel Vérand's report, no. 16A, October 1904. Almost four decades later, his statement was echoed in a German army order: "the population must be more frightened of our reprisals than of the partisans." Otto Heilbrunn, *Partisan Warfare* (New York, 1967), 150, cited in Kalyvas, *Logic of Violence in Civil War*, 150.

151. Records in the French archives concerning the "Kouklish affair" include detailed reports by the Russian gendarmerie captain who happened to be in the area when the incident occurred; MAE, Constantinople, E 147, February 28, 1905; Constantinople, E 147, March 10, 1905. This officer's reports can also be found in BOA, TFR.I.A 19/1828, which includes complaints about the conduct of troops in the Serres region from December 1904 to February 1905. The largest dossier about the incident in the Ottoman archives is in BOA, TFR.I.SL 96/9540, February, 1905. which includes inquiry questions posed by the Austrian General Schostak, Ottoman military investigation reports, autopsy records, and testimony by survivors.

16, 1905, after the commander had been alerted about the possible presence of a band in the village. The forces they commanded consisted of soldiers from the First Company of the Second Battalion of the 36th Troops and of the gendarmes from the post in Usturumca, and totaled about 120 men. They were also accompanied by a policeman named Kostaki.[152] After the soldiers and gendarmes surrounded the village, the lieutenants Mahmud and Hasan, and Kostaki, the policeman, proceeded into the village with twenty men. Hasan Efendi told one of the gendarmes to talk to the villagers and summon the village head and members of the council of elders. When the village head and two council members came by, Hasan Efendi asked them whether there were "brigands" in their village, to which they replied no, and agreed to sign a statement to that effect, also agreeing to the consequences if there were indeed "brigands" hiding there. The gendarmes and soldiers were then divided into four groups led by lieutenants Mahmud and Hasan, Kostaki, and Corporal Seyfeddin and started to search the village. Shortly after the groups had separated from each other, Hasan Efendi heard one of the soldiers at a distance shouting, "they are firing," at which instant bullets started whizzing about him; gunfire was coming from the school building as well as several houses. After he managed to meet up with Mahmud Efendi's group, they decided they had to evacuate and sent word to the major. They started slowly withdrawing behind walls surrounding the village and tried to prevent the "brigands from escaping until the Major arrived."

At approximately 5 p.m., Captain Cimetierre, the Russian gendarmerie officer, whose presence and testimony to the events would be of importance in the aftermath of the incident, arrived at the scene.[153] He had arrived in Usturumca earlier that day and had heard about the battle and spoken with one of the injured, Second Lieutenant İsmail Efendi, who gave him an account of the day's events; this coincided with the later testimony of lieutenants Mahmud and Hasan. İsmail Efendi also stated that they had made an announcement to the villagers to separate themselves and come forward if they were not armed, so that the troops could pursue the "bad ones."[154] When Captain Cimetierre reached the village with his translator, an intense gun battle was going on and smoke was coming out of the village from several locations, suggesting, according to Captain Cimetierre, that the fires had broken out simultaneously in several places.

What Captain Cimetierre saw that evening and described in his report to General Schostak was a somber scene, but things would get even worse after his departure late in the evening, as was revealed the next day when

---

152. Interviews with Lieutenants Mahmud and Hasan were conducted and transcribed on February 19, 1905; TFR.I.SL 96/9540.
153. Lieutenant Hasan Efendi mentions the arrival of a certain "French officer"; he was probably confused by the language spoken by Captain Cimetierre, who was of French origin.
154. MAE, Constantinople, E 147, March 10, 1905.

the soldiers withdrew and a final tally of the damage was taken. About a quarter of an hour after Cimetierre's arrival, the first of the reinforcement troops arrived from Usturumca under the command of Major Arif Bey. The prefect told Captain Cimetierre that night would be falling soon and that he was afraid the *komitadjis* might escape; he wanted to know what Cimetierre's opinion was on launching an attack on the house. Cimetierre, obviously hesitant to assume responsibility, first refused to state his opinion, but then he conceded that launching an attack on a "barricaded and well-defended house might cost many lives." His answer, which can be deemed ill-advised by the benefit of hindsight, seems to have given the prefect all the pretext he needed to not continue with this risky mission on a frigid night.

Captain Cimetierre, worried about those still trapped in their houses, insisted on making another announcement to the "honest" villagers to surrender. Apparently in agreement, the prefect, Ahmed Faik Bey, made an attempt to send two of the villagers who had been arrested earlier into the village on the mission. When Captain Cimetierre suggested having them escorted by soldiers, the prefect refused, explaining that they had already lost three soldiers who had tried to pick up the corpse of one their own but that the "brigands" had stopped firing when they sent in some of the villagers to retrieve the body. Cimetierre reluctantly agreed to sending the villagers unescorted. The two villagers returned from their foray into the village a little later unaccompanied. He then noticed some soldiers had detained seven more villagers and were in the process of pushing and hitting them with rifle butts.

It was getting dark at this point, and fires continued to burn at several locations in the village. The shooting was concentrated in the upper part of the village, but its intensity was tapering off. Some of the women and children who had left for the plains started coming back toward the village; their lamenting cries mixed with the dogs' howling and an intense smoke rising from the now raging fire would have unnerved even a seasoned soldier. The young Captain Cimetierre, who described the scene as "grim," was obviously shaken. He twice attempted to leave their shelter behind a wall to take a look at the other side of the village, but he was stopped by the prefect and Hasan Efendi. The prefect concluded that there was not much they could do and suggested that they call it a day: "you can send your report from town," he told Cimetierre; "why stay here?" Because we know that at least a couple of the soldiers suffered frostbite that night, it is not hard to understand why the prefect, who obviously was not the most dedicated official on the (unreliable) payroll of the Ottoman state, was so eager to leave the scene of a battle in which two hundred soldiers were engaged and three had already died.[155] More surprising, and rather appalling, is the company he had during his trek

---

155. BOA, TFR.I.SL 96/9540, February 19, 1905.

back to a warm dinner and bed: Major Arif Bey, the highest-ranking military commander in place, and Mehmed Efendi, the captain of the gendarmes. They all took off for the night, leaving behind a horde of hungry, scared, and freezing soldiers and gendarmes, with only a lieutenant, a second lieutenant, and several ill-disciplined sergeants in charge. Quite conveniently for the authorities, this made it easier to pin the blame for what ensued on several low-ranking soldiers and gendarmes.[156]

Captain Cimetierre stayed on long enough to overhear Lieutenant Hasan Efendi ask one of the gendarmerie sergeants what had happened to the house of Petre; his response was "we burned it." He also witnessed the arrival of reinforcements from Yenice, about fifty soldiers and two gendarmes under the command of a lieutenant.[157] He and Hasan Efendi then left their shelter to join Lieutenant Mahmud Efendi as he was patrolling the village, and they saw two corpses on the ground. One of the gendarmes indicated there was another one not far from these two, but before they could proceed, Mahmud Efendi escorted them back. Around 9 p.m., because it was pitch dark and the sound of gunfire had diminished to an intermittent shot or two, Captain Cimetierre also left for the town.

The next morning, Captain Cimetierre left town accompanied by two cavalrymen named Nicolas and Arif. On their way, they ran into several groups of soldiers wrapped in blankets and rugs and carrying sacks that appeared to be filled with stolen effects. On arriving in the village, they found Lieutenant Mahmud writing (presumably a report) in the shelter of a house while his subordinates were busy roasting two chickens in the courtyard. There was also a group of soldiers gathered around a pile of looted property, sharing the spoils. Cimetierre and the two cavalrymen left the scene, following a patrol going along the periphery of the village to find the other lieutenant, Hasan Efendi. The scenes they saw did not produce optimism about what had happened during the night. All along the way, houses were still burning, and there were several groups of soldiers gathered around piles of linens and other goods looted from the houses. They did not seem to mind the presence of a lieutenant and the two gendarmes. In fact, one of the gendarmes was also sporting a strange cap fashioned out of a towel. When Cimetierre inquired about it, he claimed he had found the towel on the ground and wrapped it around his head because it was cold. It was certainly cold, but Cimetierre noticed that this gendarme also had an overcoat with a hood. They next turned a bend on the road and saw two soldiers wringing the neck of a chicken; they took off after the lieutenant yelled at them. Cimetierre and

---

156. It is worth noting that, during the investigation after the incident, the soldiers and gendarmes of sergeant and lower ranks were addressed in the second person singular and were often confronted with their contradicting accounts, whereas the lieutenants were addressed with the more respectful second person plural. The major, on the other hand, was not even directly addressed but given a set of general questions; ibid.

157. According to one of the corporals interviewed, this number was forty, not fifty; ibid.

his companions followed these soldiers into a house where they discovered the destination of the chicken; a group of soldiers was fixing up a cauldron over a brazier, obviously getting ready for a feast. Among them was a gendarme, Mehmed Çavuş, who had been spotted the day before beating one of the villagers.[158] As they continued looking for Hasan Efendi, they ran into the partially burned body of a man who was later identified as Gligor Nicola, a shepherd from Popchevo, who had come with his flock to stay with his sister and brother-in-law. Gligor Nicola's pants had been torn where a bullet had penetrated his left thigh, and his hands were tied behind him with a rope. He appeared to have been thrown into the burning house while he was still alive.

Cimetierre's party eventually found Hasan Efendi, who indicated that the bugler had already sounded assembly and they were all getting ready to leave. Cimetierre asked to be shown the scene of the battle and the house where the *komitadjis* had been barricaded. As Hasan Efendi led them through the village, they saw a couple of corpses lying about, not far from one another; one of them had burns on the soles of his feet, possibly from a brazier they noticed nearby. When they reached the stone house that had been turned into a makeshift fortress the night before, Cimetierre wanted to observe the scene for himself. As they were inspecting the house, they heard cries "aman aman" (mercy) followed by gun shots. The translator asked whether there were still *komitadjis* in the areas who could be shooting, but Hasan Efendi assured him that the only armed people in the village by that time were the soldiers. He was concerned that the soldiers might actually shoot at them. He started shouting, "soldiers, soldiers here, don't shoot," as they came out of the house. They soon found the target of the shots: a few steps away lay the still warm and quivering corpse of Pande Traiko. Nearby was the corpse of Velko Poiras, also still warm, and an open purse with just a seal in it that had been left on the ground. When Cimetierre's party had taken this same path only a few minutes earlier there had been no sign of a disturbance. The two men had clearly been killed recently, which also explained the cries followed by gunshots. The open and empty purse suggested that the motive for the crime was robbery.

As Cimetierre and his companions were inspecting the crime scene, they heard more shots nearby. When they looked in the direction that the shots had been fired, they saw "soldiers fleeing through the trees and houses." Cimetierre urged Hasan Efendi to send a couple of gendarmes in pursuit to stop further attacks. Then, he noted:

> The shots went on for some more minutes, and in the direction of the shots new fires set by criminal hands spread rapidly. Rushing and trying not to lose time

---

158. He denied all these charges during his questioning; ibid.

Logic and Legitimacy in Violence → 275

needlessly so that we could immediately see everything for ourselves, we made our way, from one corpse to another pointed out by women who looked wild with terror. We were accompanied by Lieutenant Hassan Effendi, Nicolas, our *souvari*, and the villager called Nicoli, who our souvari had arrested shortly before. Few steps away from the body of Velko Païras, was lying the body of Risto Bekiar, near which Nicolas, our souvari, picked an empty mauser cartridge belonging to the army; an exhibit that we took the liberty of putting in the pocket, while showing it to Hassan Effendi. As we were walking at a brisk pace, we didn't have the time to look for more empty cartridges; as we kept walking we heard heartbreaking cries of women; we entered the yard of a house where we found the body of Helen, daughter of Jone Parode who—according to the mourning women—had been killed the day before when she tried to flee her home. A house was burning nearby; it is the school and the fire has just been set; in front of the school a villager called Tonce Pande, born in Strumnitza but living in Kuklitch since he was a child, had just been killed by the soldiers by four shots, according to the women sitting not far from there; we noted that the corpse was still warm. Some steps away from there, curled in a haystack, an old peasant Ilo Pehlivan, was lying down groaning; he had been beaten by the soldiers with rifle butts a few minutes earlier. As we followed our way, on the left, near a house that had started to burn, [was] the corpse, still warm, of Georghi Dulgher killed by a bullet, further in the middle of the road a very young man was lying dead; he was killed by a bullet and his corpse was cold; he was probably killed during the night, his identity has not yet been established.[159]

Even though it had been hours since assembly had been called, there were still soldiers walking about the village, apparently not quite done with their looting. Cimetierre learned from a group of lamenting women that several of them had been raped and robbed by the soldiers. Civilian marauders from neighboring Svidovica, Hamzali, and Bansko followed the soldiers, picking over any of the villagers' worldly belongings that had miraculously survived the battle, the fires, and the previous round of looting. Cimetierre had five of these arrested and their weapons seized. They noticed some of them were herding cattle and oxen from Kuklish to Svidovica. A lieutenant of the military happened to be passing by the scene with twenty soldiers on the way to their barracks in nearby Kolesh (Koulechino), and told Captain Cimetierre that he would have the stolen animals returned. Observing that all the soldiers under his command had also been carrying what appeared to be sacks of booty, Cimetierre did not find the lieutenant's words quite reassuring.

---

159. The villager, Nicoli, had specifically asked to be arrested by the gendarmes accompanying Cimetierre because one of them was a Christian and Nicoli apparently estimated that he was better off arrested by a Christian gendarme and a foreign officer than left at the mercy of the soldiers terrorizing the village; MAE, Constantinople, Serie E 147, March 10, 1905.

Captain Cimetierre's testimony and the reports he filed surely contributed to the detailed investigation that followed (which, alas, did not result in anything other than a denial of responsibility on the part of the military authorities). Among the most damning details of his testimony concerned a man named Eftim Poiras, whom Cimetierre had seen alive and well on the morning of February 4/17. Later on the same day, this man was discovered by Cimetierre and the prefect, dying of gun wounds, leaving no doubt that he had been shot well after the guerrillas had already left the scene.[160] Some of the questions posed to the accused gendarmes and soldiers, such as the origin of the fires, were inspired entirely by Cimetierre's findings, but questions about other breaches of discipline, not to mention the use of excessive force and cruelty, were also based on events that Cimetierre was not even aware of, such as the killing of a three-month-old by a soldier who, the mother alleged, had tossed the infant on the floor as they were ostensibly searching for weapons. The damage would have been difficult to contain even if the Russian officer had not been there. As convinced and smug as Cimetierre was about his role in preventing an even worse degree of abuse, there was not much in the interview transcripts of the soldiers and the gendarmes to suggest that they had paid any degree of attention to Cimetierre's presence or attenuated their actions accordingly, assuming that they even knew about it.[161]

One of the rather unexpected conclusions to be drawn from comparing Cimetierre's notes with the interview transcripts and post-mortem reports compiled by the Inspectorate is that the transcripts and post-mortem reports actually contained more inculpatory evidence against the military than the Russian officer's testimony because they contained eye-witness accounts and first-hand testimony obtained from the gendarmes and the soldiers, some of whom were questioned several times because of the inconsistencies in their accounts; from the villagers who survived the ordeal; and from the bodies of those who did not. Given the weight of this evidence produced by no other authority than the Ottoman state, it is hard not to be flabbergasted by the speed with which the same evidence was spun into a cynical narrative exonerating the military from any wrongdoing in the matter.

In contrast to Captain Cimetierre's report, the evidence compiled by the Inspectorate does not constitute a coherent narrative related by one person: it is choppy, it does not provide a linear chronology, and the events are described by people who have good reasons to leave out some of the details. Second Lieutenant Mahmud Efendi, who, according to Captain Cimetierre, had displayed an extraordinary neglect of his duty, and carried most of the blame for what had happened, was one such person. His interview was

---

160. Ibid.
161. See, for instance, the statements of Corporal Mustafa of Ankara; BOA, TFR.I.SL 96/9540, February 19, 1905.

relatively brief considering the role he played (or rather did not play) in the encounter between the troops and the guerrillas and its aftermath.[162] He gave an account of how the troops went to the village, received the village council's assurances, and then engaged in a battle after they were fired on as they were searching the village. The time he gave for the start of the fire approximately coincided with Captain Cimetierre's account, but he claimed that they also heard some bombs go off at this time. When asked if they made any attempt to control the fire, he explained that they could not because it was impossible for the soldiers to get into the village because guerrillas were shooting "from all the houses in the village." He was not questioned at all about the most glaring blunder (from a military, rather than a humanitarian, perspective) about the operation—namely, how the guerrillas had managed to slip out of a village that had been cordoned off by hundreds of troops. Mahmud Efendi's insistence that there were no troops left inside the village once the shooting started must have been true because they figured out that the "bandits" had already fled only when the shooting stopped and some of the soldiers started going about, yelling "they are fleeing." The question, of course, is what the soldiers positioned outside the village had been doing at this moment, which was not directly posed to any of the three officers questioned after the incident.

Gendarmerie Lieutenant Hasan Efendi, questioned after Mahmud Efendi, volunteered the only statement that might explain why nobody detected the guerrillas' exit; he claimed that the descending fog had given the bandits an opportunity to get out to the hills. Both affirmed that they saw armed people from neighboring villagers come onto the scene of the battle; Mahmud Efendi mentioned that the majority were Muslims but that there were also some Jews among them. He vehemently denied that any of the soldiers or the gendarmes had taken part in the looting, but neither he nor Hasan Efendi provided a sound statement as to what precautions they had taken to keep these armed and dangerous individuals outside the perimeter of the village. One rather disturbing detail provided by Hasan Efendi was that these villagers were milling about because it was *Kurban Bayramı* (the Feast of Sacrifice), one of the most important religious holidays of Islam. It appears that these people had no qualms about stealing their neighbors' property, including their sheep, which they conceivably intended to "sacrifice" for the occasion.

It is also interesting to note that neither Mahmud nor Hasan Efendi were asked detailed questions about the time that had elapsed between the conclusion of the battle and the sounding of the assembly the next day, which would have been critical in understanding why and how the operation had veered so widely off course, assuming there had been a planned course of

---

162. BOA, TFR.I.SL 96/9540, Mahmud Efendi's statement, February 19, 1905.

action to begin with. The scattered details in the accounts provided by the interrogated soldiers and gendarmes suggest that this was not the case and that, once the soldiers realized that the enemy had escaped, they turned their ire on the villagers who had apparently given the guerrillas shelter. Hasan Efendi, when questioned about the people found dead after the conclusion of the battle, claimed that he did not have any information about these because it had been impossible to enter the houses at the time of the encounter, and he added, "In any case, these [the villagers] are allied with the bandits. It could be that there were those who were killed in order to have some losses for putting blame [on the government]. Just as they first said there are no bandits, and then it turned out this way."[163]

The notion that all the villagers were allied with the guerrillas and deserved what had happened was shared across the ranks of the military present during the incident in Kuklish. Major Arif, during his "interview," revealed without a doubt that the engagement was viewed as an "uprising" when he was talking about how the church and school buildings were set on fire; he was adamant that the soldiers had had no part in this: "I cannot say whether the church was burned down because of a bomb or not. However, it is said that it was burned by the rebelling locals and the bandits who came from outside and were under their protection."[164] Nor, according to the major, were the soldiers involved in any act of looting or abuse of the villagers. The soldiers had made every effort to protect the village from pillage by their neighbors. Those who had somehow managed to steal property despite these measures had been apprehended and handed over to justice. As for the presence (or not) of weapons in the houses where there were dead bodies, the major was rather vague in stating that they had found several guns, including some Mannlichers (typically used by the guerrillas), but he was not sure how many had been found. The guns had already been handed over to the district commander's office, conveniently making it impossible to match them with the houses where they had been found and thus refute or support the theory that all the dead villagers had been killed in combat. The number and position of the bodies, and, more important, their time of death, were in fact sufficient to dismiss this theory. When the issue was raised that some of the corpses found the day after the encounter were still warm, the major stated that he had not personally seen these corpses but that it was quite possible that they had been injured the night before and had only passed away recently.

---

163. "*Bunlar zaten eşkiya ile müttefikdirler. Olabilir ki: itham içün bazı tazyiat olmak üzere öldürtülenler bulunsun. Nitekim evvela eşkiya yoktur dediler sonra da böyle çıktı.*" BOA, TFR.I.SL 96/9540, Hasan Efendi's statement, February 19, 1905.

164. The first page of this transcript does not mention the name of the person being interviewed, and the last page does not contain a seal and oath, which are present on all the other statements. But, judging from his narrative of events, it is safe to conclude that the person was Major Arif Efendi; BOA, TFR.I.SL, 96/9540 (undated).

Playing the three wise monkeys was the dominant theme in the interrogation transcripts of lower-ranking soldiers and gendarmes: they saw nothing, heard nothing, and said nothing. Mito Kostadi, one of the gendarmes who had accompanied the detachment that first arrived on the scene with Hasan Efendi, however, volunteered more information than the formulaic denial, probably because he felt he did not have anything to hide. The first part of his testimony was in agreement with Hasan Efendi's and Mahmud Efendi's accounts telling of the ambush they found themselves in after entering the village. Concerning the fires and the presence of marauders from neighboring villages, on the other hand, Mito Kostadi had other things to say. Hordes of these marauders had already appeared and had been going in and out of the village in the evening soon after the shooting was over and a bugler came by to tell the soldiers and gendarmes to stay where they were for the night. It was the marauders, Mito said, who had set the *kocabaşı's* house on fire. Most of these people were from Svidovica and Mito recognized the ex-convict Hüseyin among them.[165] Mito also testified that the soldiers had burned the other houses, on the side of the village where they were positioned. He was not sure who had set the church on fire. When the investigator demanded to know whether Mito and his fellow gendarmes had informed the officers about these arsons by the soldiers and the marauders, Mito Kostadi's response was utterly convincing in its naïveté: "No sir, I did not inform. We were already stupefied by the terror of the situation. What information should I present while the soldiers themselves were burning the houses?"[166]

The majority of the soldiers and gendarmes vehemently denied so much as stepping into the village all night, when it was freezing outside.[167] Many of their narratives had large blocks of time when they could not reasonably explain what they were doing, and some verged on the absurd. One of them creatively argued that it took him six to seven hours to go from the town to the village because he proceeded "lying in ambush, very slowly, observing and resting."[168] Another one claimed that he had been singled out by the village women (presumably as one who had abused them) because he had chased one woman into her house to retrieve a cartridge she was hiding and that, after successfully seizing it, he informed the soldiers of what he had done but did not show them the cartridge. The mysterious cartridge

---

165. Significantly, some of the pillagers came from *muhacir mahallesi* (the neighborhood of refugees), probably from Bulgaria.
166. BOA, TFR.I.SL 96/9540, Mito Kostadi's statement, February 23, 1905.
167. One of them admitted that they had entered a house to warm up around the fire but denied that they had kicked the family's children outside.
168. "*Ben köye gittikten sonra pusu ala ala, yavaş yavaş, seyir tutarak, dinlene dinlene gezdim....*" BOA, TFR.I.SL 96/9540, Statement of Borizan Halil of Karahisar, February 23, 1905.

was never found.[169] One of the most salient features that emerges out of these disparate narratives is that the soldiers and gendarmes had been let loose entirely without command, without directive, and without any kind of restraint or structure with regard to their conduct, in and around a village, the residents of which they held responsible for killing three of their own, not to mention supporting an "uprising" against the government, which was the sole reason for their deployment in the dead of winter.

As soon as the botched military operation was over, another one conducted by the civilian authorities was underway to minimize the consequences. The post-mortem reports, interviews with survivors, medical examinations of the injured and the raped women carried out by the district attorney's assistant and municipality's physician illustrate that the motive was to deflect blame onto the guerrillas rather than identify those responsible for the carnage that took place *after* the guerrillas left. It is telling that the gun wounds were almost invariably identified as the work of "either a Mauser or a Mannlicher rifle," the two weapons of choice favored by the Ottoman military and the revolutionary bands, respectively, with the implication that the deceased could have been killed by either side. It is curious how the bullets all seemed to penetrate and then exit the different body parts they ripped apart; not one of them was left behind to be extracted and identified by the medical examiner.

The medical examination reports of the raped women are not for the faint-hearted to read, and their details present a compelling case for the locals' mistrust of any initiative from the Ottoman government that was ostensibly meant to improve their lot. Not one of the cases was officially declared "rape" by the physician, who would only go so far as to say that the findings were "inconclusive."[170] His conclusion about one case that "the presence of blood could also be attributed to the said woman's menses" gives new meaning to the term "expert opinion," leaving us cold in astonishment. The survivors, most of whom displayed signs of their testimony to the events, either on their persons in the form of bruises, burns, and wounds or in their missing possessions and smoldering dwellings, could describe clearly and in detail what had transpired and were almost unanimous in their statements that most of the damage had been done *after* the battle by pillaging soldiers and marauders. They were equally unanimous, however, in their insistence that they would not be able to identify these soldiers if they were confronted. Given that these were the same soldiers who would still be stationed in their region, and that they had little hope of assistance from the

---

169. "Kadını evin içine kadar kovaladım. Kadın içeri girdi, ben bu fişengi alarak geri döndüm, askerin yanına geldim, askere ben bu Hristiyan kadından bir fişeng aldım dedim ama fişengi askere göstermedim." BOA, TFR.I.SL 96/9540, Corporal Mustafa's statement, February 23, 1905.

170. BOA, TFR.I.SL 96/9540, Physician's report, February 19, 1905.

government in case the same soldiers sought revenge, now that their village had been branded as "rebellious," it is not hard to understand why they were reluctant to identify the soldiers and gendarmes, some of whom they probably even knew by name.[171]

The final tally of the "Kuklish incident" is sobering, to say the least. The Ottoman forces lost three members as the encounter started. In the village thirty-six corpses were found, and two others died later of wounds sustained. It was not clearly determined how many of those dead had actually been killed in combat, but only three of them had been taken out of the house where the guerrillas were barricaded. At least twelve of the victims had been killed on Friday, and seven had been killed on Thursday evening, after the battle was over. One woman who had been raped suffered a miscarriage—the medical examiner, needless to say, determined that the miscarriage could have been due to other factors. Sixty-seven houses, including the church building, had been entirely burned. The survivors were without shelter and food in the middle of winter. The resulting scene, extraordinarily chilling even by the standards of the time and place, should not have come as a shock to the military authorities, who had unleashed the reprisal through their criminal neglect of duty and willful blindness to the "rowdiness" of their subordinates. Informed about his soldiers' acts of looting, Lieutenant Mahmud Bey's comment was that they were *terbiyesiz* (ill-behaved), as if he was speaking about a bunch of anti-social teenagers.[172] These events were not simply about lack of discipline or training (although they certainly had to with this lack) but about counterinsurgency. The Ottoman military authorities were draining the sea to get to the fish swimming in it. Their efforts to contain the insurgency thwarted, the activities of the bands on the rise, and the (justifiable) fear that Rumeli was indeed slipping away with no real rescue plan in sight becoming real, the Ottoman authorities were trying to improvise as they went along. Punishing the population that harbored and supported the guerrillas, and giving the Greek committees free reign to intimidate the Bulgarian element were the two cornerstones of this ad hoc strategy of counterinsurgency. Although this strategy was certainly counterproductive, it was by no means unique, repeated as it had been countless times in similar experiments of counterinsurgency.[173] It even seemed to work, at least in the short run, as the examples of Smardesi and Mogila, villages in western Macedonia illustrate. In April 1903, these villages had been the target of troops and *başıbozuks* after the troops failed to capture the large bands of guerrillas taking shelter there. Seeing the ruins and the dead after these attacks, locals were less willing to harbor the guerrillas, which

---

171. It is clear from the interviews that some of the gendarmes had been sent into the village before.
172. MAE, Constantinople, E 147, Captain Cimetierre's second report, March 10, 1905.
173. Kalyvas, *Logic of Violence in Civil War*, 146–61.

made it very difficult for the bands to move.[174] This was a short-lived victory for the Ottoman troops, however, because the bands moved back in as soon as the threats were over and the peasants, tired of the exactions of the guerrillas, on the one hand, and of the reprisals they suffered, on the other, naturally split their ire between the two. Their frustration and despair are captured in the words of the inhabitants of Leshko, a village in the district of Cuma-i Bâlâ. A group of IMRO guerrillas had entered the village on July 20, 1907, set four houses on fire, and shot two women escaping from the conflagration, leaving one dead and the other seriously injured. The act was apparently carried out to punish this Exarchist village for failing to comply with the demands of the Organization and not paying their "taxes." The French officer reporting on the incident heard the following plea over and over: "We pay high taxes to the government, even higher taxes to the *comitadjis*, we are beaten by soldiers, and pillaged by the *başıbozuk*, we don't know any more what [will] happen."[175]

In August 1907, an encounter between Ottoman forces and IMRO guerrillas took place in Dere Müslim, a village located not far from Melnik.[176] The series of events leading up to and following the encounter formed a familiar pattern and almost duplicated the Kuklish incident. According to the report drafted by Captain Sarrou, the French gendarmerie officer in charge of the Melnik district, on August 12, a gendarme and twelve soldiers who were on patrol duty paid a routine visit to Dere Müslim. While the soldiers waited outside the village by a stream at the bottom of a ravine, the gendarme spoke with the village elders and the *muhtar* (headman). The gendarme noticed an uneasiness as they affirmed that all was calm in the village and, his suspicions raised, asked the *muhtar* whether he would be willing to provide a written and sealed statement attesting that there were no "brigands" in the village. The *muhtar* could not turn down this demand and produced the document, as had his counterpart in Kuklish. This time, however, the gendarme took the *muhtar*'s word, and the patrol left without further inquiry. Only a few hours later, local officials alerted military authorities that three bands might be hiding in Dere Müslim. A detachment of 150 soldiers and 9 gendarmes was immediately dispatched to the area. Gendarmerie Lieutenant Salih Ağa, who was in charge of the operation, went into the village accompanied by a policeman, a gendarme, a few soldiers, and a civil official. They called on the elders to reassemble and asked them to tell the truth. When they reaffirmed that there were indeed no "bandits" hiding in the village, Lieutenant Salih Ağa said they knew this was not the case and that the village had already been put under siege so as not to allow the bandits to escape. He wanted to negotiate their surrender, he said, because there would be much bloodshed

---

174. Dakin, *Greek Struggle in Macedonia*, 97–98.
175. MAE, Constantinople, E 144, List of crimes committed in July 1907, August 1907.
176. MAE, Constantinople, E 144, August 1907.

on both sides otherwise. When they repeated that they knew nothing, Salih Ağa had his subordinates ask the villagers to leave their dwellings. As they were gathering, Salih Ağa noticed that an old man seemed willing to help. With this man as the guide, they started knocking on doors, and when they reached the second house, shots were fired from inside.

The battle and the ensuing explosions and fire consumed the village almost entirely.[177] Six peasants were killed, two of them by the guerrillas, including the old man who had been guiding the troops. There were three casualties on the Ottoman side, two soldiers and a gendarme. The injured included a certain Mehmet Sadık, ex-Stoianoff, a former bandleader, who apparently had changed his religion to go along with his political transformation.[178] In his report, Captain Sarrou noted that Mehmet Sadık not only had managed to shoot Mitza Vranali, one of the guerrilla leaders, but also had saved Salih Ağa's life as he caught a bullet from the guerrillas himself. Sarrou was able to see some of the documents seized from the dead guerrillas. These included orders issued by Mitza Marikostinali, carrying the seal of the Interior Committee for the killings of five individuals.[179] Two of the orders had already been executed; among the luckier three was the Bulgarian priest of Ploska, a "village that was hostile to the Committee."[180] According to the lieutenant, the three bands had assembled in preparation for a major attack that involved the burning of several villages while they blocked the narrow passes of Demirhisar region. Another source, whom Captain Sarrou esteemed as "very well informed" said that Sandansky himself had been waiting with eighty men under his command to meet with the three bands that had been ambushed for some "flashy act."[181]

The Dere Müslim incident was in many ways a smaller-scale version of the events in Kuklish, but there were also significant differences between the two. The most important distinction was in the way the authorities dealt with the situation after the event. Captain Sarrou's assertion that the conduct of the police, gendarmes, and soldiers was stellar should be considered

---

177. BOA, TFR.I.A 37/3649, August 16, 1907.
178. Although it was not uncommon for former bandits to enlist with the Ottoman gendarmerie, Stoianoff seems to have gone one step further by converting to Islam. I was not able to locate more specific information about Stoianoff, but Draganoff mentions a certain Petre Stoianoff who was the member of a Bulgarian band in the province of Üsküb. This person reportedly declared himself Serbian after disagreements with his comrades and then turned himself in to the Ottoman authorities, denouncing and causing the arrest of a large number of Bulgarians; Draganoff, *Macédoine et les Réformes*, 176.
179. Marikostina and Vrana were both located in Menlik district, not far from Dere Müslim; BOA, TFR.I.A 37/3649, Serres Prefecture to Menlik Subprefecture, August 14, 1907; MAE, Constantinople, E 144, Captain Sarrou to Colonel Vérand, August 19, 1907.
180. This is probably one of the two villages named Ploski in Menlik. Mishev mentions that both villages, made up of 456 and 448 households, were entirely Exarchist; Brancoff [Mishev] *La Macédoine et sa Population Chrétienne*, 192.
181. MAE Constantinople, E 144, Captain Sarrou to Colonel Vérand, August 19, 1907.

along with the fact that he arrived at the scene after the battle was over.[182] We do know, however, that the authorities reacted to his investigation immediately after the incident took place with unusual *sangfroid,* in sharp contrast to the defensive spin campaign that followed the attack on Kuklish. In fact, when the Prefecture of Serres asked the local authorities in Menlik to prevent Sarrou from taking photographs of the burned houses "in a suitable manner" and copied the Inspectorate on the correspondence, the response they received did not follow the routine procedure of damage control. Instead, the memo recommended that the French captain be allowed to proceed as he pleased because there was nothing of "harm or significance" in taking photographs.[183]

More significantly, the investigation report prepared immediately after the incident by gendarmerie Lieutenant Tayyar Bey and the Demirhisar District Commander Colonel Hamdi Bey recommended that "aid" should be provided to the owners of twenty-six houses that had been burned down in the form of government grants based on the value of their houses. The pair did not officially acknowledge that the fire had been started by the military, instead choosing deliberately vague language as to the source of the first fire and emphasizing a fatal combination of high winds, tightly built structures, large amounts of *raki* and grain alcohol kept in the houses, and finally the countless explosions set off by the brigands. Nevertheless, they did note that of the twenty-nine houses that had been incinerated, three had been deliberately set on fire by the "brigands," and because their owners were "unworthy of mercy" having been in cahoots with the brigands, they should not benefit from financial aid, implicitly conceding that compensating for the damage done to the other houses was the responsibility of the government.[184] They added that hay depots had been converted to temporary dwellings for the victims, where they were distributed food, and that "thanks to the beneficence of his Excellency the Sultan" they were ensuring the rest and recovery of the wounded through all means necessary. The beneficence of his excellency could only go so far, apparently, considering Sarrou's observation that the provisions sent for the victims were inadequate. Be that as it may, the list detailing the names of homeowners and the value of the property they lost in the fire was prepared with great expedition and

---

182. Ibid. In his report, Sarrou relates several acts of courage by the police and the gendarmes, which he could not have witnessed personally. Although it does not mean that these were entirely made up by the Ottoman officials he interviewed, the record about similar incidents calls for a note of caution.

183. BOA, TFR.I.A 37/3649, Copy of Inspectorate's letter to the Serres Prefecture, August 14, 1907. The mentioned photos indeed reached their destination. They can today be found in the same folder that contains Captain Sarrou's report to Colonel Vérand; MAE, Constantinople, E 144, Captain Sarrou to Colonel Vérand, August 19, 1907.

184. It is interesting to note that the word they used for the financial assistance to be offered to the victims was *iane* ("aid") rather than *tazminat* ("compensation").

presented to the Inspectorate by August 1907.[185] The list itself obviously did not mean much in the absence of funds to allocate for the purpose, estimated at 84,700 *guruş*. It is a testament to the importance placed on carrying through with the aid plan that on September 11, 1907, the Grand Vezir notified the Inspectorate that the Council of Ministers had authorized the release of the necessary funds from the aid earmarked for flood victims and that an imperial decree had been issued to that effect.[186] Furthermore, in March 1908, the Sublime Porte extended the three-year tax exemption to victims of attacks by Greek bands in Melnik, Zihna, and Serres, including the residents of Dere Müslim who had lost their houses.[187]

What had happened in the course of two years that inspired the Ottoman administration to adopt a different policy in dealing with the aftermath of an attack on a village harboring guerrillas? First of all, following the bad publicity following previous similar encounters, the Ottomans were strongly motivated to preempt critical reports before they surfaced. This point was explicitly stressed several times in the correspondence of the Inspectorate with the Sublime Porte. "If there are measures the government would need to take," one such letter noted, "initiative should be taken before the claims and complaints of outsiders and malicious [people]."[188]

"Damage control" was obviously the primary motive behind the changed and relatively more benevolent state attitude. And, we might expect, this change in attitude was in no small degree enabled by the declining strength of the revolutionary bands in the region as the Ottoman forces increased their efforts to eradicate them. Thanks to a new strategy relying on smaller flying columns, adopted in 1907, the Ottoman military had achieved considerable success in curbing insurgent activity in summer 1907.[189] The region of the Struma Valley was still host to numerous bands, but, as the Dere Müslim incident revealed, these were small groups under the control of local men that were limited in their capacity to enforce committee orders or stage impressive attacks unless they joined forces under the guidance of leaders such as Sandansky, which was getting progressively harder as a result of

---

185. BOA, TFR.I.A 37/3649, Serres Prefecture to the Inspectorate, August 17, 1907.
186. BOA, TFR.I.A 37/3649, Grand Vezir to the Inspectorate, September 11, 1907.
187. BOA, TFR.I.A 37/3649, Grand Vezirate to the Inspectorate, March 6, 1908.
188. *"hükümetce ittihâzı lazım gelecek tedâbir var ise agyâr ile bedhahâtın müracaat ve şikayâtından evvel mukteziyâtına teşebbüs edilmek üzere...."* BOA, TFR.I.A 37/3649, Inspectorate to the Grand Vezirate, August 21, 1907.
189. MAE, Constantinople, E 144, Colonel Vérand's Report, August 26, 1907; Dakin, *Greek Struggle in Macedonia*, 340–41. Among the leaders captured and killed that summer was the notorious Mitros Vlach, who had long been fighting against the Greeks in the region of Kastoria and was rumored to be responsible for the death of Pavlos Melas, the legendary young martyr of the Greek struggle in Macedonia. Melas had been killed in an ambush by Ottoman forces that was intended for Mitros Vlach, who had set up the trap for Melas; Dakin, *Greek Struggle in Macedonia*, 190. In the end, it was the information and guides provided by Bishop Karavangelis, another champion and hero of the Greek cause in Macedonia, that led to the capture and killing of Mitros Vlach by the Ottoman forces.

increased surveillance in the countryside, on the one hand, and the presence of Greek bands, on the other. It might well be that their progress in counterinsurgency made the Ottoman authorities adopt a more positive outlook about the future of the region, which was manifested in their dealings with the inhabitants of Dere Müslim. The band in Kuklish had escaped but not their comrades in Dere Müslim.

Violence and Political Power

In this chapter, I have analyzed violence as a historical force in its own right and established its role in the creation of something that was presumably its cause—national identity. The conflict in Ottoman Macedonia at the turn of the twentieth century is an important chapter in the histories of national liberation in Bulgaria, Greece, and Macedonia. It created national heroes for all parties involved—including the Ottomans, who ended up losing not just any territory, but Rumeli, the lands that had transformed the small principality established by the followers of a warlord named Osman into an empire and once a world power. It was indeed a formative event for all the nation-states mentioned, not only as a struggle to redeem what rightfully belonged to the nation, as official histories would have it, but for placing the inhabitants of Macedonia into national molds in the first place. In other words, it was not the people who fought for the nation, but the nation-states that fought for the people.

Analyzing violence at the local or micro level allows the disaggregation of events collectively defined as ethnonationalist violence from the broader narrative of national liberation. The range of circumstances that motivated people to take up arms, as we have seen, was not limited to ideological commitment or animosity against members of the other group. There was no single explanation for collaboration or resistance, nor was the distinction between victim and perpetrator as clear as we might assume. The way people were subsumed by this fight did not follow a linear script of rebellion against the government and reclaiming territory for the nation. The contingencies in the way the events unfolded, people's ambiguities about what course of action to take, and the ease with which they went from being noncommittal to participatory and back, become visible elements of this episode in history only after we take a closer look at the presumably ubiquitous acts of violence. References to tyranny, murderous campaigns of destruction, and calamities that people suffered just as a result of the group they belonged to constitute center stage in "heroes and traitors" style of histories of the struggle for Macedonia. Political histories, on the other hand, follow the interaction of states and assume that people's actions to mimic those of the political actors that made the decisions for insurgency or war. The mundane details of the experiences of the masses that were claimed by the fighting parties do not figure prominently in these accounts, and when they do, they are stylized to fit the master narrative. There is no place for the uncertainty, the messiness, and the contradictions of actual human experience in macro narratives of national emergence, and that is exactly why it is important that we bring them to light. The examples we have seen here demonstrate that violence contributed to the process of nation-building as a marker of boundaries and a means of consolidating disparate groups of people into members of a community that they knew extended well beyond their immediate environment. What compounded that effect was its simultaneous action as a mechanism for mass mobilization, without which there would not be a nation. This is not to argue that violence was the uniquely generative force in nation-making. Nation-making relies on other forces, forces that derive, above all, from the social and political changes that are mutually constitutive with the emergence of the modern state, forces such as new technologies of government, industrialization, and new mechanisms of legitimation that made mass political participation (which should not be confused with pluralist democracy) not only possible but also necessary. Violence, however, should not be explained away as a by-product of this process; it functioned more as a cause than a result of the hardening of national boundaries.

Was Hanna Arendt right, then, in suggesting that violence is utterly incapable of creating power?[190] Or should we conclude with a nod to Mao Zedong, who asserted that political power comes from the barrel of a gun? What we have seen about the capacity of violence to change people's worldviews and actions might make it seem that Mao was right on this subject, but I would argue differently. Nor do I completely agree with Arendt's dictum. It is true that violence is not real power; it is just an instrument of coercion. Nevertheless, it is in fact capable of helping create something that has actual power—in this case, the nation.

---

190. "Violence can destroy power; it is utterly incapable of creating it." Hannah Arendt, *On Violence* (New York, 1969), 56.

Conclusion

The conditions described in this book were to a large extent shaped by the vacuum left by a failing state. It is a challenge to gauge the degree of that failure, however, because the actions of the Ottoman government did not exactly duplicate those of a completely defunct state nor was its legitimacy, eroded as it was, entirely absent in the minds of its subject populations. This was a state that had a difficult time feeding its army, half of which happened to be stationed in Macedonia, but that still had officials who prepared detailed post-mortem reports after an attack on a village and undertook ambitious projects such as a detailed population count in the middle of an insurgency. The erosion of its legitimacy, especially in the eyes of its Christian population, was a process that had started much earlier and that was more the result of shifts in the fiscal/military administrative system and the concomitant abuse of rights over the peasantry than of that peasantry's evolving national consciousness.

This is not to argue that the Christian subjects of the Ottoman Empire had already started on a course that would inevitably result in irredentist state-seeking movements as early as the eighteenth century and finally had found in nationalism an ideal cause around which to rally the masses. No one with a scholarly interest in the Ottoman Empire would nowadays think of its Christian subject populations as religious or ethnic minorities primarily occupied with preserving the privileges accorded to them by the sultan until they could strike out on their own. Nevertheless, this assumption held sway for so long that it is still necessary to pause and reconsider the complex matrix that defined the relationship of the Ottoman center with its subjects—Muslim and non-Muslim—for most of the history of the empire. It is also necessary to remember that the framework formed by parallel alignments of religiously defined communities linked by separate threads to the center, known as the *millet* system, was a product of the *Tanzimat* era and even then was not an all-encompassing model that explained the nature of the relationship of the Ottoman state to its subjects. The key point here is that maintaining and managing difference—between religious groups, between men and women, between tax payers and collectors, between those with access to the means of coercion and those without, and, most important, between center and periphery—are the activities that define an empire and distinguish it from other forms of rule, especially those whose legitimacy is predicated on an imagined sense of belonging to a greater community of co-nationals. That the transition from the one form of rule to the other would occur only through convulsions of the social and political order is perhaps obvious. But exactly how deep those convulsions would be and what horrors they would bring to the surface before subsiding, not even the most perceptive visionaries of the Age of Revolution could have foreseen.

By the mid-nineteenth century, the notion that mass political participation was the principal tool of legitimation had become the norm, not only in the (geopolitical) core of Europe but also among the emergent political dissidents in its periphery. Nationalism was an exceptionally suitable ideological framework for expanding the political base without necessarily challenging relations of economic production or dominant class structures. At the same time, defining and classifying the demographic base according to national criteria worked harmoniously with the apparatuses of the modern state, such as statistical approaches to population management, cartography in the service of governance, huge armies of draftees, and bureaucracies and workforces emanating from unified school curricula, to name a few. The modern nation-state not only was the product of these new technologies of rule but also contributed to their development and proliferation in a mutually reinforcing process.

The societal balance the Ottomans had maintained through the cultivation of heterogeneity across their territories and communities was irrevocably unsettled as the combined momentum of mass politics and the needs of state modernization rendered obsolete established methods of association, alliance building, and derivation of legitimacy. This process, more than the mediation of intellectuals, be they the Young Ottomans or the Philiki Etaireia (who were ostensibly disseminating ideas sourced from Europe), destabilized the Ottoman social order. A new set of internal dynamics challenged the status quo of the state elites and, for the first time, demanded that they be held accountable.

This book has focused on the period that followed this initial challenge to empire. The events that eventually culminated in the resolution of the Eastern Question were set in motion, and the tension between empire and the formation of nation-states came to a head, not only for the Ottomans but also for the neighboring empires. Between 1850 and 1918, the "key dilemma of empire," as Dominic Lieven put it, was how control over vast territories could be squared with the "demands of nationalism, democracy and economic dynamism."[1] While the geopolitical realities of Europe were shifting as a result of these challenges, one of the fundamental changes that took place was the redefinition of the relationship between territory and the people. That relationship now favored the political and the national unit

---

1. Dominic Lieven, "Dilemmas of Empire: 1850–1918. Power, Territory, Identity," *Journal of Contemporary History* 34, no. 2 (1999), 165.

being the same and emphasized the use of new technologies of state power that favored a more homogenous population. These notions clashed with the agendas of hegemony of the European Powers, on the one hand, and gave political actors at the periphery of the European state system hope that they could achieve political and economic modernization through the nation-state model, on the other.

The Ottoman Empire entered this era as a defeated power with considerably less prestige and limited means in the face of vicious economic and territorial competition. The efforts to redirect power from the hands of provincial powerbrokers to the center, such as the move against semi-autonomous warlords in Rumeli, had uneven levels of success, with this "success" arguably deepening the tensions it aimed to resolve. The efforts to address social inequality, streamline tax collection and expand the draft army met with resistance both from Muslims, who viewed themselves as bearing the burden of reforms that mainly benefited the "infidels," and from non-Muslims, who were not satisfied with unsubstantiated rhetoric about government sensitivity to their plight. This is not to say that there was no intercommunal conflict before the Ottoman state started making efforts to implement modern methods of statecraft and redefine its source of legitimacy, but these conflicts were now linked to politics on a larger scale and had a significance that went well beyond the local. In fact, the growing dependency of the Ottoman Empire on the European Powers for the preservation of its territorial integrity and its gradual transformation into an outpost of European capitalism meant that local conflicts became international matters, with each power treating a chosen community as its proxy in the Ottoman Empire.

Mark Mazower identifies the decade from the Balkan Wars (1912–1913) to 1922–1923 as "the catalyst for genocide, ethnic cleansing, and massive forced population movements for the first time in history."[2] I propose that the starting date of this long period be moved back even further in time, to 1878, when the Congress of Berlin sought to repair the European status quo while leaving the resolution of the knotty Eastern Question to the future, thereby ensuring that the unresolved tensions would prove ever more difficult to contain. Revolutionary movements in southeast Europe and eastern Anatolia were directly influenced by the rivalry among the Great Powers, which alternated between pressure and appeasement in their dealings with the Ottoman Empire. After 1914–1918, when this diplomatic rivalry spilled over into a devastatingly prolonged war, the consequences were tragic for the entire continent, and especially for the people scattered throughout the territory stretching from Eastern Europe, through the Black Sea littoral and

---

2. Mark Mazower, "Violence and the State in the Twentieth Century," *American Historical Review* 107, no. 4 (2002), 1175.

Asia Minor, and into the Fertile Crescent.[3] The messy confluence of state modernization, imperialism, and nationalism indeed heralded an epoch of unprecedented levels of violence.

During this period, which witnessed a novel instrumentality of violence that distinguished it from older expressions of imperial hegemony, the Ottoman polity lurched further and further away from an imperial framework at pivotal moments, even as its statesmen were deploying those very same instruments of state violence to save the empire. The expiration date of the Ottoman Empire was 1923, but the Young Turk revolution of 1908 should be considered one of those moments that signified the end of empire before its life was officially over. This is not because the revolution ostensibly brought back the constitution and the parliament, turning the sultan into a figurehead, but because one of the trademarks of the new constitutional era (even including the brief interlude when the Ottoman Committee of Union and Progress, CUP, was in opposition) was its leaders' willingness to abandon former policies that had accommodated difference in favor of those that enforced uniformity, such as ending the old practice of allowing the rotation of church space among Christian communities of different sects. The paternalism of the Hamidian period was replaced with the presumably more "modern" and impersonal rigidity of bureaucratic rules and ostensible attachment to legalism. Soon enough, the Young Turk leadership proved to be at least as authoritarian as (if not more authoritarian than) the arbitrary rule of Abdülhamid II. The crisis in the Balkans was sufficient to abandon all pretense of parliamentary government, and the leadership cadre of the CUP, which had never completely abandoned its formative identity as members of a clandestine network, steered the empire to its demise, which, by that point had become all but inevitable. No vestiges of imperial heterogeneity were around after 1908: the fate of Ottoman Armenians in 1915 should be a clear indication that national uniformity had indisputably prevailed. The ethnically cleansed and heavily militarized nation-state of Turkey, built on this foundation, is still a work in progress, not having made its peace with its past or with the ethnic complexity of its population. Lately, the Ottoman past has experienced a revival after decades of languishing in oblivion, although it is hard to say whether the scholarly debates about the empire have any chance of influencing public perceptions when pitted against the growing obsession of the popular media with the opulence and grandeur of the Ottoman palace. Most worrisome is the recent fascination in Turkey with empire, not out of an interest with cultural plurality but out of a thinly disguised desire for restored hegemony.

---

3. One of the worst consequences of this clash was the near-total annihilation of Ottoman Armenians. On the role of Great Power competition in the development of the Armenian genocide, see Donald Bloxham, *The Great Game of Genocide: Imperialism, Nationalism and the Destruction of Ottoman Armenians* (Oxford, 2005).

What happened in Macedonia in the period between the Congress of Berlin and the Balkan Wars directly influenced the subsequent CUP policies. This is not simply because the 1908 revolution itself was organized and initiated in Macedonia but because the lessons that the CUP cadres drew from the process through which Rumeli was taken away from the empire informed the steps they would take to contain that damage and make sure that the same scenario did not play out in Anatolia. The same process also shaped the aggressively territorial and ethnically exclusive nation-states that replaced the Ottoman Empire in the Balkans, with consequences that reverberate to this day. This is not to suggest that it was the same ethnic fault line that collapsed in the Balkans in the 1990s — to the contrary, one of the main lessons of this study is that it is *not* a static ideology based on an immutable ethnic core that drives people to kill their neighbors but the instrumentality of violence in the service of politics that turns the illusion of hard ethnic boundaries into reality.

Years ago, as I was completing work on the dissertation project that later became the basis of this book, I spent a summer in Oxford, England. I quickly settled into a routine: days spent reading and writing at the Radcliffe Camera usually concluded at one of the many pubs in town, eating and drinking with friends, old and new. At the end of one such evening I climbed into a taxi, told the driver my destination, and was immediately greeted with the question, "Where are you from?" I regretted my answer to him because I was certain that my "exotic" place of origin had brought my chances of a quiet ride back home to nearly zero. The driver was silent for a second and his gaze, fixed on the rearview mirror, was one of confusion or, I feared, anger. As I was contemplating the possible subsequent conversations, each more uncomfortable than the other, he broke his silence. "Really?" he said. "You're Turkish? I could swear you're Macedonian!" Now it was my turn to stare in bemusement. I knew I had not drunk enough to hallucinate, and even a vivid imagination would be hard pressed to come up with such — at least, as I saw it — an absurd exchange. Soon the source of his speculation became clear. As he was waiting in line, he had seen me saying good-bye to my friends (all of whom happened to be from lands that used to be part of the Ottoman world); he could not hear what I said, but my intonation, gestures, and the way I looked, he explained, made him think that I was Macedonian for sure. Historians, unlike anthropologists, rarely go "local," and I am not even sure how I could project a Macedonian "look" as opposed to, say, a "Bulgarian" look with my obvious lack of a knack for appreciating the subtle differences in Balkan morphology. In fact, his guess about which specific Balkan national group I belonged to did not have much to do with the way I looked but everything to do with his own background — Slobodan, my chatty taxi driver, was a Serb from Croatia.

I doubt it was serendipity that made a stranger tell me I "look Macedonian" while I was spending days preoccupied with the fates of the residents of that region a century earlier, but in a way it encapsulated what nation-ness is all about: belonging to a community that is imagined but by no means imaginary. Slobodan and I had our separate sets of assumptions about each other's backgrounds, and certain cues he was conditioned to read as signs indicative of belonging to a specific nation had led him to conclude that I must be Macedonian. To him, my appearance was uncanny, familiar but not quite known, close yet somewhat distant. In his imagined system of associations, this pegged me as Macedonian. Imaginary as the roots of these associations may be, his having been born a Serb in Croatia had had extremely real consequences. He had been displaced during the war, had quit his studies, and had started a new life as a refugee. All national groups rely on myths of shared culture, history, and common descent. People's sense of who they are and where they belong is shaped from an early age by the allegory of belonging to one big family, the nation. But the ties that bind them together, it seems, are not in the blood they imagine they share but in the blood that spills in the name of the family.

Bibliography

ARCHIVES

Başbakanlık Osmanlı Arşivleri (Prime Ministry Ottoman Archives) (BOA), Istanbul, Turkey
BEO: Bab-ı Ali Evrak Odası
HRT: Harita
I.DH: İradeler Dahiliye
I.TAL: İradeler Taltifat
TFR: Teftişat-ı Rumeli Evrakı (Papers of the Inspectorate of Rumeli)
TFR.I.ŞKT: Arzuhaller
TFR.I.A: Sadaret Evrakı
TFR.I.AS: Jandarma Müşiriyet ve Kumandanlık Evrakı
TFR.I.KV: Kosova/Kosovo
TFR.I.M: Müteferrik
TFR.I.MN: Manastır/Monastir
TFR.I.SL: Selanik/Salonika
Y.A.RES: Yıldız Sadaret Resmi Maruzat Evraki
Y.PRK.MK: Yıldız Perakende Müfettişlikler ve Komiserlikler Tahriratı

Archives du Ministère des Affaires étrangères (MAE), Quai d'Orsay, Nantes, France
Correspondence Politique et Commerciale "Nouvelle Série"
Dossiers Thématiques

Public Records Office, Foreign Office (PRO), London, UK
FO 195: Embassy and Consulates, Turkey (Ottoman Empire) General
  Correspondence

PUBLISHED SOURCES AND PAPERS

Abbott, George F. *Macedonian Folklore.* Cambridge, UK: Cambridge University Press, 1903.
——. *Songs of Modern Greece.* Cambridge, UK: Cambridge University Press, 1900.
——. *The Tale of a Tour in Macedonia.* London: Edward Arnold, 1903.
Adanır, Fikret. *Die Makedonische Frage: Ihre Entstehung und Entwicklung bis 1908.* Wiesbaden: Steiner, 1979.
——. *Makedonya Sorunu.* Translated by İhsan Catay. Istanbul: Tarih Vakfı Yurt Yayınları, 1996 [1979].

Aksakal, Mustafa. *The Ottoman Road to War in 1914: The Ottoman Empire and the First World War*. Cambridge, UK: Cambridge University Press, 2008.
Anastasoff, Christ. *The Tragic Peninsula*. St. Louis: Blackwell Wielandy, ca.1938.
Anderson, Benedict. *Imagined Communities*. Rev. ed. London: Verso, 1991.
Appadurai, Arjun. "Number in the Colonial Imagination." In *Orientalism and the Postcolonial Predicament: Perspectives on South Asia*, edited by Carol A. Breckenridge and Peter van der Veer, 314–40. Philadelphia: University of Pennsylvania Press, 1993.
Arendt, Hannah. *On Violence*. New York: Harcourt, Brace & World, 1969.
Arnakis, George. "The Role of Religion in the Development of Balkan Nationalism." In *The Balkans in Transition: Essays on the Development of Balkan Life and Politics since the Eighteenth Century*, edited by Charles Jelavich and Barbara Jelavich, 115–44. Berkeley: University of California Press, 1963.
Augustinos, Gerasimos. "'Enlightened Christians and 'Oriental' Churches: Protestant Missions to the Greeks in Asia Minor, 1820–1860." *Journal of Modern Greek Studies* 4, no. 2 (1986): 129–42.
Baines, Athelstane. "The Census of the Empire, 1911." *Journal of the Royal Statistical Society* 77, no. 4 (March 1914): 381–414.
Baker, James. *Turkey in Europe*. London: Cassel Petter & Galpin, 1877.
Baleva, Martina, and Ulf Brunbauer, eds. *Batak: Ein Bulgarischer Erinnerungsort*. Berlin: Geschichtswerkstatt Europa, 2008.
Barkan, Ömer L. "Essai sur les Données Statistiques des Registres de Recensement dans l'Empire Ottoman aux XVème et XVIème Siècles." *Journal of the Economic and Social History of the Orient* 1 (1957): 9–36.
———. "Tarihi demografi araştırmaları ve Osmanlı tarihi." *Türkiyat Mecmuası* 10 (1953): 1–26.
———. "Türkiye'de İmparatorluk devirlerinin büyük nüfus ve arazi tahrirleri." *Iktisat Fakültesi Mecmuası* 1–2 (1940): 1–40.
Barnes, Barry. *The Elements of Social Theory*. Princeton: Princeton University Press, 1995.
Barth, Fredrik. "Enduring and Emerging Issues in the Analysis of Ethnicity." In *The Anthropology of Ethnicity: Beyond Ethnic Groups and Boundaries*, edited by in Hans Vermeulen and Cora Govers, 11–32. Amsterdam: Het Spinhuis, 1994.
———, ed. *Ethnic Groups and Boundaries: The Social Organization of Cultural Difference*. London: Allen and Unwin, 1969.
Bechev, Dimitar. *The Historical Dictionary of the Republic of Macedonia*, Plymouth and Maryland: Scarecrow Press, 2009.
Behar, Cem. *Osmanlı İmparatorluğu'nun ve Türkiye'nin Nüfusu, 1500–1927*. Ankara: State Institute of Statistics, 1996.
———. "Qui Compte? 'Recensement' et Statistiques Démographiques dans L'Empire Ottoman, du XVIe au XXe Siècle." *Histoire et Mesure* 13, no. 1–2 (1998): 135–46.
Belia, Eleni D. "Ē Ekpaideutikē Politikē tou Ellinikou Kratous pros tēn Makedonia kai o Makedonikos Agōn" [The Educational Policy of the Greek State toward Macedonia and the Macedonian Struggle]. In *O Makedonikos Agōnas: Symposio* [Macedonian Struggle, Symposium Proceedings], 29–40. Thessaloniki: Idryma Meletōn Xersonisou tou Aimou, 1987.

Bell, Morag, Robin Butlin, and Michael Heffernan, eds. *Geography and Imperialism, 1820–1940.* Manchester: Manchester University Press, 1995.
Berghaus, Heinrich. *Geographische Verbreitung der Menschen-Rassen.* Gotha: Justus Perthes, 1848.
Bernal, Martin. *Black Athena: The Afroasiatic Roots of Classical Civilization.* 2 vols. New Brunswick, NJ: Rutgers University Press, 1991.
Bianconi, F. *Ethnographie et Statistique de la Turquie d'Europe et de la Grèce.* Paris: A. Lassailly, 1877.
Billig, Michael. *Banal Nationalism.* London: Sage, 1995.
Black, Jeremy. *Maps and History.* New Haven: Yale University Press, 1997.
Bloxham, Donald. *The Great Game of Genocide: Imperialism, Nationalism and the Destruction of Ottoman Armenians,* Oxford: Oxford University Press, 2005.
Boissonnas, Frédéric. *La Macédoine Occidentale.* Geneva: Editions d'Art Boissonnas, 1921.
Boué, Amie. *Receuil d'Itinéraires dans la Turquie d'Europe, Détails Géographiques, Topographiques, et Statistiques cur cet Empire.* Vienna: Libraire de L'Académie Impériale des Sciences, 1854.
———. *La Turquie d'Europe, ou Observations sur la Géographie, la Géologie, l'Histoire Naturelle, la Statistique, les Moeurs, les Coutumes, l'Archéologie, l'Agriculture, l'Industrie, le Commerce, les Gouvernements Divers, le Clergé, l'Histoire, et l'État Politique de cet Empire.* 4 vols. Paris, 1840.
Boyer, Christine. *The City of Collective Memory.* Cambridge, MA: MIT Press, 1994.
Brailsford, Henry N. *Macedonia, Its Races and Their Future.* London: Methuen & Co., 1906.
Brancoff D. M. [Dimitar Mishev] *La Macédoine et sa Population Chrétienne.* Paris: Librairie Plon, 1905.
Braude, Benjamin. "Foundation Myths of the Millet System." In *Christians and Jews in the Ottoman Empire: The Functioning of a Plural Society.* Vol. 1, *The Central Lands,* edited by Benjamin Braude and Bernard Lewis, 69–88. New York: Holmes and Meier, 1982.
Brown, Keith. *The Past in Question: Modern Macedonia and the Uncertainties of Nation.* Princeton: Princeton University Press, 2003.
———. "A Rising to Count On: Ilinden between Politics and History in Post-Yugoslav Macedonia," in *The Macedonian Question: Culture, Historiography, Politics,* edited by Victor Roudometof, 143–72. Boulder: East European Monographs, 2000.
Brubaker, Rogers. "The Manichean Myth: Rethinking the Distinction between 'Civic' and 'Ethnic' Nationalism." In *Nation and National Identity: The European Experience in Perspective,* edited by Hanspeter Kriesi, Klaus Armingeon, and Hannes Siegrist, 55–71. Zürich: Verlag Rüegger, 1999.
———. *Nationalism Reframed: Nationhood and the National Question in the New Europe.* Cambridge, UK: Cambridge University Press, 1996.
Brubaker, Rogers, and David D. Laitin. "Ethnic and Nationalist Violence." *Annual Review of Sociology* 24 (1998): 423–52.
Brunnbauer, Ulf. "Historiography, Myths and the Nation in the Republic of Macedonia." In *(Re)Writing History: Historiography in Southeast Europe after Socialism,* edited by Ulf Brunnbauer, 176–86. Münster: Lit Verlag, 2004.

———, ed. *(Re)Writing History: Historiography in Southeast Europe after Socialism.* Münster: Lit Verlag, 2004.
Calhoun, Craig. "Nationalism and Ethnicity." *Annual Review of Sociology* 19 (1993): 211–39.
———. *Nations Matter: Culture, History, and the Cosmopolitan Dream.* New York: Routledge, 2007.
Carpenter, Teresa. *The Miss Stone Affair: America's First Modern Hostage Crisis.* New York: Simon & Schuster, 2003.
Carte des Écoles Chrétiennes de la Macédoine, Paris: Erhard Frères, 1905.
Cartes Ethnographiques des Vilayets Salonique, Cossovo et Monastir. Sofia: L'Institute Cartographique à Sophia, 1901.
Clarke, Hyde. "On the Supposed Extinction of the Turks and Increase of the Christians in Turkey." *Journal of the Statistical Society* 28, no. 2 (1865): 261–93.
Clarke, James F. *The Pen and the Sword: Studies in Bulgarian History,* edited by Dennis Hupchick. Boulder: East European Monographs, 1988.
Cohn, Bernard S. "History and Anthropology: The State of Play." In *An Anthropologist among the Historians and Other Essays,* 18–49. Delhi and Oxford: Oxford University Press, 1987. [Originally published in *Comparative Studies in History and Society* 22 (1980).]
———. "The Census, Social Structure and Objectification in South Asia." In *An Anthropologist among the Historians and Other Essays,* 224–54. Delhi and Oxford: Oxford University Press, 1987.
Colocotronis, V. *La Macédoine et l'Hellenisme, Étude Historique et Ethnologique.* Paris: Berger-Levrault, 1919.
Cosgrove, Denis. "Contested Global Visions: One-World, Whole Earth, and the Apollo Space Photographs." *Annals of the Association of American Geographers* 84, no. 2: 270–94.
———. "Tropic and Tropicality." In *Tropical Visions in an Age of Empire,* edited by Felix Driver and Luciana Martins, 197–216. Chicago: University of Chicago Press, 2005.
Couisinéry, E. M. *Voyage dans la Macédoine, Contenant les Recherches sur l'Histoire, la Géographie et les Antiquités de ce Pays.* Paris: Imprimerie Royale, 1831.
Cowan, Jane K., and Keith S. Brown. "Introduction: Macedonian Inflections." In *Macedonia: The Politics of Identity and Difference,* edited by Jane K. Cowan, 1–28. London: Pluto Press, 2000.
Crampton, Jeremy. "The Cartographic Calculation of Space: Race Mapping and the Balkans at the Paris Peace Conference of 1919." *Social & Cultural Geography* 7, no. 5 (October 2006): 731–52.
Crampton, Richard J. *A Concise History of Bulgaria.* Cambridge, UK: Cambridge University Press, 1997.
Cvijić, Jovan. *Questions Balkaniques.* Neuchâtel: Attinjer, 1916.
———. *Remarks on the Ethnography of the Macedonian Slavs.* London: Horace Cox, 1906.
———. "Remarques sur l'Ethnographie de la Macédoine." *Annales de Géographie* 15, no. 80 (1906): 115–32; no. 81 (1906): 249–66.
Dakin, Douglas. *The Greek Struggle in Macedonia, 1897–1913.* Thessaloniki: Institute for Balkan Studies, 1966.

Danforth, Loring M. *The Macedonian Conflict: Ethnic Nationalism in a Transnational World*. Princeton: Princeton University Press, 1995.
Darrow, David W. "Census as a Technology of Empire." *Ab Imperio* 4 (2002): 145–76.
Davis, Natalie Z. "The Rites of Violence: Religious Riot in Sixteenth-Century France." *Past and Present* 59 (May 1973): 51–91.
Davison, Roderic H. "Ottoman Diplomacy and Its Legacy." In *The Imperial Legacy*, edited by L. Carl Brown, 174–201. New York: Columbia University Press, 1996.
Deringil, Selim. "They Live in a State of Nomadism and Savagery: The Late Ottoman Empire and the Post-Colonial Debate." *Comparative Studies in Society and History* 45, no. 2 (2003): 311–42.
———. *The Well-Protected Domains: Ideology and the Legitimation of Power in the Ottoman Empire, 1876–1909*. London: I. B. Tauris, 1999.
Derlugian, Georgi. *Bourdieau's Secret Admirer in the Caucasus*. Chicago: University of Chicago Press, 2005.
Dimara, K. Th. *Kōnstantinos Paparrēgopoulos, ē epochē tou, ē Zōē tou, to ergo tou*. Athens: Morfōtiko Idryma Ethnikēs Trapezēs, 1986.
Dirks, Nicholas. *Castes of Mind: Colonialism and the Making of Modern India*. Princeton: Princeton University Press, 2001.
Dominian, Leon. "The Turk, Casual of Geography." *Journal of Geography* 18, no. 1 (1919): 3–13.
Doumani, Beshara B. "The Political Economy of Population Counts in Ottoman Palestine: Nablus, circa 1850." *International Journal of Middle East Studies* 26, no. 1 (February 1994): 1–17.
Draganoff. *La Macédoine et les Réformes*. Paris: Librairie Plon, 1906.
———. *Macedonia and the Reforms*. Translated by Victor Bérard. London: Hazell, Watson and Vinery, 1908.
Dragostinova, Theodora. *Between Two Motherlands: Nationality and Emigration among the Greeks of Bulgaria, 1900–1949*. Ithaca: Cornell University Press, 2011.
Dragoumis, Iōnos. *Ta Tetradia tou Ilinten*. Edited by Giōrgos Petsivas. Athens: Ekdoseis Petsiva, 2000.
Driault, Edouard. *La Question d'Orient depuis ses Origines jusqu'a nos Jours*. 5th ed. Paris: Librairie Félix Alcan, 1912.
Dündar, F. Fuat. *Modern Türkiye'nin şifresi: Ittihad ve Terakki'nin Etnisite Mühendisliği, 1913–1918*. Istanbul: Iletişim Yayınları, 2008.
du Val, Pierre. "Carte de l'Empire des Turcs et de les Contins." In *European Cartographers and the Ottoman World, 1500–1750: Maps from the Collection of O.J. Sopranos*, edited by Ian Manners, 42. Chicago: Oriental Institute Museum Publications, 2007.
Les Écoles Chrétiennes de Macédoine. Paris: A. Pedone, 1905.
Edney, Matthew H. *Mapping an Empire: The Geographical Construction of British India, 1765–1843*. Chicago: University of Chicago Press, 1997 [1990].
———. "Mapping Parts of the World." In *Maps: Finding Our Place in the World*, edited by James R. Akerman and Robert W. Karrow Jr., 117–58. Chicago: University of Chicago Press, 2007.

Eldem, Edhem "Ottoman Financial Integration with Europe: Foreign Loans, the Ottoman Bank and the Ottoman Public Debt." *European Review* 13, no. 3 (2005): 431–45.

Eliot, Sir Charles. *Turkey in Europe*. 2nd ed. New York: Barnes and Noble, 1907 [1900].

The English Blue Book regarding Macedonia, Comments by A.K. Athens, 1891 [commentary on the Blue Book No. 3, 1889, Turkey].

"Ethnology and Ethnography." In *Encyclopædia Britannica*, 11th ed., Vol. 9: 849. New York: Cambridge University Press, 1910.

Exertzoglou, Chares. *Ethnikē Tautotita stēn Kōnstantinoupolē tou 19o Aiōna: O Ellēnikos Syllogos Kōnstantinoupoleōs, 1861–1912*. Athens: Nephelē 1996.

Fabian, Johannes. *Time and the Other: How Anthropology Makes Its Object*. New York: Columbia University Press, 1983.

Fall, Juliet J. "Artificial States? On the Enduring Myth of Natural Borders." *Political Geography* 29, no. 3 (2010): 140–47.

Fearon, James D., and David D. Laitin. "Ethnicity, Insurgency, and Civil War." *American Political Science Review* 97, no. 1 (2003): 75–90.

Febvre, Lucien. "*Frontière:* The Word and the Concept." In *A New Kind of History from the Writings of Febvre*, edited by Peter Burke, translated by K. Folca, 208–17. London: Routledge & Kegan Paul, 1973.

———. *A Geographical Introduction to History*. Translated by E. G. Mountford and J. H. Paxton. New York: Alfred A Knopf, 1925.

Fermor, Patrick L. *Roumeli: Travels in Northern Greece*. New York: New York Review of Books, 2006 [1966].

Finkel, Caroline. *Osman's Dream: The Story of the Ottoman Empire, 1300–1923*. New York: Basic Books, 2006.

Fortna, Benjamin. *The Imperial Classroom: Islam, the State, and Education in the Late Ottoman Empire*. Oxford: Oxford University Press, 2002.

Friedman, Victor. "Language in Macedonia as an Identity Construction Site." In *When Languages Collide: Perspectives on Language Conflict, Language Competition, and Language Coexistence*, edited by Brian D. Joseph, Johanna Destefano, Niel G. Jacobs, and Ilse Eliste, 257–98. Columbus: Ohio University Press, 2003.

———. "Macedonian Language and Nationalism during the Nineteenth and Early Twentieth Centuries." *Balkanistica* 2, no. 98 (1975): 83–98.

Friendly, Michael, and Gilles Palsky. "Visualizing Nature and Society." In *Maps: Finding Our Place in the World*, edited by James R. Akerman and Robert W. Karrow Jr., 207–54. Chicago: University of Chicago Press, 2007.

Frussetta, James. "Common Heroes, Divided Claims: IMRO between Macedonia and Bulgaria." In *Ideologies and National Identities: The Case of Twentieth-Century Southeastern Europe*, edited by John Lampe and Mark Mazower, 110–30. Budapest: Central European University Press, 2004.

Gagnon, Valère P. *The Myth of Ethnic War: Serbia and Croatia in the 1990s*. Ithaca: Cornell University Press, 2004.

Gandolphe, Maurice. *La Crise Macédonienne: Enquête dans les Vilayets Insurgés (Sept.–Dec. 1903)*. Paris: Perrin, 1904.

Gazi, Effi. "Revisiting Religion and Nationalism in Nineteenth-Century Greece." In *Making of Modern Greece: Nationalism, Romanticism, and the Uses of the Past (1797–1896)*, edited by Roderick Beaton and David Ricks, 95–106. Aldershot, UK: Ashgate, 2009.

Gellner, Ernest. *Nations and Nationalism*. Ithaca: Cornell University Press, 1983.

———. *Thought and Change*, London: Weidenfeld and Nicolson, 1964.

Geographische Verbreitung der Menschen-Ranssen. Gotha: Justus Perthes, 1848.

Gingeras, Ryan. *Sorrowful Shores: Violence, Ethnicity, and the End of the Ottoman Empire, 1912–1923*. New York: Oxford University Press.

Gladstone, William E. *The Bulgarian Horrors and the Question of the East*. London: John Murray, 1876.

Göçek, Fatma M., and Şükrü Hanioğlu. "Western Knowledge, Imperial Control and the Use of Statistics in the Ottoman Empire." Center for Research on Social Organization Working Paper no. 500, Department of Sociology, University of Michigan, Ann Arbor, 1993.

Gopčević, Spiridon. *Makedonien und Alt-Serbien*. Vienna: Verlag von L. W. Seidel & Sohn, 1889.

Gourgouris, Stathis. *Dream Nation*. Stanford: Stanford University Press, 1996.

Guha, Sumit. "The Politics of Identity and Enumeration in India c. 1600–1990." *Comparative Studies in Society and History*, 45 (2003): 148–67.

Guys, Charles Édouard. *Le Guide de la Macédoine*. Paris: Benjamin Duprat, 1857.

Hacısalihoğlu, Mehmet. *Jön Türkler ve Makedonya Sorunu*. Istanbul: Tarih Vakfı Yurt Yayınları, 2008.

———. *Die Jungtürken und die Makedonische Frage (1890–1918)*. Munich: R. Oldenburg Verlag, 2003.

Hall, John A. "Conditions for National Homogenizers." In *Nationalism and its Futures*, edited by Umut Özkırımlı, 15–32. New York: Palgrave Macmillan, 2003.

———, ed. *The State of the Nation: Ernest Gellner and the Theory of Nationalism*. Cambridge, UK: Cambridge University Press, 1998 [1988].

Hanioğlu, Şükrü. *A Brief History of the Late Ottoman Empire*. Princeton: Princeton University Press, 2008.

———. *Preparation for a Revolution*. Oxford: Oxford University Press, 2001.

Hanssen, Jens. *Fin de Siècle Beirut: The Making of an Ottoman Provincial Capital*. Oxford: Oxford University Press, 2005.

Harley, J. Brian. "Maps, Knowledge, and Power." In *The Iconography of Landscape: Essays on the Symbolic Representation, Design and Use of Past Environments*, edited by Denis Cosgrove and Stephen Daniels, 277–312. Cambridge, UK: Cambridge University Press, 1988.

Hirsch, Francine. *Empire of Nations: Ethnographic Knowledge and the Making of the Soviet Union*. Ithaca: Cornell University Press, 2005.

———. "The Soviet Union as Work-in-Progress: Ethnographers and the Category Nationality in the 1926, 1937 and 1939 Censuses." *Slavic Review* 56 (1997): 251–78.

Hobsbawm, Eric J. *Nations and Nationalism since 1780: Programme, Myth, Reality*. Cambridge, UK: Cambridge University Press, 1990.

Hosoon, David J. M. "The Development of Geography in Pre-Soviet Russia." *Annals of the Association of American Geographers* 58 (1968): 250–72.

Ignatieff, Michael. *Blood and Belonging*, New York: Farrar, Straus and Giroux, 1993.

Ignotus, Paul. "Czechs, Magyars, Slovaks." *Political Quarterly* 40, no. 2 (1969): 187–204.
Illustrations of the Principal Varieties of the Human Race, Arranged According to the System of Dr. Latham. Descriptive notes by Ernest Ravenstein. London: James Reynolds, ca. 1850.
Inalcık, Halil. "Review of Kemal H. Karpat 'Ottoman Population: Demographic and Social Characteristics.'" *International Journal of Middle East Studies* 21, no. 3 (1989): 422–24.
Ishirkov, Anastas. *Études Ethnographiques sur les Slaves de Macédoine*. Paris: Gauthier-Villars, 1908.
——. *La Macédoine et la Constitution de l'Exarchat bulgare*. Lausanne: Librairie Centrale de Nationalités, 1918.
——. *Le Nom de Bulgare: Eclaircissement d'Histoire et d'Ethnographie*. Lausanne: Librairie Centrale des Nationalités, 1918.
Ivanoff, J. *La Question Macédonienne au Point de Vue Historique, Ethnographique et Statistique*. Paris: Librairie J. Gamber, 1920.
Jelavich, Charles, and Barbara Jelavich. *The Establishment of the Balkan National States, 1804–1920*. Seattle: University of Washington Press, 1986 [1977].
Joerg, W. L. G. "The New Boundaries of the Balkan States and Their Significance" *Bulletin of the American Geographical Society* 45 (1913): 819–30.
Judson, Pieter. *Guardians of the Nation: Activists on the Language Frontiers of Imperial Austria*. Cambridge, MA: Harvard University Press, 2006.
Kafadar, Cemal. *Between Two Worlds: The Construction of the Ottoman State*. Berkeley: University of California Press, 1995.
Kaiser, Robert. "Geography." In *The Encyclopedia of Nationalism*, edited by Alexander Motyl, 315–33. San Diego: Academic Press, 2000.
Kakar, Sudhir. *The Colors of Violence: Cultural Identities, Religion and Conflict*. Chicago: University of Chicago Press, 1996.
Kalyvas, Stathis. *The Logic of Violence in Civil War*. Cambridge, UK: Cambridge University Press, 2006.
——. "The Ontology of 'Political Violence': Action and Identity in Civil Wars." *Perspectives on Politics* 1, no. 3 (2003): 475–94.
Kaplan, Robert D. *Balkan Ghosts: A Journey through History*. New York: St. Martin's Press, 1993.
Karakasidou, Anastasia. *Fields of Wheat, Hills of Blood: Passages into Nationhood in Greek Macedonia, 1870–1990*. Chicago: University of Chicago Press, 1997.
Karavas, S. "Oi Ethnografikes Peripeteies tou Ellēnismou." *Ta Istorika* 19 (2002): 23–74.
Karpat, Kemal. *Ottoman Population 1830–1914: Demographic and Social Characteristics*. Madison: University of Wisconsin Press, 1985.
——. "Ottoman Population Records and the Census of 1881/1882–1893." *International Journal of Middle East Studies* 9 (1978): 237–74.
Kasaba, Reşat. *Ottoman Empire and the World Economy, the Nineteenth Century*. Albany: SUNY Press, 1988.
Kasasis, Néoclès. *L'Hellénisme et la Macédoine*. Paris: Imprimerie de la Renaissance Latine, 1903.

Kechriotis, Vangelis. "The Modernization of the Empire and the Community 'Privileges': Greek Orthodox Responses to Young Turk Policies." In *The State and the Subaltern: Modernization, Society and the State in Turkey and Iran*, edited by Touraj Atabeki, 53–70. London: I. B. Tauris, 2007.

Kedouri, Elie. *Nationalism*. London: Hutchison University Library, 1960.

Kelbechova, Evelina. "The Short History of Bulgaria for Export." In *Religion, Ethnicity, and Contested Nationhood in the Former Ottoman Space*, edited by Jørgen Nielsen, 223–48. Leiden: Brill, 2012.

Kertzer, David, and Dominique Arel. "Censuses, Identity Formation, and the Struggle for Political Power." In *Census and Identity*, edited by David Kertzer and Dominique Arel, 10–32. Cambridge, UK: Cambridge University Press, 2002.

Kiepert, Heinrich. *Ethnographische Übersichtskarte des Europäischen Orients*. Berlin: D. Reimer, 1876.

———. *Notice Explicative sur la Carte Ethnogratique des pays Helleniques, Slaves, Albanais et Roumains*. Berlin: Imprimerie de Kerskes & Hohmann, 1878.

———. *Tableau Ethnocratique des Pays du Sud-est de l'Europe*. Berlin: Imprimerie de Kerskes & Hohmann, 1878.

King, Jeremy. *Budweisers into Czechs and Germans: A Local History of Bohemian Politics*. Princeton: Princeton University Press, 2002.

Kıray, Emine. *Osmanlı'da Ekonomik Yapı ve Dış Borçlar*. Istanbul: İletişim, 1995.

Kitromilides, Paschalis. *The Enlightenment as Social Criticism: Iosipos Moisiodax and Greek Culture in the Eighteenth Century*. Princeton: Princeton University Press, 1992.

———. "'Imagined Communities' and the Origins of the National Question in the Balkans." In *Modern Greece: Nationalism and Nationality*, edited by Martin Blinkhorn and Thanos Veremis, 23–64. Athens: ELIAMEP, 1990.

———. "On the Intellectual Content of Greek Nationalism: Paparrigopoulos, Byzantium and the Great Idea." In *Byzantium and the Modern Greek Identity*, edited by David Ricks and Paul Magdalino, 25–33. Brookfield, VT: Ashgate, 1998.

Kivelson, Valerie A. *Cartographies of Tsardom: The Land and Its Meanings in Seventeenth-Century Russia*. Ithaca: Cornell University Press, 2006.

Kofos, Evangelos. "Attempts at Mending the Greek-Bulgarian Ecclesiastical Schism (1875–1902)." *Balkan Studies* 25 (1984): 347–68.

———. "Patriarch Joachim (1878–1884) and the Irredentist Policy of the Greek State." *Journal of Modern Greek Studies* 4, no. 2 (1986): 107–20.

Kohn, Hans. *A History of Nationalism in the East*. New York: Harcourt Brace, 1929.

———. *The Idea of Nationalism: A Study in Its Origins and Background*. New York: Macmillan, 1944.

Korzybski, Alfred. *Science and Sanity: An Introduction to Non-Aristotelian Systems and General Semantics*. 5th ed. Englewood, NJ: Institute of General Semantics, 1994.

Koulouri, Christina, ed. *Clio in the Balkans: The Politics of History Education*. Thessaloniki: Center for Democracy and Reconciliation in Southeast Europe, 2002.

———. *Dimensions Idéologiques de l'Historicité en Grèce, 1834–1914: Les Manuels de l'Histoire et de Géographie*. Frankfurt am Main: Peter Verlag, 1991.
Kropotkin, Peter. "The Fifty Years' History of the Russian Geographical Society." *Geographical Journal* 10 (July 1897): 53–56.
Kŭnchov, Vasil. *Makedonia: Ethnographia i Statistika*. Sofia: Bulgarskoto kn. Druzhestvo, 1900.
Lamouche, (Colonel) León. *Quinze Ans d'Histoire Balkanique*. Paris: Payot, ca. 1928.
Lange-Akhund, Nadine. *The Macedonian Question 1893–1908 from Western Sources*. Boulder: East European Monographs, 1998.
Laoudras, Vasileios. *To Ellinikon Genikon Proxeneion Thessalonikēs*. Thessaloniki: Etaireia Makedonikōn Spoudōn, 1961.
Lejean, Guillaume. "Ethnographie de la Turquie d'Europe." In *Peterman's Geographische Mittheilungen*. Gotha: Justus Perthes, 1861.
Liakos, Antonis. "The Construction of National Time: The Making of the Modern Greek Historical Imagination." *Mediterranean Historical Review* 16 (2001): 27–42.
Lieven, Dominic. "Dilemmas of Empire: 1850–1918. Power, Territory, Identity," *Journal of Contemporary History* 34, no. 2 (1999): 163–200.
Lilova, Desislava. "Barbarians, Civilized People and Bulgarians: Definition of Identity in Textbooks and the Press (1830–1878)." In *We, the People: Politics of National Peculiarity in Southeastern Europe*, edited by Diana Mishkova, 181–206. Budapest: Central European University Press, 2009.
Lory, Bernard. "Schools for the Destruction of Society: School Propaganda." In *Conflicting Loyalties in the Balkans: The Great Powers, the Ottoman Empire and Nation-Building*, edited by Hannes Grandits, Natalie Clayer, and Robert Pichler, 46–63. New York: I. B. Tauris, 2011.
———. "Soloun, Ville Slave?" In *Salonique, 1850–1918: La "Ville des Juifs" et le Réveil des Balkans*, edited by Gilles Veinstein, 129–37. Paris: Autrement, 1993.
Lowry, Heath. *The Nature of the Early Ottoman State*. Albany: SUNY Press, 2003.
———. "The Ottoman Tahrir Defterleri as a Source for Social and Economic History: Pitfalls and Limitations." In *Studies in Defterology: Ottoman Society in the Fifteenth and Sixteenth Centuries*, 3–18. Istanbul: Isis Press, 1992.
———. *The Shaping of the Ottoman Balkans, 1350–1550*. Istanbul: Bahçeşehir University, 2008.
La Macédoine et les Reformes, Mémoire du Syllogue Macédonien. Athènes: Imprimerie Sakellarios, 1903.
"Macedonia." In *Encyclopædia Britannica*, 11th ed., Vol. 17: 216. New York: Cambridge University Press, 1910.
Macedonia, Documents and Material. Sofia: Bulgarian Academy of Sciences, 1978.
Mackridge, Peter. *Language and National Identity in Greece, 1766–1976*. Oxford: Oxford University Press, 2009.
———. "Ottoman Orientalism." *American Historical Review* 107, no. 3 (2002): 768–96.
———. "Rethinking Ottoman Imperialism: Modernity, Violence, and the Cultural Logic of Ottoman Reform." In *The Empire in the City: Arab Provincial Cap-*

itals in the Late Ottoman Empire, edited by Jens Hanssen, Thomas Philippe, and Stefan Weber, 29–48. Beirut: Orient Institut der Deutschen Morgenländischen Gesellschaft, 2002.
Mann, Michael. *The Dark Side of Democracy: Explaining Ethnic Cleansing.* Cambridge, UK: Cambridge University Press, 2005.
Manners, Ian. *European Cartographers and the Ottoman World 1500–1750.* Chicago: Oriental Institute Museum Publications, 2007.
Marinov, Tchavdar. *La Question Macédonienne de 1944 à Nos Jours: Communism et Nationalisme dans les Balkans.* Paris: l'Harmattan, 2010.
———. "We, the Macedonians: The Paths of Macedonian Supranationalism (1878–1912)." In *We, the People: Politics of National Peculiarity in Southeastern Europe,* edited by Diana Mishkova, 107–38. Budapest: Central European University Press, 2009.
Markova, Zina. "Bulgarian Exarchate 1870–1879." *Bulgarian Historical Review* 16, no. 4 (1988): 39–55.
———. *Bŭlgarskata Ekzarhiya, 1870–1879.* Sofia: BAN, 1989.
Marriott, John A. R. *The Eastern Question: An Historical Study in European Diplomacy.* Oxford: Clarendon Press, 1947.
Marx, Anthony. *Faith in Nation: Exclusionary Origins of Nationalism,* Oxford: Oxford University Press, 2003.
Matalas, Paraskevas. *Ethnos kai Orthodoxia: Oi Peripeties mias Scheseis apo to "Elladiko" sto Voulgariko Schisma.* Irakleio: Panepistimiakes Ekdoseis Krētēs, 2002.
Mathieu, Henri. *La Turquie et ses Différents Peuples.* Paris: E. Dentu, ca. 1857.
Mazower, Mark. *The Balkans: A Short History,* New York: The Modern Library, 2002.
———. *Salonika, City of Ghosts: Christians, Muslims and Jews, 1430–1950.* New York: Alfred Knopf, 2004.
———. "Violence and the State in the Twentieth Century." *American Historical Review* 107, no. 4 (2002): 1158–78.
McCarthy, Justin. *Death and Exile: The Ethnic Cleansing of Ottoman Muslims, 1821–1912.* Princeton: Darwin Press, 1996.
———. *Muslims and Minorities: The Population of Ottoman Anatolia and the End of the Empire.* New York: New York University Press, 1983.
———. *Population History of the Middle East and the Balkans,* Istanbul: İsis Press, 2002.
McCrone, David. *The Sociology of Nationalism.* New York: Routledge, 1998.
Mearsheimer, John J., and Stephen Van Evera. "Redraw the Map, Stop the Killing." *New York Times,* April 19, 1999.
Megas, Giannis. *Oi "Varkarides" tēs Thessalonikēs: Ē Anarchikē Voulgarikē Omada kai oi Vomvistikes Energeies tou.* Athens: Trochalia, 1994.
Meininger, Thomas A. *Ignatiev and the Establishment of the Bulgarian Exarchate, 1864–1872.* Madison: State Historical Society of Wisconsin, 1970.
Michaēlidēs, Iakōvos D., and Kōnstantinos S. Papanikolaou, eds. *Aphaneis Gēgeneis Makedonomachoi (1903–1913).* Thessaloniki: University Studio Press, 2008.
Mishew, Dimitur [Dimitar Mishev]. *America and Bulgaria and Their Moral Bonds.* Bern: Paul Haupt, Akademische Buchhandlung, 1918.

Moore, Lorrie. "In the Life of 'The Wire.'" *New York Review of Books* 57, no. 15 (October 14, 2010): 23–31.

Morgan, E. Delmar. "Russian Geographical Work in 1886 from Russian Sources." *Proceedings of the Royal Geographical Society and Monthly Record of Geography* 9 (July 1887): 423–37.

Nordman, Daniel. "From the Boundaries of the State to National Borders." In *Rethinking France: Les Lieux de Mémoire*. Vol. 1, *The State*, edited by Pierre Nora, translated by Mary Trouille, 105–32. Chicago: University of Chicago Press, 2001.

Ofeicoff, A. [A. Shopov]. *La Macédoine au Point de Vue Ethnographique, Historique, et Philologique*. Constantinople: E. Heyrich, 1887. [Also published in Phillippoli: Imprimerie Centrale, 1887.]

Paillarès, Michel. *L'Imbroglio Macédonienne*. Paris: P. V. Stock, 1907.

Pallis, A. A. "Racial Migrations in the Balkans during the Years 1912–1924." *Geographical Journal* 66, no. 4 (October 1925): 315–31.

Palmer, Stephen E., Jr., and Robert R. King. *Yugoslav Communism and the Macedonian Question*. Hamden, CT: Archon Books, 1971.

Pantazopoulos, Nikolaos J. *Church and Law in the Balkan Peninsula during the Ottoman Rule*. Thessaloniki: Institute for Balkan Studies, 1967.

Panzac, Daniel. "L'Enjeu du Nombre: La Population de la Turquie de 1914 à 1927." *Revue de l'Occident Musulman et de la Méditerranée* 50, no. 4 (1988): 45–67.

———. "La Population de la Macédoine au XIXe Siècle." *La Revue du Monde Musulman et de la Méditerranée* 66 (1992): 113–29.

———. *La Population de l'Empire Ottoman*. Aix-en-Provence: Travaux et Documents de l'IREMAM, 1993.

Papazoglou, Leōnidas. *Phōtographika Portraita apo tēn Kastoria kai tēn periochē tēs tēn periodo tou Makedonikou Agōna*. Thessaloniki: Mouseio Phōtographias Thessalonikēs, 2004.

Peabody, Norbert. "Cents, Sense, Census: Human Inventories in Late Precolonial and Early Colonial India." *Comparative Studies in Society and History* 43 (2001): 819–50.

Perry, Duncan. *The Politics of Terror: The Macedonian Liberation Movements, 1893–1903*. Durham: Duke University Press, 1988.

———. *Stefan Stambolov and the Emergence of Modern Bulgaria, 1870–1895*. Durham: Duke University Press, 1993.

Philliou, Christine M. *Biography of an Empire: Governing Ottomans in an Age of Revolution*. Los Angeles: University of California Press, 2010.

Picot, M. E. *Les Roumaines de la Macédoine*. Paris: Ernest Leroux, 1875.

Plamenatz, John. "Two Types of Nationalism." In *Nationalism: The Nature and Evolution of an Idea*, edited by Eugene Kamenka, 23–36. London: Edward Arnold, 1976.

The Population of Macedonia: Evidence of the Christian Schools. London: Ede, Allon and Townsend, 1905.

Poulton, Hugh. *Who Are the Macedonians?* Bloomington: Indiana University Press, 2000 [1995].

Pouqueville, F. C. H. L. *Voyage en Morée, à Constantinople, en Albanie, et dans Plusieurs Parties de l'Empire Othoman, pendant les Années 1798, 1799, 1800 et 1801*. Paris: Gabon, 1805.

Pundeff, Marin V. "Bulgarian Nationalism." In *Nationalism in Eastern Europe*, edited by Peter F. Sugar and Ivo J. Lederer, 98–103. Seattle: University of Washington Press, 1969.
Ravenstein, Ernst G. "Distribution of the Population in the Part of Europe Overrun by Turks." *Geographical Magazine* 3 (October 1876): 259–61.
———. "Lands of the Globe Still Available for European Settlement." *Proceedings of the Royal Geographic Society and Monthly Record of Geography* 13, no.1 (January 1891): 27–35.
———. "The Population of Russia and Turkey." *Journal of the Statistical Society* 40 (September 1877): 433–67.
"Recent Russian Geographical Literature." *Geographical Journal* 6 (December 1895): 554–58.
Reclus, Elisée. *The Earth and Its Inhabitants*. Vol. 1, *Greece, Turkey in Europe, Rumania, Serbia, Montenegro, Italy, Spain and Portugal,* edited by Ernst G. Ravenstein. New York: D. Appleton and Company, 1882.
Reed, John. *The War in Eastern Europe*. New York: C. Scribners and Sons, 1916.
Rodogno, Davide. "The European Powers' Intervention in Macedonia, 1903–1908: An Instance of Humanitarian Intervention?" In *Humanitarian Intervention: A History*, edited by Brendan Simms and David J. B. Trim, 205–25. Cambridge, UK: Cambridge University Press, 2011.
Roshwald, Aviel. *Ethnic Nationalism and the Fall of Empires: Central Europe, Russia and the Middle East, 1914–1923.* London: Routledge, 2001.
Roudometof, Victor. *Nationalism, Globalization, and Orthodoxy, the Social Origins of Ethnic Conflict in the Balkans.* Westport, CT: Greenwood Press, 2001.
Routier, Gaston. *La Macédoine et les Puissances, l'Enquête du Petit-Parisien*. Paris: Dujarric, 1904.
Sack, Robert D. *Human Territoriality: Its Theory and History.* Cambridge, UK: Cambridge University Press, 1986.
Sahlins, Peter. "Natural Frontiers Revisited: France's Boundaries since the Seventeenth Century." *American Historical Review* 95, no. 5 (1990): 1423–51.
Sarrou, Auguste, ed. *Le Capitaine Sarrou, un Officier Français au Service de l'Empire Ottoman*. Istanbul: Les Éditions Isis, 2002.
Sax, Carl. "Ethnographische Karte der Europäischen Türkei und ihrer Dependenzen zu Anfang des Jahres 1877." *Mittheilungen der Kaiser Königlichen Geographischen Gesellschaft in Wien*. Wien, 1878.
Schopoff, A. *Les Reformes et la Protection des Chrétiens en Turquie*. Paris: Librairie Plon, 1904.
Scott, James C. *Seeing like a State*. New Haven: Yale University Press, 1998.
———. *Weapons of the Weak: Everyday Forms of Peasant Resistance*. New Haven: Yale University Press, 1985.
Shaw, Stanford J. "The Nineteenth-Century Ottoman Tax Reforms and Revenue System." *International Journal of Middle East Studies* 6, no. 4 (1975): 421–59.
———. "The Ottoman Census System and Population 1831–1914." *International Journal of Middle East Studies* 9 (1978): 325–38.
Sherman, Laura B. *Fires on the Mountain: The Macedonian Revolutionary Movement and the Kidnapping of Ellen Stone*. Boulder: East European Monographs, 1980.

Skopetea, Ellē. To "Protypo Vaseileio" kai ē Megalē Idea, Opseis tou ethnikou provlēmatos stēn Ellada, 1830–1880. Athens: Polytypes, 1988.
Smith, Woodruff D. "Friedrich Ratzel and the Origins of Lebensraum." German Studies Review 3, no.1 (February 1980): 51–68.
Somel, Selçuk Akşin. The Modernization of Public Education in the Ottoman Empire, 1839–1908. Leiden: Brill, 2001.
Sonnichsen, Albert. Confessions of a Macedonian Bandit. New York: Duffield & Company, 1909.
Sowards, Steven. Austria's Policy of Macedonian Reform. Boulder: East European Monographs, 1989.
Spiliotopoulos, A. T. La Macédoine et l'Hellénisme. Athènes: Imprimerie Apostolopoulos, 1904.
Stamatopoulos, Dēmētrios. Metarrythmisē kai Ekkosmikeusē: Pros mia Anansynthesē tēs Istorias tou Oikumeniku Patriarcheiu ton 19o aiōna. Athens: Ekdoseis Alexandria, 2003.
——. "The Splitting of the Orthodox Millet as a Secularizing Process." In Griechische Kultur in Südosteuropa in der Neuzeit: Beiträgezum Symposium in Memoriam Gunnar Hering, Wien, 16–18 Dezember 2004, edited by Maria A. Stassinopoulou und Ioannis Zelepos, 243–70. Vienna: Byzantina et Neograeca Vindobonensia, 2008.
Stanford, Edward [I. Gennadius]. Ethnological Map of European Turkey and Greece with Introductory Remarks on the Distribution of Races in the Illyrian Peninsula and Statistical Tables of Population. London: 1877.
Stavrianos, Leften Stavros. The Balkans since 1453. New York: New York University Press, 2000 [1965].
Stephanopoli, Ioanna Z. Grecs et Bulgares en Macédoine. Athens: Imprimerie Anestis Constantinidis, 1903.
——. Macédoine et Macédoniens. Athens: Imprimerie Anestis Constantinidis, 1903.
Stoianovich, Traian. "The Conquering Balkan Orthodox Merchant." Journal of Economic History 20, no.2 (1960): 234–313.
Stoyanova-Boneva, Bonka, Stephan Nikolov, and Victor Roudometof. "In Search of 'Bigfoot': Competing Identities in Pirin Macedonia, Bulgaria." In The Macedonian Question: Culture, Historiography, Politics, edited by Victor Roudometof, 237–58. Boulder: East European Monographs, 2000.
Sugar, Peter F. "External and Domestic Roots of Eastern European Nationalism." In Nationalism in Eastern Europe, edited by Peter F. Sugar and Ivo J. Lederer, 28–33. Seattle: University of Washington Press, 1969.
——. Nationalism and Religion in the Balkans since the 19th Century. Seattle: University of Washington, 1996.
Suny, Ronald G. "Constructing Primordialism: Old Histories for New Nations." Journal of Modern History 73, no. 4 (2001): 862–96.
——. The Revenge of the Past: Nationalism, Revolution, and the Collapse of the Soviet Union. Stanford: Stanford University Press, 1993.
Svolopoulos, Kōnstantinos. "Kōnstantinos Paparrēgopoulos kai ē Chartografēsē tēn Chersonēsou tou Aimou apo ton Heinrich Kiepert." In Afierōma eis ton Kōnstantinon Vavouskon. Thessaloniki: Ekdoseis Sakkoula, 1992.
Synvet, A. La Carte Ethnographique de la Turquie d'Europe et Denombrement de l'Empire Ottoman. Paris: A. Lassailly, 1877.

———. *Les Grecs de L'Empire Ottoman: Etude Statistique.* Constantinople, 1878.
Tilly, Charles. *The Contentious French: Four Centuries of Popular Struggle.* Cambridge, MA: Harvard University Press, 1986.
———. *The Politics of Collective Violence.* Cambridge, UK: Cambridge University Press, 2003.
Tishkov, Valery A. "Forget the 'Nation': Post-Nationalist Understanding of Nationalism." *Ethnic and Racial Studies* 23, no. 4 (2000): 625–50.
Tongchai, Winichakul. *Siam Mapped: A History of the Geo-body of a Nation.* Honolulu: University of Hawaii Press, 1994.
Toumarkine, Alexandre. *Les Migrations des Populations Musulmanes Balkaniques en Anatolie.* Istanbul: İsis Press, 1995.
Tozer, Henry F. *Researches in the Highlands of Turkey.* 2 vols. London: John Murray, 1869.
Trajanovski, Alexandar. "L'Activité Politico-Educatrice de l'Exarchat en Macédoine dans les Premieres Années avan et après la Fondation de l'Organisation Revolutionnaire Macedo-Adrinienne Secrete." *Macedonian Review* 1 (1981): 187–97.
Tsanoff [Tsanov], Radoslav A. "Bulgaria's Case." *Journal of Race Development* 8, no. 3 (1918): 296–317.
Ubicini, A. *Lettres sur la Turquie.* Paris: J. Doumaine, 1853 [1851].
Valtchinova, Galia. "Nationalism at Symbolic Work: Social Disintegration and the National Turn in Melnik and Stanimaka." In *Conflicting Loyalties in the Balkans: The Great Powers, the Ottoman Empire and Nation-Building,* edited by Hannes Grandits, Nathalie Clayer, and Robert Pichler, 225–50. London: I. B. Tauris, 2011.
Verković. *Narodne Pesme Makedonski Bugara* [Folk Songs of Macedonian Bulgars]. Belgrade, 1860.
Viquesnel, Auguste. *Voyage dans la Turquie d'Europe.* Paris: Arthus Bertrand, 1868.
Volkan, Vamik. "Psychoanalytic Aspects of Ethnic Conflicts." In *Conflict and Peacemaking in Multiethnic Societies,* edited by Joseph V. Montville, 81–92. Lexington, KY: Lexington Books, 1991.
von Mach, Richard. *The Bulgarian Exarchate: Its History and the Extent of Its Authority in Turkey.* London: T. Fisher Unwin, 1907.
———. *Der Machtbereich des Bulgarischen Exarchats in der Türkei.* Leipzig, 1906.
Vouri, Sophia. *Pēges gia tēn Istoria tēs Makedonias: Politikē kai Ekpaideusē* [Sources for the History of Macedonia: Politics and Education]. Athens: Paraskinio, 1994.
Walker, Mary A. *Through Macedonia to the Albanian Lakes.* London: Chapman and Hall, 1864.
Wilkinson, Henry R. *Maps and Politics: A Review of the Ethnographic Cartography of Macedonia.* Liverpool: Liverpool University Press, 1951.
Wills, Martin. *A Captive of the Bulgarian Brigands, Englishman's Terrible Experiences in Macedonia.* London: Ede, Allon & Townsend Ltd., 1906.
Wolff, Larry. *Inventing Eastern Europe: The Map of Civilization on the Mind of the Enlightenment.* Stanford: Stanford University Press, 1994.
Wood, Denis. *The Power of Maps.* New York: Guilford Press, 1992.
Wood, Elisabeth J. "Armed Groups and Sexual Violence: When Is Wartime Rape Rare?" *Politics & Society* 37 (March 2009): 131–62.

——. "Variation in Sexual Violence during War." *Politics & Society* 34 (September 2006): 307–41.
Xenos, Nicholas "Civic Nationalism: An Oxymoron?" *Critical Review* 10, no. 2 (1996): 213–31.
Yack, Bernard. "The Myth of the Civic Nation." *Critical Review* 10, no. 2 (1996): 193–211.
Yasamee, Feroze. A. K. *Ottoman Diplomacy: Abdülhamid II and the Great Powers*. Istanbul: İsis Press, 1996.
Yosmaoğlu, İpek K. "*Ekmek Parası:* The Allatini Brothers and the Ottoman Army in Macedonia at the Turn of the Twentieth Century." Paper presented at the conference on Local and Imperial Histories: Approaches to Ottoman/Greek Civilization, Chios, Greece, September 2000.
——. "Marching on an Empty Stomach: Practical Aspects of Gendarmerie Reform in Ottoman Macedonia." *Economy and Society on Both Shores of the Aegean*, edited by Lorans Tanatar Baruh and Vangelis Kechriotis, 277–96. Athens: Alpha Bank Historical Archives, 2010.
Zannas, Alexandros D. *O Makedonikos Agōn (Anamnēseis)*. Thessaloniki: Etaireia Makedonikōn Spoudōn, 1960.
Zeman, Z. A. B. "Four Austrian Censuses and Their Political Consequences." *The Last Years of Austria-Hungary*, edited by Mark Cornwall, 31–41. Exeter, UK: University of Exeter Press, 1990.
Ziya Karal, Enver. *Osmanlı İmparatorluğu'nda ilk Nüfus Sayımı*. Ankara: İstatistik Umum Müdürlüğü, 1943.

Index

Abbott, George F., 49, 115
Abdülaziz, Sultan, 22
Abdülhamid II, Sultan, 10–11, 22, 27, 30, 33, 46, 106, 136, 229, 292
abortion, 131–32
Adana, 33
Adanır, Fikret, 33
Adrianople, 23, 26, 35
Adriatic Sea, 106–7
Aegean Sea, 23, 43, 106, 109
Ağa, Salih, 282–83
Ahmed Faik Bey, 272
Albania, 9, 34, 39, 51, 68, 123, 128, 139, 156–58, 246, 266
Alexander, Prince, 25, 26
Alistrat, 199, 222, 267–68
Allatini brothers, 41
Anadolu, 20, 24, 42, 80–81, 104–5, 108, 291, 293. *See also* Anatolia
Anatolia, 20, 24, 42, 80–81, 104–5, 108, 291, 293. *See also* Anadolu
andartes, 39, 231, 262, 269. *See also* Greece: insurgent bands
Anderson, Benedict, 146, 170–71
Andrássy, Count, 21
Anglo-Ottoman Convention, 43
Anthimos VI, 53, 58
Anthimos VII, 64
anthropology, 79, 89–90, 95, 141, 293
Apostol, 223–25, 234, 256, 264, 269
Appadurai, Arjun, 146
April Uprising, 21
Aprilov, Vasil, 75
Ardahan, 25
Arel, Dominique, 146–47, 168
Arendt, Hanna, 287
Arif Bey, 272–73
Armenia, 22, 24, 27, 140, 232, 292
Arsenyev, K. I., 96
Aryans, 87, 114–15, 117
Athanas, Vano Orde, 231
Atlas Universel, 85–86
Austria, 23–25, 33, 36, 54, 95, 167
Avrethisar, 182

Baer, Karl, 96
Balkan Wars, 1, 14, 81, 104, 127, 137, 267–68, 293

Bansko, 275
Barakova, 255
Baravitçe, 224
başibozuks, 21
Batak, 21
Batandzhiev, Hristo, 27, 78
Batum, 25
Bavaria, 27
Behar, Cem, 166
Berghaus, Heinrich, 88–89, 91
Berlin, Congress of, 1, 24–25, 36, 94, 101, 122, 291, 293
Bernal, Martin, 87
Besarya Efendi, 203
Besika Bay, 23
Bessarabia, 25
Bianconi, F., 94, 133
Bismarck, Otto von, 24, 94, 125
Bithynia, 80
Bitola, 58, 61, 63–64
Black, Jeremy, 84, 87
Black Sea, 1, 23, 97, 106, 291
Blunt, John Elijah, 141
Bogdantzi, 264
Bohemia, 2, 12
Bomboki, 259
Boré, Eugene, 136
Boscovich, Ruggiero Giuseppe, 173–74
Bosnia, 20–22, 25, 158
Bosphorus, 11, 80
Boué, Amie, 91–92, 100, 113
bourgeoisie, 5, 50, 62, 99, 120, 206–7
Boursouk, 246
boycotts, 188, 232–33, 250
Brailsford, Henry Noel, 109, 116–17, 139–40, 169–70, 173–75, 188
Brancoff, D. M., 66, 98, 268–69
Britain
  Bulgaria, relations with, 24, 54
  cartographic representation, 85, 118, 133
  census systems, 147
  commercial interests, 42–44
  Cyprus, control of, 25
  India colonization, 146
  military activity, 23
  Russia, relations with, 23, 45–46

Britain (*continued*)
  Salonika, presence in, 38
  Stanford Map, 118
  Sublime Porte, relations with, 45–46, 232
Brubaker, Rogers, 6, 210
Bulgaria
  Austria, relations with, 24–25, 54
  Britain, relations with, 24, 54
  cartographic representation, 92–94, 96, 100–101, 109, 161
  Eastern Rumelia, 24–25, 60, 122, 154
  education system, 27, 51–52, 61–68, 71–78, 98–99, 141–44, 175
  Exarchate, role of, 26, 53–62
  ferman, 53, 57–59
  Greece, relations with, 59–60, 67–68, 119–23, 178, 198–99, 266–67
  gymnasia, 65–67, 69, 71, 76
  insurgent bands, 27, 30–31, 64, 78, 121, 178, 197–201, 218, 243
  irâde, 61
  military activity, 25, 29, 31
  paramilitary groups, 27, 39, 41
  Patriarchate, role of, 35, 53–60, 143, 158–59
  political environment, 22, 26–27, 32, 56
  population statistics, 94, 96, 99, 153
  Principality, 24–25, 154
  racial relations, 91, 115–18
  Russia, relations with, 24–27, 29, 32, 60, 62
  San Stefano treaty, effects of, 23–24, 100
  Serbia, relations with, 25
  stereotypes, 115–17, 119–20
  Sublime Porte, relations with, 26–27, 29, 55
  unification, 25–26
Bulgarski Knizhitsi, 61
Byzantine dynasty, 79, 174

Calhoun, Craig, 8–9
Calice, Heinrich Freiherr von, 33, 42, 45
Capety, Constantine, 144
Carpathian Mountains, 24, 113
Carte de France, 84–85
cartography
  Albania, representation of, 123, 128
  Austria, representation of, 95
  authority, role of, 125–26
  boundaries as approximations, 81–82, 108–10, 127–28
  Britain, representation of, 85, 118, 133
  Bulgaria, representation of, 92–94, 96, 100–101, 109, 161
  Carte de France, 84–85
  choropleth technique, 89, 94, 99, 133
  color distinctions, 93–94, 96, 100, 105, 108, 123–25
  Darwinian geopolitics, 82, 84, 111
  early Macedonian representations, 91–95, 98–101, 119–23
  ethnography, relation to, 10, 82–83, 87–90, 121, 126, 129–30
  geography, relation to, 82, 85–87, 106–12
  Greece, representation of, 94–95, 99, 109
  measuring implements, 84–85
  moral attributes, 83, 107, 120
  natural boundaries, 108–11, 121
  organic boundaries, 111–12
  origins, 84–85, 88
  Ottoman, 85–86, 102–6
  political influences, 82–83, 102, 108, 112, 126, 130
  population counts, 88–89, 94, 96, 98–100, 105, 108, 133–34
  race, representation of, 88–90, 95–96, 108–9, 120–22, 127
  Russia, representation of, 85, 96–97
  Serbia, representation of, 97–98
  Stanford Map, 94, 118–20, 133
  statistical tables, 88, 99–100
  Syllogos involvement, 122
  territoriality, assertions of, 83–84, 102, 105, 118, 125, 129–30, 133
  thematic maps, 88–89, 99–100
Cassandra, 261–62
Cassini family, 84–85
Catholicism, 53–54, 162, 173, 235
Caucuses, 2, 21, 23
census. *See* population counts
Census of 1903, 134, 136–37, 147–55, 159–60, 165–66. *See also* population counts
Çerkes Said Efendi, 232
Chernopeyef, 182
chetas, 30–31, 35. *See also* militias
Chomakov, Stoian, 58
choropleth technique, 89, 94, 99, 133. *See also* cartography
Christianity, 12, 21–24, 31, 33, 46, 98, 113, 131–32, 137–39, 153–55, 173, 249–50, 289. *See also* religion
Cimetierre, Captain, 271–77
Clarke, James F., 68, 70, 93
Cohn, Bernard, 146
Committee for Support of Greek Church and Education, 63, 70–71
Concert of Europe, 17, 19, 25
Constandi, Risto, 263–64
Cosgrove, Dennis, 84

Cousinéry, E. M., 91, 100
Crampton, Jeremy, 127
Crete, 19, 32, 34, 79, 154
Crimean Wars, 17, 19, 22
Croatia, 293–94
Cuma-i Bâlâ, 32–33, 61, 149, 177, 235, 249–50, 253, 255, 269, 282
Cvijić, Jovan, 92, 95–96, 100–101, 127–28
Cyprus, 25
Cyrill and Methodios, Saints, 59, 116, 189

Dakin, Douglas, 76, 143
Dalyan, 180
Danev, Stoyan, 32, 34
Danube River, 23–24
Darrow, David W., 162
Darwinian geopolitics, 82, 84, 111
Davis, Natalie, 226
Degiorgis, Emilio, 37
Delchev, Georgi "Gotse", 27, 30–31
Deliyannis, Theodoros, 77
Demirhisar, 184, 188–89, 191–92, 206, 249, 283
Dere Müslim, 282–83, 285–86
Deringil, Selim, 148
Diarko Ethniko Symvoulio, 56
Dimitrov, Andon, 27, 78
Dionysios V, 177
Dnieper, 113
Dolmabahçe Palace, 58
Doubnitza, 40
Doumani, Beshara, 166
Doyran, 61, 158, 196–97
Draganoff, 36
Dragashevitch, Colonel, 98
Dragoumis, Ion, 70–72
Drama, 39, 61, 183–85
Driault, Eduard, 115
Dupin, Baron Charles, 89

Eastern Rumelia, 24–25, 60, 122, 154
Ecumenical Patriarchate. *See* Patriarchate
Edirne, 23, 33, 80
Edney, Matthew, 126
education
    Albania, 68
    building disputes, 63–64, 193–95
    Bulgaria, 27, 51–52, 61–68, 71–78, 98–99, 141–44, 175
    class differentiation, 65–72
    curriculum, 66–67, 71–72, 75
    drop-out rates, 143
    Exarchate, role of, 49, 61–62, 142, 144
    facilities, 63–64, 66–67, 72, 193–95
    funding, 61–64, 66, 69, 74
    Greece, 50–52, 63, 66–78, 98–99, 141–44
    language options, 50–51, 64–66, 70, 75–77, 141
    national sentiment, 52, 67–78, 145, 193, 219
    Patriarchate, role of, 51
    religion, connection with, 49, 52, 61–62, 64, 70–71, 142, 145, 175, 192–95
    Romania, 51, 68
    school structures, 49–50
    Serbia, 51–52, 68, 99
    student enrollment, 49, 66–67, 141–45
    teacher requirements, 61–62, 65, 70–71, 159
Edward VII, 46
Eğridere, 221–22, 242, 244, 267–68
Egypt, 85
Eliot, Sir Charles, 108
Elsan, 151
empires
    defined, 289–90
    balance of power, 19–20, 24–25, 290–91
    frontiers, role of, 80
    Habsburg Empire, 2, 23, 86, 167
    Roman Empire, 114
    Russian Empire, 97, 156–57
    transition to nation-state, 2, 14, 106, 165, 290
Enlightenment, 50, 81, 87–88, 99, 114, 170, 207
Epirus, 25, 122–23
Erzurum, 23
Eskice, 181
Esmen Ağa, 196
ethnicity. *See* race and ethnicity
Ethnographische Übersichtskarte, 121–22
ethnography, 82–83, 87–90, 112–14, 121, 126, 129–30, 147–49. *See also* cartography
ethnology, 89–90, 141
ethnophyletism, 53
European Concert, 44
Exarchate
    authority, 176, 182
    base expansion, 27
    Bulgaria, role in, 26, 53–62
    church rotation, 188–92, 202, 242–43
    education, role in, 49, 61–62, 142, 144
    ferman, 53, 57–59
    identity cards, 151
    IMRO, relations with, 15, 30
    newspaper publishing, 26
    origins, 53–55, 61
    Patriarchate, dispute with, 52–60, 172, 178–79, 183–85, 190–95, 198–205, 236, 242–44
    population counts, role in, 149, 157–59

Exarchate (*continued*)
    Sublime Porte, relations with, 29–30, 59
    terminology, 12
    See also religion

Falconetti, Leon, 63
Farr, William, 131
Ferdinand, Prince, 26–27
Fermor, Patrick Leigh, 79, 81
Fertile Crescent, 1, 292
Ferzi, Georghi, 245–46
Ficker, Adolf, 95
Fifth Department of Science, 103–4
Fortna, Benjamin, 102, 104–5
Fourka, 158–59
France, 3, 20, 53, 76–77, 84–85, 89, 112, 207
French Revolution, 207

Gabrovo, 75
Galicia, 2, 161–62
Gandolphe, Maurice, 9–10
Garvanov, Ivan, 39–40
Gellner, Ernest, 2–5
Gemidzis, 34
Gennadius, Ioannis, 96, 118–20, 125, 130, 133
geography, 82, 85–87, 106–13, 132. *See also* cartography
Germany, 21, 39, 43, 45, 111–12
Gevgeli, 234–35
Giesl, Wladimir, 37
Giorgieva, Helen, 245–46
Gladstone, William, 22
Golo Bardo, 9
Goluchowski, Agenor Maria, 33, 45
Gopčević, Spiridon, 97–98
Gorice, 228
Gorki, Christo, 201
Goroyif, Konstantin, 229
Graçen, 198–200, 221–22, 267–68
Grand Vezir, 80
Great Powers, 2, 16, 19–20, 22, 24, 32–37, 42–45, 78, 82, 153, 291
Greece
    Bulgaria, relations with, 59–60, 67–68, 119–23, 178, 198–99, 266–67
    cartographic representation, 94–95, 99, 109
    cultural monopoly, 51–52, 55, 76–77
    école normale, 66
    education system, 50–52, 63, 66–78, 98–99, 141–44
    Enlightenment thought, 81, 87
    insurgent bands, 39–41, 64, 199, 201, 218, 224, 232, 261, 265–66
    language reach, 49–50, 63, 70, 72–73, 77
    military activity, 40–41
    Ottoman Empire, war with, 32, 34
    population statistics, 94–95, 141, 153, 156
    Russo-Ottoman war involvement, 23
    San Stefano treaty, effects of, 23
    Serbia, relations with, 64
    Sublime Porte, relations with, 177, 285
    Greek Orthodox, 49–55, 61–67, 140, 155, 165, 169, 171, 176–79, 184–90, 197, 205, 243. *See also* religion
Grey, Sir Edward, 45
Griesebach, August Heinrich Rudolf, 100
Gruev, Damian "Dame", 27–28, 78
Guadalquivir, 34
guerrilla warfare, 31, 35, 78, 95, 130, 209, 217, 219–20, 226, 228–29, 234, 243–44, 256–63, 276–81. *See also* insurgent bands
Guha, Sumit, 147, 171
Gulf of Orfano, 23, 269

Habsburg dynasty, 2, 23, 86, 167
Hadgi-Yorgi, Catherina, 234–35, 263
Hadzi Nikolov, Ivan, 27, 78
Hall, John, 8
Hamdi Bey, 284
Hamidian regime, 11, 102, 104–5, 228, 264, 292
Hamzali, 275
Hanioğlu, Şükrü, 24
Harley, J. B., 83–84, 130
Hasan Efendi, 270–75, 277–79
Helle, Zur, 132
Hellenism, 12, 13, 25, 61–64, 69–70, 73, 76, 113, 123, 140, 154
Hercegovina, 20–24, 25
Hisarbey, 180–81
History of the Greek Nation, 122
Hobsbawm, Eric, 3
Homondos, 231
Hristo, Gorgi, 245
Hungary, 23, 25, 36–45, 107–8, 167
Huseyin Ali, 229–30
Hüseyin Efendi, 151–52

identity cards, 136, 148–49, 151, 155, 159–60, 166. *See also* population counts
Ignatieff, Count Pavel, 22
Ignatieff, Michael, 6
Ignatiev, Nikolai, 57–58
Ilarion of Loftza, 59
Ilarion of Macariopolis, 56–59
Ilinden Uprising, 10, 34–36, 39, 144, 157, 174, 202, 205, 247, 249, 253, 260, 270
Imperial Classroom, The, 102

India, 85, 146, 233
insurgent bands, 27, 30–31, 39, 46–47, 64, 78, 121, 149–50, 157, 178, 197–201, 218, 224, 232, 243, 261, 265–66. *See also* guerilla warfare
Internal Macedonian Revolutionary Organization (IMRO)
  chetas, 30–31, 35
  Exarchate, relations with, 15, 30
  founding members, 27, 78
  fundraising methods, 30–32
  Ilinden Uprising, effect of, 34–36, 39
  kidnappings, 31–32
  leadership, 15, 27, 31, 39–40, 78
  organizational structure, 15, 30, 39–40
  origins, 15, 27, 78
  secret networks, 30–31, 40
  Supreme Committee, relations with, 30–32
  Vrhovists, conflict with, 267, 270
  See also Sandansky, Jane
International Commission for Financial Control, 43
Invention of Eastern Europe, The, 107–8
Ioachim III, 59–60, 64, 70, 177
Irby, Adeline Paulina, 100
Ireland, 85
Ishirkov, Anastas, 56, 101, 117–18
İskirçova, 222, 236, 267–68
İşkodra, 33
Islam, 21, 80, 277
İsmail Efendi, 271
Istanbul, 22, 27, 37, 53–55, 59–60, 105, 151, 259
Italy, 37–38, 149

Jaucourt, Louis de, 114–15
Joerg, W. L. G., 127
Jonction Salonique-Constantinople, 133
Joseph, Francis, 23–24
Judaism, 131, 150, 154, 232, 277. *See also* religion

Kakar, Sudhir, 233–34, 240
Kakaraska, 151
Kalendra, 255
Kalyvas, Stathis, 220, 234, 238, 240–42
Kaplan, Robert, 6
Karaca Dağ, 123
Karacaköy, 255
Karakasidou, Anastasia, 206
Karasu Çiftlik, 253
Karatheodori, Stephanos, 56
Karavangelis, Germanos, 35, 40
Karavelov, Petko, 26
Karlikovo, 182–85, 199, 244–45, 267–68
Karpat, Kemal, 136
Kars, 25

Kastoria, 38, 40
Katiboff, Georgi, 238–39
Kavaklı, 160–63
Kavala, 23
Kazim Daouli, 264–65
Kemal Efendi, 196
Kertzer, David, 146–47, 168
Kiatibof, Giorgi, 230
kidnappings, 31–32, 235, 252, 261
Kiepert, Heinrich, 94–96, 100, 104, 108, 118, 121–26
King, Jeremy, 12
Kiro, Angos, 235
Klepousna, 184, 236–37, 267–68
Kofos, Evangelos, 69
Kohn, Hans, 7
Kokoschka, Oskar, 95
Kolesh, 275
Komarov, V. V., 96
komitadjis, 199, 265, 267, 272, 274
komites, 196–98, 200–201, 205
Konboti, Vasil, 243
Konstantin, Avram, 190
Köprülü, 61
Kornitza, 236
Koromilas, Lambros, 40–41, 48, 161–63
Korzybski, Alfred, 83
Kosovo, 33, 38–39, 66, 246
Kostadi, Mito, 279
Kostur, 61
Koukoush, 61
Koula, 178–79
Koutzo-Vlachs, 113
Krastevič, Gâvril, 56–57
Kruševo, 35
Külahlı, 246–47
Kûnchov, Vasil, 99

Laitin, David, 210
Lamouche, Captain, 76–78
Lamsdorff, Vladimir, 33, 45
Lancaster, Joseph, 75
Landsowne, Lord, 42
Langaza, 160, 262
Lebensraum, 111
Lejean, Guillaume Marie, 93, 96, 100
Lemnos, 43
Leonidas, 200
Leshko, 253, 282
Lieven, Dominic, 290
Limpasa, 261
Loftzo, 58
Lovichta, 246–47

Mackenzie, Georgina Mary Muir, 100
Madjaroff, Ivan, 151
Mahmud Efendi, 270–71, 273, 276–77, 279

Makariopolis, 58
Mala Prespa, 9
Manastir, 26, 58
Mann, Michael, 8
Mao Zedong, 218, 287
mapping. *See* cartography
Marikostina, 245-46
Marikostinali, Mitza, 283
Marinov, Tchavdar, 15
Marmara Sea, 23
Martin, Henry, 113-14
Mathieu, Henri, 133
Mavrogenis, Alexander, 202-3
Mazower, Mark, 291
Mehmed Bey, 263-64, 281
Mehmed Efendi, 273
Melas, Pavlos, 40
Melnikitch, 151, 243
Menlik, 61, 177, 184, 189, 191-92, 257, 270
Methodii, Bishop, 175-76
Methodios, 59
Mihal, Yovan Gilo, 230, 238
Miladinov brothers, 72-73
militias, 30-31, 35, 217-19, 226, 231
millet system, 56, 145, 154-56, 162, 169, 176
Miloyevitch, M. S., 98
Mishev, Dimitar, 66, 144, 152, 161
Mogila, 281
Moglena, 58, 61
Monastir, 33, 35, 38, 40, 63, 66, 209, 228, 260, 269
Mongolia, 114, 119-20
Montenegro, 22-23, 25, 123
Morava valley, 22-23
Moravia, 2
Moscow Benevolent Society, 62
Mount Lebanon, 19
Mravintza, 263-65
Müller, Joseph, 100
Murad V, 22
Mürzsteg Reform Program, 36-39, 42, 46, 134, 150, 153-54
Museum of Macedonian Struggle, 48-49
Muslims, 21, 25, 31, 33, 35, 39, 46, 98, 113, 132, 137-39, 154, 161, 184, 231, 249-50, 291. *See also* religion
Mytilene, 43

Nablus, 166
Nano, Hristo, 196
nations
  transition from empire, 2, 14, 106, 165, 290
  boundaries, 1-11, 46, 80, 101, 108-12, 154
  capitalism, role of, 4
  ethnicity, role of, 16
  modernization, model of, 2, 90
nationalism
  civic, 7-8
  class differentiation, 2-3, 68-71, 193
  consolidation, path to, 2
  defined, 2-4, 14, 72
  ethnic, 6-8
  goals, 8-9, 23, 68-69
  indoctrination, 48-50, 62, 67
  modernist understandings of, 2, 5
  primordialism and, 6, 170-71
  religion and, 4-6, 9, 53-55, 60, 141, 169-73, 208
Negorçe, 148
Negovan, 160
Nevrekop, 59, 183-84, 186-87, 206, 259, 261-62
Nicolaides, C., 98
Nicolas, Jovan, 236
Nicolas II, 46

Ohrid, 13, 26, 59, 61, 177
Orta Dağ, 123
Ottoman Bank, 20, 33-34, 42
Ottoman Committee of Progress and Union (CPU), 46-47
Ottoman Committee of Union and Progress (CUP), 292-93
Ottoman Freedom Society, 46

Pallavicini, Johann Markgraf von, 44
Pallis, A., 2
Panagiurishte, 21
Panaretos, 59
Panayiot, Nico Dimitri, 231
Panitsa, Kosta, 26
Panteli, Anton, 238-40
Panzac, Daniel, 137
Paparrigopoulos, Konstantinos, 64, 69, 76, 122-26
Papzoglou, Leonidas, 50, 209, 228
Paris Treaty, 19, 101
Pasha, Enver, 47, 220
Pasha, Hasan Fehmi, 260
Pasha, Hüseyin Hilmi, 33, 36, 41-43, 150-55, 157, 162-63, 185, 188, 191, 267
Pasha, Karatheodoris, 24
Pasha, Mareşal Ibrahim, 270
Pasha, Mirliva Salih, 250, 253-55
Patriarchate
  authority, 176-77
  Bulgaria, role in, 35, 53-60, 143, 158-59
  church rotation, 188-92, 202, 242-43

education, role in, 51
  Exarchate, dispute with, 52–60, 172, 178–79, 183–85, 190–95, 198–105, 236, 242–44
  komitajis menace, 39
  population counts, role in, 149, 152–53, 157–59
  Sublime Porte, relations with, 153, 176
  terminology, 12
  See also religion
Peabody, Norbert, 147
peasants, 3–5, 12, 20, 31, 60, 68–71, 101, 113, 156, 159–66, 218–19, 241
Peloponnese, 122, 132
Pen and the Sword, The, 93
Peninsule Balkanique, La, 101
Perry, Duncan, 32, 78
Petermann, August Heinrich, 93
Petermann's Mittheilungen, 91–93, 98
Petre, Nikola, 232–33
Petriç, 177, 265
Petrov, Gorce, 30–31
Petrov, Racho, 34
Peucker, Karl, 99, 105
Phanariots, 56–57
Phillippopoli, 58
Physicalischer Atlas, 88–89, 91
Picot, M. E., 113
Piraeus, 76, 95
Pirava, 265
Pirin Macedonia, 9
Pirolik, 180–81
Plamenatz, John, 7
Pleven, 23
Plovdiv, 13
Poiras, Eftim, 276
Poiras, Velko, 274–75
Pokrovnik, 249–50, 253
Poland, 162
political actors, 3, 219, 286, 291
political entrepreneurs, 219–20, 241, 245, 253–54
Polyanino, 61
Poparsov, Petûr, 27, 78
population counts
  Abdülhamid II, Sultan, role of, 136
  Albania, 156–58
  Bulgaria, 94, 96, 99, 153
  cartographic representation, 88–89, 94, 96, 98–100, 105, 108, 133–34
  Census of 1903, 134, 136–37, 147–55, 159–60, 165–66
  early counts, 135–36, 146–47
  Exarchate, role of, 149, 157–59
  foreign traveler observations, 132–33, 141
  Greece, 94–95, 141, 153, 156
  identity cards, 136, 148–49, 151, 155, 159–60, 166
  military purposes, 136–38, 154, 160, 163
  Mürzsteg Reform Program, effect of, 150, 153–54
  political factors, 134, 141, 155, 161, 166–67
  propaganda efforts, 149–50, 161
  reliability, 132–33, 137–38, 141, 144–45
  religion, connection with, 25, 98, 131–32, 137–39, 149, 154–59, 161–66
  Russia, 156–57, 161–62
  salnâmes, role of, 135–36, 138
  school enrollment, 141–45
  Serbia, 156–57
  taxation purposes, 136–38, 154–55, 160, 163
  territoriality, assertions of, 105, 133–34
  Turkey, 131–33
Population of Macedonia, Evidence of the Christian Schools, The, 71, 143
Poroy, 247
Porter, James, 173
Pouqueville, François C. H. L., 100, 132
Power of Maps, The, 127–28
Preobrazhenie, 35
Prilep, 74
Prosenik, 151
Protestantism, 53–54, 173, 252
Ptolemy, 93, 130
Public Debt Administration, 20
public executions, 222, 224–31
Purlichev, Grigor, 72–73

race and ethnicity
  Bulgaria, 91, 115–18
  cartographic representation, 88–90, 95–96, 108–9, 120–22, 127
  ethnic cleansing, 14
  ethnography, role in, 90, 112–14
  ethnophyletism, 53
  group definitions, 112
  hierarchical ranking, 90, 113–14, 120
  intermingling, 2, 109, 112, 119
  Mürzsteg Reform Program, effect of, 134
  nationality, compared to, 112–13
  physical characteristics, 89, 113, 116
Rangavis, Alexandros Rizos, 58, 73
rape, 251–53, 255, 264, 280–81
Ratzel, Friedrich, 82, 111
Ravenstein, E. G., 132–33
Ravna, 198, 208
Razlog, 31, 261–62
Reclus, Elisée, 102–3, 106–8

Reed, John, 1–2
Reichstadt Convention, 23
religion
    Catholicism, 53–54, 162, 173, 235
    Christianity, 12, 21–24, 31, 33, 46, 98,
        113, 131–32, 137–39, 153–55, 173,
        249–50, 289
    church rotation, 188–92, 197, 205,
        242–44
    education, connection with, 49,
        52, 61–62, 64, 70–71, 142, 145,
        175, 192–95
    ferman, role of, 53, 57–59
    Greek Orthodox, 140, 155, 165, 169,
        171, 176–79, 184–92, 197, 205, 243
    holidays, 176–80, 187, 190, 205–6, 242,
        244–45, 277
    Judaism, 131, 150, 154, 232, 277
    millet system, 56, 145, 154–56, 162,
        169, 176
    moral authority, 175–76
    Muslims, 21, 25, 31, 33, 35, 39, 46, 98,
        113, 132, 137–39, 154, 161, 184,
        231, 249–50, 291
    ownership of churches, 202–5
    political influences, 170, 179, 200, 219
    population counts, connection with, 25,
        98, 131–32, 137–39, 149, 154–59,
        161–66
    Protestantism, 53–54, 173, 252
    ranking categories, 114
    rituals, 174, 187, 200
    sacred spaces, 171–72, 200, 233
    stabilizing influence, 170–71
    symbolism, 172–73, 177, 182, 184
    Uniates, 54, 62, 162, 265
    violence, role of, 170, 178, 189,
        196–202, 242–46
    See also Exarchate
    See also Patriarchate
Rhodope Mountains, 23
Rila Monastery, 40
Ritter, Carl, 88
Romania, 23, 25, 51, 68, 139
Romanov dynasty, 2
Rondi-i Bâlâ, 201, 230, 238
Roudometof, Victor, 207
Roumains de la Macédoine, Les, 113
Rumeli, 20, 33, 79–82, 104–5, 286,
    291, 293
Rumeli Vilâyetleri Müfettiş-i Umûmîsi,
    33
Russia
    Austria, relations with, 36
    Britain, relations with, 23, 45–46
    Bulgaria, relations with, 24–27, 29, 32,
        60, 62

cartographic representation, 85, 96–97
colonialism, 148
Imperial Geographic Society, 156
Macedonia reform, role in, 33
population statistics, 156–57, 161–62
Russo-Ottoman war, 22–24
Sublime Porte, relations with, 22

Sachtouris, Antonios, 41
Sack, Robert David, 83–84
Sadık, Mehmet, 283
salnâmes, 135–36, 138. *See also*
    population counts
Salonika, 14, 21, 23, 27, 33–34, 38–40,
    52, 66, 140, 142, 180, 205, 232–33,
    261, 269
San Stefano, 23
Sandansky, Jane, 16, 31, 40, 47, 220, 252,
    257–59, 269–70, 283, 285. *See also*
    Internal Macedonian Revolutionary
    Organization (IMRO)
Sanson, Nicolas, 81
Sarafov, Boris, 31, 39–40
Sarakatsani, 79–80
Savati, Yovan, 239
Sax, Carl, 95, 118, 132
Saxe-Coburg-Gotha, 26
Schafarik, Pavel, 91–92
Schools of Macedonia, 145
Scott, James, 146
Selânik, 144
Selichte, 249, 253
Semënov, P. P., 96
Serbia
    Bulgaria, relations with, 25
    cartographic representation, 97–98
    claims to Macedonia, 39, 139
    education system, 51–52, 68, 99
    Greece, relations with, 64
    independence, 25
    insurgent bands, 39
    peasant rebellion, 20
    population statistics, 156–57
    Russo-Ottoman war involvement, 23
    San Stefano treaty, effects of, 23
    war declaration, 22
Serfice, 38
Serres, 13, 39–41, 61, 66–68, 144, 158,
    177, 179, 201, 205, 238, 249
Siam Mapped, 84
Skopje, 38, 40, 59, 96, 177, 269
Skrijovo, 236–37, 267–68
Smardesi, 281
Society for the Dissemination of Greek
    Letters, 52, 61, 63–64, 69, 76, 122
Sofia, 27, 29, 40, 98, 255
Sonnichsen, Albert, 209

Sowards, Steven, 44
Spatovo, 188–92, 195
Stambolov, Stefan, 26–27, 29
Stanford Map, 94, 118–20, 133. *See also* cartography
Statistical Society of London, 132
Steeg, Louis, 37, 259
Stephanopoli, Ioanna, 78, 120–21
Stone, Ellen, 31, 252
Strandja, 35
Strumnitza, 40, 58, 61, 270–71. *See also* Usturumca
Struma Valley, 14, 266–67, 285
Sublime Porte
   Britain, relations with, 45–46, 232
   Bulgaria, relations with, 26–27, 29, 55
   custom duty rates, 42
   Exarchate, relations with, 29–30, 59
   Great Powers, relations with, 19–21, 36–38, 43
   Greece, relations with, 177, 285
   Mürzsteg Reform Program, acceptance of, 36
   Patriarchate, relations with, 153, 176
   reforms, role in, 20, 22, 42–45
   Russia, relations with, 22
Sukutlu, 181
Supreme Committee, 29–33, 39–40
Svidovica, 275, 279
Switzerland, 16
Syllogos. *See* Society for the Dissemination of Greek Letters
Synvet, A., 94–95

Tableau Ethnocratique, 113, 118, 121–22
Tachino, 49
Tantcheff, Constandine, 151
Tanzimat, 51, 176, 226, 289
Tartars, 114, 116
Tatarchev, Hristo, 15–16, 27
Tatarpazarcık, 255
Tayyar Bey, 284
taxation, 20–21, 30, 136–38, 154–55, 160, 163, 243–44, 282, 289, 291
Tchirka, Dimitri, 236
tezkeres, 151, 159–63
Theodorides, J. M., 179, 203–4
Thessaloniki Museum of Photography, 209
Thessaly, 25, 122
Thrace, 15, 24, 52, 94, 105, 119, 122, 173
Tilly, Charles, 219, 224, 241, 255
Tirnovo, 208
Todor, Jovan, 237
Todorak, 246
torture, 151, 165, 222, 224–26, 280
Touranians, 114–16

Tozer, Henry F., 116, 187
Traiko, Pande, 274
Trandafil, Dimitri, 230, 238–39
Transylvania, 2
Trikoupis, Charilaos, 69
Tsilka, Catherine, 31, 252
Turkey, 81–84, 87, 93, 99, 119, 131–33, 154, 266, 292
Turquie d'Europe, La, 92
Turquie es ses Différents Peuples, La, 133
Turtsiia, 63
Tzinzars, 113

Uniates, 54, 62, 162, 265
United States, 21, 31, 54
Ural Mountains, 97
Uskub, 26, 30
Usturumca, 40, 58, 61, 270–71. *See also* Strumnitza
Uvać-Mitrovico railroad, 45

Val, Peirre du, 81
Valandova, 158, 196–98
Vanguel, Bougdan, 236–37
Vardar, 23
Vardiçe, 180
Vasil, Vlad, 148–49
Vehdi Pazar, 180
Veles, 59, 61, 183
Veliko Turnovo, 12
Velo, Pavlo, 246
Vérand, Colonel, 68, 153–54, 246, 250–51, 270
Verković, Stefan, 96
Veselinovitch, M., 98
Vienna, 24
violence specialists, 220, 245, 251
Viquesnel, Auguste, 113
Visoçen, 178
Vladya, 158–59
Voden, 61
Vodine, 152–53
Vogoridis, Stephan, 56–57
Von Czörnig, Carl, 95
Von Humboldt, Alexander, 88
Von Mach, Richard, 98
Vranali, Mitza, 283
Vrhovists, 267, 270

Wallachia, 123
War in Eastern Europe, The, 1
Weigand, Gustave, 98
Wiener Punktation, 33, 36
Wilkinson, Henry Roberts, 10, 91–92, 118, 125–26, 129
Wilson, Woodrow, 127

Winichakul, Tongchai, 84
Wolff, Larry, 86, 99, 107–8
Wood, Denis, 84, 127–28
World War I, 2, 16, 147
World War II, 16, 82

Yanya, 33
Yemen, 33, 248
Yenice, 180, 229, 266, 273

Yorgi, Marko, 242–43
Young Turks, 17, 106, 153, 292

Zalokostas, Mr., 64
Zarjanko, N. C., 96
Zervi, 164
Zihna, 151, 182–85, 236, 267, 269
Zinoviev, I. A., 33, 42, 44
Zolotas, G. I., 69, 76

www.ingramcontent.com/pod-product-compliance
Lightning Source LLC
Chambersburg PA
CBHW021846300426
44115CB00005B/36